The
BERKSHIRE
Book
A Complete Guide

THE
BERKSHIRE
BOOK
A Complete Guide

SIXTH EDITION

Lauren R. Stevens

Berkshire House Publishers
Lee, Massachusetts

The Berkshire Book: A Complete Guide
Copyright © 1986, 1991, 1994, 1997, 1999, 2000 by Berkshire House Publishers
Cover and interior photographs © by credited photographers

Library of Congress Cataloging-in-Publication Data

Stevens, Lauren R.
    The Berkshire book : a complete guide / Lauren R. Stevens.—6th ed.
       p.   cm. — (Great destinations, ISSN 1056-7968)
    Rev. ed. of: The Berkshire book / Jonathan Sternfield and Lauren R. Stevens. 5th ed. c1999.
    Includes bibliographical references and index.
    ISBN 1-58157-015-5
      1. Berkshire Hills. (Mass.)—Guidebooks. I. Sternfield, Jonathan. Berkshire book. II. Title. III. Great destinations series.

    F72.B5 S83 2000
    917.44'1—dc21
                                                    99-067015

ISBN: 1-58157-015-5
ISSN: 1056-7968 (series)

Editor: Rodelinde Albrecht. Managing Editor: Philip Rich. Design and composition: Dianne Pinkowitz. Cover design and composition: Jane McWhorter. Maps: Ron Toelke Associates. Index: Diane Brenner.

Berkshire House Publishers
480 Pleasant St., Suite 5; Lee, Massachusetts 01238
800-321-8526

Manufactured in the United States of America
First printing 2000
10 9 8 7 6 5 4 3 2 1

No complimentary meals or lodgings were accepted by the author or reviewers in gathering information for this work.

Berkshire House Publishers'
Great Destinations™ travel guidebook series

Right on the money.

— THE NEW YORK TIMES

. . . a crisp and critical approach, for travelers who want to live like locals.

— USA TODAY

Great Destinations™ guidebooks are known for their comprehensive, critical coverage of regions of extraordinary cultural interest and natural beauty. The authors in this series are professional travel writers who have lived for many years in the regions they describe. Each title in this series is continuously updated with each printing, in order to insure accurate and timely information. All of the books contain over 100 photographs and maps.

Neither the publisher, the authors, the reviewers, nor other contributors accept complimentary lodgings, meals, or any other consideration (such as advertising) while gathering information for any book in this series.

Current titles available:
The Adirondack Book
The Berkshire Book
The Charleston, Savannah & Coastal Islands Book
The Chesapeake Bay Book
The Coast of Maine Book
The Hamptons Book
The Monterey Bay, Big Sur & Gold Coast Wine Country Book
The Nantucket Book
The Newport & Narragansett Bay Book
The Napa & Sonoma Book
The Santa Fe & Taos Book
The Sarasota, Sanibel Island & Naples Book
The Texas Hill Country Book
Wineries of the Eastern States

If you are traveling to, moving to, residing in, or just interested in any (or all!) of these enchanting regions, a **Great Destinations™** guidebook is a superior companion. Honest and painstakingly critical, full of information only a local can provide, **Great Destinations™** guidebooks give you all the practical knowledge you need to enjoy the best of each region. Why not own them all?

Contents

CHAPTER ONE
From the Glaciers to the Present
HISTORY
1

CHAPTER TWO
Getting Here, Getting Around
TRANSPORTATION
17

CHAPTER THREE
The Keys to Your Room
LODGING
28

CHAPTER FOUR
Pleasing the Palate
RESTAURANTS & FOOD PURVEYORS
80

CHAPTER FIVE
What to See, What to Do
ARTS & PLEASURES
144

CHAPTER SIX
Spas & the Spiritual Life
BODY & SPIRIT
206

CHAPTER SEVEN
For the Fun of It
OUTDOOR RECREATION
217

CHAPTER EIGHT
Fancy Goods
SHOPPING
261

CHAPTER NINE
Practical Matters
INFORMATION
292

Acknowledgments

The sixth edition of *The Berkshire Book* was perpetrated on an unsuspecting public by a dubious cast of characters who have in common that they live, work, and play in Berkshire County. These include first of all the card-carrying Berkshire County Mealmen: Carol Bosco Baumann (honorary), Jean Cowhig, Sean Cowhig, Wally Graves, Henrietta Graves, Molly Jackel, Maxeme Kupperman-Guinals, Judith Monachina, Katherine Myers, Gerard Smith, Philip Rich, Jean J. Rousseau, Sarah Shepard, Edith Stovel, and Lauren R. Stevens. These folks undertook to make the *Restaurants* chapter digestible. Never before did so few eat so much in the service of their county.

Carol Bosco Baumann and Charlie Moore also aided by investigating many of the galleries in Chapter Five, *Arts & Pleasures*. Judith Monachina, who served as photo editor, also wrote Chapter Six, *Body & Spirit*. Maryjane Fromm wrote Chapter Eight, *Shopping*. Seth Rogovoy wrote the "Nightlife" section of *Arts & Pleasures*. Thanks to them all for their wealth of knowledge and professionalism.

Mary Osak at Berkshire House contributed to almost every part of the text from her wealth of county lore. Laura Gratz and Charlie Moore checked and rechecked facts throughout, and Rodelinde Albrecht edited the whole, pulling both text and pictures together admirably. Philip Rich served as patient and exacting managing editor. Publisher Jean Rousseau kept his vigilant eye on every aspect of the book. Berkshire Book Six is more of an ensemble production than the work of any individuals. Fortunately, this group worked well together. Any errors, however, should be attributed to me. Readers could help by forwarding comments to Berkshire House.

— LRS

Jonathan Sternfield completed his tour of duty with Berkshire Book Five. He and David Emblidge concocted this special guide to a special place, the first edition dated 1986. Jonathan contributed most of the writing and photographs, although he modestly shared credit with "28 Berkshire friends." The book has evolved since, but much of the heaviest lifting was done initially — for which Jonathan deserves all our thanks.

Growing up in New York City and attending the University of Pennsylvania, Jonathan has made Berkshire County his real home. He published *The Complete Book of Mopeds* (Funk & Wagnalls), *Starring Your Love Life* (Lynx), *The Look of Horror* (Running Press), and numerous articles for the former *Berkshire Magazine*, as well as pieces on electric cars and solar energy for other publications. Berkshire House published his book, *Firewalk*, in 1992. As a photographer, he has created images for advertising, for actors, for book illustrations, and for rock videos. When he's not writing or photographing, he is a tennis pro at Canyon Ranch in Lenox.

Berkshire House and the crew of Berkshire Book Six wish him well.

The Way This Book Works

ORGANIZATION

Entries are located by subject in the appropriate chapters. Among the chapters, arrangements vary to suit the needs of subject matter. Most material is arranged in three geographical groupings, with South County offerings first, followed by those in Central County, and finally North County. A few nearby listings that are located Outside the County are given as well.

Within these geographic groupings, listings are arranged alphabetically — first by town or topic, and then by establishments' names. Some entries, such as those in *Shopping*, are arranged by type; hence all the craft shops appear together. Each chapter has its own introduction, and the specific arrangement of that chapter is spelled out there.

Factual information was researched at the latest possible time before publication, but be advised that chefs and innkeepers come and go, hours change, shops appear and disappear. When in doubt, phone ahead.

Specific information (such as address and location, telephone number, hours of business, and a summary of special features or restrictions) is presented in the lefthand column or is otherwise shown separately, adjacent to descriptions of various entries throughout the book.

PRICES

With few exceptions, specific prices are not given. Because pricing is constantly changing, generally we have noted price ranges.

Lodging prices are on a per-room rate, double occupancy, in the high season (summer, fall foliage, and ski months). Low-season rates are likely to be 20–40% less. We urge you always to phone ahead for updated prices and other information and for reservations.

Restaurant prices indicate the cost of an individual's meal, which includes appetizer, entrée, and dessert but does not include cocktails, wine, tax, or tip. Restaurants with a prix fixe menu are noted accordingly.

Price Codes

	Lodging	*Dining*
Inexpensive	Up to $65	Up to $15
Moderate	$65 to $100	$15 to $25
Expensive	$100 to $175	$25 to $40
Very Expensive	$175 or more	Over $40

Credit cards are abbreviated as follows:

AE — American Express   DC — Diner's Club
CB — Carte Blanche   MC — MasterCard
D — Discover   V — Visa

AREA CODE

There is one telephone area code for all of Berkshire County: **413**.

INFORMATION BOOTHS

Volunteers in several Berkshire towns staff tourist Information Booths in the summer and early fall. Often information is available at the site even when volunteers aren't. Year-round tourist information can be obtained from the *Berkshire Visitors Bureau,* Berkshire Common, bottom level, Crowne Plaza Hotel, West St., Pittsfield (413-443-9186). The bureau is open Mon.–Fri., 8:30–4:30.

For a more detailed list of information sources, see "Tourist Information" at the end of Chapter Nine, *Information.*

North County
Adams (population 8,768)
Cheshire (3,421)
Clarksburg (1,674)
Florida (729)
New Ashford (190)
North Adams (15,496)
Savoy (693)
Williamstown (7,948)

Central County
Becket (1,501)
Dalton (6,854)
Hancock (575)
Hinsdale (1,855)
Lanesborough (3,035)
Lenox (5,180)
Peru (757)
Pittsfield (45,513)
Richmond (1,628)
Washington (621)
Windsor (759)

South County
Alford (407)
Egremont (1,226)
Great Barrington (7,592)
Lee (5,657)
Monterey (801)
Mount Washington (130)
New Marlborough (1,253)
Otis (1,060)
Sandisfield (654)
Sheffield (2,956)
Stockbridge (2,293)
Tyringham (363)
West Stockbridge (1,445)

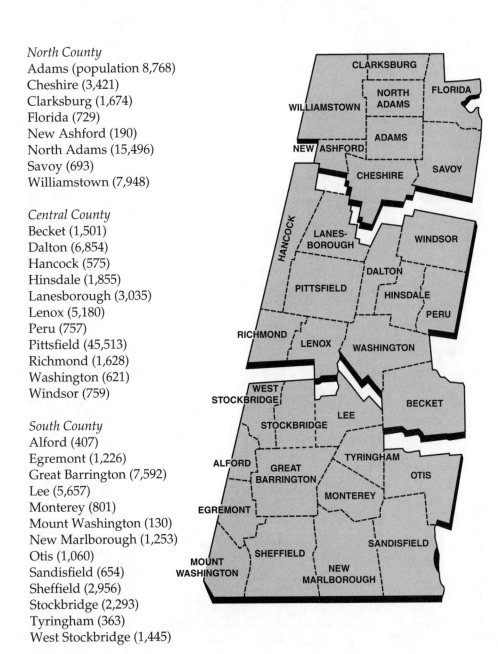

BERKSHIRE TOWNS

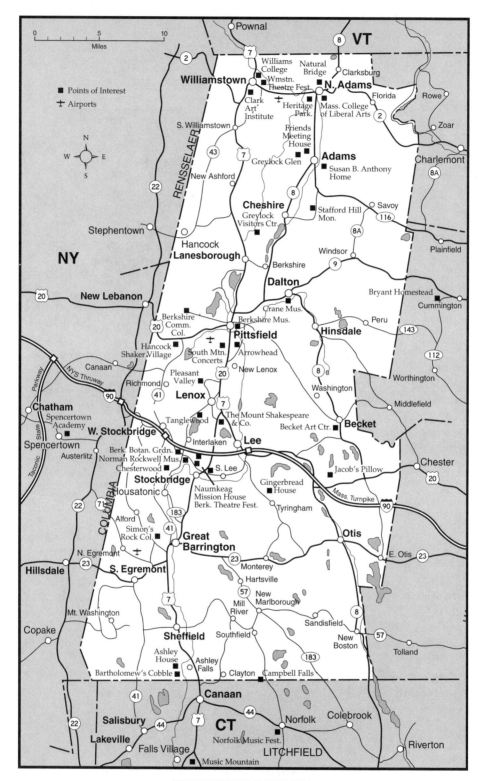

BERKSHIRE COUNTY

The
BERKSHIRE
Book
A Complete Guide

CHAPTER ONE
From the Glaciers to the Present
HISTORY

To the hard-working Berkshire settlers, much of what we prize as beauty — these rolling hills — was at the least unproductive, and at the most an absolute impediment to making a living. Jeremiah Wilbur, who in 1767 at the age of 14 began farming on the sides of Mount Greylock, could not have had a lot of time to admire the view. This prodigious worker built a carting road over the Notch between Ragged Mountain and Greylock into Adams, built a road

Judith Monachina

The village of Tyringham rises in a wooded dell.

to near the summit of Greylock (the forerunner of today's Notch Road), cleared enough land to grow and cut 100 tons of hay in a year, tapped enough maples to produce 1,800 pounds of sugar in a year, protected his herd of free-roaming cattle from wolves, maintained the best sheep herd in the county, built a cider mill, a grist mill, and a sawmill on Notch Brook, increased his holdings to 1,600 acres, and died in 1813 a relatively wealthy man. Water power may have lured this early farmer out of the valley and onto the wildest land around, but that same water was a constant threat to his road, wild animals threatened to destroy his livelihood, and the steep terrain was hard to negotiate and tough to plow.

We're fortunate to know a bit about Wilbur. One eyewitness was Timothy Dwight, who toured upstate New York and New England in 1800, after retiring from the presidency of Yale College, and published *Travels in New England and New York* in 1822. At that time people traveled to settle, trade furs, convert Indians, survey boundaries, or fight wars. The concept of taking a recreational spin through remote and unsettled places was unheard of. Dwight may, in fact, have been America's first tourist. Our good fortune is that he was an intelligent, observant, literate man.

When Dwight rode into Williamstown in October, he looked up Ebenezer Fitch, president of Williams College, who had written about Wilbur's remarkable sheep farm, and suggested a trip up Mount Greylock. Fitch led the way to Wilbur's home, partway up the mountain. Wilbur not only allowed the men to cross his land, but he accompanied them up the road he had built to carry salt to his cattle.

"We alighted from our horses within 20 feet of the summit," Dwight wrote, "and found our path better than a great part of the town and country roads throughout the hill country of New England." The summit of Mount Greylock was covered with trees; no one, as yet, had built a tower there. So to obtain a view, the farmer and the two college presidents each picked out a wind-battered fir tree, and shinnied up.

"The view was immense and of amazing grandeur," Dwight recalled. "You will easily suppose that we felt total superiority to all the humble beings who were creeping on the footstool beneath us. The village of Williamstown shrunk to the size of a farm; and its houses, church, and colleges appeared like the habitation of martins and wrens."

Dwight recognized the Adirondacks, the Green Mountains, Mount Monadnock, Mount Tom, and the Catskills. He discovered the joy of the third dimension — height — which we, who so easily drive over hills or fly above them, take for granted. To Dwight's generation and those to follow, Mount Greylock was spectacular, as most people did not visit higher peaks; just as Bash Bish Falls, at the southwest corner of Berkshire, inspired awe in the days when few had seen Niagara.

Berkshire, The Berkshires, The Berkshire Hills

What is the name of this place, anyway? The original Berkshire is in England, south of Oxford. There it's pronounced "Bark-shuh." "Shire" refers to an Anglo-Saxon administrative district.

Purists refer to the "Berkshire Hills," meaning specifically what this book calls the southern Taconics, including peaks in New York State. The logic of calling all hills in Berkshire County the Berkshire Hills seems to be gaining acceptance.

Berkshire residents — and visitors — refer to the area variously as "Berkshire County," as simply "Berkshire," and as "the Berkshires," actually a 20th-century term created to publicize the area. This book does likewise.

Forty-four years later, when writer/naturalist Henry David Thoreau climbed past the old Wilbur homestead, Mount Greylock was still wild country, still an adventure. He exchanged a few words about reaching the summit that night with Smith Wilbur, Jeremiah's grandson. Thoreau used the trip to overcome his grief over his brother's death, his disappointment at being

Foresters examine an old-growth specimen on Mt. Greylock.

Lauren R. Stevens

rejected as a suitor by a cousin, his remorse at having accidentally burned 300 acres of woodlands in Concord, and his need to find his own transcendental vision. All these things, he implies, he put behind him on his walk up Greylock, awakening the next morning to an inspiring sunrise above the clouds. The trip was his preparation for Walden, pond and book.

(Thoreau must have read Dwight, for he made the same mistake of identifying Williamstown from the summit. Can't be done: Mount Prospect is in the way. Thoreau admitted, in his account of the trip in *A Week on the Concord and Merrimack Rivers,* that he had only a very quick view out before the sun set.)

What Dwight began, and 19th-century writers and painters continued, was to instruct hard-working, practical folk like farmer Wilbur in the appreciation of the landscape. For a farmer occupied with the daily grind of producing food for his family, someone had to say — as Thoreau did more than once — slow down, enjoy, observe the values nature maintains without any human labor.

Thus the Hudson River School of painters created large, inspiring landscapes and touted them through the towns and cities. "Look what we have here!" they exclaimed to frontierspeople who had seen little beyond the back forty. Furthermore, these artists transformed the religious view of the landscape. When the Puritans arrived on these shores, they saw the woods as dark, evil, aligned with the devil. When Thoreau described his July sunrise or Thomas Cole painted the sun breaking through the clouds, we realize that it is really heaven that is in cahoots with the trees, fields, and falling water around us. Thoreau came to terms with his own problems on Greylock, but he also taught his readers to appreciate the marvels of this godly place.

Building on this tradition, excelling and expanding in their seasons, the arts in Berkshire are still teaching residents and visitors to pay attention to our magnificent surroundings.

NATURAL HISTORY

Tell me your landscape and I will tell you who you are.

— Ortega y Gasset

Erosion gentled the Berkshire landscape in much the same way that culture has smoothed the rough edges of its people — whom Edith Wharton once called her "granite outcroppings." Artists taught us to appreciate this gentled landscape.

Six hundred million years ago this area was flatter, covered by a shallow sea. Lapping waves built up beaches that turned to sandstone, which in turn metamorphosed into quartzite — the erosion-resistant backbone of many county ridges. Shelled marine animals built coral reefs, which calcified over eons into limestone. Deposits of this alkaline agent, which are mined on the side of Mount Greylock today, buffer the area against the worst ravages of acid precipitation. Some of the limestone recrystallized into marble, snowy chunks of which grace hiking trails and can be examined at Natural Bridge, in North Adams. Offshore, muddy sediments settled to form shales and then schists, crystalline rocks that fracture into clean layers. All of these rocks are still present in Berkshire County.

Then at a speed of an inch a year over 150 million years, the land masses that would one day be North America, Africa, and Europe moved toward each other, closing the proto-Atlantic Ocean. Several arcs of offshore volcanic islands were shoved onto the continent in a series of slow but cataclysmic collisions known as the Taconic Orogeny (orogeny means "mountain building"). The entire continental shelf was squeezed into a series of enormous folds, the monumental forerunners of the Appalachian Mountains. Then, slowly, the continents began to pull apart, as they are still doing.

Even as the mountains were rising, to several miles in elevation, the process of erosion began. Rain fell, forming streams that raged through a landscape mostly free of vegetation. Over the eons, water and wind tamed the rugged landforms and sculpted the hills of Berkshire.

Less than two million years ago, the first in a succession of four ice sheets ground down in response to a cooling climate. These mile-high glaciers deposited debris, gravel, and rocks around the relative nubbins of mountains that remained. Glacial lakes covered Great Barrington, Tyringham, and the basin from Williamstown to Adams, and when they drained left gravel beaches on the mountainsides. But the glaciers did not create these mountains; they only iced the Berkshire cake. The great work of diminution had begun — and continues — through everyday erosion. Two great landslides on Mount Greylock in the summer of 1990 were simply more dramatic instances. The Hoosic, Housatonic, and Westfield river valleys remained largely the same as

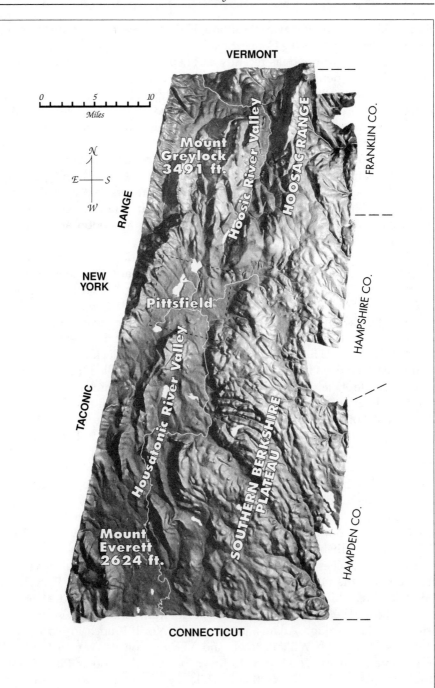

VERMONT

0 5 10
Miles

N
E S
W

RANGE

NEW
YORK

TACONIC

Mount
Greylock
3491 ft.

Hoosic River Valley

HOOSAC RANGE

FRANKLIN CO.

HAMPSHIRE CO.

Pittsfield

Housatonic River Valley

SOUTHERN BERKSHIRE
PLATEAU

HAMPDEN CO.

Mount
Everett
2624 ft.

CONNECTICUT

From the relief map by Bartlett Hendricks, courtesy Berkshire Museum they had been before the glaciers, although glacial debris forced the Farmington River to swing north to the Connecticut.

As the region warmed, as recently as 11,000 years ago, vegetation returned and further tempered the climate. From boggy marshlands the evergreen forest moved north, lingering now only on the tops of the highest ridges. In its place the broad-leaved deciduous forest moved in, characterized by oak and its associated species in South County and the sugar maple farther north.

As the glaciers withdrew, animals returned — and humans arrived. Perhaps a few of the earliest North Americans, whose ancestors had boated or walked across the land bridge from Asia, were in Berkshire to watch the glacial lakes drain. The first Americans in the region were foragers, but after developing tools they crafted weapons and became hunters. In South Egremont not long ago were found the remains of a 12,000-year-old mastodon and, around it, arrowheads of the same age.

Seen from above, Berkshire County presents its ridges as north-south-running folds: the Taconics along the New York boundary, the Green Mountains protruding south from Vermont, the Hoosacs filling the northeast quadrant, and the Southern Berkshire Plateau in the southeast. Tributaries of the two major Berkshire rivers, the Housatonic and the Hoosic, nearly meet at Brodie Mountain and then flow in opposite directions to form the extended north-south valley that U.S. Route 7 now follows. The Greylock massif stands as a peninsula, as indeed it was when glacial Lake Bascom filled the Hoosac Valley to the 1,300-foot elevation. Greylock rises 3,491 feet, the highest point in southern New England, visible from most of the county. Mount Everett is the 2,264-foot sentinel of South County. It is possible to see the one from the other.

The rocky steepness of the county does not lend itself to leisurely flowing water and big lakes. With the exception of the southern reach of the Housatonic River, which meanders through Sheffield, Berkshire rivers rush to their destinations. With the exception of Stockbridge Bowl, we owe the county's present-day lakes to 19th-century industrialists, who either dammed small ponds to make them larger, as with Otis, Pontoosuc, and Onota, or created reservoirs out of rivers, as with Cheshire Reservoir. They wanted a supply of water available to turn the mill wheels in low-water times.

The two branches of the Housatonic River rise in the Greylock range and in Washington, the northernmost part of the Southern Berkshire Plateau. They meet in Pittsfield and flow south to enter Long Island Sound at Stratford, Connecticut. The Hoosic River flows north from Cheshire Reservoir (a.k.a. Hoosac Lake) through Adams, joins with its North Branch in North Adams, and passes through Williamstown and Vermont on its way to the Hudson River above Albany. The Westfield River forms in the Hoosac Plateau, joining the Connecticut River in Westfield, while the Farmington River forms in the Southern Berkshire Plateau, mostly in Otis Reservoir, the largest recreational body of fresh water in the Commonwealth.

Although settlement and deforestation of the county once drove off the larger animals, today they are returning. One hundred years ago the county was 75 percent cleared. Now, as the farms grow in, it is 75 percent wooded, providing habitat for deer, black bear, red and gray fox, coyotes, bobcats, beavers, mink, and the occasional moose. Tales of eastern cougar sightings are making the rounds; the last cougar in these parts was thought to have been shot in Vermont 100 years ago. Berkshire hosts rare salamanders who thrive only in these wetlands because of the area's high lime content. Wild turkey flap about in the woods, while in 1999 a bald eagle was born in Sandisfield. Giant blue herons, with wings six feet across, can be seen here on isolated ponds; ruffed grouse and quail occupy the woods.

Although formal gardens at historic homes are beautiful, so are the ephemeral spring flowers at Bartholomew's Cobble and the delicate boreal blooms on Greylock. A gentled, cultivated Berkshire awaits your exploration.

This geology follows Lauren R. Stevens's *Hikes & Walks in the Berkshire Hills*, for which Williams College geologist Paul Karabinos consulted. The pamphlet *A Canoe Guide to the Housatonic* comments on the local ecology. Berkshire Sanctuaries Director René Laubach, in his *Guide to Natural Places in the Berkshire Hills*, invokes the flora, fauna, geology, and ecology. The Berkshire Museum, the county's center for natural history study, displays Bartlett Hendricks's wall-sized raised-relief topographic map of the country. For field trips, try any of the "Outdoor Sites" (see Chapter Seven, *Outdoor Recreation*). And in the summer the Appalachian Mountain Club runs excellent nature study programs at sky-high Bascom Lodge atop Mt. Greylock.

SOCIAL HISTORY

History is to the community what memory is to the individual.

— Shaker saying

As recent archeological digs in South County have confirmed, American Indians settled and farmed this area before the time of Europeans. The words *housatonic* and *hoosic* have a similar linguistic root, which may have meant "beyond-place," beyond the Hudson. The Mahican Indians entered the area from the Hudson Valley by way of the Green and Hoosic rivers to hunt and fish, in prehistory. They fished for shad, herring, and salmon in the springtime. The Mahicans built weirs to trap fish in Housatonic tributaries and also fished with hand nets from dugout canoes on the river. They gathered mussels from the rocky river bottoms and smoke-cured them, together with their surplus fish, for winter storage. They hunted duck and geese, and they maintained gardens in the river's floodplain, which was fertilized annually by the spring flood.

After the Dutch established a fur-trading outpost at Fort Orange (now Albany, NY) in 1624 the Mahicans fell into conflict and then went to war with the neighboring Mohawks over the valuable fur trade. By 1628 the Mahicans had been driven to the east of the Hudson, some settling in Berkshire.

In 1676 the first European of record set foot in Berkshire, when Major John Talcott overtook a raiding band of about 150 Indians "neare onto Ousatunick" (Great Barrington) and won the last significant battle of King Philip's War. Smallpox brought by the Europeans dramatically reduced Mahican ranks by the late 17th century.

As the numbers of Indians shrank, a few Dutch settlers came from the Hudson Valley to what is now the town of Mount Washington. Dutch town names such as Van Deusenville (in Great Barrington) still exist in South County, and traces of Dutch architecture linger in the square gable ends of certain old buildings.

In 1724 a small band of Mahicans led by chiefs Konkapot and Umpachenee sold their lands along the Housatonic River, including what is now Sheffield, Great Barrington, Egremont, Mount Washington, Alford, and parts of Lee, Stockbridge, and West Stockbridge. The price: "£460, 3 bbls. of cider, and 30 qts. of rum." While the first land-buyers were speculators from the Bay Colony (Massachusetts), the first settlers tended to come from Connecticut, because it was easier to move north along the river valleys than from east to west over the mountains.

English settlers moved to the Sheffield grant, building the first homesteads at some distance from the Housatonic, on the second river terrace. This allowed the fertile floodplain to be used for agriculture and kept homes away from the malarial lowlands and safely distant from floods. In the mid-1730s, the Rev. John Sergeant came from Yale College to proselytize and educate the hundreds of Mahicans who lived around *W-nahk-ta-kook* ("Great Meadow"), later called Indian Town and then Stockbridge. He learned their language and won their respect.

In 1744 Berkshire was opened to cross-country travel for the first time, when the "Great Road" was laid out between Boston and Albany, crossing the county at Great Barrington. Five years later, John Sergeant died, and two years after that, Rev. Jonathan Edwards came to Stockbridge. With his fiery preaching style, Edwards had stirred up the "Great Awakening," a religious revival that swept New England. His zeal, however, had offended parishioners at his previous pulpit in Northampton, resulting in his dismissal. Exiled to Stockbridge, he got along less well with the Indians than Sergeant had. One of America's earliest religious philosophers, Edwards published *Freedom of the Will*, Berkshire's first book, in 1754.

After the British victory over the French at Quebec marked the end of the French and Indian Wars in 1759, western Massachusetts was less vulnerable to Indian attack and considered safer for settlement. The county was created as a political entity on July 1, 1761, when the royal governor, Sir Francis Bernard, struck off a section from the already-existing Hampshire County and declared this one "Berkshire," after his home county in England. The county's boundaries corresponded in an unusual degree to its topography (although the boundary with New York wasn't settled until the 1790s).

In early 1773 a group of townspeople and lawyers met in the Sheffield study of Colonel John Ashley. There, in one of the earliest public assertions of American freedom, they drafted the "Sheffield Declaration," stating to Great Britain and all the world that "Mankind in a State of Nature are equal, free, and independent of each other. . . ."

During the following year, ferment against the British intensified in the county. In July a county convention met under the chairmanship of Colonel Ashley. From this meeting the "Stockbridge Non-Intercourse Articles" of 1774 were drafted, complaining that "whereas the Parliament of Great Britain have of late undertaken to give and grant away our money without our knowledge or consent, . . . we will not import, purchase, or consume" any British goods.

British oppression mounted. On August 16, some 1,500 Berkshire citizens staged a peaceful sit-down strike around the Great Barrington Courthouse, preventing the royal judges from meeting. It was the first open resistance to British rule in America.

In April 1775 a regiment of Berkshire Minutemen under Colonel John Paterson of Lenox started out for Cambridge to aid in the Revolutionary effort. And in May, former Sheffield resident Ethan Allen led his Green Mountain Boys, with 57 Berkshire men, in a successful surprise attack on Fort Ticonderoga on Lake Champlain. That winter (1776), General Henry Knox with Continental troops and over 100 oxen dragged captured Ticonderoga cannon through Berkshire to General George Washington in Cambridge. With the help of this additional weaponry, Washington was able to drive the British from Boston.

After the Revolution, Daniel Shays led a revolt of Western Massachusetts veterans disappointed in their lot. In 1786 they closed court houses and released debtors from jail. An attempt to take the Springfield arsenal the following January failed. Most of the Regulators were killed or captured. Mum Bett, then employed by the Sedgwicks, hid the family silver during the fighting.

With peace and prosperity, the 1790s saw the beginnings of a number of long-term county institutions. The Shakers established colonies in Hancock and Tyringham, and marble quarrying started in West Stockbridge. Williams College's faltering beginnings in 1793 led, eventually, to its position as one of the finest liberal arts colleges in the United States.

The Native American community in Berkshire had meanwhile collapsed socially and economically. As Konkapot's tribe dwindled to fewer than 400 members, in 1771 at age 94 he had stepped down as chief of the rechristened "Stockbridge Indians" — Mahicans plus the remnants of several other tribes. Beginning in 1784 the Stockbridge were forced into westward migration, leaving only their Housatonic legends — and a Bible — behind them. Their descendants returned to the Mission House for the Bible 200 years later.

Elkanah Watson introduced Spanish Merino sheep — and, incidentally, the agricultural fair — into Berkshire in 1807, tethering two of the animals on the Pittsfield common. Their wool, spun into fine worsted yarn and woven into Berkshire broadcloth in the county's state-of-the-art mills, was fashioned into President Madison's inauguration suit in 1807. Shortly thereafter, the first stage route in the county was established, running from Greenfield to North Adams, Williamstown, and Albany.

Judith Monachina

The village of Housatonic, long known for its busy mills, is now home to many art galleries as well.

The mill on the farm became the mill in the town. Driven by plentiful water power, industry took a firm hold in Berkshire when Zenas Crane began paper production in Dalton and David Estes opened the first textile mill in North Adams.

Writers and painters arrived soon after. William Cullen Bryant spent a year at Williams College and then practiced law in Great Barrington, attempting simultaneously to divine the art of poetry. His friend Catherine Sedgwick published her first novel, *A New England Tale*, in 1820 to critical acclaim. Hudson River School artist Thomas Cole painted Mount Greylock over Pontoosuc Lake, while others depicted the lower Housatonic and Bash Bish Falls. Alexis de Tocqueville visited the Sedgwicks by stagecoach in Stockbridge in 1831. Not long after, trains huffed into the hills, one of them carrying Mr. and Mrs. Henry Wadsworth Longfellow to honeymoon in Pittsfield. Dr. Oliver Wendell Holmes, "the autocrat of the breakfast table," built a home on family property at Canoe Meadows in order to spend his summers in Berkshire. Nathaniel Hawthorne moved from Salem to Lenox and took up residence at a property he called Tanglewood. Then in 1850 Herman Melville bought Arrowhead Farm in Pittsfield. David Dudley Field introduced Melville to Hawthorne on the occasion of a climb up Monument Mountain; the two great writers' imaginations were entwined thereafter.

Hawthorne and Thoreau

Nathaniel Hawthorne was one of 19th-century Berkshire's greatest admirers. During his year-and-a-half residence in the "Red Cottage" at "Tanglewood," overlooking Stockbridge Bowl, he kept a journal that recorded the fullness of his affection for the landscape.

October 16, 1850

A morning mist filling up the whole length and breadth of the valley, betwixt here and Monument Mountain; the summit of the mountain emerging. The mist reaches to perhaps a hundred yards of our house, so dense as to conceal everything, except that, near its hither boundary, a few ruddy or yellow tree-tops emerge, glorified by the early sunshine; as is likewise the whole mist cloud.

Henry David Thoreau shared Hawthorne's reverence for these hills, praising Williams College's position at the foot of Greylock — or anyone's willingness to learn from nature.

It would be no small advantage if every college were thus located at the base of a mountain, as good at least as one well-endowed professorship.... Some will remember, no doubt, not only that they went to college, but that they went to the mountain.

In 1851 construction began on the Hoosac Tunnel between the Berkshire towns of Florida and North Adams, a project that was to take 24 years and cost 195 lives. At 4.75 miles it was the longest railroad tunnel in America and the one in which nitroglycerine was used for the first time.

Before those explosions were silenced, shells were fired in hate in the Civil War. Five days after the Confederate forces opened fire on Fort Sumter, Berkshire militiamen were on their way south to defend the Republic. Those first county recruits stayed three months and saw little action, but other Berkshire regiments took their place, fighting through 1865 as far south as the state of Florida.

After two unsuccessful attempts, in 1866, Cyrus Field of Stockbridge and his engineers laid a cable across the Atlantic Ocean, connecting America with Europe. A year later in America's leading paper town, Lee, paper fabrication from wood pulp rather than rags was demonstrated for the first time in the United States.

Industry was booming in the Berkshires, with textile and paper plants lining the rivers. Fueled by the county's abundant forests, iron smelters, railroads, and other heavy industries cut deep into the Berkshire woodland. Before long nearly 75 percent of the county's timber was gone, and the hills were nearly bald.

In 1875 the Hoosac Tunnel was finally completed, opening North County to interstate commerce. Shortly thereafter, in 1879, Crane & Co. of Dalton obtained an exclusive contract with the federal government involving a lot of money — producing U.S. currency.

In 1886, William Stanley installed the world's first commercial electric system, lighting 25 shops along Main Street in Great Barrington. The General Electric Company visited Stanley in his Pittsfield workshop and, soon after, moved nearby. Five years later, an electric trolley system was introduced in Pittsfield, running from Park Square to Pontoosuc Lake. Soon this quiet, reliable transport would connect most of the towns in the county, and the county with the region.

The 1880s ushered in Berkshire's Gilded Age during which millionaires came to the hills to play and to build their dream "cottages." Mrs. Searles had just completed her $2.5 million castle in Great Barrington; Anson Phelps Stokes had spent nearly as much in completing the largest home in America just then, his 100-room Shadowbrook in Stockbridge. A mile away, the 33-room Italianate palazzo called Wheatleigh was being finished, a gift of H. H. Cook to his daughter on the occasion of her marriage to Count Carlos de Heredia. The 50-room Elm Court was nearby in Lenox, built by rug magnate W. D. Sloane; and across town, Giraud Foster had erected his multimillion-dollar likeness of the French Petit Trianon at his estate, Bellefontaine. In Stockbridge was Naumkeag, Ambassador Choate's homey mansion, along with sculptor Daniel Chester French's splendid Chesterwood. Soon Robert Paterson constructed Blantyre and Edith Wharton built The Mount, both in Lenox. In all, some 75 extraordinary mansions graced the Berkshire landscape. European and urban tastes had arrived in the hills.

Yet William C. Whitney, secretary of the Navy under Grover Cleveland, acquired more land than all of these. In 1896, Whitney established an 11,000-acre game preserve in the Berkshire town of Washington and stocked it with buffalo, moose, Virginia deer, and elk. The estate later became October Mountain State Forest, a giant reserve in the center of the county. Two years later, North Adams industrialists donated 400 acres at the top of Mount Greylock to the Commonwealth, creating the first state reservation.

In North Adams a "Normal School" or teachers' college was established in 1894. Over the following century it evolved into the Massachusetts College of Liberal Arts.

President James Garfield was assassinated on his way to his 25th Williams

The Mount today, terrace side/east elevation, following recent restoration.

College reunion, so his vice president, Chester A. Arthur, took over. Both men had taught in the same one-room school in Pownal, Vermont, in the 1850s. In the fall of 1902, President Theodore Roosevelt visited Berkshire, sustaining minor injury after his coach overturned near the Pittsfield Country Club. That next summer, both ex-president Grover Cleveland and humorist Mark Twain summered in Tyringham. Eight years later, as Pittsfield observed its gala 150th anniversary on July 4, 1911, President Taft spoke before a crowd of 50,000 at the railroad station. Later that same year, Edith Wharton's novella *Ethan Frome* was published, a critical and popular success that derived many of its dramatic and scenic details from life in the Berkshires.

The 20th century in Berkshire has been marked by events principally in industry and the arts. Since 1903 General Electric has played a significant role in the county's industry. In 1914, GE established a high-voltage laboratory in Pittsfield, and seven years later, the lab made electrical history by producing a million-volt flash of artificial lightning. While GE developed a large trans-former business and produced naval armaments, Sprague Electric met the country's enormous need for capacitors during World War II and expanded to

The Ted Shawn Theatre at Jacob's Pillow. The Pillow celebrated its 65th anniversary in 1999.

Gary Gunderson, courtesy Jacob's Pillow

occupy former mills in North Adams. Both manufacturers were to decline significantly in the second half of the century.

In the arts, the Stockbridge Playhouse (now the Berkshire Theatre Festival) opened in 1928 with Eva LeGallienne in *Cradle Song*. Ted Shawn established a School of Dance at Jacob's Pillow in Becket in 1932. The 1930s heard the first Berkshire Symphony Festival concerts, a prelude to Tanglewood.

Downhill skiing debuted in Berkshire in 1935 as Bousquet opened runs in Pittsfield and arranged "ski trains" from New York City. Then the Thunderbolt Trail on Greylock, carved by the Civilian Conservation Corps, became the scene of Eastern downhill ski championships, before and after World War II. Soon half a dozen mountains in the county were crisscrossed by trails.

The 1950s saw the arrival of artist Norman Rockwell in Stockbridge and the creation of the Sterling and Francine Clark Art Institute in Williamstown, with its collection and library of international import. The Williamstown Theatre Festival began performances, enlivening all of Berkshire with star-studded drama. In the 1960s, two more colleges joined Williams and Mass College: Berkshire Community College in Pittsfield, the first in a series of state junior colleges; and Simon's Rock Early College in Great Barrington, a progressive school that is now part of Bard College. Arlo Guthrie, scion of a folk legend and former student at Stockbridge School, wrote a song about littering, the draft, and a community of friends living in Stockbridge.

The last Shaker sisters left their "village" in Hancock in 1960. A group of visionary citizens led by Amy Bess Miller managed to purchase their property and turn it into a living museum, today one of the county's premier attractions.

In the mid-'60s, General Electric made another breakthrough, this time in plastics, and the company subsequently developed a new family of polymers that diversified the corporation. In the 1990s, Lockheed Martin purchased the defense systems, and soon after they were purchased by General Dynamics Defense Systems, which is now developing liquid propellant technology for military and civilian use.

The great estates of the past have been recycled since the mid-20th century, increasingly in recent years, opening Berkshire's fiefs to the public. In addition to uncounted B&Bs and restaurants, the arts are leading in adaptive reuse of former manors. The Mount, now owned by Edith Wharton Restoration, Inc., is open to tours in season, sponsoring lectures and other events. Shakespeare & Company is moving from The Mount to Springlawn, another former estate. Bellefontaine has become a sophisticated spa, Canyon Ranch in the Berkshires. In the Glendale section of Stockbridge, the gracious Linwood estate has been transformed into the home of the Norman Rockwell Museum. Looking back toward Tanglewood from this splendid site provides a fresh view of an unspoiled 19th-century Berkshire.

Tanglewood has expanded on another former estate, creating the $10-million Seiji Ozawa Hall, where 1,200 music lovers can enjoy both intimacy and acoustic fidelity. In North County, the arts are reclaiming not so frequently estates but abandoned mills, most spectacularly the former textile mills that became Sprague Electric Co., now the Massachusetts Museum of Contemporary Art (Mass MoCA), in North Adams. It opened in the summer of 1999 to large crowds and international press coverage. Critics, even those who had reservations about the enormous pieces of art displayed, gave bravos to the space created and to the imaginative series of film, theater, dance, and music presented.

Berkshire citizens discuss the changes in their county: condos, shopping malls, bypasses, and the Greylock Glen sustainable development project. The Wal-Marting of Berkshire has begun, first up in North Adams and then in Pittsfield. Some say Wal-Marts create jobs and bring low prices; others point out that the Berkshire Mall has drained life from downtown Pittsfield, as Prime Outlets has pulled business away from the Lenox shops.

Environmental issues are being addressed head-on. A variety of ecologically aware groups are mobilizing to clean up Berkshire's principal river, the Housatonic. The Hoosic River appears to be on its way to be cleansed of PCBs for good.

The Berkshire Natural Resources Council and other environmental protection groups guard and preserve the splendor of the landscape. With the gradual shrinking of industry here, and with tourism becoming among the most stable of Berkshire businesses, protecting the rolling hills makes economic and aesthetic sense. Once the hills were decimated, shaved bald by paper and lumber mills and charcoal manufacturers. Now the hills are once more alive, fully forested and soothing to the eye.

MASS MoCA, writ large, opened to acclaim in 1999.

CHAPTER TWO
Getting Here, Getting Around
TRANSPORTATION

Judith Monachina

Berkshire Regional Transit Authority bus, here in Williamstown, helps bind the county together.

Although bus lines bring some visitors to and from Berkshire County, and the B Bus (Berkshire Regional Transit Authority) carries some through the county, most people rely on automobiles. Travel was more colorful, if less comfortable, in the past.

First we walked or rode horseback on county roads that were choked with dust, buried in snow, or clogged with bottomless mud, depending on the season. The Hudson and Connecticut rivers carried passengers toward Berkshire aboard sailing ships and, after 1825, steamboats. Both Albany and Hartford were connected to New York City by regular steamboat runs. The upper Connecticut River was outfitted with an elaborate system of locks to bypass the rapids.

With the harnessing of steam for riverboat power, it wasn't long before the iron horse galloped into the Berkshire Hills. The Housatonic Railroad brought visitors from New York City and southern New England. Two lines competed to the west: the Albany-West Stockbridge Line and the Hudson and Berkshire Line.

From Boston, construction of the Western Railway up from Springfield was reportedly "delayed by competition between Stockbridge and Pittsfield for fixing of the route through their town. After surveys, Pittsfield won." During the summers of 1840–41, workers made deep cuts in the hills and built many bridges. When the lines were completed, Berkshire was nine hours by train from Boston and about three hours from Albany. Many who had come to work on the railroads never took the train back. Hundreds of Irish rail laborers from cities east and west stayed on.

Sons of these rail workers may have labored on a remarkable system of electric trolley track and overhead wires running from Williamstown east to North Adams and south through Adams, Pittsfield, Lenox, Lee, Great Barrington, and Sheffield. Quiet and reliable, this Berkshire Street Railway grew so popular that opulent parlor cars were constructed and put into service, running till 1932. When automobiles and buses were refined, the possibilities for public transport changed: paved roads were improved, and unpaved ones were surfaced. Passenger rail and trolley service to and within the Berkshires withered.

PRESENT POSSIBILITIES

The roads to Berkshire are smooth and scenic, so an automobile, if available, is useful to explore the back roads and byways. Buses run regularly from New York, Hartford, Boston, and Albany. If you're in a hurry to get to these hills, you can fly in, but, alas, only by private or charter plane to Great Barrington, Pittsfield, or North Adams. Major airlines with regular service fly into Bradley International near Hartford and into the Albany County Airport; from there, car rentals or limousine and bus service are available. For your convenience, a host of details about Berkshire transportation follows; none of it as up-to-date as your telephone call, however.

GETTING TO THESE HILLS

BY CAR

From Manhattan: Take the Major Deegan Expressway or the Henry Hudson Parkway to the Saw Mill River Parkway, then proceed north on one of the most beautiful roadways in the world, the Taconic State Parkway. For southern Berkshire, exit the Taconic at "Hillsdale, Claverack, Rte. 23" and follow 23 east, toward Hillsdale and on to Great Barrington. For Stockbridge, Lee, and Lenox, proceed up Rte. 7. For Pittsfield and northern Berkshire, exit the Taconic at Rte. 295, following Rte. 22 to Rte. 20 for Pittsfield or to Rte. 43 through Hancock to Williamstown and North Adams.

BERKSHIRE ACCESS

Using Tanglewood (on the Stockbridge-Lenox line) as the Berkshire reference point, the following cities are this close. (Newly increased speeds on the interstates bring Berkshire somewhat closer to the rest of the world than this table indicates.)

CITY	TIME	MILES
Albany	1 hr	50
Boston	2.5 hrs	135
Bridgeport	2 hrs	110
Danbury	1.75 hrs	85
Hartford	1.5 hrs	70
New Haven	2.5 hrs	115
Montreal	5 hrs	275
New York City	3 hrs	150
Philadelphia	4.5 hrs	230
Providence	2.5 hrs	125
Springfield	.75 hr	35
Waterbury	1.5 hrs	75
Washington, DC	7 hrs	350
Worcester	1.75 hrs	90

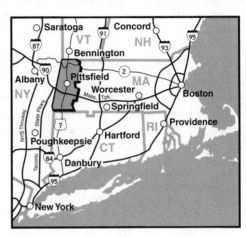

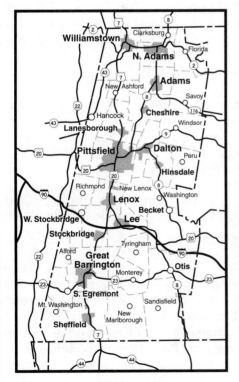

Berkshire County is 56 miles in length from Sheffield to Williamstown, and, depending on the season and the weather, it normally takes 1.5 hours to drive along Rte. 7. Because of the mountain ranges that also run north to south, east-west travel across the county remains more difficult. All of the county's east-west routes (2 in the north, 9 midcounty, and 23 in the south) are tricky drives in freezing or snowy weather. Back roads in particular vary tremendously in condition and type, ranging from smooth macadam to rough dirt. On these back roads especially, drivers should keep an eye out for bicyclists, horseback riders, hikers, joggers, rollerbladers — and deer, bear, moose, and bobcat.

From New Jersey, Pennsylvania, and south: If local color is high on your list or you'd rather ramble northward, Rte. 22 north is a good choice, and you can pick it up as far south as Armonk or Bedford in Westchester County, NY. Rte. 22 is a road still proud of its diners: of particular note is the Red Rooster in Brewster, just north of I-684's end. Further upstate on Rte. 22, turn right at Hillsdale on Rte. 23 east toward Great Barrington, Rte. 20 to Pittsfield, and Rte. 43 to Williamstown. For the most direct route from New Jersey, Pennsylvania, and south, take the New York Thruway to I-84 east; at the Taconic Parkway, turn north, following instructions "From Manhattan."

From Connecticut and/or the New York metro area: Rte. 7 north was an early stagecoach thoroughfare to Berkshire, and you join the same trail at Danbury, via I-684 and I-84. Driving up Rte. 7, you'll wend your way along the beautiful Housatonic River, north through New Milford, Kent, and Canaan and into Massachusetts through Ashley Falls (an especially good ride for picnics and antiques). To arrive in southeastern Berkshire, Rte. 8 is a quick and scenic drive as it follows the Farmington River north.

From Boston and east: The scenic Massachusetts Turnpike is the quickest and easiest route west to south Berkshire and Pittsfield. From Boston, there's no better bet, especially as tolls at the western end have been dropped. For the best route to Otis Ridge, Butternut Basin, and Catamount ski areas, you can leave the turnpike at Exit 3 west of the Connecticut River, take Rte. 202 south to Rte. 20 west, and pick up Rte. 23 west at Woronoco. Most people stay on the turnpike right into the Berkshires, exiting either at Lee or at West Stockbridge.

A less rapid but more colorful route westward from Boston is Rte. 20, which cuts across southern Massachusetts, connecting with Lee. If you're coming west to the Berkshires from more northern latitudes, Rte. 9 from Northampton is a splendid drive, a high road with long lovely vistas and few towns. Still farther to the north, eastern entry to Berkshire County can be gained by driving the spectacular Mohawk Trail, originally an Indian byway. Also known as Rte. 2, this is the most direct way to North Adams, Williamstown, and the ski slopes at Jiminy Peak and Brodie Mountain.

From Hartford: The quickest route is I-91 north to the Massachusetts Turnpike west. Then proceed as in the directions for Massachusetts Turnpike travel from Boston. A slower but more pleasant drive is Rte. 44 west, up through Avon, Norfolk, and Canaan, where you take Rte. 7 north into Berkshire County.

From Montreal and Albany: Leaving Canada, take I-87 (known as "the Northway") south to Albany. Exit at either Rte. 7 to Rte. 2 toward Williamstown or Rte. 20 to Pittsfield; or continue on I-87 south to I-90 east, which becomes the Massachusetts Turnpike. Exit either at Canaan, NY, or, Lee. (There is no eastbound exit from the Mass Pike at West Stockbridge.)

BY BUS

From Manhattan (3.5 hours): Bonanza (800-556-3815) serves the Berkshires out of New York City's *Port Authority Bus Terminal* (212-564-8484) at 40th St. between 8th and 9th Aves. Tickets may be purchased at the Greyhound ticket windows (800-231-2222), near 8th Ave. Several buses a day. Boarding is down the escalators at the center of the terminal, and then to the right, usually at Gate 13. Berkshire locales marked with an asterisk (*) are Flag Stops, where you must wave to the bus driver in order to be picked up.

Berkshire Phone Numbers for New York Buses

Canaan, CT	Brooks Pharmacy, Main St.	860-824-5481
Gt. Barrington	Bill's Pharmacy, 362 Main St.	413-528-1590
Hillsdale, NY	*Junction Rtes. 22 & 23	800-556-3815
Lee	McClelland Drug Store, 43 Main St.	413-243-0135
Lenox	Lenox News & Variety, 39 Housatonic St.	413-637-2815
New Ashford	*Entrance to Brodie Mt. Ski Area, Rte. 7	800-556-3815
Pittsfield	Bus Terminal, 57 S. Church St.	413-442-4451
Sheffield	First Massachusetts Bank (ATM), Rte. 7	800-556-3815
S. Egremont	*Gaslight Store	800-556-3815
Stockbridge	Information Booth, Main St.	800-556-3815
Williamstown	The Williams Inn, 1090 Main St.	413-458-2665

From Boston (3.5 hours): *Bonanza* and *Greyhound* serve the Berkshires from Boston out of the *Greyhound Terminal* at 10 St. James Ave. (800-231-2222). *Peter Pan/Trailways* runs daily to Pittsfield and North Adams-Williamstown out of the Trailways Terminal at South Station. Berkshire-bound passengers change buses at Springfield. Call 800-343-9999 for prices and schedules.

Berkshire Phone Numbers for Boston Buses

Lee	McClelland Drug Store, 43 Main St.	413-243-0135
Lenox	Lenox News & Variety, 39 Housatonic St.	413-637-2815
Pittsfield	Bus Terminal, 57 S. Church St.	413-442-4451
Williamstown	The Williams Inn, 1090 Main St.	413-458-2665

From Hartford (3 hours): The *Greyhound Line* runs two buses to Pittsfield daily, with a transfer in Springfield, from the *Greyhound Terminal* at 1 Union Place (in the train station), Hartford (860-522-9267).

From Montreal (6 hours): *Greyhound* runs south to the Albany Greyhound Terminal. Connect to Pittsfield as noted below.

From Albany (1 hour): *Bonanza* runs two buses daily from Albany to Pittsfield. *Greyhound* runs one bus daily.

BY TRAIN

From Manhattan: You can ride at the commuter rate, a fraction of the regular, if you get off at Dover Plains, NY. Call *Metro-North* (800 METRO-INFO) for fares and schedules. Buses complete the trip to Great Barrington on weekends. *Amtrak* (800-USA-RAIL or 800-872-7245) can also help you get to the Berkshires. Their turboliner from Grand Central Station runs frequently and smoothly along the Hudson River, a splendid ride. For southern Berkshire, stay aboard till Hudson, NY, a river town recently restored; for northern Berkshire, carry on to Rensselaer, NY. For travel connections from Dover Plains, Hudson, or Rensselaer to the Berkshires, see "By Limousine or Taxi."

From Boston: Amtrak continues to run a single train daily through the Berkshires, starting from Boston's South Station. To find the Pittsfield shelter: take West St. west past the Crowne Plaza Hotel; at the first light, turn right onto Center St.; take the next right onto Depot St.; the shelter is on the left. Anyone boarding the train in Pittsfield must purchase tickets on the train. The round-trip ticket prices vary, depending on time of travel and seat availability. Private compartments are available.

From Montreal: Amtrak runs one train daily from Montreal through Albany. There is no same-day train connection from this run to the Berkshires; see "By Limousine or Taxi"; or see "By Bus."

From Albany: Amtrak runs a single daily Pittsfield-bound train from the Albany/Rensselaer Depot on East St. (2 miles from downtown Albany), stopping at Pittsfield's Depot St. shelter (see directions above under "From Boston").

BY PLANE

If you own a small airplane or decide to charter one, you can fly directly to the Berkshires, landing at Great Barrington, Pittsfield, or North Adams airports.

From New York City: Feeling rich, traveling high with some friends, or riding on the corporate account? There are several charter air companies in the metropolitan New York area that will fly you from La Guardia, JFK, or other airports near New York to any of the Berkshire airports. Charters currently flying these routes include:

Airborne Inc.	800-553-3590
Business Air Services, Oxford, CT	800-226-6022
Chester Charter, Chester, CT	800-752-6371
Executive Airlines & Aviation	800-645-9572

and from Westchester County:

Panorama (White Plains airport)	914-328-9800
if calling from New York City:	718-507-9800
Richmor Aviation	800-331-6101 or
	518-828-9461

From Boston: There are several charter flight companies that fly from Beantown to Berkshire. Some of those you can try are:

Bird Airfleet	508-372-6566
Wiggins Airways	718-762-5690 Ext. #251

From Hartford: Bradley Airport in Hartford handles numerous domestic and international airlines, so you can fly to Bradley from nearly anywhere. From there, charter air service to the Berkshires is available through the companies listed under "From Boston" or through the Berkshire County companies listed below.

From Albany: Albany is terminus for a substantial volume of domestic jet traffic and, being less than an hour from the Berkshires by car, is the closest you can get to these hills by jet. Charter connector flights from Albany to the Berkshires are available through Signature Flight Support (518-869-0253) or through the Berkshire County companies listed below.

In Berkshire County: There are two aviation companies in Berkshire County which operate air taxi service to just about any other northeastern airport.

Berkshire Aviation	Gt. Barrington Airport	413-528-1010 or 528-1061 or 528-2030
Esposito Flying Service	Harriman & West Airport, N. Adams	413-663-3330

BY LIMOUSINE OR TAXI

If you're with a group or want to pamper yourself, a limousine direct to Berkshire is the smoothest approach. There are many limousine services that will whisk you away from urban gridlock to the spaciousness of this hill country.

From New York and its Airports:

Carey	212-935-9700
Kabot	718-545-2400

From Boston and Logan Airport:

Cooper	617-482-1000 or 800-343-2123
Fifth Avenue	781-286-0555

From Hartford and Bradley Airport:

Carey Elite Limousine	860-666-9051 or 800-RE:LIMOS (735-4667)
Ambassador	860-633-7300 or 800-395-LIMO (395-5466)

From Albany, Albany Airport, and Rensselaer:

Diamond Limousine 518-283-8000

To northern Berkshire (by reservation only):

Norm's Limousine Service 413-663-8300 or 413-663-6284

From Hudson, NY, and its Amtrak Station:

Star City Taxi 518-828-3355

GETTING AROUND THE BERKSHIRES

Note: Individual town maps of Great Barrington, Stockbridge, Lenox, Pittsfield, North Adams, and Williamstown can be found at the back of this book.

Rte. 7 is Berkshire County's main roadway, connecting cities and towns from south to north. Driving in winter, you'll certainly need snow tires. In summer, the cruising is easy; but on certain weekends during Tanglewood season and fall foliage, temporary traffic delays in popular villages are likely. Whenever possible, park and walk. Friendly but firm traffic police will suggest outlying parking areas. And motorists beware: state law requires a full stop for pedestrians in crosswalks, and for a school bus flashing red lights.

BY BUS

Berkshire County is no longer served by the electrified Berkshire Street Railway, but the "*B*," a public bus system, has in some ways filled the gap. The buses run from early in the morning to early in the evening. Buses are fitted with bicycle racks. Information can be obtained from the **Berkshire Regional Transit Authority** (413-499-2782 or, from Massachusetts phones, 800-292-2782). Fares vary by distance. If you're visiting without a car, the "*B*" will provide plenty of access to other communities, but Sunday service is not available.

BY RENTED CAR

Car rental agencies abound in Berkshire. Most will not deliver cars — you must first go to their place of business to do the paperwork. An exception is *Enterprise*. Its drivers will pick you up from the train, bus, or wherever, and then drive you back to the office to complete the paperwork. Berkshire car rentals are available through the following agencies:

Adams	Enterprise Rent-A-Car	413-743-7805
Gt. Barrington	AA Livery & Car Service	413-528-3906 or 877-528-3906

Gt. Barrington	Enterprise Rent-A-Car	413-644-9644
	Larkin's Car Store	
	(used only)	413-528-2156
	Pete's Ford	413-528-0848 or 800-698-0848
Lee	R.W.'s, Inc.	413-243-0946
Pittsfield	Enterprise Rent-A-Car	413-433-6600 or 800-325-8007
	Hertz Rent-A-Car	800-654-3131
	Pete's Leasing, Inc.	413-443-1406 or 413-445-5795
	Rent-A-Wreck	413-447-8117 or 800-499-8117
N. Adams	Rent-A-Wreck	413-664-1000
Williamstown	B&L Service Station	413-458-8269

BY TAXI OR LIMOUSINE

Numerous taxi and limo companies serve Berkshire County. The following is a listing by town, with notations indicating if they have only taxis (T), only limos (L), or both (B).

Gt. Barrington	Taxico	413-528-0911 or 528-0567 (T)
Lee	Abbott's Limousine	
	& Livery	413-243-1645 (L)
	Park Taxi	413-243-0020 (T)
Lenox	Alston's	413-637-3676 (L)
	Tobi's Limousine Service	413-637-1224 (L)
N. Adams	Berkshire Livery Service	413-662-2609 or
		800-298-2609 (L)
	Norm's Limousine Service	413-663-8300 or 663-6284 (B)
Pittsfield	Aarow Taxi	413-499-8604 (T)
	Airport & Limousine	413-443-7111 (L)
	Rainbow Taxi	413-499-4300 (T)
Stockbridge	Stockbridge Livery	413-298-4848 (T)

BY BICYCLE

Bicycling in the Berkshires gives an exciting intimacy with the rolling landscape. Depending on your willingness to bundle up, biking from town to town is possible nearly year around. Bike rental prices vary widely, with bikes available through:

Canaan, CT	Bike Doctor	860-824-5577
Gt. Barrington	Berkshire Bike & Blade	413-528-5555
Lenox	Arcadian Shop	413-637-3010
Pittsfield	Plaine's Bike, Golf, Ski	413-499-0391

ON FOOT

The Appalachian Trail enters southern Berkshire in the town of Mount Washington and runs over hill and dale, past Great Barrington, through Monterey, and down into Tyringham Valley, then up through the town of Washington, through Dalton and Cheshire, over Mt. Greylock, and toward Vermont. If you've got the time, we've got the trail. See "Walking, Camping, Cross-Country Skiing" in Chapter Seven, *Outdoor Recreation*.

Many Berkshire towns are small enough for walking exploration, and four in particular are well suited to visiting without a vehicle: Stockbridge, Lenox, Lee, and Williamstown. All are lovely villages, with good accommodations, fine dining, interesting shopping, and first-rate cultural attractions within easy walking distance.

NEIGHBORS ALL AROUND

Although we tend to think of the Berkshires as a place apart, the county and its people have close ties to their neighboring communities, counties, and states. Travelers as well will want to connect with these neighbors, for Berkshire is surrounded by areas of extensive natural beauty. Many nearby towns are loaded with good restaurants, old inns, and cultural attractions.

TO THE SOUTH

The Litchfield Hills of northwest Connecticut are gentler than the Berkshire Hills, but they still make for good hiking. There is lovely architecture in this area, with many stately homes in Salisbury, Lakeville, Sharon, Litchfield, and Norfolk. And there are music festivals as well, such as the ones at Norfolk and at Music Mountain in Falls Village. See "Music" in Chapter Five, *Arts & Pleasures*.

TO THE EAST

Between the Housatonic River valley and the Connecticut River lies the jagged eastern county border, shared with Franklin, Hamden, and Hampshire counties. Besides its natural splendor, this eastern area boasts an attractive array of cultural possibilities. The "Five College Area" of Amherst, South Hadley, and Northampton offers all the aesthetic and academic action anyone could want, with Amherst, Hampshire, Mt. Holyoke, and Smith colleges and the University of Massachusetts.

TO THE NORTH

The Green Mountains of Vermont offer great skiing, hiking, and camping. The town of Bennington makes an interesting stopover with The Bennington Museum (featuring Grandma Moses paintings), fine colleges, and Robert Frost's grave behind the historic Old Bennington Church. There is also the extraordinary Bennington Pottery, where you can both buy and dine on the handsome stoneware. Rte. 7 continues north as the spine of the Green Mountains. A ride to architecturally stunning Manchester is worth the time, even if you decide to dawdle along Historic Route 7A.

TO THE WEST

The farms and small towns of Columbia County, in New York State, hold treasures for antiques and "untiques" hunters. Berkshire is not far from the Hudson Valley, an area rich with history and with vineyards worth visiting. Then there's Albany, which offers big-city cultural entertainment such as the touring New York Metropolitan Opera, performing at the capital city's structurally unique theater, The Egg. A bit farther north is Saratoga with its spas, its springs, its own summer arts festival (known as SPAC), and its elegant and justly famous racecourse.

CHAPTER THREE
The Keys to Your Room
LODGING

As stagecoach travel through the Berkshires developed in the 18th century, the need for roadside lodgings grew. The *New Boston Inn*, in Sandisfield, still welcoming travelers, was likely the first. Built in 1737, this restored inn is about as authentic an early-American lodging experience as you can find in New England. Close in age and attention to period detail is the *Old Inn on the Green* (1760), in New Marlborough. This inn served as a tavern, a

Judith Monachina

The gracious porch of the Red Lion Inn.

store, and later as a post office. Today it comforts travelers with a small number of authentically Colonial rooms and a superlative restaurant. Next came the *Red Lion Inn* (1773), in Stockbridge, which provided not only housing for sojourners but also a meeting place for pre-Revolutionary political activists eager to communicate their grievances to Britain. More than 200 years later, distinguished guests still communicate from the Red Lion . . . around the world.

There are many other 18th-century Berkshire inns continuing to offer warmth, hospitality, and a good night's sleep, often in a four-poster bed. Among them, the *Village Inn* in Lenox, built as a farmhouse in 1771; the *Egremont Inn* (1780) and the *Weathervane Inn* (1785) in South Egremont, the *Elm Court Inn* (1790) in North Egremont, and the *Williamsville Inn* in West Stockbridge, originally a farmhouse dating from 1797.

Or, if the 19th century's sumptuous Gilded Age stirs your stirrup cup, Berkshire offers, among other possibilities, an Italian palazzo called *Wheatleigh* and a Tudor castle called *Blantyre,* both in Lenox. Strikingly different in style, these palatial estates-turned-hotels share the ability to satisfy even the most refined of tastes and to do so with panache.

About 300 Berkshire lodgings exist today, some shorter perhaps on romance but more reasonably priced than others. Berkshire Visitors Bureau Executive Director William R. Wilson Jr. estimates 4,000 pillows available for guests to the county. There is an ever-growing number of guest houses, both in town and out, many offering bed and breakfast ("B&B"); there are simple inns where precious quiet is an everyday experience; and there are modern hotels and all grades of motels on main highways.

We present a representative sampling, in terms of price, geography, and architecture. To evaluate lodgings, we place a high value on hospitality, the personal attention and sincere care that can turn a visit into an unforgettable sojourn. We also assign value and significance to the architectural qualities of a property; to its history and traditions; its care in furnishing and use of antiques or other art; to the views and the natural beauty right at its doorstep. As always, we would appreciate hearing about disappointments — or pleasant surprises.

BERKSHIRE LODGING NOTES

Rates

Rate cards are generally printed in the spring and will change slightly from year to year. Reminder: Price codes are based on a per-room rate, double occupancy, during the high seasons (summer, fall foliage, skiing). Off-season rates are usually a few dollars lower. Many establishments adjust for midweek as well.

Inexpensive	Up to $65
Moderate	$65 to $100
Expensive	$100 to $175
Very Expensive	Over $175

These rates exclude required room taxes or service charges that may be added to your bill.

Minimum Stay

Many lodgings require a minimum stay of two or three nights on summer or autumn weekends. For a single night's stay in Berkshire at such times, motels are the best bet. During the off season, minimum-stay requirements relax and in most instances no longer apply.

Deposit/Cancellation

Deposits are usually required for a confirmed reservation. Policies regarding deposits, cancellations, and refunds vary. It is always wise to inquire about these in advance. In the high season, including college graduation weekends in late May and early June, lodging demand occasionally exceeds supply, so reservations for the more popular places need to be made months or even years ahead.

Special Features

Wherever pertinent, we mention special features of lodgings, along with any caveats, such as restrictions on smoking or pets. We also suggest the ages of children for whom the inn might be appropriate, based on information provided by the establishments themselves. This is intended as a general guide only, and it is always best to call and inquire, as policies are often flexible and subject to change according to the season.

Web Sites

We have included web sites for the establishments that have them; since lodgings can almost always be reached via their web sites, we have given e-mail addresses only for lodgings lacking web sites.

If you find it difficult to access a web site with an "html" suffix, try going to the main "dot.com" or "dot.org" site first. From there, you can usually get to the inn you're trying to reach.

If you're browsing for accommodations, try some of the general lodging or community sites, such as www.berkshirelodging.com, leelodging.org, berk shireweb.com, or greatbarrington.org.

Other Options

For last-minute or emergency lodging arrangements in Berkshire, here are some numbers to phone:

> **Berkshire Bed & Breakfast Reservation Service:** 413-268-7244
> **Berkshire Lodgings Association:** 413-298-4760, 800-298-4760
> **Berkshire Visitors Bureau:** 413-443-9186

Information Booths

For single-night stays in the high season or for spur-of-the-moment arrangements at other times, visit any of the tourist information booths listed in Chapter Nine, *Information*.

LODGING SOUTH COUNTY

Egremont

North Egremont

ELM COURT INN
Managers: Urs & Glee Bieri.
413-528-0325.
227 Rte. 71, P.O. Box 95, N.
    Egremont, MA 01252.
Center of town.
Price: Moderate.
Credit Cards: AE, MC, V.
Special Features: No pets.

Three immaculate, comfortable rooms above one of the more popular restaurants in South Berkshire invite the traveler, even if they are a sideline for the inn. One room has a private bath; the other two share a bath. They reside in the center of a quaint, quiet hamlet.

South Egremont

**BALDWIN HILL FARM
    B&B**
Owners: Richard & Priscilla
    Burdsall.
413-528-4092; 888-528-4092;
    fax 413-528-6365.
www.berkshirelodging.
    com/baldwinhill.html.
121 Baldwin Hill Rd. N.-S.,
    Gt. Barrington, MA
    01230.
From Taconic Parkway,
    Rte. 23 E. to S. Egremont,
    left on Baldwin Hill Rd.,
    1.5 mi. to inn on left.
Price: Moderate to
    Expensive.
Credit Cards: AE, D, MC, V.
Special Features: Pool; No
    smoking; No pets;
    Children over 12 welcome.

Baldwin Hill provides a 360-degree view of its magnificent surroundings. The establishment includes an 1820s farmhouse-turned-B&B and barns galore. It provides an opportunity for guests to stay at what they think farms were like. Peace, quiet, and tranquility abound on 500 acres perfect for hiking, cross-country skiing, or simply observing the wildlife. Guests enjoy reading by the fieldstone fireplace in winter or on the screened porch in summer. Four rooms, two with private bath, have views across fields to the mountains beyond. Full breakfast, from a menu with numerous choices, is served by friendly innkeepers. They take pride in this farm that has been in the family since 1910.

EGREMONT INN
Owners: Steven & Karen
    Waller.
413-528-2111, 800-859-1780.
www.egremontinn.com.
10 Old Sheffield Rd., P.O.
    Box 418, S. Egremont,
    MA 01258.
Side street off Rte. 23 in
    center of village.

Coziness, low ceilings, fireplaces, broad porches, 19 delightful rooms (some newly renovated) furnished with antiques: these set the tone for this historic 1780 stagecoach inn nestled on a quiet side street in the heart of a classic old village. All rooms have private baths. Both two-room suites have fold-out sofas. Scenery ranges from lovely to gorgeous. Tavern and fine restaurant are located on

Price: Expensive.
Credit Cards: AE, D, MC, V.
Special Features: Pool; 2
  tennis courts.

WEATHERVANE INN
Owners: Maxine & Jeffrey
  Lome.
413-528-9580, 800-528-9580;
  fax 413-528-1713.
www.weathervaneinn.com.
P. O. Box 388, S. Egremont,
  MA 01258.
Rte. 23, just E. of the village.
Price: Expensive to Very
  Expensive.
Credit Cards: AE, MC, V.
Handicap Access: Limited.
Special Features: Pool; No

the main floor. Some newly renovated rooms and bathrooms.

This is a comfortable, clean, and well-run operation set within a 1785 farmhouse. All 12 rooms have private baths and air conditioning. Your hosts are skilled at their trade and provide their version of Colonial lodging and catered fine dining for groups of 10 or more. Location is convenient to some of the best antiques shopping in the Berkshires, including one shop just behind the inn. Note that weekends in July and August have a three-night minimum stay.

Great Barrington

**COFFING-BOSTWICK
  HOUSE**
Proprietors: Diana &
  William Harwood.
413-528-4511.
www.greatbarrington.org/
  GBaccom.html.
98 Division St., Gt.
  Barrington, MA 01230.
Corner Rte. 41 & Division
  St., 2 mi. N. of town.
Price: Moderate.
Credit Cards: None.
Special Features: No pets.

The sleepy village of Van Deusenville was once a bustling town with mills, factories, and a train station. Little remains except Isaac Van Deusen's own large 1825 mansion, now a six-room bed & breakfast. The guest rooms are spacious and well appointed, as are the public rooms. Breakfasts, prepared by local caterer Diana Harwood, are sumptuous. Just down the street is the church, now owned by Arlo Guthrie, where Alice of "Alice's Restaurant" fame lived.

GREENMEADOWS
Owners: Frank Gioia &
  Susie Kaufman.
413-528-3897;
  fax 413-528-6334.
www.greatbarrington.org/
  GBaccom.html.
117 Division St., Gt.
  Barrington, MA 01230.
0.25 mi. W. of Rte. 41, 1.5
  mi. N. of town.
Open: Mid-May–end Oct.
Price: Moderate to Expensive.
Credit Cards: AE, MC, V.
Special Features: No
  smoking; No pets.

A rural setting on a quiet country road in what is still a farming area, although close to the center of Great Barrington. The four rooms include private baths, cable TV, and air conditioning. The owners serve full breakfast on a sunny, glass-enclosed porch.

**SEEKONK PINES INN
B&B**
Owners/Innkeepers:
Lefkowitz Family.
413-528-4192; 800-292-4192.
www.seekonkpines.com.
142 Seekonk Cross Rd.
(Rte. 23), Gt. Barrington,
MA 01230.
Between S. Egremont &
Gt. Barrington.
Price: Moderate to
Expensive.
Credit Cards: MC, V.
Special Features: Pool;
Bicycles; No smoking;
No pets.

Originally the main house for a large estate, this nearly 170-year-old house surrounded by meadows and well-groomed acreage keeps getting better and better. Furnished in country antiques and collectibles, the six guest rooms, all with private baths, are filled with personal touches. A recently added guest pantry has a refrigerator, hot-water dispenser, and sink, with complimentary beverages available. Guests can take a dip in the swimming pool on hot summer days and walk or read in the formal gardens. A hearty breakfast is served.

THORNEWOOD INN
Owners/Innkeepers: Terry
& David Thorne.
413-528-3828, 800-854-1008;
fax 413-528-3307.
www.thornewood.com.
453 Stockbridge Rd.,
Gt. Barrington, MA
01230.
Rte. 7, just N. of
Gt. Barrington.
Price: Expensive to Very
Expensive.
Credit Cards: AE, D, MC, V.
Special Features: Pool; No
pets; No smoking;
Children over 11.

Creativity and imagination are evident throughout this inn. Having purchased an old, run-down, but handsome Dutch Colonial, the Thornes have restored and expanded it to create 10 guest rooms, all with private bath, and four public rooms — picturesque right down to the uneven floors. The antiques used throughout include canopy beds, pier mirrors, and original sinks. Refurbished in 1992, the two-room carriage house, which sleeps four, is convenient for families. The restaurant has a view of the Berkshire hills, and the full breakfast might include strawberry-stuffed French toast or apple pancakes. The inn enjoys hosting banquets and weddings.

TRAIL'S END GUESTS
Owner: Anne Hines.
413-528-3995.
678 S. Egremont Rd., Gt.
Barrington, MA 01230.
Rte. 23, just E. of town.
Closed: Nov.–Apr.
Price: Moderate.
Credit Cards: None.
Special Features: No pets.

This large modern Colonial is neat and trim inside and out. Set back from Rte. 23, it has three rooms, all with private bath, air conditioning, and TV. Full continental breakfast is served. Look for the handsome sleigh on the porch or in the yard. In summer the large screened porch is a popular spot for reading, as is the sun room. Children are welcome.

TURNING POINT INN
Owners: Dennis, Rachel &
Teva O'Rourke.
413-528-4777.
www.berkshirelodging.
com/turningpoint.html.

Very well regarded lodging in a handsome brick-and-clapboard former stagecoach inn that's nearly 200 years old. Informal atmosphere. Full breakfast and Saturday evening dinner served to guests; Rachel is a chef and Teva a pastry chef

3 Lake Buel Rd., (Rte. 23),
    Gt. Barrington, MA 01230.
E. of town.
Price: Moderate to
    Expensive.
Credit Cards: None.
Special Features: Children
    welcome.

WAINWRIGHT INN
Innkeepers: Anne & David
    Rolland.
413-528-2062.
www.wainwrightinn.com.
518 S. Main St. (Rte. 7), Gt.
    Barrington, MA 01230.
1 block S. of jct Rte. 23.
Price: Moderate to
    Expensive.
Credit Cards: MC, V.
Handicap Access: Yes.
Special Features: No
    smoking; Dining room
    reserved for guests;
    Children welcome, crib
    available.

WINDFLOWER INN
Owners: Liebert & Ryan
    families.
413-528-2720, 800-992-1993.
www.windflowerinn.com.
684 S. Egremont Rd. (Rte.
    23), Gt. Barrington, MA
    01230.
Just E. of S. Egremont.
Price: Expensive.
Credit Card: AE.
Handicap Access: Limited.
Special Features: Pool; No
    pets.

Housatonic

BROOK COVE
Managers: Clifford &
    Barbara Perreault.
413-274-6653.
30 Linda Ln. (Rte. 41),
    Housatonic, MA 01236.
Rte. 41., 5.7 mi. S. of Mass.
    Pike Exit l.

(they also do catering). Six inn rooms (four with private baths) and a separate two-bedroom cottage perfect for families. The popular Butternut Basin ski area is a third of a mile down the road.

A gracious year-round inn, this beautiful gabled house, built by Peter Ingersoll in 1766, was the Tory Tavern and Inn until David Wainwright purchased it in 1790. It passed down through his descendants as a family home. David and Anne bought it in 1993, remodeling it to eight guest rooms/suites with private baths, some with fireplaces. One guest room has been renovated to be entirely wheelchair accessible.

O ne of the prettiest settings in South Berkshire complements the soothing, comfortable interior of this gracious and respected inn. Antiques furnish the common rooms as well as the bedrooms. All 13 rooms have private bath and six have fireplaces. Full breakfast. Afternoon tea and cookies. The inn and its restaurant are available for special catered occasions. The inn is across from the country club, which is open to the public.

D efinitely not your typical guest house. The Perreaults have one large ground-floor apartment with full kitchen, which they rent by the night. The apartment sleeps four, with more beds available. Since the country property meanders down to the Williams River, the setting seems ideal for longer stays. The room price is for two, with an

Price: Moderate.
Credit Cards: None.
Handicap Access: Yes.
Special Features: No
smoking, Pets permitted.

CHRISTINE'S B&B
Innkeepers: Steve &
Christine Kelsey.
413-274-6149, 800-536-1186;
fax 413-274-6296.
www.christinesinn.com.
325 N. Plain Rd. (Rte. 41),
Housatonic, MA 01236.
About 4 mi. N. of Gt.
Barrington.
Price: Expensive.
Credit Cards: MC, V.
Special Features: No
smoking; No pets;
Children over 11.

$8 charge for each additional person. No breakfast served.

A little jewel (three rooms, all with private bath), off the beaten path between Great Barrington and West Stockbridge. The rooms and the innkeepers are delightful. One room is decorated in white wicker, one has a queen canopy bed, and the other a four-poster. All are filled with antiques. All are air conditioned. Full breakfast. Occasional wine tastings. Those who book for a holiday weekend, such as Mothers' Day or Fathers' Day, can get a holiday dinner/package.

Lee

(See also South Lee)

APPLEGATE
Owners: Len & Gloria
Friedman.
413-243-4451, 800-691-9012.
www.applegateinn.com.
279 W. Park St., Lee, MA
01238.
Off Rte. 7, betw.
Stockbridge & Lenox.
Price: Expensive to Very
Expensive.
Credit Cards: MC, V.
Special Features: Pool; No
pets; Children over 12.

This magnificent white-pillared Colonial is special in every way. A stay at Applegate will be a cherished treat. Public rooms are large, with fireplaces and bay windows. The puppets that appear to be part of the decor are also for playing. Guests are greeted in their room by brandy-filled crystal decanters and Godiva chocolates. Six large guest rooms all have private bath and five have fireplaces; one boasts a sauna/shower. The carriage house has a two-room suite with Jacuzzi. The house has central air conditioning. From the screened-in porch filled with wicker furniture, a tranquil view across the pool reveals six landscaped acres. If anyone wishes to go farther afield, the Friedmans have four bicycles to loan.

AUNTI M'S B&B
Owner: Michelle Celentano.
413-243-3201.
www.leelodging.org/
auntim.html.
60 Laurel St. (Rte. 20), Lee,
MA 01238.

Aunti M's is a restored Victorian within walking distance of a historic downtown. All five comfortable rooms have period furnishings, floral wallpapers and borders, and oak floors. One has a private bath and the others share two baths. There is a homey feeling here. As Michelle Celentano

Price: Moderate to
  Expensive.
Credit Cards: None.
Special Features: No
  smoking; No pets;
  Children over 15.

**BEST WESTERN BLACK
  SWAN INN**
Owner: Shatish Desai.
413-243-2700,
  800-876-SWAN.
435 Laurel St. (Rte. 20), Lee,
  MA 01238.
On Laurel Lake, N. of town.
Price: Moderate to Very
  Expensive.
Credit Cards: AE, D, DC,
  MC, V.
Handicap Access: Yes.
Special Features: Pool;
  Exercise room and sauna;
  No pets.

says of her guests, "Whatever is ours is theirs." A piano in the foyer is the focal point for after-breakfast camaraderie. A full breakfast with home-baked treats is served.

From the outside, this 52-room inn looks decidedly like a motel, but its location on placid Laurel Lake, its private balconies, Colonial decor, and hospitality provide an inn-like atmosphere. Lovely restaurant, swimming pool, and exercise room with sauna. There are boat rentals for boating on the lake. Close to Tanglewood, hiking trails, countless other Berkshire amenities. Conference facilities available. Meals are not included in the summer; in winter a continental breakfast is served.

Judith Monachina

Chambéry Inn in Lee, once a school, still has chalkboards in the guest rooms on which visitors write and draw to express gratitude.

CHAMBÉRY INN
Owners: Joe & Lynn Toole.
413-243-2221, 800-537-4321.
www.berkshireinns.com/
   chambery.html.
199 Main St. (Rte. 20), Lee,
   MA 01238.
Price: Moderate to Very
   Expensive.
Credit Cards: AE, MC, V.
Handicap Access: Yes.
Special Features: No
   smoking; No pets;
   Children over 15.

The Chambéry Inn began life as a schoolhouse in 1885, when five nuns arrived from France to teach the youngsters of St. Mary's Parish in Lee. Joe Toole's grandfather was in the first class. Concerned that it was scheduled for the wrecker's ball and enchanted by its history, Joe moved the schoolhouse to its present location. He left the proportions of the rooms as they were, which is *big*, with 13-foot ceilings and massive windows. There are nine rooms (six are suites; eight have fireplaces); all have large private baths with whirlpools, and king or queen beds. The furniture, including canopy beds, is Amish handcrafted cherry. All the rooms have central air conditioning, telephones, and cable TV. Breakfast is delivered to the room. The original blackboards in the suites are a charming feature.

CRABTREE COTTAGE
Owner: Janis Monachina.
413-243-1780.
www.crabtreecottage.com.
65 Franklin St., Lee, MA
   01238
Off Main St.
Price: Moderate to
   Expensive.
Credit cards: None.
Special features: Pool;
   Children over 12.

This lovely Greek-revival home on a quiet residential street is handsomely garbed in Victorian furnishings. The four rooms all have private baths, air conditioning, and TV. The option of a kitchen goes with one of the two suites. Guests have the use of a common room, deck, and swimming pool. Janis's husband, contractor Jeffrey Keenan, who grew up in the home, has done much of the extensive refurbishing. Full continental breakfast.

DEVONFIELD
Owners/Managers: Jim &
   Pam Loring.
413-243-3298, 800-664-0880;
   fax 413-243-1360.
www.devonfield.com.
85 Stockbridge Rd., Lee,
   MA 01238.
Off Rte. 20 just outside of
   town.
Price: Expensive to Very
   Expensive.
Credit Cards: AE, D, MC, V.
Special Features: Heated
   pool; Tennis; Bicycles;
   Children over 10 in
   July–Aug.

No expense was spared in renovating this 1800s house, built by a Revolutionary War soldier and initially restored by George Westinghouse in the early 1900s. The small estate became the 1942 summer sanctuary for Queen Wilhelmina of the Netherlands, her daughter Princess Juliana, and granddaughters Beatrix and Irene. The house is secluded, with 10 air-conditioned rooms, all with private bath and phone. Full breakfast.

INN AT LAUREL LAKE

Owners: Thomas & Heidi
  Fusco.
413-243-9749;
  fax 413-243-2936.
www.laurellakeinn.com.
615 Laurel St. (Rte. 20), Lee,
  MA 01238.
2 mi. N. of Mass Pike Exit 2.
Price: Expensive to Very
  Expensive.
Credit Cards: AE, D, MC, V.
Handicap Access: Limited.
Special Features: Private
  beach, with canoes,
  paddleboats for guests;
  Tennis; Sauna; No
  smoking.

On the shore of Laurel Lake, this 98-year-old country property has attracted a loyal following with its 19 comfortable bedrooms (17 with private bath) and two sitting rooms filled with an impressive collection of record albums, books, and games. The tennis court, sauna, and private beach add to guests' playtime possibilities. Full breakfast buffet served; at an additional cost, owners can provide a picnic, which can be held in the inn's back yard.

MORGAN HOUSE INN

Owners: Heidi & Thomas
  Fusco, Wesley &
  Kimberly Bookstaver
413-243-3661;
  fax 413-243-3103.
www.morganhouseinn.com.
33 Main St. (Rte. 20), Lee,
  MA 01238.
0.8 mi. N. of Mass Pike Exit 2.
Price: Expensive.
Credit Cards: AE, MC, V.
Special Features: No pets;
  Children welcome; Beach
  privileges at Laurel Lake
  Inn.

This full-service inn was totally refurbished when its new owners took over in 1999. Built in 1817 and a stagecoach stop beginning in 1853, the Morgan House has a bustling and convenient in-town location and 12 comfortable rooms in a variety of shapes and sizes, seven with private bath. The dining room has been spruced up, with a new menu; light fare is available in the tavern. While the old hotel registers that served as wallpaper in the lobby could not be saved, the spirit of former guests remains to provide a patina for a modern inn. Lunch and dinner are served seven days a week; brunch on Sunday.

PARSONAGE ON THE GREEN

Innkeepers: Barbara & Don
  Mahoney.
413-243-4364.
E-mail: parsonage@
  berkshire.net.
20 Park Place, Lee, MA 01238
On town green, adj. to
  Congregational Church.
Price: Expensive.
Credit Cards: None;
  personal checks accepted.
Special Features: No
  smoking; No pets;
  Children over 12; Access
  to beach on Laurel Lake.

This 1851 colonial, originally the parsonage for the church next door, was refurbished entirely by the present owners, who have run it since 1997. Four sunny rooms upstairs with private bath (one bath detached) have comfortable four-poster beds, family memorabilia, and other nice touches. Coffee and tea are available upstairs at 7am, and a formal breakfast is served in the dining room downstairs. Also downstairs are a formal parlor and a library (with games and TV), both filled with pictures of the Mahoney family and early occupants of the house. Though the inn is smack dab in the middle of Lee, it's set on the opposite side of the green from the main drag, so visitors enjoy quiet as well as easy access to town.

Judith Monachina

The imposing façade of the Federal House.

South Lee

FEDERAL HOUSE
Owners: Robin & Kenneth
  Almgren.
413-243-1824, 800-243-1824;
  fax 413-243-1828.
www.federalhouseinn.com.
1680 Pleasant St. (Rte. 102),
  P.O. Box 288, S. Lee, MA
  01260.
Just E. of Stockbridge.
Price: Moderate to Very
  Expensive.
Credit Cards: AE, D, MC, V.
Special Features:
  Restaurant; No pets.

This brick Federal house, built in 1824, has been beautifully restored. In this historic property, the 10 guest rooms sit above a respected restaurant. Graceful and charming rooms feature antique furnishings. All have private bath and air conditioning. Full breakfast included. Owned and operated by a dynamic young couple who combine good taste and culinary talents.

HISTORIC MERRELL INN
Innkeepers: Faith & Charles
  Reynolds
Asst. Manager: Mary Palmer.
413-243-1794, 800-243-1794;
  fax 413-243-2669.

Those who walk through the massive door of this striking 1794 brick inn will find themselves transported back in time. For years it served as a stagecoach stop on the busy Boston-Albany Pike. It lay idle and boarded up for over 100 years until purchased by the Reynoldses in late 1980. Now

www.merrell-inn.com.
1565 Pleasant St. (Rte. 102),
   S. Lee, MA 01260.
Just E. of Stockbridge.
Closed: Christmas and
   week preceding.
Price: Moderate to Expensive.
Credit Cards: MC, V.
Special Features: No
   smoking; No pets;
   Inquire about children.

New Marlborough

**OLD INN ON THE
GREEN & GEDNEY
FARM**
Innkeepers: Bradford
   Wagstaff & Leslie Miller.
413-229-3131, 800-286-3139;
   fax 413-229-8236.
www.oldinn.com or
   www.gedneyfarm.com.
Star Rte. 70 (Rte. 57), New
   Marlborough, MA 01230.
Center of village.
Price: Expensive to Very
   Expensive.
Credit Cards: AE, MC, V.
Special Features:
   Restaurant; No pets.

RED BIRD INN
Innkeepers: Barbara &
   Doug Newman.
413-229-2349;
   fax 413-229-2972.
16 Adsit Crosby Rd. (Rte.
   57), New Marlborough.
Mail: 16 Adsit Crosby Rd.,
   Gt. Barrington, MA 01230.
From Gt. Barrington, Rte.
   23 E. to Rte. 57.
Price: Expensive to Very
   Expensive.
Credit Cards: AE, MC, V.
Handicap Access: Limited.
Special Features: No
   smoking; No pets.

lovingly and carefully restored, the inn is listed on the National Register of Historic Places. Of the nine bedrooms and one suite, some are furnished with four-poster and canopy beds, and all have private baths, air conditioning, TV, and telephones; four have fireplaces. The Old Tavern Room features the original circular Colonial bar. A groomed lawn in back leads to the banks of the Housatonic River, where there is a screened gazebo. A full breakfast is served from a menu.

A beautiful village rich in unaffected nostalgia is the setting for this 18th-century inn. The five rooms, each with private bath, have been lovingly restored and furnished in a simple American country style. Gedney Farm, a short walk from the inn, has 16 guest rooms with four suites, carved out of a Normandy-style barn, which was built around 1900 as a showplace for Percheron stallions and Jersey cattle. All suites feature fireplaces in the living rooms, large bedrooms, and whirlpool tubs in the master baths. Thayer House has an additional five rooms, while Stebbins House can be leased by the week or longer. The restored second horse barn serves as a space for weddings, parties, meetings, an art gallery, and concerts. The inn's restaurant is one of the finest in the Berkshires.

A former stagecoach stop, the 1791 Red Bird Inn is located on 10 ten acres on a quiet country road. The eight rooms currently have six private baths, with another two being added to the remaining rooms. They are furnished with antiques and retain their original wide-plank floors, fireplaces, and old ironwork. Luxurious linens and bathrobes are laid out. A separate cottage suite has one huge room with a queen bed, two twins, a sitting area, and private bath. The inn is available only to persons wishing to reserve five rooms on Friday and Saturday nights. The large screened porch is a popular feature with warm-weather guests. Doug, a chef, prepares a full country breakfast.

Sandisfield

NEW BOSTON INN
Innkeepers: Susan &
  Conrad Ringeisen
413-258-4477.
Rtes. 8 & 57, P.O. Box 601,
  Sandisfield, MA 01255.
Village of New Boston.
Price: Moderate.
Credit Cards: AE, MC, V.
Special Features: 1737 pub
  and full-service
  restaurant.

Built in 1737, this remarkable old stagecoach inn is listed on the National Register of Historic Places, and the owners continue to make improvements. The six guest rooms are — true to the period — snug. Low ceilings, wide-board floors, and multipaned windows hark back to the 18th century and, in most cases, are original. All rooms feature private baths and are decorated with early pine furniture and stenciling. All closets are cedar lined.

After wandering through the cozy bedrooms on the second floor, you enter the spacious ballroom — now called the Gathering Room — complete with pool table, large-screen TV, and barrel-vaulted ceiling. The matching fireplaces at either end accent the sense of openness and grace.

Another historic delight is the taproom, now open as a pub, that adjoins the low-ceilinged dining room. The 22-inch-wide pine boards on the wall are called "king's wood." The trees were cut by the colonists in spite of being marked for masts for the royal navy. In this room as throughout the inn the wooden molding, plaster walls, slanted floors, venerable windows and doorways (there is hardly a right angle in the place) provide a powerful charm and sense of history. What's more, the New Boston Inn has a resident ghost. She is real enough to have been reported in *Yankee* magazine: an Irish maiden, dressed in bridal black, who was shot by a scorned suitor in an upstairs room.

Sheffield

**CENTURYHURST
  ANTIQUES & B&B**
Managers: Ronald & Judith
  Timm.
413-229-8131.
175 Main St. (Rte. 7), P.O.
  Box 486, Sheffield, MA
  01257.
Price: Moderate.
Credit Cards: AE, MC, V.
Special Features: No
  smoking; No pets;
  Children over 11.

This grand 1800 home, nestled among towering trees, together with the center of Sheffield, is listed on the National Register of Historic Places. The inn features four guest rooms that share two baths. The rooms are named for previous owners of the home. A new post-and-beam barn behind the house serves as an antiques shop, specializing in American clocks, early 19th-century furniture, and Wedgwood. As we go to press, Sandra Rossi is acquiring the inn, but the Timms will continue to manage the antique shop.

**IVANHOE COUNTRY
  HOUSE**
Managers: Carole & Dick
  Maghery.
413-229-2143.

Set along one of the most scenic roads of South Berkshire, the Ivanhoe provides nine comfortable rooms, all with private bath and refrigerator. Two units — one a one-bedroom unit, the other a

254 S. Undermountain Rd.
  (Rte. 41), Sheffield, MA
  01257.
4 mi. S. of jct. Rte. 23; 10 mi.
  N. of Lakeville, CT.
Price: Expensive.
Credit Cards: None.
Special Features: Pool; Pets
  welcome; No young
  children July–Aug.
  weekends.

two-bedroom unit — have kitchenettes. Continental breakfast is served at your door. Take a dip in the pool before dinner, play the piano if you wish, enjoy the fire in the chestnut-paneled public room, and select from the many fine local restaurants for your evening meal. At the base of Race Mountain, traversed by the Appalachian Trail, 20 wooded acres hug this 1780-vintage country house. Golden retrievers are raised on the property, and guests are welcome to bring their own dogs (no cats!) for an additional $10.

ORCHARD SHADE
Owners: Debbie & Henry
  Thornton.
413-229-8463, 877-672-4233;
  fax 413-229-2711.
www.orchardshade.com.
999 Hewins St., P.O. Box
  669, Sheffield, MA 01257.
E. side of the Housatonic,
  between County Rd. &
  Rte. 7.
Price: Moderate to
  Expensive.
Credit Cards: AE, D, MC, V.
Special Features: No
  smoking; No pets;
  Children welcome.

The Thorntons moved their B&B from a larger house to a smaller one, built in 1850, also previously operated as a bed & breakfast. They took their better antiques to the three bedrooms and common room with fireplaces to ward off the chill on cooler evenings. One room has a private bath. The large screened-in porch is perfect for relaxing after a busy day of Sheffield antiquing. So are the two acres and gardens.

**RACE BROOK LODGE
  B&B**
Innkeeper: David
  Rothstein.
413-229-2916, 888-RBLODGE;
  fax 413-229-6629.
www.rblodge.com.
864 S. Undermountain Rd.
  (Rte. 41), Sheffield, MA
  01257.
2 mi. S. of Berkshire School.
Price: Moderate to
  Expensive.
Open: Year-round.
Credit Cards: AE, MC, V.
Handicap Access: Ground-
  level entry to many rooms.
Special Features: No
  smoking; Children
  welcome; Well-behaved
  dogs accepted.

This rustic lodge beside Race Brook has its own trail leading to a state forest with waterfall, ravine, and the Appalachian Trail. A large rambling barn, dating from the 1790s and recently renovated, embraces rooms and suites in what were once haylofts, with exposed original beams, stenciling, nooks and alcoves, and windows and stairs in unexpected places. The variety of bedroom, bathroom, and entrance arrangements can work for couples, family groups, or friends traveling together. With a garage converted into the Meeting House, the lodge emphasizes team-building retreats for organizations.

The interiors have been specifically designated a "chintz-free zone" to maximize informality. More rooms and suites, 21 in all, are in nearby cottages. All rooms have private baths and air conditioning.

In the lofty common rooms at the heart of the barn is the well-stocked, always-open, help-yourself kitchen, along with tables, a TV corner, and a horseshoe bar run on the honor system. The lodge will produce lunch and suppers for groups, on request. A hearty breakfast buffet is served.

RAMBLEWOOD INN
Owners: Harry & Holly
  Desmond.
413-229-3363, 800-854-1862.
www.ramblewoodinn.com
400 S. Undermountain Rd.
  (Rte. 41), P.O. Box 729,
  Sheffield, MA 01257.
5 mi. S. of Gt. Barrington.
Price: Expensive.
Credit Cards: MC, V.
Handicap Access: Limited.

Up a short hill off scenic Rte. 41, this Alpine structure at the edge of the woods has an attractive rustic look, with all the comforts of home, including central air conditioning. The Ederers offer six guest rooms (four with private bath) and a ground-floor suite with full kitchen, bedroom, living room, and bath. June, an English teacher, has named each room for a character in the *Canterbury Tales*. The Miller's Room on the first floor has its own deck and, not surprisingly, the Wife of Bath's Room on the second floor is the largest in the house. The inn owns pond-front property across the road, where guests may swim, canoe, and fish.

A full gourmet breakfast is served. The Berkshire School, site of the Berkshire Choral Institute (see "Music" in Chapter Five, *Arts & Pleasures*), is a mile down the road.

STAGECOACH HILL INN
Innkeeper/Manager:
  Sandra MacDougall.
413-229-8585;
  fax 413-229-8584.
854 S. Undermountain Rd.
  (Rte. 41), Sheffield, MA
  01257.
N. of Lakeville, CT.
Closed: First two weeks in
  March.
Price: Inexpensive to
  Expensive.
Credit Cards: AE, MC, V.
Special Features: Pool; Access
  to Appalachian Trail.

A time machine. Nostalgia for bygone eras (especially Colonial times as evident in the decidedly English pub and restaurant), plus charm and comfort greet the fortunate visitor to this ideally situated hostelry. Choice of 11 rooms in the main house or cottage, nine with private bath. Continental breakfast on weekends only. Meals separately priced. (Although originally the same property, the inn is not related to Race Brook Lodge.)

STAVELEIGH HOUSE
Innkeepers/Owners:
  Dorothy Marosy &
  Marion Whitman.
413-229-2129.
www.berkshirelodging.
  com/staveleigh.html.
59 Main St. (Rte. 7), P.O.
  Box 608, Sheffield, MA
  01257.

This vintage 1821 house is set in the heart of Sheffield. Your hostesses believe in old-fashioned hospitality and have succeeded in creating a warm and comfortable interior, with hooked rugs and patchwork quilts in the five guest rooms (private and shared baths). A full breakfast and an afternoon tea, with imaginative specialties. The grounds feature perennial beds, an herb garden,

Just S. of village.
Price: Moderate to
   Expensive.
Credit Cards: None.
Special Features: No
   smoking; No pets;
   Children over 12.

and a place to sit under the trees. There is one resident cat. During the off-season, needlecraft (quilts, rug-hooking, and needlepoint) workshops are offered.

Stockbridge

ARBOR ROSE B&B
Owner: Christina Alsop.
413-298-4744.
www.arborrose.com.
8 Yale Hill Rd., P.O. Box
   114, Stockbridge, MA
   01262.
Off E. Main St. (Rte. 102).
Price: Moderate to
   Expensive.
Credit Cards: MC, V.
Special Features: No
   smoking; No pets; Well-
   behaved children
   welcome.

The first thing you hear on entering the driveway to Arbor Rose is the soothing sound of rushing water. The house sits on a hill overlooking an early 1800s sawmill and millpond. The large white house has five guest rooms and one efficiency that sleeps four, all with private bath and air conditioning, including three rooms in the mill. The charming decor is highlighted by colorful paintings by the owner's mother, Suzette Alsop, a noted local artist. A horse poses in the fields on occasion.

Full breakfast includes magnificent muffins. A downstairs room has been converted into a gift shop.

BERKSHIRE THISTLE
Owners: Gene & Diane
   Elling.
413-298-3188;
   fax 413-298-3549.
www.berkshirethistle.com.
19 East St. (Rte. 7), P.O. Box
   1227, Stockbridge, MA
   01262.
N. of village.
Price: Moderate to
   Expensive.
Credit Cards: None.
Special Features: Pool; No
   smoking; No pets;
   Children 8 and older.

The owners of one of the truly impressive homes on Rte. 7 have had years of training in the bed & breakfast business, filling in for Gene's parents at their B&B. This location, midway between Lenox and Stockbridge, is unbeatable. Although the house is a recently built Colonial, it is comfortable and beautifully sited, with a cozy fireplace in the guest living room and a wraparound deck to take advantage of the views. All five rooms have private baths and air conditioning. Easy access to theater, Tanglewood, and great hiking trails. Swimming pool and picturesque pasture with grazing horses on five acres.

CONROY'S B&B
Owners: James & Joanne
   Conroy.
413-298-4990, 888-298-4990;
   fax 413-298-5188.
www.conroysinn.com.
11 East St. (Rte. 7), P.O. Box
   191, Stockbridge, MA
   01262.

Located just north of Stockbridge in a handsome 1830s Federal-style house, Conroy's B&B is close to, but acoustically insulated from, the Mass Pike. Therefore it is well situated for cultural attractions. Owner-proprietors Jim and Joanne serve in the same capacity at the justly well-known Cactus Cafe Mexican restaurant in downtown Lee.

About 1.5 mi. N. of village.
Price: Moderate to
  Expensive.
Credit cards: AE, D, MC, V.
Special Features: No
  smoking; No pets;
  Special events catering;
  Two weeks' notice of
  cancellation.

INN AT STOCKBRIDGE
Innkeepers: Alice & Len
  Schiller.
413-298-3337; 888-466-7865;
  fax 413-298-3406.
www.stockbridgeinn.com.
Rte. 7, P.O. Box 618,
  Stockbridge, MA 01262.
About 1 mi. N. of village.
Price: Expensive to Very
  Expensive.
Credit Cards: AE, D, MC, V.
Handicap Access: Limited.
Special Features: Pool; No
  smoking; No pets;
  Children over 12.

The B&B's dining and lounging rooms are located in a spacious addition behind the original house, so period charm is not compromised. The Conroys offer five double rooms in various configurations, some with private baths, some shared. Three rooms and a seasonally available apartment/suite are located in the barn. Full breakfast is included.

A marvelous, secluded inn run by friendly, professional people. The large, white-columned 1906 house is decorated with impeccable taste, featuring priceless antiques and many thoughtful touches. All 12 rooms (including four fireplace rooms and three whirlpool rooms) have private baths and are air conditioned. Wine and cheese are served in the living room (warmed by a fire in chilly weather) and the full breakfast in the formal dining room includes homemade pastries, with croissants, French toast, and cinnamon buns possible offerings. Special private dinners can be arranged on request.

Judith Monachina

The back porch at the Red Lion Inn.

THE RED LION INN
General Manager: C.
  Brooks Bradbury.
413-298-5545;
  fax 413-298-5130.
www.redlioninn.com.

In Colonial America, three years before the States became United, the Red Lion Inn first opened its doors to travelers on the stagecoach route linking Albany, Hartford, and Boston. More than two centuries later the Red Lion still welcomes visitors and

30 Main St., P.O. Box 954,
Stockbridge, MA 01262.
Village center, Rtes. 7 & 102.
Price: Expensive to Very
Expensive.
Credit Cards: AE, D, DC,
MC, V.
Handicap Access: Yes.
Special Features: Pool;
Exercise Room; Massage
therapist.

locals with consummate Colonial charm. The present inn, rebuilt in 1897 after a fire in 1896, is a Berkshire icon, representing graceful country lodging at its best.

Antique furniture and a fine collection of china teapots adorn the lobby. Each private room is decorated with unique period appointments, carefully coordinated by the inn's owner, Jane Fitzpatrick, also owner of Country Curtains. Recent improvements have concentrated on creating larger rooms and increasing the number of suites (bedroom plus living room), consistent with guest requests. Throughout, loving attention to detail is evident in every aspect of the inn's operation. It's easy to feel at home here because all the top-quality services are offered by a vibrant, eager-to-please staff. In summer, porch or courtyard company may be an actor or actress of note who spends evenings nearby on the boards of the Berkshire Theatre Festival.

The atmosphere is faithful to the rhythms of a simpler, slower time while providing all contemporary comforts. Sipping a cool drink on a hot summer's day on the famous porch of the Red Lion, or meeting a companion in front of the cheery fireplace in the lobby in winter, is to beat to the heart of the Berkshires. The Red Lion Inn is not, however, a particularly tranquil place. The main building is full of activity and people, and the street right outside (Rtes. 7 & 102) is sometimes noisy with traffic. There's a conviviality and gaiety about the lobby that some folks love. Others might prefer the cottages that form a complex around the inn: Stafford House, O'Brien House, Yellow Cottage, Stevens House, Fire House, McGregor House, and Two Maple Street.

Reservations should be made in advance, especially in the summer. An excellent formal dining room; the Lion's Den, a pub featuring nightly entertainment; a courtyard for summer meals under the trees, surrounded by bushels of impatiens; the Pink Kitty, an outstanding gift shop; and a Country Curtains retail store complement the rooms.

ROEDER HOUSE
Innkeepers: Vernon &
Diane Reuss.
413-298-4015;
fax 413-298-3413.
www.roederhouse.com.
Rte. 183, P.O. Box 525,
Stockbridge MA 01262.
Just S. of Glendale village
center.
Price: Expensive to Very
Expensive.
Credit Cards: AE, D, MC, V.
Special Features: Pool; No
smoking; No pets; No
children.

A delightful hideaway, in a small village far from the crowds, but close to summer attractions and just three-quarters of a mile from the new Norman Rockwell Museum. Awaiting lucky house guests are seven large, exquisitely furnished air-conditioned rooms, all with private bath and filled with antiques and four-poster, queen-sized beds. The entire house reflects the impeccable taste of the owners, who also run an antiques shop. A full breakfast is served on tables set with china, silver, and crystal on the charming screened-in porch, weather permitting.

SEASONS ON MAIN B&B
Innkeepers: Pat & Greg
O'Neill.
413-298-5419;
fax 413-298-0092.
www.bedandbreakfast.com
47 Main St. (Rte. 7), P.O.
Box 634, Stockbridge,
MA 01262.
E. end of town center.
Price: Expensive to Very
Expensive.
Credit cards: AE, MC, V.
Special features: No
smoking; No pets; No
children; 3-night
minimum during
Tanglewood season.

TAGGART HOUSE
Owners: Hinckley & Susan
Waitt.
413-298-4303.
www.taggarthouse.com.
18 Main St. (Rte. 102),
Stockbridge, MA 01262.
Price: Very Expensive.
Credit Cards: AE, CB, D,
DC, MC, V.
Special Features: No
smoking; No pets;
Inquire about children.

This gracious house is within an easy walk of Stockbridge shops, restaurants, and the Berkshire Theatre Festival. Downstairs the inn offers three sitting rooms with Victorian-inspired furnishings and wallpaper, and a dining room with a Duncan Phyfe–style dining table and Larkin sideboards. The four air-conditioned guest rooms upstairs follow a seasonal motif; one has a king-size sleigh bed, a fireplace, TV, and a large bathroom. Guests have the use of a comfortable, west-facing porch that affords a view of Main Street and handsome gardens. A full hot breakfast is served.

A stunning array of art and antiques in the richly detailed architectural setting of a 19th-century mansion, with a fireplace around just about every corner, a billiards room, a paneled library, a music room, and three secluded acres of gardens and field: the description of a romantic country manor house in a Victorian novel. Actually, the Taggart House is right on Main Street in Stockbridge, where resident owners Hinckley and Susan Waitt have transformed fiction into reality. Their personal collection of antique furnishings and artwork, with dramatic choices of color and texture, artfully blend elegance and whimsy, opulence and coziness.

Throughout the downstairs living rooms and the upstairs bedrooms are a variety of fabulous faux effects painted on walls and ceilings, including bois and tortoiseshell finishes. In the butler's pantry, trompe-l'oeil painting merges a real garden scene with an illusory one. The abundance of imaginative details also includes fabrics and wallpaper with William Morris designs, a birch-bark canoe suspended from a frescoed ceiling over the billiards table, curtains drawn back with antlers, a collection of Native American artifacts in the library, and a pillowed nook halfway up the stairs. The cavernous music room has hosted chamber concerts from Bach to Gershwin — and an 18-foot Christmas tree. The four bedrooms feature rich and restful color themes, fireplaces, and luxurious antique beds; each room's private bath is equally sumptuous, with antique furnishings, heated towel racks, and even bath salts. Morning brings gourmet breakfasts, and there are some self-serve options, too. Afternoon tea can be provided, as well as early-evening hors d'oeuvres.

West Stockbridge

CARD LAKE COUNTRY INN
Owners: Ed & Lisa Robbins.
413-232-0272;
   fax 413-232-0294.
www.cardlakeinn.com.
29 Main St., P.O. Box 38, W. Stockbridge, MA 01266.
Price: Moderate to Expensive.
Credit Cards: MC, V.
Special Features: No pets.

The inn offers eight guest rooms featuring brass and iron beds. All have private bath. Village shops across street are artsy-craftsy. Guests may want to ask for a room at the back of the inn. Restaurant and tavern on the premises.

SHAKER MILL INN
Innkeepers/Owners: Lori Bashour & Michael Lee.
413-232-4600;
   fax 413-232-4601.
www.shakermillinn.com.
2 Oak St. (Rte. 102), P.O. Box 61, W. Stockbridge, MA 01266.
Price: Expensive to Very Expensive.
Credit Cards: AE, MC, V.
Special Features: Children and pets welcome.

The inn offers nine enormous, modern deluxe rooms, all with patio or balcony, queen or king beds, and complete with small kitchens and living rooms. The suite has two full bedrooms, two full baths, a large fully equipped kitchen, living room, two TVs, laundry, and just about anything else you might want. All accommodations are in a converted barn. Continental breakfast is served.

Early in 2000, Lori Bashour and Michael Lee purchased the inn. They will continue to run it as an inn, providing yoga (Phoenix Rising) on one floor. See Chapter Six, *Body & Spirit*.

The colonial charm of the 18th-century Williamsville Inn.

Jonathan Sternfield

WILLIAMSVILLE INN
Owners: Gail & Kathleen Ryan.

This gracious white Colonial home was built in 1797 and retains the charm of a bygone era. There are 10 guest rooms in the main house, two

413-274-6118;
fax 413-274-3539.
www.williamsville.com.
Rte. 41, P.O. Box 138, W.
Stockbridge, MA 01266.
5 mi. N. of Gt. Barrington
and 5 mi. S. of W.
Stockbridge.
Price: Expensive.
Credit Cards: AE, MC, V.

with fireplaces. Two units, available in the summer, and four more units, all with wood stoves, in the converted barn, bring the room total to 16. All rooms have private baths and air conditioning. The fine restaurant on the main floor, pool, and clay tennis court give the inn an added dimension. Summer guests will enjoy the sculpture garden with its changing exhibits. In winter there are Sunday evening storytelling programs. The inn is available for meetings and conferences.

LODGING CENTRAL COUNTY

Becket

LONG HOUSE B&B
Owners: Roy & Joan
Simmons.
413-623-8360.
155 High St., P.O. Box 271,
Becket, MA 01223.
Off Rte. 8.
Price: Moderate.
Credit Cards: MC, V.
Special Features: No
smoking; No pets.

The Simmonses have been welcoming bed & breakfast guests since 1966. Their 1820 country home, listed on the National Register of Historic Places, has four cozy rooms, one with private bath. Convenient to Jacob's Pillow, hiking, and nature trails. Full breakfast offered. Groups are welcome.

Dalton

DALTON HOUSE
Hosts: Gary & Bernice
Turetsky.
413-684-3854;
fax 413-684-0203.
www.thedaltonhouse.com.
955 Main St., Dalton, MA
01226.
Price: Moderate to
Expensive.
Credit Cards: AE, MC, V.
Special Features: Pool; No
smoking; No pets;
Children over 10.

The rooms in the main house and carriage house, 11 altogether, all have private baths, telephones, and TVs. Set in a small New England village, the house has been partially furnished with antiques. Summer guests enjoy air conditioning, a pool, extensively landscaped lawn and flower gardens, and a picnic area. Breakfast is served, with blueberry pancakes when in season.

Hancock

HANCOCK INN
Owners: Joe & Gail
  Mullady.
413-738-5873;
  fax 413-738-5719.
hancockin@aol.com
102 Main St. (Rte. 43),
  Hancock, MA 01237.
Betw. Williamstown &
  Stephentown, NY.
Price: Moderate.
Credit Cards: AE, D, MC, V.
Special Features: No
  smoking; No pets;
  Children under 5 free.

New owners have not changed a cozy Victorian inn set in a village that seems unaware of the 21st century's arrival. A tastefully furnished, family-run establishment, the inn has the charm of a delightful, forgotten keepsake discovered one day in your grandmother's attic. Six comfortable rooms, all with private baths and air conditioning, above a respected restaurant for fine dining. A full breakfast is included.

JIMINY PEAK
General Manager: Paul
  Maloney.
413-738-5500, 800-882-8859
  (outside MA).
www.jiminypeak.com.
Brodie Mountain/Corey
  Rd., Hancock, MA 01237.
Betw. Rtes. 7 & 43, 10 mi.
  N. of Pittsfield.
Price: Very Expensive.
Credit Cards: AE, D, DC,
  MC, V.
Handicap Access: Yes.
Special Features: Pool;
  Tennis; Health club;
  Trout fishing; Alpine
  slide; Downhill skiing;
  No pets.

This relatively new, full-service resort truly has it all. In the Country Inn, all 105 suites feature kitchen, living room with queen-size sofa bed, bath with powder room, and a master bedroom with king bed. Most of the units can be rented for one night, weekdays, or two nights on weekends. There are also one-, two-, and three-bedroom condominiums for rent. Add to that the Founders Grille, Christiansen Tavern, and two cafeterias during ski season; tennis, swimming, health club, trout fishing, an Alpine slide for summer, and — best of all — *great* downhill skiing, and you've got one of the Berkshire's most complete resorts. Conference facilities are available. Meals are not included.

Hinsdale

MAPLEWOOD B&B
Innkeepers: Charlotte &
  Bob Baillargeon.
413-655-8167;
  fax 760-838-7987.
435 Maple St. (Rte. 143),
  P.O. Box 477, Hinsdale,
  MA 01235.
Price: Moderate.
Credit Cards: None.
Special Features: No
  smoking; No pets.

Country setting; country style. The 1770s house is set on six acres with a small pond and has two rooms with private baths and a two-bedroom suite with private bath. Full breakfast might feature fresh trout caught by Bob or corn pancakes with fresh, locally made maple syrup; special diets can be accommodated. Antiques in many rooms. Guests have a common room with library, dining room, and separate entrance.

Lanesborough

TUCKERED TURKEY
Managers: Dan & Marianne
  Sullivan.
413-442-0260.
30 Old Cheshire Rd., P.O.
  Box 638, Lanesborough,
  MA 01237.
From Rte. 7, turn E. on
  Summer St., then N. on
  Old Cheshire Rd.
Price: Moderate.
Credit Cards: None.
Special Features: No
  smoking; No pets.

A restored 19th-century Colonial farmhouse, set on close to four acres, with spacious views. Three antique-furnished rooms share baths. Guests are welcome to bring their children to play with the owner's children. Full breakfast served.

Lenox

APPLE TREE INN
Owners: Sharon Walker &
  Joel Catalano.
413-637-1477;
  fax 413-637-2528.
www.appletree-inn.com.
10 Richmond Mtn. Rd. (Rte.
  183), P. O. Box 699,
  Lenox, MA 01240.
Just S. of Tanglewood's
  Main Gate.
Price: Expensive to Very
  Expensive.
Credit Cards: AE, D, MC,
  V.
Special Features: Pool;
  Tennis; No pets.

Magically set, the Apple Tree Inn is indisputably the lodging that lies closest to the front gates of Tanglewood. The 14 guest rooms in the main house are down-comforter dainty, some with antique brass beds and fireplaces, two with shared baths. The Lodge, with 21 additional rooms, is less charming, though the rooms are convenient and clean, bringing the total number of units to 35.

The Apple Tree would be worth a visit for the views alone: a magnificent Berkshire panorama from the south rooms, from poolside, or from the gazebo, which now serves as a restaurant. There is also dining on the deck. The downstairs parlor is thoughtfully appointed and very comfortable; the bar has rich wood paneling, stained glass windows, and a huge hearth. A crowning touch is the landscaping, boasting hundreds of varieties of roses set among the apple trees — truly a visual feast throughout late spring and summer. Continental breakfast included.

BIRCHWOOD INN
Owner: Ellen Chenaux.
413-637-2600, 800-524-1646;
  fax 413-637-4604.
www.birchwood-inn.com.
7 Hubbard St., P.O. Box
  2020, Lenox, MA 01240.
Corner of Main St.
Price: Moderate to Very
  Expensive.

The elegant 1767 mansion high on the hill overlooking the charm of Lenox continues renovations under a new owner. There are 10 rooms in the main house, eight with private bath, and two rooms and one suite in the carriage house. Rooms have either ceiling fans or air conditioners. A magnificent library extends along one side of the house, with books, magazines, and games galore. The

Credit Cards: AE, D, MC, V.

Special Features: No smoking; No pets; Children over 12.

wicker-furnished front porch is a popular spot in summer. A full gourmet breakfast is included.

Drawing © Carol Wallace, 1998, the Preserve America™ Collection of Crane & Co.

Blantyre.

BLANTYRE
Manager: Roderick Anderson.
413-637-3556; fax 413-637-4282 .
www.blantyre.com.
16 Blantyre Rd., Lenox, MA 01240.
Off Rte. 20, 3 mi. N. of Mass Pike Exit 2.
Closed: Early Nov. to early May.

Regally set amidst over 100 conscientiously groomed acres of lawns, trees, and hedges, Blantyre offers its guests attentive and even ingenious service, great natural and architectural beauty, palatial furnishings, and magnificent vistas.

New York City businessman Robert Paterson built Blantyre in 1902 as a replica of his wife's ancestral home in the Scottish village of the same name. Blantyre went through several hands in midcentury and fell into disrepair. In 1980 Jack and Jane

Price: Very Expensive.
Credit Cards: AE, DC, MC, V.
Handicap Access: Limited.
Special Features: Pool; Tennis; Croquet; Sauna; Hot tub; No pets; Children over 12.

Fitzpatrick bought the property and, with their daughter Ann, restored it to its present excellent condition: a baronial yet hospitable place — massive but comfortable, grand yet delicately appointed.

A member of the prestigious Relais et Châteaux, Blantyre has been recognized by *Condé Nast Traveller* magazine as the third highest ranked of all small hotels in the United States, and one of the finest in the world. High praise, but well deserved. It has also been awarded AAA's four diamonds for dining and Mobil Travel Guide's four stars. The five original suite-size bedrooms, with four-poster beds, fireplaces, and magnificent bathrooms, are the true "jewels" in Blantyre's crown. There are three other rooms on the same floor, created in the "nanny's wing" on a different scale, smaller but just as elegant. Twelve more rooms are neatly tucked away in the original Carriage House. There are also two cottages on the grounds, both cozy, endearingly whimsical, and brilliantly situated.

In addition to its superb accommodations, Blantyre has a magnificent gourmet dining room. The hotel maintains four Har-Tru tennis courts and two tournament-size bent-grass croquet courts. A delightful exercise room fashioned out of a former potting shed provides a sauna and hot tub. Nearby is a lovely, landscaped swimming pool. Tanglewood is a mere three miles to the west. Conferences and small meetings are welcome. (Please note that the grounds and buildings are *not* open to the public for casual viewing.)

BROOK FARM INN
Owners/Innkeepers: Joe & Anne Miller.
413-637-3013, 800-285-POET; fax 413-637-4751.
www.brookfarm.com.
15 Hawthorne St., Lenox, MA 01240.
Just off Old Stockbridge Rd.
Price: Expensive to Very Expensive.
Credit Cards: D, MC, V.
Special Features: Pool; No smoking; No pets.

The Millers bought this inn in January 1992. Each day has it own poem, displayed in the 1,400-volume library and supplemented by 75 poets on tape. A reading takes place for guests every Saturday at 4pm, accompanied by tea and scones. A buffet breakfast and afternoon tea are served daily to guests; on Sunday mornings in season musicians from the nearby Tanglewood Institute perform during breakfast. Twelve antique-furnished rooms — all with private bath, air conditioning, and telephones — are offered in this large Victorian home, close to many Berkshire attractions. All of the rooms have been renovated, with special attention lavished on the two large rooms at the front of the house, both with four-posters, sitting areas, and new bathrooms.

CANDLELIGHT INN
Innkeeper/Owner: Rebecca Hedgecock.

This comfortable, antique-furnished inn has eight large guest rooms, all with private bath, some retaining their original fixtures. Like the

413-637-1555, 800-428-0580;
fax 413-637-1594.
www.candlelightinn-
lenox.com.
35 Walker St. (Rte. 183),
P.O. Box 715, Lenox, MA
01240.
Corner of Walker & Church
Sts., near village center.
Price: Moderate to
Expensive.
Credit Cards: AE, D, MC,
V.
Special Features: No pets;
Children over 10.

rooms, a small upstairs lounge is furnished in period style. Centrally located in the heart of Historic Lenox Village, the inn features a charming restaurant on the main floor. Beside that is a storied wooden bar, once part of the former Curtis Hotel and prior to that, scorched in a fire that destroyed a famous old Boston hotel. Delightfully and professionally run. Continental breakfast is included.

CLIFFWOOD INN
Owners: Scottie & Joy
Farrelly.
413-637-3330, 800-789-3331;
fax 413-637-0221.
www.cliffwood.com.
25 Cliffwood St., Lenox,
MA 01240.
Just off Main St., in village.
Price: Expensive to Very
Expensive.
Credit Cards: None.
Special Features: Indoor &
outdoor pools; No
smoking; No pets;
Children over 11.

This special inn, on a quiet residential street, was built for an ambassador to France in the early 1890s. The elegant public rooms have tall ceilings, polished inlaid hardwood floors, and grand fireplaces. The seven guest rooms have private baths and air conditioning; six come with their own fireplaces. The inn features an outdoor pool and an indoor countercurrent pool and spa. In summer, a copious continental breakfast is served on the spacious veranda overlooking the gardens and pool. On winter Sunday mornings, breakfast is served by a warming fire in the oval dining room with its ornate wood-carved fireplace mantel. Wine, hors d'oeuvres, and friendly conversation served early evening.

CORNELL INN
Innkeepers: Billie & Doug
McLaughlin.
413-637-0562, 800-637-0562;
fax 413-637-0927.
www.cornellinn.com.
203 Main St. (Rte. 7A),
Lenox, MA 01240.
Just N. of town center.
Price: Expensive to Very
Expensive.
Credit Cards: AE, CB, D,
DC, MC, V.
Handicap Access: Yes.
Special Features: Pub; No
smoking; No pets;
Children 13 and over.

Written in the guest book at the Cornell Inn: "Charming home. The pancakes were delicious." The home began life in 1888 as a large, well-built Victorian, and the owners keep making all the right improvements. Each of the 13 bedrooms in the main house has its own bath and is furnished with brass or four-poster beds; several have wood-burning fireplaces. There are eight additional rooms in the converted carriage house and 11 in the adjacent MacDonald House. The MacDonald House rooms have fireplaces and whirlpool tubs. Phone, color TV in all rooms. Full breakfast is included Sundays; extended continental breakfast the rest of the week.

CRANWELL RESORT & GOLF CLUB

General Manager: Victor Capadonio.
413-637-1364, 800-272-6935.
www.cranwell.com.
55 Lee Rd. (Rte. 20), Lenox, MA 01240.
3.5 mi. N. of Mass. Pike Exit 2, S. of Lenox center.
Price: Expensive to Very Expensive.
Credit Cards: AE, CB, D, DC, MC, V.
Handicap Access: Yes.
Special Features: Pool; Smoking permitted in a few rooms; Tennis; Golf; No pets.

Cranwell is a 380-acre estate high on a hill with one of the finest views of the Berkshire Hills. The 1893 Tudor mansion is surrounded by lawns, gardens, and a par-70 championship golf course. Guest rooms are in the Mansion (Cranwell Hall); Beecher's Cottage (the farmhouse built on the property in 1853 by Henry Ward Beecher); the Carriage House; Olmsted Manor; Founder's Cottage; and a group of one-bedroom cottages (totaling 105 units). The most luxurious bedrooms in the Mansion are spacious and individually decorated in the Victorian stylè, with private marble baths. In the various outbuildings, accommodations are slightly simpler and more contemporary, but some have the advantages of wet bar, refrigerator, and/or galley kitchens. Two dining rooms, Sloane's Tavern, and numerous conference rooms complete the full-service offerings of this property.

EASTOVER

Owners: Susan & Bob McNinch, Ticki Windsor.
413-637-0625, 800-822-2386; fax 413-637-4939.
www.eastover.com
430 East St., P.O. Box 2160, Lenox, MA 01240.
From Rte. 7 in Lenox, take Housatonic St. E., then left onto East St. for 1 mi.
Price: Moderate (AP); weekly rates also.
Credit Cards: AE, D, MC, V.
Special Features: Indoor & outdoor pools; Tennis; Exercise room; Sauna; Driving range; Miniature golf; Xc skiing; Toboggan run; No pets.

Eastover makes no bones about its informality. It is a picturesque, amiable place, admirably free of pretension. What would William Fahnestock, the original owner, say? As another of the celebrated Lenox "cottages," this grand Gilded Age house is obviously living out of character but seems to be thriving. The sprawling grounds present tennis, swimming, biking, volleyball, sauna, exercise room, horseback riding, and all sorts of winter activities, including cross-country skiing, and the longest tobogganing run in New England.

Inspired by the remarkable spirit of the late founder, George Bisacca, the staff is up for anything as long as it's fun. To add to the festivities, there is dancing to live music during happy hour and again later in the evening. No liquor license here, so it's BYOB, but the band can play into the wee morning hours. This is not the place for the shy, the reclusive, or those who don't quite feel dressed without a jacket and tie or a skirt and heels. For the good sport, the incurably casual, or the curious, Eastover means relaxation, silliness, and whatever the weekend's theme may be. Special weekends are organized for couples, singles, and families. Prospective guests should call ahead. Eastover has some fun planned.

While wandering the grounds, guests may catch a glimpse of American buffalo, geese, and other pets. The founder's collection of Civil War artifacts and the museum in the Heritage Room will fascinate boys. The 165 guest rooms are large in the main house and of various sizes elsewhere.

GABLES INN
Owners: Frank & Mary
  Newton.
413-637-3416.
www.gableslenox.com.
81 Walker St. (Rte. 183),
  Lenox, MA 01240.
Price: Moderate to Very
  Expensive.
Credit Cards: D, MC, V.
Special Features: Pool;
  Tennis; No Pets; Children
  over 12.

Charming 1885 home in the center of Lenox where Edith Wharton summered while her "cottage," The Mount, was being built. Visitors can stay in her room or in that of her husband, Teddy. He stayed there until 1928, long after she'd taken off. The Newtons discuss the Whartons knowledgeably. The inn is fully air conditioned, with TV and VCR. There are 19 bedrooms, all with private baths; nine with fireplaces. A handsome house. Full breakfast. (A sister inn, called the Summer White House, is at 17 Main St., Lenox.)

GARDEN GABLES INN
Owners: Mario & Lynn
  Mekinda.
413-637-0193;
  fax 413-637-4554.
www.lenoxinn.com.
135 Main St., P.O. Box 52,
  Lenox, MA 01240.
Price: Expensive to Very
  Expensive.
Credit Cards: AE, D, MC,
  V.
Special Features: Pool; No
  pets; Children over 13.

The Mekinda family has brought new life to this inn since purchasing it in 1987. All 18 rooms have been upgraded to include air conditioning and private baths (three have whirlpools); all have telephones and answering machines; eight rooms have fireplaces; some have private porches; and some have TV. The five acres of landscaped grounds include the largest outdoor pool in Berkshire County. Walking distance to Lenox shops and restaurants, and even to Tanglewood for the hardy. Breakfast buffets are extra special.

GATEWAYS INN
Owners: Fabrizio &
  Rosemary Chiariello.
413-637-2532,
  800-GWAYINN;
  fax 413-637-1432.
www.gatewaysinn.com.
51 Walker St. (Rte. 183),
  Lenox, MA 01240.
Just off Main St., in center
  of village.
Price: Expensive to Very
  Expensive.
Credit Cards: AE, D, DC,
  MC, V.
Special Features:
  Restaurant; No smoking;
  No pets; Children over 13.

Built in 1912 by Harley Procter of Procter and Gamble fame, this Berkshire "cottage" received a complete facelift in 1999. Up a graceful, skylit mahogany staircase from an award-winning restaurant (new chef J. Steven Brockman was formerly at Rancho Encantada in Santa Fe) are 12 spacious, elegant rooms, each with bath, three with fireplaces, a four-poster here, a canopy there, and peace and quiet everywhere. Arthur Fiedler, who stayed here when performing at Tanglewood, gave his name to the lovely Fiedler Suite. TV, telephone, voice-mail, and modem jack in each room; air conditioned throughout; a Jacuzzi in the suite.

HAMPTON TERRACE
Owners: Stan & Susan
Rosen.
413-637-1773 (phone/fax),
800-203-0656.
www.hamptonterrace.com.
91 Walker St., Lenox, MA
01240.
Price: Expensive to Very
Expensive.
Credit cards: AE, D, DC,
MC, V.
Special features: No pets;
Children 10 years and
over.

The Rosens arrived from Georgia to teach Yankees hospitality. They located an 1882 "cottage" in town that was designed to be a year-round home and to accommodate guests — on a paying basis — for 70 years. When we visited, remodeling was underway. As this book goes to press, five rooms are available in the main house, plus a two-room suite, and eight more should be ready in the carriage house. All rooms have private baths, several including spa tubs and fireplaces. The Rosens' hospitality extends to — and beyond — daily tea, complimentary bar, late-night guest kitchen, wine and cheese, and an enhanced continental breakfast. Cooking weekends are available with their nephew, who is the chef at Bistro Zinc.

Susan Rosen, a much-sought-after furniture painter, and Stan, formerly the director of development at the National Music Center, finding the house in good condition, have been redecorating. They are capitalizing on the crystal chandeliers, linen wall covering, balcony, three-story suspended stairs, and two porches. One of the porches will be available for breakfasts, as will the grounds.

HARRISON HOUSE
Innkeeper/Owner: Viola
Fish.
413-637-1746;
fax 413-637-9957.
www.harrison-house.com.
174 Main St., Lenox, MA
01240.
Across from Kennedy Park.
Price: Expensive to Very
Expensive.
Credit Cards: AE, D, MC, V.
Handicap Access: Limited.
Special Features: No pets.

A charming country inn, with six elegant guest rooms and splendid public areas. The attractive Victorian, at the crest of Main St., has a wraparound porch and a handsome sitting/breakfast room overlooking the back lawn. The bedrooms are air conditioned, each with a private bath, period fixtures and decor, fireplace (many with the original Victorian tiles), and cable TV. Duvets and cutwork linens add a romantic touch. The Norman Rockwell suite has a canopy bed, a sitting room with sofa-bed, and an especially splendid bathroom. A lavish buffet breakfast is served. As this book goes to press, three new rooms are in the works.

KEMBLE INN
Innkeepers/Owners:
Richard & Linda
Reardon.
413-637-4113, 800-353-4113.
www.kembleinn.com.
2 Kemble St. (Rte. 7A),
Lenox, MA 01240.

A new luxury bed & breakfast inn in Lenox is named for the actress Fanny Kemble, who once lived on the street named for her. It occupies yet another Berkshire "cottage" — this one the Georgian mansion built in 1881 by Chester Arthur's secretary of state, Frederick T. Frelinghuysen. Richard Reardon, a contractor, has supervised the

Judith Monachina

The Kemble Inn, seen from Trinity Church, Lenox.

Price: Expensive to Very Expensive.
Credit Cards: MC, V.
Handicap Access: Yes.
Special Features: No smoking; No pets; Children over 12.

complete renovation of the house, which included adding several bathrooms. Each of the 15 guest rooms has a private bath and air conditioning. The furnishings throughout the house are period reproductions. The master suite has a bedroom with fireplace and a bathroom with Jacuzzi — and another fireplace. The most impressive features of the inn are the elegant and spacious common areas on the ground floor — foyer, reception room, dining room — all with magnificent Adam-style paneling — and the views of the mountains to the back and historic Trinity Church to the front. Continental breakfast is included in summer.

PINE ACRES B&B
Owner: Karen Fulco.
413-637-2292.
137 New Lenox Rd., Lenox, MA 01240
Price: Moderate.
Credit Cards: None.
Special Features: No smoking; No children.

A bed & breakfast on a quiet back road, close to all the Berkshire highlights. Three rooms, shared bath, have a pleasant Colonial decor. In summer, coffee and juice are served on the sun porch.

ROOKWOOD INN

Owners: Stephen Lesser &
Amy Lindner-Lesser.
413-637-9750, 800-223-9750;
fax 413-637-1352.
www.rookwoodinn.com.
11 Old Stockbridge Rd.,
P.O. Box 1717, Lenox,
MA 01240.
Just off Main St. in center of
town.
Price: Expensive to Very
Expensive.
Credit Cards: AE, D, MC.
V.
Handicap Access: Limited.
Special Features: No
smoking; No pets;
Children welcome.

The Lessers purchased the inn in the fall of 1996. It's a grand 166-year-old Victorian lady on a quiet street in back of the Town Hall. All 19 rooms and one suite have private bath and eight include fireplaces. The two-level turret room is a marvelous secluded aerie, and the three rooms in the new addition at the back of the house are particularly comfortable.

A gourmet chef prepares full breakfasts. Children are welcome as guests; babysitting can be arranged.

SEVEN HILLS INN

Owners: Jim & Patty Eder.
413-637-0060, 800-869-6518.
www.sevenhillsinn.com.
40 Plunkett St., Lenox, MA
01240.
Jct. Rtes. 7 & 20, just
beyond The Mount.
Price: Moderate to Very
Expensive.
Credit Cards: AE, D, DC,
MC, V.
Handicapped Access: Yes.
Special Features: Fireplaces
in many rooms; Pets
accepted; Outdoor pool;
Tennis court.

In 1993, after years in the financial world, the Eders purchased a Berkshire "cottage" that formerly belonged to Emily Spencer. It had been a summer house, on 27 well-landscaped acres. They kept the lovely main building largely intact but gutted and redid the Terrace House to make it more useful as an inn. All 52 rooms in both buildings have private baths. Each comfortable and welcoming room is imaginatively decorated in a different style and all look out on the wooded scene that surrounds Edith Wharton's Mount. Patty Eder kept much of the original furnishings and traveled to auctions to pick up the rest.

When we visited the stucco inn, it was entertainingly decorated for the holidays with stuffed creatures between the banister rails. Jim describes the tone as less formal than at Wheatleigh or Blantyre.

As well as the attractive dining room on the first floor of the main building, public spaces include a banquet room suitable for weddings and other functions and a bar from which wafts music on summer evenings. A full breakfast is included in the room rent for a night's stay or guests may choose other combinations of meals and lodgings.

SUMMER HILL FARM

Owners: Sonya Chassell
Wessel & Michael
Wessel.
413-442-2057, 800-442-2059.

Enjoy the countryside, away from the busy village. Here is a piece of the old Berkshires, before the days of the grand "cottages" and the influx of New York society. The historic ca. 1750

www.summerhillfarm.com.
950 East St., Lenox, MA
    01240.
Off Rtes. 7 & 20 at Holmes
    Rd.; right on Chapman
    Rd. (becomes East St.) to
    red farmhouse on left.
Price: Moderate to
    Expensive.
Credit Cards: AE, MC, V.
Handicap Access: Yes.
Special Features: No pets;
    Well-behaved children
    by arrangement.

farmhouse has five rooms year-round, seven in the summer with a one-bedroom suite in a cottage behind the house. All the rooms have private baths, color TVs, and Wessel family antiques. A third building, the lower farmhouse, has a self-catering apartment with three bedrooms and two baths, available year-round. It rents by the week or the month. Michael is English, and Sonya lived in England for 36 years, which makes for an appealing, cosmopolitan atmosphere. Twenty acres of peaceful countryside at the foot of October Mountain, at the northern edge of Lenox, provide a peaceful stopping place away from the busy village. Wildflower walks, canoeing, and bicycling are just a few of the possible pastimes in the area. Horses board at the farm. Lessons are available down the road. Full country breakfast included (continental breakfast in the cottage).

VILLAGE INN
Proprietors: Clifford
    Rudisill & Ray Wilson.
413-637-0020, 800-253-0917;
    fax 413-637-9756.
www.villageinn-lenox.com.
16 Church St., P.O. Box
    1810, Lenox, MA 01240.
Off Walker St. in the center
    of town.
Price: Expensive to Very
    Expensive.
Credit Cards: AE, D, DC,
    MC, V.
Handicap Access: Yes.
Special Features: No
    smoking; No pets;
    Children over 6.

Innkeepers Cliff Rudisill and Ray Wilson are cultivated, hospitable hosts whose personal warmth complements this old, highly respected hostelry. Their pride in restoration and furnishings is evident. Of the 32 guest rooms (some newly renovated), all with private bath and telephone, six have fireplaces. The suite has a kitchenette. The smoking ban extends to public rooms.

The inn was built in 1771 as a farmhouse; four years later, its original owner started to put up weary travelers arriving by horse-drawn coach. By 1815 he had sold his surrounding land, presumably having become exclusively an innkeeper.

Full breakfasts served on the sunny all-season porch and the English afternoon tea for which the Village Inn is justly famous (neither is included in the room rate). The full-scale restaurant as well as a downstairs tavern feature English ales.

WALKER HOUSE
Innkeepers: Peggy &
    Richard Houdek.
413-637-1271, 800-235-3098;
    fax 413-637-2387.
www.walkerhouse.com.
64 Walker St. (Rte. 183),
    Lenox, MA 01240.
Price: Moderate to Very
    Expensive.

Comfortable, well-furnished, 1804-vintage Federal house operated by two friendly people. The three acres of garden and woods behind the house are gorgeous. Eight rooms all have private baths; five have fireplaces. The decor in each is an impression of the composer for whom the room is named. Have the Houdeks explain. Sitting rooms offer an impressive collection of music and books, and a 12-foot video

Credit Cards: None.
Handicap Access: Limited.
Special Features: No smoking; Well-mannered pets with prior approval.

screen in the Library Theatre — wonderful for opera, films, and sports events. Generous continental breakfast. Within walking distance of Tanglewood, Lenox shops, and restaurants.

Judith Monachina

The Italianate entrance to Wheatleigh.

WHEATLEIGH
Owners: Susan & Linfield Simon.
Manager: François Thomas.
413-637-0610;
   fax 413-637-4507.
www.wheatleigh.com.
Hawthorne Rd., P.O. Box 824, Lenox, MA 01240.
From Rte. 183 in Lenox, left on Hawthorne Rd. to Wheatleigh sign.
Price: Very Expensive.
Credit Cards: AE, DC, MC, V.
Special Features: Restaurant; Outdoor pool; Tennis; Fitness room; Massage room; No pets; Children over 10.

Wheatleigh is pure romance. An estate built for heiress Georgie Bruce Cook, wife of "Count" Carlos de Heredia, it encourages flights of imagination. The grounds and setting captivate. From the broad terrace, the manicured lawns slope down to a grassy stairway and then to a fountain. Straight ahead is a view of the Stockbridge Bowl with the Berkshire hills in the distance. The heated pool is hidden away in a knoll surrounded by trees, and the tennis court is off in another direction.

Owners Linfield and Susan Simon have preserved the expansive luxury of the interior space and decorative details in this turn-of-the-century mansion. The approach is by way of a winding driveway, then through an enclosed courtyard with a circular drive — reminiscent of a 16th-century private palazzo in the hills outside Florence.

Inside, the Great Hall is impressive with its magnificent Tiffany windows lining the grand staircase, newly added antique furnishings, and original brass chandelier. The dark-wooded Conservatory with its cooling breezes is perfect for summer dining.

The 19 guest rooms, newly renovated, are baronial in size. Nine have working fireplaces. All have TV, VCR, and personal portable telephones.The bathrooms are splendid, several with original fixtures. Wheatleigh contains an award-winning, prix-fixe restaurant, complemented by an award-winning wine list. The premises are available for business meetings, weddings, and parties.

WHISTLER'S INN
Managers: Richard & Joan
  Mears.
413-637-0975;
  fax 413-637-2190.
www.whistlersinnlenox.
  com.
5 Greenwood St., Lenox,
  MA 01240.
Cor. of Rte. 7A &
  Greenwood St.
Price: Expensive to Very
  Expensive.
Credit Cards: AE, D, MC,
  V.
Special Features: No pets.

Charming, much-admired guest house created within a seven-acre, 1820s English Tudor summer estate within walking distance of the town center. Cultivated, accommodating hosts (Richard is an author; Joan is an artist) will put you at ease. The inn is furnished with antiques, chandeliers, and Persian rugs, resulting in an Old-World Victorian atmosphere. A seasonal suite features an African motif. The interior is full of pleasant surprises, including an extensive library. The 14 bedrooms, all with private bath, are quaint and cozy. From the stone-walled terrace it's possible to walk among gardens and woodland — or wind through the kudzu maze. The town center is within walking distance. Full breakfast is provided.

The spiral staircase at the Crowne Plaza.

Judith Monachina

Pittsfield

CROWNE PLAZA HOTEL
General Manager: Vince
Barba.
413-499-2000, 800-227-6963.
www.berkshirecrowne.com.
One West St., Pittsfield, MA
01201.
Berkshire Common, just off
Park Square.
Price: Expensive to Very
Expensive.
Credit Cards: AE, D, DC,
MC, V.
Handicap Access: 8 units.
Special Features: Indoor
pool; Sauna; Jacuzzi;
Parking garage.

The Crowne Plaza crowns downtown Pittsfield, having completed a major renovation. Friendly and spacious, it is a big hotel (179 rooms) with all the comforts. Located within striking distance of central, north, and south Berkshire, it is a good choice for travelers who prefer modern amenities over rustic charm.

Children appreciate the Sony Play Stations (video games) in each room and the TV channels are beyond counting. Rooms, rugs, and drapes are fancy; the beds spacious and comfortable. Rockwell's is the formal dining room, Dewey's the lounge adjacent to the indoor pool. The Park Square Grille is available for special functions. From a grand ballroom to small meeting rooms, Crowne Plaza is prepared for business needs.

*The White Horse Inn,
Pittsfield.*

Judith Monachina

WHITE HORSE INN
Innkeepers: Joe & Linda
Kalisz.
413-442-2512;
fax 413-443-0490.
www.regionnet.com/
colberk/whitehorse.html.
378 South St. (Rtes. 7 & 20),
Pittsfield, MA 01201.
S. of town center.
Price: Moderate to
Expensive.
Credit Cards: All major.
Special Features: No
smoking; No pets.

An attractive 1907 Colonial Revival set back from the busy main street, south of the center of Pittsfield. All eight rooms have private baths, air conditioning, phones and TV (and fax and computer capability). The rooms have been redecorated with linens and wallpapers. Guests may use a kitchenette and a small sitting room on the second floor. A full breakfast is served in the dining room, where guests have individual tables, or on the deck in summer. Perennial gardens and a picnic table complete the picture.

Richmond

**BERKSHIRE HILLS
  COUNTRY INN**
Owner: Ann Meyer.
413-698-3379.
673 Dean Hill Rd.,
  Richmond, MA 01254.
Off Rte. 41.
Closed: Nov.–May.
Price: Inexpensive.
Credit Cards: None.
Special Features: No
  smoking; No pets;
  Children over 17.

Great view of the Berkshires from this 147-acre hilltop property. Three comfortable rooms share a bath. Another has a private bath. Continental breakfast is served. Tanglewood and Hancock Shaker Village, just a hop, skip, and a jump . . . such as the resident chicken and sheep might make.

**ECHEZEAUX, A
  COUNTRY B&B**
Proprietors: Ronald Barron
  & Ina Wilhelm.
413-698-2802
  (winter 617-965-3957).
180 Cheever Rd.,
  Richmond, MA 01254.
2.25 mi. N. on Swamp Rd.
  (from W. Stockbridge),
  then rt. on Cheever to end.
Closed: Labor Day to last
  weekend in June.
Price: Moderate.
Credit Cards: None.
Special Features: Pool; No
  smoking; No pets.

Delightful country retreat, owned by a member of the Boston Symphony Orchestra and his wife and frequently rented to other BSO members, this house often fills the surrounding hills with music. Just two miles from the front gate of Tanglewood, the main house has three antique-furnished rooms, sharing a bath. A fourth room in a separate building is available for weekends or weekly rental. An elegant continental breakfast is served on weekends.

Washington

BUCKSTEEP MANOR
Manager: Mark Pitsch.
413-623-5535, 800-645-BUCK.
www.berkshireweb.com/
  bucksteep.
885 Washington Mtn. Rd.,
  Washington, MA 01223.
Off Rte. 8 N. from Becket.
Price: Moderate to
  Expensive.
Credit Cards: AE, D, MC, V.
Handicap Access: Limited.
Special Features: Xc ski
  center; Pool; No pets;
  Children welcome.

Deep in the Washington woods, a cross-country skier's paradise. Of the 22 comfortably furnished rooms in the inn itself, several share baths. Fourteen rooms in the lodge have private baths. In the summer nine cabins plus campgrounds increase the number of accommodations and add to the rustic feeling of the property. Hiking, biking, and birding opportunities abound. Pool and hot tub. Great dancing. Rock, country, bluegrass, and reggae concerts in the Barn and on the lawn on summer weekends. Good vibes, funky buildings, and that mellow, laid-back feeling predominates. Continental breakfast is served.

LODGING NORTH COUNTY

Bascom Lodge, atop Mt. Greylock.

Lauren R. Stevens

Adams

BASCOM LODGE
Manager: Glen Oswald,
  Appalachian Mtn. Club.
413-443-0011, ext. 10
  (9–5 daily).
www.outdoors.org (AMC).
Summit Rd., Adams, MA
  01220.
From Rte. 7 take North
  Main St. to Rockwell Rd.,
  or Notch Road from N.
  Adams, to the summit of
  Mt. Greylock.
Closed: Mid-Oct.–
  mid-May.
Price: Inexpensive.
Credit Cards: MC, V.
Handicap Access: Yes.
Special features: Rustic
  lodge; Extraordinary
  view.

Bascom Lodge, atop Mt. Greylock, is a marvel of dramatic beauty, adventure, and good food. Operated by the Appalachian Mountain Club and owned by the Massachusetts Department of Environmental Management, the lodge at the 3,491-foot summit of the state's highest peak was built of stone and wood by the Commonwealth and by the Civilian Conservation Corps during the Depression. Generations of hikers, birders, and canny travelers have celebrated the accommodations, returning often.

The stone fireplace and hand-cut oak beams cultivate a sense of adventure, which the magnificent hills and trails confirm. This is lodging for the hearty, or at least the sporting. Although linen is supplied, you might want to bring a sleeping bag or an extra blanket. The guest rooms are private or dormitory style, with bathrooms down the hall, so plan accordingly. In all, the lodge can accommodate 36 in its private rooms and bunk rooms. Breakfast and dinner (open to the public) are served family style at a set time.

Workshops and field trips on topics ranging from bird watching and backpacking to geology and photography are offered throughout the hiking season. Appalachian Trail through hikers, campers from Sperry Road Campground, naturalists, and tourists rub elbows in a friendly way. The price is cheap. It is even possible to exchange trail-clearing labor for a five-day stay.

Cheshire

HARBOUR HOUSE INN
Owners: Terri & Jay
  Cooper.
413-743-8959.
www.harbourhouseinn.
  com.
725 N. State Rd. (Rte. 8),
  Cheshire, MA 01225.
Price: Moderate to
  Expensive.
Credit Cards: AE, D, MC, V.
Special Features: No
  smoking; Full breakfast.

The Coopers purchased what had been the main farmhouse for Rolling Acres Farm in 1998, converting it to a B&B with five guest rooms, two with private baths, one with half bath, and one with a working fireplace. The rooms, which are artfully decorated with curtains, wall coverings, and canopies, all have names, such as Field of Dreams for the bridal room, Country Sunshine, and Imagination — which is a family-sized room. Guests have the use of a spacious common room, music room, and formal dining room, where full breakfasts are served.

The house has a colorful history, from its 18th-century origins through massive 1903 additions, having served as a tavern, stagecoach stop and possibly a stop on the Underground Railway — for which it is named. Set on an eminence among sweeping fields, its views of Mount Greylock and the Hoosac Valley are immense.

North Adams

BLACKINTON MANOR
Hosts: Dan & Betsy
  Epstein.
Manager: Don Haines.
413-663-5795.
www.blackinton-
  manor.com.
1391 Massachusetts Ave.,
  N. Adams, MA 01247.
One block off Rte. 2,
  minutes from
  Williamstown.
Price: Expensive.
Credit Cards: MC, V.
Special Features: Pool;
  Chamber music concerts
  throughout the year —
  call for schedule; Hiking;
  No smoking; No pets;
  Children over 7.

This handsome Federal mansion offers the most elegant and romantic B&B experience in North Berkshire County. Reopened in 1993 after a complete renovation by new owners, the 1849 house is notable for its Italianate features — including intricate wrought-iron balconies, floor-to-ceiling pocket windows, and a spacious bay window. The five bedrooms, all now with private baths (one with Jacuzzi), have furnishings, fabrics, and wallpaper appropriate to the period; yet the entire building is air conditioned. A full gourmet breakfast is served in the formal dining room or, in summer, on the screened porch or pool patio. Ironed linen.

Dan is pianist for the Raphael Trio and Betsy is an opera singer and invested cantor, so house concerts and chamber music workshops are a regular part of life at Blackinton Manor. Hiking weekends are also a specialty, since the Appalachian Trail is out the back door .

HOLIDAY INN BERKSHIRES
General Manager: Edward Bassi.
413-663-6500.
www.holidayberkshires.com.
40 Main St., N. Adams, MA 01247.
Price: Moderate.
Credit Cards: All major.
Handicap Access: Yes.
Special Features: Indoor pool; Sauna; Jacuzzi; Full workout center; No pets.

Centrally located in the heart of town and convenient to numerous area attractions, the completely renovated former North Adams Inn calls itself "the newest full-service hotel in the Berkshires." The 86 air-conditioned rooms, all with private bath, TV, and telephone, are large and decorated in soft tones of purple and mauve. Due Baci, a full-service restaurant, serves breakfast, lunch, and dinner. Conference and meeting facilities are available; tours are welcome; the gymnasium is available to local membership as well as to guests.

TWIN SISTERS INN
Owner: Jae H. Chung.
413-663-6933.
1111 S. State St. (Rte. 8), P.O. Box 193, N. Adams, MA 01247.
2 mi. S. of N. Adams City Hall.
Price: Inexpensive.
Credit Cards: None.
Handicap Access: Limited.
Special Features: No pets; Children welcome.

The owner, who also owns the Miss Adams Diner in Adams and a restaurant chain in the Boston area, is poised to invest $500,000 to turn Twin Sisters into the upscale Jae's Inn, including ten rooms, a 45-seat full-service restaurant and bar, a health club and spa in the basement, tennis courts, and swimming pool.

In the meanwhile this former carriage house, set on 10 lovely acres, serves guests as a bed & breakfast. Four rooms share two baths. All have TV. The large living room has a fireplace. The porch has a great view of the eastern Hoosac Range, looking toward the Mohawk Trail. Continental breakfast is served.

Williamstown

BUXTON BROOK FARM
Innkeeper: Nancy B. Alden.
413-458-3621;
fax 413-458-3640.
91 Northwest Hill Rd., Williamstown, MA 01267.
Between W. end of Main & Bulkley Sts.
Price: Expensive.
Credit Cards: AE, D, MC, V.
Special features: Pool; No smoking; No pets; No small children.

Situated on 70 country acres adjacent to 2,500-acre Hopkins Memorial Forest, Buxton Brook Farm is one of the most gracious B&Bs in these pages. The roomy Federal house has three rooms, all with private bath and air conditioning. The furnishings and appointments, although related to individuals in the family, are of the 1820s, tasteful without being fussy.

Common space on the first floor focuses on three fireplaces and a woodstove. The grounds include an outdoor pool. Nancy serves a full homemade breakfast, either in the stylish dining room or on the terrace in the summer. Buxton Brook Farm is within two scenic miles of the Williamstown

Theatre Festival, the Clark Art Institute, and the Williams College Museum of Art. Miles of the best hiking and cross-country skiing trails in town are out the back door.

FIELD FARM GUEST HOUSE
Managers: Jean & Sean Cowhig.
413-458-3135.
www.thetrustees.org (Trustees of Reservations).
554 Sloan Rd., Williamstown, MA 01267.
From jct. Rtes. 43 & 7, 1 mi. on rt.
Price: Expensive.
Credit Cards: D, MC, V.
Special Features: Pool; Tennis; Hiking/skiing trails; No pets.

A property of The Trustees of Reservations, Field Farm comprises 254 acres, excellent for hiking and cross-country skiing, and a house built in 1948 in the American Modern style. Five guest rooms all have private bath, two have working fireplaces, and three have sun decks. Country living with views of Mt. Greylock and the Taconic Range, just minutes from the attractions of Williamstown. Under the hands of an experienced chef, the breakfasts are to be admired.

GOLDBERRY'S
Innkeeper: Mary Terio.
413-458-3935.
39 Cold Spring Rd. (Rtes. 7 & 2), Williamstown, MA 01267.
Near Williams Inn.
Price: Moderate.
Credit Cards: None.
Special Features: No smoking; No pets; Children over 3.

J.R.R. Tolkien fans will recognize the name. Hobbits are welcome. This bed & breakfast opened in 1991 in an ideal location within three blocks of the Williams College campus, the Williamstown Theatre Festival, and the Clark Art Institute. The 1830s Georgian house is comfortably furnished with antiques and appropriate companion pieces, and guests are invited to use the living room, dining room, sun porch, and back porch overlooking the perennial gardens. The three bedrooms have private baths. Mary's breakfast might include baked apple French toast or crumb pancakes. She serves tea with pastries in the afternoon and, sometimes, a late-night snack. This is a popular stopping place for Williams College alumni and parents.

THE HOUSE ON MAIN STREET
Innkeepers: Phyllis, Bud & Regina Riley.
413-458-3031;
fax 413-458-2254.
www.houseonmainst.com.
1120 Main St., Williamstown, MA 01267.

Once known as Victorian Tourist & Antique House, this bed & breakfast has been taking guests since the 1930s. The Rileys became innkeepers in 1991 and are proud of the comment of one satisfied guest: "You have achieved a great combination of Victorian charm and modern comfort."

Near jct. Rtes. 2 & 7, W. of
   Williams Inn.
Price: Moderate.
Credit Cards: MC, V.
Handicap Access: Limited.
Special Features: No
   smoking; No pets;
   Children welcome.

This home began in the 18th century, with a major Victorian addition in the 1870s. The six guest rooms are light and spacious, with accents of antique furnishings, pretty country prints, and braided rugs. A healthful and hearty breakfast — fruits in season and eggs or pancakes — is served in the country kitchen. Guests may use the parlor and the wicker-laden screened porch. The congenial Rileys are well versed on the attractions of Williamstown, all within walking distance.

LE JARDIN
Manager: Walter Hayn.
413-458-8032.
777 Cold Spring Rd. (Rte. 7),
   Williamstown, MA
   01267.
S. of town.
Price: Moderate.
Credit Cards: AE, D, MC, V.
Special Features:
   Restaurant; No pets.

On a wooded hillside just south of the heart of Williamstown, Le Jardin offers six cozy rooms, all with private bath, in a large country farmhouse. Well-known restaurant on the first floor.

ORCHARDS
Owner: Sayed M. Saleh.
413-458-9611, 800-225-1517;
   fax 413-458-3273.
www.orchardshotel.com.
222 Adams Rd. (Rte. 2),
   Williamstown, MA
   01267.
E. of town center.
Price: Expensive to Very
   Expensive.
Credit Cards: AE, CB, DC,
   MC, V.
Handicap Access: Yes.
Special Features:
   Restaurant; Pool;
   Exercise center with
   sauna, environmental
   chamber, whirlpool; No
   pets.

This small luxury hotel, a member of Preferred Hotels & Resorts Worldwide, is reminiscent of an English country inn. Antique furnishings, complimentary afternoon tea, and enormous guest rooms featuring four-poster beds with down pillows are just a few of the amenities. Many rooms have wood-burning fireplaces and bay windows. The Orchards' award-winning restaurant features a menu that reflects New England's heritage and the chef's distinctive international talents. In summer al fresco patio dining is available overlooking the pond in the nicely landscaped inner courtyard. Chocolate chip cookies are a regular bedtime treat. Private conference and meeting rooms.

RIVER BEND FARM
Owners: David & Judy
   Loomis.
413-458-3121.

A stay at River Bend Farm, an authentic 1770 home listed on the National Register of Historic Places and featured on PBS's "This Old House," comes as close to an 18th-century lodging experience as one can have, but with heat and

643 Simonds Rd. (Rte. 7), Williamstown, MA 01267.
0.75 mi. N. of jct. Rtes. 7 & 2.
Price: Moderate.
Credit Cards: None.
Closed: Nov.–Mar.

water. Col. Benjamin Simonds built the house as a tavern. Thanks to the Loomises' painstaking work, original features are intact: wide pine floorboards, magnificent paneling, corner cupboards, and a central chimney containing five separate fireplaces, two ovens, and an attic smoking chamber. Furnishings, accessories, and fabrics used throughout the house are from the period or appropriate to it. Four guest rooms share two very large bathrooms (one was the buttery of the house and its walls are lined with crocks, paddles, and other implements). Breakfast (homemade breads, jams, and granola, with River Bend's own honey) is served in the keeping room at the back of the house, and the former taproom is a guest parlor. In summer, lawn furniture and a hammock are placed among the perennial and herb gardens, which feature a variety of 18th-century plants.

STEEP ACRES FARM

Owners: Mary, Marvin & Daniel Gangemi
413-458-3774.
520 White Oaks Rd., Williamstown, MA 01267.
From Rte. 7, E. on Sand Springs Rd., N. on White Oaks Rd.
Price: Moderate to Expensive.
Credit Cards: None.
Special Features: Pond for swimming, boating, fishing; Hiking trails; No smoking; Children 5 and up; No pets.

Two miles from the center of Williamstown, Steep Acres offers country lodging up a long gravel drive. The 1900 stone-and-shingle house sits on a hilltop on the Vermont state line, overlooking Mount Greylock. The Gangemis's 50 acres include a 1.5-acre pond for canoeing, trout fishing, and swimming (there are a diving board and raft), and trails for hiking and cross-country skiing. A patio off the sun porch — great for summer breakfasts or reading — seems to be perched at the top of the world. The house features an attractive decor combining late Victorian oak, wicker, and handsome fabrics. Two or four possible guest rooms available, depending on preference of party; three baths. Next door, in a contemporary house, The Birches at Steep Acres offers three more rooms, twin, queen, and king with Jacuzzi. A full gourmet breakfast and afternoon refreshments are included.

WILLIAMS INN

Owners: Carl & Marilyn Faulkner.
413-458-9371; 800-828-0133.
www.williamsinn.com.
Main St., Williamstown, MA 01267.
On the town green, jct. Rtes. 7 & 2.
Price: Expensive.

The generous Faulkners are much respected for making their inn a hub of town activities. Although its architecture is not exactly in keeping with the classic Williamstown, the Williams Inn and its staff please a great many North County travelers — and take the hassle of being an interstate bus stop as well. Vast and modern, the facility offers 103 rooms, each with a telephone and TV.

The Williams Inn greets travelers arriving by bus or by automobile.

Judith Monachina

Credit Cards: AE, D, DC, MC, V.
Handicap Access: Yes.
Special Features: Indoor pool; Sauna, whirlpool; Full-service dining room; Banquet facilities; Pets permitted (some restrictions), $10 per night.

Sunday brunch is highly regarded. The Faulkners are energetic about organizing special events, such as horse-drawn wagon rides. On Friday evenings a guitarist provides entertainment in the Tavern; on Saturday evenings, jazz. Nearby are two of America's fine art museums and the renowned Williamstown Theatre Festival. There is no charge for children under 14 in parents' room and pets are welcome in ground-floor rooms.

WILLIAMSTOWN B&B
Owners: Kim Rozell & Lucinda Edmonds.
413-458-9202.
www.williamstown bandb.com.
30 Cold Spring Rd. (Rte. 7), Williamstown, MA 01267.
Just S. of town library.
Price: Moderate.
Credit Cards: None.
Special Features: No smoking; No pets; Children over 12.

Open for business since 1989, the Williamstown Bed & Breakfast credits its success to a central, in-town location and a high proportion of returning guests. This spacious and airy Victorian has been completely renovated and tastefully furnished with a mixture of antiques and comfortable sofas and chairs. Each of the four guest rooms has its own bath and is individually decorated in period oak, maple, or mahogany furniture. Guests have exclusive use of the living room, dining room, and broad front porch. Lingering around the table after Kim Rozell's popular breakfasts — featuring homemade breads, muffins, scones, and always a hot entrée — is standard operating procedure at Williamstown B&B. Summer guests enjoy the perennial gardens and hammocks for lazy afternoons.

LODGING OUTSIDE THE COUNTY

Salisbury, Connecticut

UNDER MOUNTAIN INN
Owners: Peter & Marged Higginson.
860-435-0242;
  fax 860-435-2379.
www.innbook.com/inns/undermnt.
482 Undermountain Rd. (Rte. 41), Salisbury, CT 06068.
4 mi. N. on Rte. 41 from center of town.
Price: Expensive (MAP).
Credit Cards: MC, V.
Special Features: No smoking; No pets; Children over 6.

Have you been longing for a quiet day in the English countryside? Save the airfare and drive to the Under Mountain Inn, a 1730s Colonial set on three acres on a picturesque country road. Owner Peter Higginson, retired from the British Merchant Navy, has recreated his heritage in Connecticut.

Continental breakfast (available at all hours) and dinner are included. The menu in the dining rooms, warmed by a fire in winter, features such English staples as steak and kidney pie, bangers and mash, and shepherd's pie. There are four fireplaces in the common rooms and the seven rooms in the inn are furnished in part with antiques. All have private baths with Gilchrist & Soames soaps. Sherry served in the rooms and afternoon tea add to the British atmosphere. A wealth of British books and videos in the parlor invite a quiet afternoon far removed from the hectic city. Tally-ho!

WHITE HART
Owners: Scott & Roxanne Bok.
860-435-0030, 800-832-0041;
  fax 860-435-0040.
www.whitehartinn.com.
The Village Green, P.O. Box 545, Salisbury, CT 06068.
Jct. Rtes. 41 & 44, in center of town.
Price: Expensive to Very Expensive.
Credit Cards: AE, CB, D, DC, MC, V.
Handicap Access: Yes.
Special Features: Pets in some rooms; Children welcome; Senior discount (weekdays).

The oldest portions of this landmark inn were built sometime prior to 1810, when records indicate the farmhouse was converted to a tavern. The public spaces display an air of country elegance and comfort. Twenty-three charming guest rooms, plus three suites, all offer private baths, air conditioning, phones, and cable TV. Meals are not included in the rate, but breakfast, lunch, and dinner are served on the premises (there are two restaurants).

Averill Park, New York

GREGORY HOUSE
Owners: Bette & Bob
Jewell.
518-674-3774;
fax 518-674-8916.
www.gregoryhouse.com.
Rte. 43, P.O. Box 401,
Averill Park, NY 12018.
Price: Moderate to
Expensive.
Credit Cards: AE, CB, D,
DC, MC, V.
Handicap Access: Limited.
Special Features: Pool; No
smoking; No pets.

The Gregory House has a clean, sophisticated country look. Twelve guest rooms, all with air conditioning and private baths, have stenciled walls and attractive country furnishings. A continental breakfast is served to guests, and the cozy bar and the restaurant are open for dinner Tuesday through Sunday. TV in common room. Averill Park is convenient to Williamstown attractions and North County ski areas as well as to the Saratoga Performing Arts Center.

Berlin, New York

SEDGWICK INN
Innkeepers: Chet & Diane
Niedzwiecki.
518-658-2334;
fax 518-658-3998.
www.sedgwickinn.com.
Rte. 22, P.O. Box 250,
Berlin, NY 12022.
Price: Moderate to
Expensive.
Credit Cards: AE, CB, D,
DC, MC, V.
Special Features: Pool;
Jacuzzi; Pets & children
in annex only.

A 1791 house with restaurant and six-room motel (the annex) attached, set on 12 acres in the country. Privately owned and operated, this quaint, well-kept property offers comfortable rooms and proximity to Berkshire attractions. The five rooms in the main house, all with private bath, are preferred. Full breakfast is included.

Hillsdale, New York

AUBERGINE
Owner: David Lawson.
518-325-3412;
fax 518-325-7089.
www.aubergine.com.
P.O. Box 387, Hillsdale, NY
12529.
Jct. Rtes. 22 & 23.
Price: Moderate to
Expensive.
Credit Cards: AE, DC, MC, V.
Special features: No
smoking; Call ahead
about pets, children.

This 1783 Dutch Colonial house strikes a noble profile above a busy intersection in a small upstate New York village. Four delightful, large rooms, all with private bath, are thoughtfully furnished. The owner/chef, a Minnesotan, operates an extraordinary restaurant on the ground floor. A "high continental" breakfast is available to residents for an additional $10.

**SWISS HÜTTE
COUNTRY INN**
Managers: Gert & Cindy
Alper.
518-325-3333, 413-528-6200.
www.swisshutte.com.
Rte. 23, P.O. Box 357,
Hillsdale, NY 12529.
2 mi. E. of town on MA-NY
border.
Price: Moderate to
Expensive.
Credit Cards: MC, V.
Handicap Access: Limited.
Special Features: Pool;
Tennis.

At the entrance to the popular South County ski area, Catamount, this property boasts several tennis courts, pool, lovely gardens, and, of course, an inviting downhill slope in its front yard. Fifteen comfortable, well-furnished rooms are split between the original wooden chalet and a newer building. An award-winning restaurant completes the picture. A modified American plan is available. Breakfast is not included with the basic room rate.

New Lebanon, New York

**CHURCHILL HOUSE
B&B**
Owners: Michele & Michael
Arthur.
518-766-5852, 800-532-2702.
www.churchillhousebb.com.
228 Churchill Rd., P.O. Box
252, New Lebanon, NY
12125.
Off Rte. 22, 0.25 mi. S. of
Rte. 20.
Price: Moderate to
Expensive.
Credit Cards: AE, D, MC, V.
Special Features: Hiking
trails; No smoking; No
pets; Children over 5
welcome.

Churchill House was built in 1797 for Rev. Silas Churchill and remained in the Churchill family until 1965. The Arthurs bought the property, which includes 18 acres of land, in 1991. Churchill House has four guest rooms with private baths. Three can have an additional bed in the room. There is a charming room under the eaves, with trails of ivy stenciled by Michele. Each room has bathrobes, and the beds are mounded high with featherbeds. The living room and wraparound front porch with views of the Taconic Hills are for the guests' use. On weekends and holidays a full breakfast is served, with dietary restrictions accommodated (picnic breakfasts available with advance notice). Exceptionally low weekday rates are available in the high season. Away from the madding crowd but handy to all Berkshire attractions.

Stephentown, New York

MILL HOUSE INN
Innkeepers: Frank Tallet &
Family.
413-738-5348, 800-563-8645;
fax 518-733-6025.
www.themillhouseinn.com.
Rte. 43, Stephentown, NY.
Mail: P. O. Box 1079,
Hancock, MA 01237.
Price: Moderate to
Expensive.

Old-world touches in a former sawmill enhance this cozy, well-regarded country inn, with refurbishing ongoing. Furnished with antiques, the rooms are warm and whimsical. A living room with fireplace offers warm comfort. Seven rooms and five suites, several with fireplaces of their own, all have private baths, air conditioning, and telephones; some have TV. Set on three peaceful, rural acres with formal gardens, stone walls, garden

Credit Cards: AE, MC, V.
Closed: Mar. 15–May 15;
Sept. 1–Oct. 1.
Handicap Access: 1 unit.
Special Features: Pool; No
smoking; No pets.

paths, and a pool, it's the perfect romantic escape — a touch of country with a European flair. Afternoon tea and continental breakfast are served; a full breakfast is available à la carte.

MOTELS

South County

Barrington Court Motel (413-528-2340; 400 Stockbridge Rd., Rte. 7, Gt. Barrington, MA 01230; N. of town) Price: Expensive to Very Expensive. AE, MC, V. Handicap access. 21 motel units, refrig. 4 suites, kitchenettes, Jacuzzi, pool. Continental breakfast.

Briarcliff Motor Lodge (413-528-3000; 506 Stockbridge Rd., Rte 7, Gt. Barrington, MA 01230; N. of town) Price: Inexpensive to Moderate. AE, D, DC, MC, V. Handicap access. 16 units. Spacious landscaped grounds, view of Monument Mtn.

Days Inn, Great Barrington (413-528-3150; 372 Main St., Gt. Barrington) Price: Moderate to Expensive. Credit Cards: AE, CB, D, DC, MC, V. Handicap access. 62 units.

Days Motor Inn (413-243-0501, 800-329-7466; Rte. 102, P.O. Box 426, Lee, MA 01238; between Stockbridge and Lee) Price: Moderate to Expensive. AE, D, DC, MC, V. 26 units. Cable TV, AC.

Gaslight Motor Lodge (413-243-9701; Greenwater Pond, Rte. 20, Lee, MA 01238; 5 mi. E. of town) Price: Moderate. MC, V. 8 units, refrig. Pond with swimming, paddleboats, rowboats, fishing, ice skating, xc skiing, hiking (Appalachian Trail crosses property). Coffee, tea in morning.

Lantern House Motel (413-528-2350, 800-959-2350; Stockbridge Rd., Rte. 7, P.O. Box 97, Gt. Barrington, MA 01230; 1 mi. N. of town) Price: Moderate (3-night weekend min. in summer). D, MC, V. Handicap access. 14 rooms. Refrig., cable TV. Pool.

Laurel Hill Motel (413-243-0813; Laurel St., Rte. 20, P.O. Box 285, Lee, MA 01238; N. of town) Price: Moderate to Expensive. AE, CB, D, DC, MC, V. 23 units. 2 efficiencies. Pool, view.

Monument Mountain Motel (413-528-3272; 249 Stockbridge Rd., Rte. 7, Gt. Barrington, MA 01230; N. of town) Price: Moderate to Expensive. AE, CB, D, DC, MC, V. Above average. 18 units. Cable TV. Heated pool, lighted tennis courts, picnic tables, 20 acres bordering Housatonic River, flower gardens. No pets.

Pilgrim Motor Inn (413-243-1328; 165 Housatonic St., Rte. 20, Lee, MA 01238; E. of town) Price: Expensive. AE, D, DC, MC, V. 34 units. Cable TV. Pool.

Pleasant Valley Motel (413-232-8511; Rte. 102, W. Stockbridge, MA 01266; sandwiched betw. Mass Pike Exit 1 & Rte. 102) Price: Inexpensive to Expensive. AE, D, MC, V. Handicap access. Cable TV. Pool. Continental breakfast incl. summer weekends.

Sunset Motel (413-243-0302, fax 413-243-2880; 150 Housatonic St., Rte. 20, Lee, MA 01238) Price: Moderate to Expensive. AE, CB, D, DC, MC, V. 27 units, 1 Jacuzzi room. Cable TV, AC. Pool. Convenient to Mass Pike Exit 2.

Super 8 Motel (413-243-0143; 128 Housatonic St., Rte. 20, Lee, MA 01238) Price: Inexpensive to Expensive. AE, D, DC, MC, V. Handicap access. 49 rooms. Cable TV. Nonsmoking rooms; free coffee, paper. Convenient to Mass Pike Exit 2.

Central County

Berkshire Inn (413-443-3000; 150 W. Housatonic St., Rte. 20, Pittsfield, MA 01201; W. of town) Price: Moderate to Expensive. AE, MC, V. 38 units, 9 with refrig. Cable TV, AC. Pool.

Berkshire North Cottages (413-442-7469; 121 S. Main St., Lanesborough, MA 01237) Price: Inexpensive to Moderate. MC, V. 5 cottages: 3 with full kitchens, 2 with refrig., hot plates. Cable TV. Closed Nov.–mid-May.

Comfort Inn (413-443-4714; 1055 South St., Rtes. 7 & 20, Pittsfield, MA 01201) Price: Moderate to Very Expensive. AE, CB, D, DC, MC, V. 58 units. Cable TV, AC. Exercise room; discount pass to Berkshire West. Pool. Deluxe continental breakfast.

Heart of the Berkshires Motel (413-443-1255; 970 W. Housatonic St., Rte. 20, Pittsfield, MA 01201; W. of town) Price: Inexpensive to Moderate. AE, D, MC, V. 16 units. Cable TV, AC.

Howard Johnson Motel (413-442-4000, 800-I-GO-HOJO; 462 Pittsfield Rd., Rtes. 7 & 20, Lenox, MA 01240; N. of town) Price: Moderate to Very Expensive. AE, D, MC, V. 44 units; some with Jacuzzi. Cable TV, AC. Pool.

Huntsman Motel (413-442-8714; 1350 W. Housatonic St., Rte. 20, Pittsfield, MA 01201; W. of town) Price: Moderate. AE, MC, V. 14 units; 1 suite with kitchen. Cable TV.

Inn at Village Square (413-684-0860; 645 Main St., Dalton, MA 01226) Price: Moderate. AE, D, MC, V. Handicap access. 15 units. Cable TV. Restaurant.

Lamp Post Motel (413-443-2979; Rte. 7, P.O. Box 335, Lanesborough, MA 01237; N. of Pittsfield) Price: Inexpensive to Moderate. AE, D, MC, V. 10 units, all with efficiency kitchens. Cable TV. Pool.

Lanesborough Mountain Motel (413-442-6717; Rte. 7, P.O. Box 335, Lanesborough, MA 01237) Price: Inexpensive to Moderate (special midweek rates). AE, D, MC, V. 10 rooms. 5 mi. to Jiminy, Brodie.

Lenox Motel (413-499-0324; Rtes. 7 & 20, P.O. Box 713, Lenox, MA 01240; N. of town) Price: Moderate to Expensive. AE, D, MC, V. 17 units. Cable TV, AC, in-room coffee. Pool.

Mayflower Motor Inn (413-443-4468; 474 Pittsfield-Lenox Rd., Rtes. 7 & 20, P.O. Box 952, Lenox, MA 01240; N. of town) Price: Inexpensive to Expensive. AE, D, DC, MC, V. 20 rooms. Cable TV. Pool, views.

Mountain View Motel (413-442-1009; 499 S. Main St., Lanesborough, MA 01237) Price: Moderate to Expensive. AE, D, MC, V. 13 rooms in motel. 3 efficiency cottages available year-round. Cable TV with HBO.

Pittsfield Travelodge (413-443-5661, 800-578-7878; 16 Cheshire Rd., Pittsfield, MA 01201; jct. Rtes. 8 & 9) Price: Inexpensive to Expensive. AE, D, DC, MC, V. Handicap access. 47 units. Cable TV. Near Berkshire Mall.

Quality Inn (413-637-4244, 800-442-4201; 130 Pittsfield Rd., Rte. 7, Pittsfield, MA 01201) Price: Inexpensive to Very Expensive. AE, D, DC, MC, V. 120 rooms. Cable TV, AC, refrig., in-room coffee. Outdoor pool, tennis courts. Deluxe continental breakfast incl. Cocktail lounge, banquet facilities.

Super 8 Motel (413-637-3560, 800-800-8000; 194 Pittsfield Rd., Rtes. 7 & 20, Lenox, MA 01240; N. of town) Price: Expensive. AE, D, DC, MC, V. 59 units. Cable TV, AC. Pool.

Wagon Wheel Motel (413-445-4532; 646 Pittsfield Rd., Rtes. 7 & 20, P.O. Box 808, Lenox, MA 01240; 3 mi. N. of town) Price: Inexpensive to Expensive. AE, D, MC, V. 18 units, 2 Jacuzzi rooms. Cable TV.

Weathervane Motel (413-443-3230; 475 S. Main St., Rte. 7, Lanesborough, MA 01237; S. of town) Price: Moderate. AE, CB, D, MC, V. 17 units.

Yankee Home Comfort Inn (413-499-3700, 800-835-2364; www.berkshireinns. com/yankee. html; 461 Pittsfield Rd., Rtes. 7 & 20, P.O. Box 829, Lenox, MA 01240; near Pittsfield line) Price: Moderate to Very Expensive. AE, D, DC, MC, V. Handicap access. 96 units (incl. 36 new units, mostly kings); 22 rooms with fireplaces; some rooms with Jacuzzis. Cable TV. Indoor pool, spa, manicured grounds. Conference center.

North County

Berkshire Hills Motel (413-458-3950; Rtes. 7 & 2, Williamstown, MA 01267; 2 mi. S. of town) Price: Moderate to Expensive. D, MC, V. Brick 2-story motel, 21 rooms. Cable TV. Nonsmoking rooms, king beds available. Heated pool. Spacious landscaped grounds. Generous continental breakfast buffet.

Carriage House Motel (413-458-5359; Rte. 7, New Ashford, MA 01237) Price: Inexpensive. AE, CB, D, DC, MC, V. Partial handicap access. 14 units. Pool, indoor tennis & racquetball, woods, brook, trails.

Chimney Mirror Motel (413-458-5202; 295 Main St., Rte. 2, Williamstown, MA 01267; just E. of town) Price: Moderate. AE, MC, V. 18 units. Cable TV. Continental breakfast incl. summer weekends.

Cozy Corner (413-458-8006; 784 Sand Springs Rd., Rte. 7, Williamstown, MA 01267; N. of town center) Price: Moderate. AE, D, DC, MC, V. 12 units. Across from convenience store at gateway to Vermont.

Dublin House Motel (413-443-4752; at Brodie Mtn., Rte. 7, New Ashford, MA 01267) Price: Moderate. AE, D, DC, MC, V. Owned by Brodie Mtn. Ski Resort. 31 units. Convenience rather than charm, but right at the base of the slopes.

Dug-Out Motel (413-743-9737; 99 Howland Ave., Rte. 8, Adams, MA 01220; N. of town) Price: Inexpensive. AE, DC, MC, V. Partial handicap access. 14 rooms, 2 efficiencies. Cable TV, AC.

Econo Lodge Springs Motor Inn (413-458-5945; Rte. 7, New Ashford, MA 01237; halfway between Pittsfield and Williamstown) Price: Moderate to Expensive. AE, D, DC, MC, V. 40 standard motel rooms, 2 small chalets with fireplaces. Cable TV, in-room coffee. Pool, tennis court. Reputable restaurant across the street. Convenient to ski resorts.

This restaurant and two motels make up the 1896 Motel complex in Williamstown.

Judith Monachina

1896 Motel Brookside (413-458-8125; 910 Cold Spring Rd., Rte. 7, Williamstown, MA 01267) Price: Moderate to Expensive. AE, D, DC, MC, V. 16 rooms. In-room coffee, tea. Cable TV. Scenic Hemlock Brook at the front door. Access to pool at 1896 Pondside. Generous continental breakfast.

1896 Motel Pondside (413-458-8125; 910 Cold Spring Rd., Rte. 7, Williamstown, MA 01267, across from 1896 House Restaurant) Price: Moderate to Expensive. AE, D, DC, MC, V. 12 rooms (each with 2 queen), 1 efficiency suite, 1 suite with Jacuzzi. Cable TV. In-room coffee, tea. Pool. Continental breakfast.

Four Acres Motel (413-458-8158; 213 Main St., Rte. 2, Williamstown, MA 01267) Price: Moderate to Expensive. AE, CB, D, DC, MC, V. Handicap access. 31 units. Cable TV. Garden area with pool. Meeting rooms. Continental breakfast.

Green Valley Motel (413-458-3864; 1214 Simonds Rd., Rte. 7, Williamstown, MA 01267; N. of town) Price: Moderate. AE, MC, V. 18 units. Cable TV. Pool. Continental breakfast.

Jericho Valley Inn (413-458-9511, 800-JERICHO; Hancock Rd., Rte. 43, P.O. Box 239, Williamstown, MA 01267) Price: Moderate. AE, MC, V. 25 units; suites, cottages available. Satellite TV, AC. Heated pool. 350 mountain acres with spectacular views, fireplace lounge. Near Jiminy, Brodie. Pets allowed in cottages.

Kerry House Motel (413-443-4753; Brodie Mtn., Rte. 7, New Ashford, MA 01267) Price: Moderate to Expensive. AE, D, DC, MC, V. 41 units, some efficiency apartments. Cable TV. Located on slopes of Brodie Mtn.

Maple Terrace Motel (413-458-9677; 555 Main St., Rte. 2, Williamstown, MA 01267; E. side of town) Price: Moderate. AE, D, DC, MC, V. 17 units, 2 efficiencies. Cable TV, AC. Heated pool. Mountain views. Spacious grounds well off the highway.

New Ashford Motor Inn (413-458-8041; Rte. 7, New Ashford, MA 01237; 1 mi. N. of Brodie Mtn.) Price: Inexpensive to Moderate. AE, MC, V. 16 units. Four channels of TV. For the skier and traveler who does not insist on old-world charm.

Northside Inn & Motel (413-458-8107; 45 North St., Rte. 7, Williamstown, MA 01267; N. of town) Price: Inexpensive. AE, D, DC, MC, V. Handicap access. 32 units. Cable TV. Pool. Coffee shop for breakfast.

Villager Motel (413-458-4046; 953 Simonds Rd., Rte. 7, Williamstown, MA 01267; N. of town) Price: Inexpensive to Moderate. D, MC, V. 13 rooms. Cable TV, AC. On main road but set well back. Expanded continental breakfast.

Wigwam & Western Summit Cottages (413-663-3205; Mohawk Trail, Rte. 2, P.O. Box 7, N. Adams, MA 01247; E. of town center) Price: Inexpensive to Moderate. AE, D, MC, V. 5 units. Color TV. Porch with fantastic view of Mt. Greylock. Gift shop. Open late May to mid-Oct.

Willows Motel (413-458-5768; 480 Main St., Rte. 2, Williamstown, MA 01267; E. of town) Price: Inexpensive to Moderate. AE, MC, V. 17 rooms. Cable TV. Above average. Heated pool.

CHAPTER FOUR
Pleasing the Palate
RESTAURANTS & FOOD PURVEYORS

Some of the county's showiest restaurants are found in the "cottages" of the Gilded Age: at Orleton, now called Gateways, and at Blantyre and Wheatleigh. Yet a great table is set as well in more humble Berkshire settings, such as pre-Revolutionary farmhouses, old mills, and inns.

The fare is no longer just American, with a dash of the continental, but has become abundant in many other cuisines including Japanese, Chinese, Indian, Vietnamese, even Finnish.

"A Taste of the Berkshires" or "Taste of Williamstown" or festivals

Judith Monachina

The Old Inn on the Green in New Marlborough is lighted entirely by candlelight.

in other towns are annual extravaganzas that celebrate the bounty of the our region. Books of Berkshire recipes are also available. The Williamstown Theatre Festival's *As You Like It* is a prize-winning compilation of the favorite recipes of the festival's stars, directors, writers, and associates. For the Berkshire County Historical Society's *Berkshire Victuals*, editor Janet Cook researched all county cooks, both dead and alive, and came up with scores of delicious local recipes. *The New Red Lion Inn Cookbook* (a revision of the original edition), honors the cuisine of the county's best-known inn, while *Best Recipes of Berkshire Chefs* by Miriam Jacobs demonstrates the culinary specialties of a range of fine contemporary county chefs. *The Kripalu Cookbook,* by Atma Jo Ann Levitt, features vegetarian recipes from the kitchen of the Kripalu Center in Lenox, suitably scaled down for home use.

The number of restaurants in the county is vast — more than 225 (37 in Williamstown alone!). To cover all of them would require a book twice this size. Diners should be guided by what we suggest, but follow their own hunches, as well. We would be pleased to hear of discoveries for a future edition. We have grouped the best of the breakfast/lunch eateries in a section of their own, pp. 129–131. There are dozens of specialty food suppliers, too, engaging alternatives to supermarkets.

We have concentrated on the establishments we have found most interesting and most successful, risking critical judgments. *De gustibus non disputandum.* A dining experience has many dimensions. The food, of course, is primary, but we have also based our judgments on other factors, such as the range of the menu, the decor and ambience of the restaurant, the quality of the service, and value for price. We note that a restaurant participates in the Berkshire Regional Food and Land Council's Berkshire Grown Restaurant Certification Program. Restaurateurs are invited to join if they "pledge to buy and utilize locally grown food and food products to the extent that [they] are able, thus supporting local farmers and food producers who preserve and sustain the beauty and the bounty of the Berkshire region." Patrons who dine at Berkshire Grown restaurants enjoy their fine meals knowing that they are also supporting the local agricultural way of life.

Reviews are organized first by section of the county, then alphabetically by town, then by restaurant name. Food purveyors are grouped alphabetically by type, then by name of establishment. Every entry appears in the general index, too. While the information is as up-to-date as we can make it, it is still wise to call ahead.

We designate each restaurant with a price code, signifying the approximate cost of a meal, including appetizer, entrée, and dessert, but not cocktails, wine, tax, or tip. Restaurants with a prix-fixe menu are noted accordingly.

Dining Price Codes

Inexpensive	Up to $15
Moderate	$15 to $25
Expensive	$25 to $40
Very Expensive	Over $40

Credit Cards

AE — American Express
CB — Carte Blanche
D — Discover
DC — Diner's Club
MC — MasterCard
V — Visa

Meals
- B — Breakfast
- L — Lunch
- D — Dinner
- SB — Sunday Brunch

RESTAURANTS SOUTH COUNTY

North Egremont

ELM COURT INN
413-528-0325.
Rte. 71, N. Egremont.
Closed: Mon. & Tues. in
    winter.
Price: Expensive.
Cuisine: Continental.
Serving: D.
Credit Cards: AE, MC, V.
Reservations:
    Recommended.
Special Feature: Fireplaces.

We probably don't consider Swiss as ethnic cuisine but the Elm Court's hosts Glee Bieri and her chef husband, Urs, maintain the Swiss tradition in Berkshire County. A former executive chef at the United Nations, Urs Bieri concentrates his substantial culinary talents on roesti potato and Wienerschnitzel, without slighting dishes from other parts of Europe. We split a duck sausage appetizer, and settled into salmon cake with asparagus and lobster chunks, and roasted duckling with a Swiss orange sauce bigarade. The lobster was a particularly happy companion to the salmon, yet many other listed appetizers and entrées would have created equal anticipation and, we're certain, nearly as much pleasure.

Elm Court is a restaurant to drool for. It gets high marks, as well, for imaginative menu items, such as crayfish and fennel ravioli; and all are served with a fine eye for color and arrangement on the plate. The dessert list pays proper homage to chocolate; we in turn paid proper homage to a banana chocolate bread pudding.

Although the menu tilts toward carnivores, on an earlier trip a vegetarian friend received a plate as delicious as it was beautiful, a grilled golden bell pepper, zucchini, string beans, and shiitake mushrooms, along with pasta in tomato basil sauce.

The Elm Court's wine list offers a nice range of French, Swiss, German, Italian, and California bottles, at surprisingly affordable prices. Many good wines are priced around $15, with some of the best up around $100. Service is superior: informative, available, but not in the diners' soup.

South Egremont

EGREMONT INN
413-528-2111, 800-859-1780.
www.egremontinn.com

The menu at the Egremont Inn might be described as "Manhattan/Provence." It is as good as it gets. Innkeeper Steve Waller explains

10 Old Sheffield Rd., S.
  Egremont.
On side street off Rte. 23 in
  center of village.
Mail: P.O. Box 418, S.
  Egremont, MA 01258
Closed: Mon. & Tues.
Price: Moderate to
  Expensive.
Cuisine: American,
  "Sophisticated Country."
Serving: D.
Credit Cards: AE, D, MC,
  V.
Reservations:
  Recommended.
Special Features: Fireplaces;
  Live entertainment
  Thurs., Sat.

that the chefs are his stepson Jonathan Taufman and Jonathan's fiancée, Vanesse Cortesi, both graduates of the Culinary Arts Institute. What a team! They do their school proud.

The sweet cornbread and focaccia (accompanied by a bottle of olive oil) started us off. A perfectly textured country pâté and a generous salad of fresh mesclun greens with pine nuts, dried cranberries, and blue cheese tossed with a red wine vinaigrette were marvelous. Our entrées were a tender sautéed duck breast with fava beans in a cabernet reduction sauce; and pan-seared sea bass with shiitakes and leeks, each served on a mound of mashed Idaho potatoes.

The wine list is one of the longest in the Berkshires, with many choices available in half bottles. We enjoyed the '96 Murphy-Goode fumé blanc. Dessert choices included banana split with a sweet-creamy sauce and a flourless chocolate cake.

A sensible meal could easily be made of the generous salad plus soup or an appetizer, but total indulgence is indicated here — unless you are fortunate enough to come frequently to work your way through the menu. These people can cook; the atmosphere enhances; c'est bon!

Completing a fine meal, at John Andrew's.

Jonathan Sternfield

JOHN ANDREW'S
413-528-3469.
Rte. 23, S. Egremont.
2.5 mi. W. of village.
Open: Daily July–Aug.; off
  season closed Weds.
Price: Moderate to
  Expensive.

John Andrew's Restaurant continues to offer one of the finest dining experiences in the Berkshires. The softly lit, cleanly decorated dining rooms make a pleasant contrast to its rustic exterior. Service is attentive, professional, and discreet. The menu is simple; the offerings, in the New American vein, are superior. Delicious freshly baked breads are

Cuisine: American.
Serving: D.
Credit Cards: MC, V.
Reservations:
Recommended.
Special Features: Glassed-
in porch in back;
Fireplace, outdoor deck,
terrace in season;
Member, Berkshire
Grown.

offered first. Appetizers and salads display executive chef/proprietor Danny Smith's imaginative side. The grilled, roasted, and braised entrées emphasize marvelous natural flavors, enhanced with perfectly executed vegetable accompaniments. The wine list has been chosen with sufficient care and taste to bring John Andrew's a *Wine Spectator* magazine Award of Excellence.

Proprietors Susan and Danny Smith are true professionals and excellent hosts. Although they have extended their reach by opening the very popular Union Bar & Grill in Great Barrington, John Andrew's continues to display every evidence of their constant care and attention.

Elegant simplicity at the Old Mill.

Jonathan Sternfield

OLD MILL
413-528-1421.
Rte. 23, S. Egremont.
Center of village.
Closed: Mon. in winter.
Price: Moderate to
Expensive.
Cuisine: American/
Continental.
Serving: D.
Credit Cards: AE, DC, MC,
V.
Reservations: Recom-
mended for parties of
5 or more.

A generous spacing of tables adds to the gracious, casual, airy feeling of this renovated 1797 grist mill. Although not brightly lighted, it is not overly dark. The service is well paced yet unhurried.

Since chef/owner Terry Morse recently returned from Italy, it was not surprising to see a few fine Italian dishes on his menu. An appetizer of airdried beef (bresaola) with mesclun, shaved Parmesan, and truffle oil, and an endive-and-pear salad with gorgonzola dressing and toasted almonds was shared. An interesting array of entrées included a tender garlic-and-herb-crusted rack of lamb with

Special Features: Private dining room; Fireplace; Member, Berkshire Grown.

mashed Yukon Gold potatoes, and manicotti with spinach, ricotta, and mozzarella; the freshness of the tomato sauce truly reminded us of Italy. A bottle of 1994 Barolo was a perfect accompaniment.

We understand that Terry makes a great tiramisú. Since it was unavailable the evening we were there, we will call ahead next time! Berkshire butter pecan ice cream and a wonderful, thin-crusted crème brûlée were worthy substitutes.

Great Barrington

BARRINGTON BREWERY & RESTAURANT
413-528-8282.
www.baygo.com; keyword: Barrington Brewery.
420 Stockbridge Rd. (Jenifer House Commons), Gt. Barrington.
Price: Inexpensive to Moderate.
Cuisine: American.
Serving: L, D.
Credit cards: AE, D, MC, V.
Special Features: Patio dining in summer; Pool tables and dartboard; Member, Berkshire Grown.

The South County entry in the burgeoning category of micro-brewery cum restaurant, Barrington Brewery is a barnlike but cozy place with a genuine and complete brewery in the hayloft section of the Tavern. Taking the distinctive feature first, Brewer Andy Mankin's "Barn Brewed™" beer is darned good. Berkshire Blonde Ale, "Hopland" Pale Ale, "Barrington" Brown Ale, and "Black Bear" Stout, in increasing order of weight, are the regulars always on tap. To assist your exploration, they offer a "sampler" of the five current offerings in 3-oz. glasses, which makes for good tasting fun in the taproom.

The luncheon menu is soups, salads, and "super" sandwiches, a plowman's lunch (sausage, cheese, chutney, and bread), or jacket potatoes with various cheese, chili, or steamed broccoli toppings. After 5pm, the luncheon menu is supplemented with such dinner offerings as the lobster pot pie (Maine lobster, traditional pot pie–style, topped with garlic mashed potatoes); shepherd's pie (a seasoned ground beef, lamb, and corn casserole covered with a mashed potato crust); or, for the vegetarian, delicious sautéed eggplant slices rolled with roasted sweet peppers and provolone, topped with marinara sauce and baked. The portions of both the sandwich plates and the main courses are quite ample. Desserts, such as the fresh fruit crisp, are fresh-baked on the premises. All in all, Barrington Brewery offers good, hearty food, and the best beer you'll drink south of Pittsfield (where you will find The Brewery on North Street).

BIZEN
413-528-4343.
17 Railroad St., Gt. Barrington.

Bizen is a first-rate Japanese restaurant and sushi bar, as perhaps shown best by its great popularity with New York City–based second-home owners here — to say nothing of numerous

A Japanese greeting in the entryway at Bizen on Railroad St. in Great Barrington.

Judith Monachina

Price: Moderate to
   Expensive.
Cuisine: Japanese.
Serving: L, D.
Credit Cards: AC, D, MC,
   V.
Handicap Access: Yes.
Reservations:
   Recommended.
Special Features: Sushi bar;
   Japanese grill; Full bar;
   Private rooms available;
   No smoking.

CASTLE STREET CAFÉ
413-528-5244; fax 413-528-
   8863.
10 Castle St., Gt.
   Barrington.
Closed: Tues.
Price: Inexpensive to
   Moderate.

sophisticated locals. Proprietor (and acclaimed potter — see p. 283) Michael Marcus and chef associate Hideo Furukawa preside over a bustling enterprise, seemingly always full — even now, after a recent doubling in size. The atmosphere is lively, the tables close together, the ceramic tableware all from Michael's own Joyous Spring Pottery. There's a full bar now, too, and a Japanese grill. The menu covers the full array of traditional Japanese cuisine, from sushi and sashimi by the piece, to varied and delicious hand rolls, excellent cooked dishes, soups, and salads. A perfect *bistrot* — in a different language.

Michael Ballon's Castle Street Café holds its own, and then some, in the ever more sophisticated Berkshire dining scene. The bistro atmosphere of exposed brick walls, frequently changing hangings of contemporary paintings, white linen tablecloths, and fresh flowers never fails to please the eye. The eclectic menu combines French, Italian, and American influences, and proudly features locally grown and produced foods, from goat

Cuisine: Continental.
Serving: D.
Credit Cards: AE, D, MC, V.
Special Features: Cruvinet wine bar; Member, Berkshire Grown.

cheese to French bread to fresh produce. Prepared by Michael himself, the fare is always finely done. The wine list, featuring mostly moderately priced French and American wines, has earned Castle Street a *Wine Spectator* magazine Award of Excellence. But service is what sets Castle Street apart. The veteran and accomplished waitstaff know their business and do it to perfection. One always feels welcome — well attended to, but perfectly undisturbed.

The adjoining Celestial Bar and Jazz Club became a Berkshire tradition almost from its first day. Offering jazz (soloists weeknights, combos on weekends) and a lighter menu six nights a week, it provides a welcome atmosphere for both the pure jazz aficionado and the more casual diner.

DOS AMIGOS
413-528-0084.
250 Stockbridge Rd. (Rte.7), Gt. Barrington.
Price: Inexpensive.
Cuisine: Mexican.
Serving: D.
Credit Cards: AE, D, DC, MC, V.
Reservations: Preferred for groups of 5 or more.
Special Features:
Vegetarian dishes;
Children's menu;
Entertainment; Member, Berkshire Grown.

Under proprietor Ari Zorn, Dos Amigos offers a pleasant, informal setting. It has always had a steady local and second-home clientele. Competition in the county from Mexican eateries has led to improvements in menu and preparation, more fresh ingredients, vegetarian offerings, fruit salsas, marinated meat dishes, and quite special specials — such as portabella mushroom fajita or grilled Cajun catfish with passion fruit salsa. Chicken and cheese chimichangas or quesadillas are typical of regular menu items. A word about spiciness: the chef will make it hot, but to get it really hot, diners must convey in graphic terms the importance of self-immolation. On this score, it's a pity that whole jalapeños are not served as a garnish. A tasty, large margarita is served in a glass the size of a birdbath, and specialty coffees are available as postprandials.

Dos Amigos presents a guitarist occasionally for the music-and-dining crowd. There's a kids' menu starting at $4. The patio is preferred on a mild summer evening. Altogether, Dos Amigos is a friend in the Berkshires.

GLORY OF INDIA
See *Paradise of India,* under *Lee.*

HELSINKI TEA COMPANY
413-528-3394.
284 Main St. (Rte. 7), Gt. Barrington.

The Helsinki Tea Company, tucked behind Great Barrington's Main Street, is a cozy little bastion of nouvelle Finnish home recipes, decorated with soft old-eccentric-aunt armchairs, throw

The Helsinki Tea Company in Great Barrington.

Judith Monachina

Price: Moderate.
Cuisine: Northern European.
Serving: L, D, SB.
Credit Cards: MC, V.

pillows, and funky art and textiles. Although Helsinki is locally known for its good-looking wait-staff, the inventive menu and great chef are just as alluring.

The house specialty is the Mad Russian, crisp potato latkes topped with a not-too-sweet, apple-wild blueberry compote and salty-good gravlax, sour cream, and caviar. In summertime, the sweet, smooth borscht runs cold, and in winter it's hot and chunky; either way it's crowned with a dollop of Helsinki's horseradish-sour cream. Tuna-melt aficionados rave about "Fellini's Favorite" and the Swedish ribs are tangy and sweet and fall-off-the-bone, melt-in-your-mouth tender with a honey-orange barbecue glaze and lots of fixin's. The salads are simple and fresh with delicious dressings and there are plenty of offerings for the vegetarian. Specials happen every night (usually a salmon and a chicken); we tried a seared tuna (not overcooked) over fresh red-pepper pappardelle (flat wide noodle) with a tomato and smoky braised spinach and basil sauce, caramelized red onion, and topped with an intense Kalamata olive tapenade.

From the small dessert menu, we sampled a dense, flourless Sachertorte — for serious chocolate lovers only. And as the restaurant's name suggests, a good pot of loose tea is available here. Sunday brunch with delightful fresh-squeezed mimosas should not be missed, nor Club Helsinki in the evening — the new intimate, ambient bar-nightclub in a space adjoining the restaurant, with live music on weekends, quality tap beer, hep decor, and dancing till the wee hours, blue-law style (that's 1am).

The creative head chef is Damian Whittaker and the pastry chef (he makes desserts and great focaccia) is Marco Belli.

HUDSON'S RESTAURANT

413-528-2002.
www.hudsonsrestaurant.
com.
50 Stockbridge Rd. (Rte. 7),
Gt. Barrington.
Price: Expensive.
Cuisine: Eclectic
Contemporary.
Open: Tues.–Sun. in
summer, Weds.–Sun. in
winter.
Serving: L, D, SB.
Credit Cards: AE, D, DC,
MC, V.
Special Feature: Member,
Berkshire Grown.

Proprietors Cindy and Geoffrey Brown, both graduates of the distinguished Culinary Institute of America, love to work in many different American and international cuisines. Thus the designation "eclectic contemporary." They have further adapted their offerings to take the fullest possible advantage of locally produced fruits, vegetables, dairy products, meat, and game. They personify the spirit of Berkshire Grown. Their dining room, like their cuisine, is contemporary, beautifully put together, and thoroughly inviting.

Hudson's thoughtful, informative menu prepared us for a wonderful meal. We were not disappointed except, perhaps, in the smallest details. We appreciated the number of vegetarian and fish entrée offerings and ordered catfish in pecan coating. It was tasty, but could have had a bit more crunch. The duck with fruit compote was also quite good, but might have used a bit more seasoning. We shared a large, crisply fresh mesclun salad with goat cheese, a tasty and rich house wine, and a taste of the mango salsa, which was delicious. The bread was light, tasty, and homemade.

Hudson's is delightful, with a lot of love going into the menu, the ambience, and the food preparation.

JODI'S

413-528-6064.
327 Stockbridge Rd. (Rte.
7), Gt. Barrington.
Price: Inexpensive to
Moderate.
Cuisine: Contemporary
American.
Serving: B, L, D, SB.
Credit Cards: AE, D, DC,
MC, V.
Reservations:
Recommended.
Special Feature: Member,
Berkshire Grown.

Consistently popular with travelers and locals alike, this "country cookery" in an old farmhouse right on Route 7 continues to turn out three squares a day for the multitudes. Although Jodi's immediate locale amid a shopping center, a car dealership, and a McDonald's may not suggest country charm, proprietors Steven and Jodi Amoruso and their partner, Carole Altman, succeed in establishing a rustic ambience inside. Both dining rooms are pleasant, spacious, and "country" feeling, while the porch that wraps around the front of the old farmhouse is popular in warmer weather.

Although the dinner menu reflects the Amorusos' Italian restaurant roots, the luncheon offerings tend more toward American. At lunch the food is well-prepared and nicely served, although a bit bland. Dinner is very good Italian, although the decor and cuisine aren't quite in sync. Dinner specials include other international offerings, such as grilled duck breast with figs and apples, and tuna au poivre.

KINTARO
413-528-5678.
287 Main St. (side
  entrance), Gt. Barrington.
Closed: Mon.
Price: Moderate.
Cuisine: Japanese,
  American.
Serving: D.
Credit cards: D, MC, V.
Reservations:
  Recommended.

Kintaro's cool, subdued decor offers diners a sanctuary from the serious shopping along Great Barrington's now chic Main Street and Railroad Street shops. We always go to Kintaro when in need of a healthy, healing meal. The waitstaff are uniformly cheerful and pleasant, helpful in explaining the intricacies of the Japanese menu. Chef Hideo Kikuchi artfully prepares each dish — all fresh, perfectly portioned, and cooked to perfection. Kintaro sushi remains outstanding, prepared at a cozy bar that seats about eight diners. California rolls are available with crabmeat, salmon, eel, or smoked tofu. Daily specials include catch of the day, prepared teriyaki, shogayaki (ginger sauce), shioyaki (sake sauce), and misoyaki (with a sweet miso sauce) and a variety of sushi bar specials. The chicken served is free-range, and the rice is organic. Kintaro presents an eclectic beverage list that includes sakes, domestic and imported wines, plum wine, beers, and a variety of healthful nonalcoholic choices. An outstanding tiramisú will complete one of Berkshire's most balanced dinners.

PAINTED LADY
413-528-1662.
785 S. Main St. (Rte. 7), Gt.
  Barrington.
Price: Moderate.
Cuisine: Northern Italian,
  Continental.
Serving: D.
Credit Cards: MC, V.
Reservations:
  Recommended.

Owners Julie and Dan Harris team up to present a comfortable atmosphere and good food. The old Victorian house that gives the place its name is painted colorfully and lovingly decorated.

Much of the extensive menu seems, as it says, to depend on the mood of the chef; that is, there are several nightly specials. The regulars, such as a good variety of pasta dishes, are also worth trying. A salad comes with all the entrées.

An enticing feature is a snack of garbanzo bean salad and a basket of warm bread, as soon as diners are seated. Pesto pasta and chicken with wild mushrooms were tasty and satisfying. Apple raspberry pie is an excellent way to end an evening . . . or, perhaps, begin one.

PANDA WEST
413-528-5330.
300 State Rd. (Rte. 23), Gt.
  Barrington.
NE of town.
Price: Inexpensive to
  Moderate.
Cuisine: Chinese.
Serving: L, D.
Credit Cards: AE, MC, V.

See Lenox for more information on Pandamonium! Berkshire has been inundated with good Chinese food. First there were no Chinese restaurants in Berkshire, then there were only ersatz Chinese. Now there are excellent Pandas everywhere, all serving Peking, Hunan, Szechuan, Shanghai, and Cantonese specialties.

SPENCER'S RESTAURANT

413-528-3828, 800-854-1008.
www.thornewood.com.
453 Stockbridge Rd., Gt.
Barrington.
Jct. Rte 183.
Open: Thurs.–Sun. in
summer; Fri. & Sat. in
winter.
Price: Moderate to
Expensive.
Cuisine: Country
Continental.
Serving: D, SB (seasonal).
Credit Cards: AE, D, MC, V.
Reservations: Preferred.
Special Features:
Vegetarian dishes.

Spencer's Restaurant in the Dutch Colonial Thornewood Inn welcomes diners in the formal, candlelit dining room with dance floor, and in the pub-like atmosphere of the library. Sunday brunch is added to the fare spring, summer, and fall. On Saturday evenings and during brunch, innkeeper David Thorne leads his jazz trio in mellow jazz and blues selections.

Chef J.D. Logan's dinner, gracefully served on crisp white table linens in the dining room, is quite good. Chef accommodated by converting a risotto appetizer into an entrée, pronounced perfectly prepared, avoiding the danger of the rice clumping. A filet of beef was also cooked correctly and nestled comfortably on garlic mashed potatoes. For appetizer we shared a brie, bruschetta, and fruit plate — which suffered a bit from the fruit being out of season. Pinot noir and chardonnay brought out the flavor of the food and the thoughts of the diners. The chocolate trifle cake was moist and tasty.

Dreams of an autumn evening included returning in the summer to sit on the deck, overlooking Taft Farm, and sampling other delightful offerings, such as mushroom charlotte with port-and-currant sauce, and eggplant rounds for appetizers; vegetable pie with a French-bread crust or salmon stuffed with scallop mousse for entrées. And, of course, others of those "fresh homemade desserts prepared on the premises."

20 RAILROAD STREET

413-528-9345.
20 Railroad St., Gt.
Barrington.
Price: Inexpensive.
Cuisine: American.
Serving: L, D, SB.
Credit Cards: MC, V.
Handicap Access: Yes.
Special Features: Open late;
Member, Berkshire
Grown.

20 Railroad Street is the restaurant granddaddy of the Railroad Street revival. In the warm, high, brick dining room, always convivial, we shared dining space with jovial families, couples young and old, as well as softball teams and ski patrol squadrons. We heard about divorces and deals, patients and quarterbacks. In story or in person, most of southern Berkshire has been in 20 Railroad. The 28-foot-long mahogany bar and backbar, built in New York City in 1883, arrived in Great Barrington in 1919. It served one of the area's speakeasies during Prohibition, referred to as "Mahogany Ridge" by those who explained to their spouses just where they were hunting.

But good food is what makes 20 Railroad chug along. For lunch, dinner, or whenever, 20 Railroad's starters, salads, sandwiches, and burgers are legendary. Unusual starters include the Plowman's Snack, a combination of brie, sopressata sausage, and French bread. Pocket sandwiches are outstanding, with the vegetarian side pocket being among our favorites. The restaurant also nurtures a whole Reuben family (available in halves), with ham (Mama Reuben), turkey (Rebecca Reuben), and roast beef (Roland Reuben). More than a dozen different burgers and an equal number of sandwiches fill out Railroad Street's printed menu.

UNION BAR & GRILL
413-528-6228.
293 Main St. (Rte. 7), Gt.
  Barrington.
Open: Daily.
Price: Moderate.
Cuisine: New American.
Serving: L daily in summer
  & Fri.–Mon. in winter, D
  year-round.
Credit Cards: MC, V.
Handicap Access: Yes.
Reservations: Not
  accepted.
Special Features: Smoking;
  40-foot bar; Kids' menu;
  Food served to 1am;
  Member, Berkshire
  Grown.

The successful owners of John Andrew's Restaurant in South Egremont also presents the Union Bar & Grill, a spare, urban, brushed-aluminum space — considerably less expensive than John Andrew's, although just as committed to high quality, innovative dishes, and creative presentation. Serving lunch and a sophisticated, pancultural menu until 11pm every night, with a reasonable kids' menu and a lively bar scene, make the Union one of the most popular hangouts in all of Berkshire County.

We started with the mussels, which were fresh and abundant in a buttery sake-and-lime broth. The soup, tomato-basil with leeks, had a caramelized sweetness and a harking-back-to-summer tomato flavor. The grilled pizza was thin and crisp, with fresh mozzarella and roasted tomato. Though the menu changes often, the regulars will not allow the grilled flank steak sandwich to go, prepared as it is with grilled red onion, smoked Gouda, and an Asian barbecue sauce on flatbread. The plantain-wrapped salmon on a beet-and-apple salad was a little dry, but the tarragon-cream and salmon-roe sauce was creamy and flavorful. The black-peppercorn steak had great taste, a velvety sauce, and the latke-like potato-cheesecake served alongside was outstanding.

All hail the pastry chef: we tried the apple tart, which was polished off in a resounding clash of forks; it was made from a homemade, flaky, crisp, buttery, golden puff pastry round, topped with microthin sliced apples sitting atop a raspberry sauce with a dollop of homemade vanilla (vanilla-y!) ice cream.

A great place for a sophisticated lunch, dinner, or late-night meal. The food is consistently good and innovative.

Housatonic

JACKS GRILL
413-274-1000.
www.jacksgrill.com.
1063 Main St., Housatonic.

Jacks Grill. No apostrophe, no *e*. "Honest Food; Satisfaction Guaranteed," as Jacks says. Jacks' weekly specials section of the menu runs from corned beef & cabbage (Tuesday) to roast pork,

Closed: Nov.–Apr.; Tues. in season.
Price: Moderate.
Cuisine: American.
Serving: D.
Credit Cards: AE, D, MC, V.
Reservations: Recommended.

cornbread, and applesauce (Sunday). Comfort is the theme here, and it is pervasive. The menu selections, the setting in a former hardware store in an old mill town, and the decor (the original store shelves full of endlessly varied collections of stuff; an operating electric train hung from the ceiling) all say "family" loud and clear. And families are welcome: there is nice selection of kids' stuff on the menu to satisfy the younger set while parents enjoy more adult fare. There are also occasional family nights during the summer season. Those who prefer a little less bustle should check ahead.

We don't disdain. The Fitzpatrick family know their hospitality. The food is seriously well prepared. Drinks are liberal and well made. Guinness and Harp are on tap. Every wine on the very serviceable wine list is available by the glass or the bottle. The waitstaff are eager and attentive. Everything about Jacks is as genuine, and as satisfying, as we could wish a place like this to be.

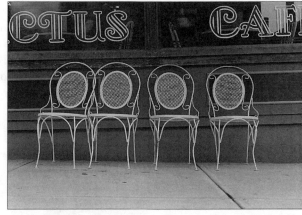

The chairs dance at the Cactus Cafe.

Judith Monachina

Lee

CACTUS CAFE
413-243-4300.
54 Main St. (Rte. 20), Lee.
Closed: Wed.
Price: Inexpensive to Moderate.
Cuisine: Mexican.
Serving: L, D.
Credit Cards: D, MC, V.

The Cactus Cafe has settled into a comfortable niche as one of the most popular dining spots in downtown Lee. Co-proprietors Joanne Conroy and spouse/chef Jim offer many of their own home-styled, Cal/Mex creations plus innovative twists on the old standards. The result is some of the best Mexican food in Berkshire!

The atmosphere is quaint but honest, tin-ceilinged, Mexican, as close to the Baja as you'll find in these parts. The selection of Mexican beers, plus a few top U.S. and German choices, or the frozen margarita or sangría, go well with the excellent, complimentary house-made chips and salsa, or perhaps even better with creamy-spicy chili con queso. For a different appetizer at dinner, sopa de lima — scallops, swordfish, and shrimp in a lime bouillon — is sensational, an oceanic meal in itself. Or the ceviche, a mix of marinated shrimp, marlin, and scallops, is up to top seaside standards, and the quinoa salad is a vegetarian delight, large enough to do as a main course. Main courses are ample — we sometimes even pass up a full appetizer. *Always* ask about the pescada del día (fish of the day) served grilled, with a mango salsa. Or try the caldo quintana-roo "Yucatan bouillabaisse" in a rich, chili-charged fish broth. But this isn't a fish restaurant; all the classic Tex/Mex (actually Cal/Mex here) classics are on offer, too, and all very interestingly done. The lunch menu is a bit less elaborate, with more emphasis on conventional Mexican choices, but still offers enough of Cactus's specialties and flair to make it worth the visit.

CORK 'N HEARTH
413-243-0535.
Rte. 20, Lee.
On Laurel Lake, N. of Lee.
Closed: Mon.
Price: Moderate.
Cuisine: New England
   Contemporary.
Serving: D.
Credit cards: AE, MC, V.
Special Features: Fireside
   ambience; View of lake.

Chef/owner Christopher Ryan continues the charm and warm hospitality of Cork 'n Hearth, on the shores of lovely Laurel Lake. While not overflowing with ambience, the restaurant's amenities include antique quilts on the walls, a profusion of flowers and plants, and attentive waitstaff.

The food is dependably good, from an extensive menu or prepared to order. Our choice of Atlantic scrod with seasoned breadcrumbs, lemon, wine, and butter, was baked to perfection and served with a delicious green salad, baked potato, and chilled sorbet.

Joe Sorrentino of Joe's Diner.

Courtesy of The Advocate Newsweeklies.

JOE'S DINER
413-243-9756.
85 Center St. (Rte. 20), Lee.
Cor. Center & Main Sts.
Closed: Sun.
Price: Inexpensive.
Cuisine: American.
Serving: B, L, D.

Joe's — the diner that time forgot but history honors, where things are just as they were and as they will be. Still bustling with the vigor of the 1940s, Joe's stocks packets of Red Man Chewing Tobacco right next to buckets of lifetime-guarantee combs; artichokes (in season) are 50 cents apiece and a real New York egg cream runs all of 65 cents. A politician wouldn't think of breezing through Berkshire without a photo op and a plate of meatloaf at Joe's.

But the secret of success is that Joe Sorrentino and his family serve good food. This ex-army cook will happily serve "breakfast at dinner, or dinner at breakfast." Joe creates a special each day. "We'll go through a whole hip of beef every Monday, 120 pounds of corned beef every Thursday," says Joe. Those serious about taking in one of Joe's specials (like a roast beef dinner with vegetable, potato, and bread for four bucks), had better arrive early. We came on corned-beef night recently and watched the last of the 120 pounds disappear quickly, leaving disappointed latecomers. Not for long. They soon wrapped their tongues around something even better they just hadn't thought of.

PARADISE OF INDIA
413-243-0500.
5 Railroad St., Lee.
Price: Moderate.
Cuisine: Indian.
Serving: L, D.
Credit Cards: AE, D, MC, V.

Casual and warm, tucked just off the Main Street of Lee, Paradise of India has tapped a vein of Indian-food lovers. Serving lunch and dinner without a break in between, the restaurant offers a treat for those in the Berkshires who have unusual schedules or just happen to find themselves thinking about lunch when everyone else seems to be having a siesta. The menu offers a wide variety of curries, vegetarian and nonvegetable, and a selection of specialties cooked in a tandoori clay oven. Breads are delicious. Desserts are mildly sweet and creamy, such as rasmalai (made from the essence of milk, garnished with nuts, and served chilled) or kulfi (sweetened cream, frozen and flavored with cardamom and pistachio). The massala tea is a treat not to be missed.

The same owners run Glory of India (413-528-312, Main St., Gt. Barrington) offering a similar menu.

SULLIVAN STATION
413-243-2082.
Railroad St., Lee.
Price: Moderate.
Cuisine: New England.
Serving: L, D.
Credit Cards: AE, D, MC, V.
Reservations: Accepted.

Located in an old New York, New Haven & Hartford Railroad depot, Sullivan Station has a convivial mahogany bar with a brass foot rail from a Methodist church. The wainscoted dining room walls are decorated with railroad memorabilia, and soft pop — the Beatles, Hall & Oates — plays over the stereo.

Special Features: Summer dining on deck or in refurbished caboose; Member, Berkshire Grown.

Chef Todd Ranolde specializes in hearty, home-style fare. For starters, a recent evening menu offered shrimp cocktail and a bean-and-barley soup. Entrées, which were accompanied by butter-nut squash and mashed potatoes, included baked scrod in lemon butter and charbroiled sirloin steak served fresh off the cowcatcher. The waitstaff is good-natured and prompt. Complete dinner for two and tip runs about $55.

South Lee

FEDERAL HOUSE INN
413-243-1824; 800-243-1824;
fax 413-243-1828.
1680 Pleasant St. (Rte. 102),
S. Lee.
1.5 mi. E. of Stockbridge.
Closed: Mon.
Price: Expensive.
Cuisine: Continental.
Credit Cards: AE, D, MC, V.
Reservations: Recommended.
Special Feature: Fireplaces.

The Federal House Inn is a handsome, columned building in a setting of beautiful old trees. The dining room, with white linen, silver, candles, and fresh flowers immediately suggests an unusual and charming experience. The owners, Robin and Kenneth Almgren, and their menu, provide just that.

Appetizers included a galantine of goose breast made with dried apricots, figs, and pistachios, served with lingonberries; and tiger shrimp with tequila-chili sauce, sauce gribiche, and watercress-aïoli. On the specials menu was an onion soup grat-inée with calvados, a very special dish indeed.

A mixed-greens salad with warm goat cheese, Granny Smith apples, walnuts, walnut oil, and fresh lemon juice prepared us for our entrées. The fresh yellowfin tuna seared rare was served with wasabi, tamari, fresh grated horseradish, pickled onions, and basmati rice. A boneless roast Long Island duckling, crisp where it should have been crisp and tender where it should have been tender, was served with fresh pear chutney, sautéed wild-rice pan-cakes, and a currant-mustard sauce. Also on the specials menu was a lattice of halibut and salmon, pleasing to the eye as well as the palate.

It was almost impossible to choose from among such tempting desserts as warm chocolate-rum cake with island sauce, banana fritters with ice cream and Bavarian cream sauce, lime mousse with raspberry sauce, and fresh fruit Napoleon with kiwi sauce. A complete prix-fixe dinner including appetizer, salad, entrée, and dessert is $38. The wine list is excellent.

SWEET BASIL GRILLE
413-243-1114.
1575 Pleasant St. (Rte. 102),
S. Lee.
Closed: Mon. in winter.
Price: Moderate.

The Sweet Basil Grille has changed its spot! Tired of the endless reconstruction of Routes 7 & 20 in front of their restaurant, owners Rick and Lynn Penna up and moved in 1999 to scenic South Lee and the handsome red-brick home of the late Hoplands Restaurant. Signs are that they will

Cuisine: Italian.
Serving: L in summer, D
  year-round.
Credit Cards: AE, DC, MC,
  V.
Reservations:
  Recommended.

remain there even if the roadwork ever is completed. Too bad for the Pittsfield/Lenox crowd; a great break for the Stockbridge/Lee/Tyringham corner of the county. As was said of The Grille in its previous home, "the restaurant is always busy because the service is good, the help familiar with the menu, the portions satisfying, the food tasty, and the price right." One almost doesn't need to know anything more about it, but it should be added that this is an Italian restaurant, though the name doesn't suggest it. We don't know if cream of garlic soup is Italian, but it alone is worth the visit. Most other offerings are more distinctly Italian, homemade, tasty, and satisfying.

New Marlborough

HILLSIDE
413-528-3123.
Rte. 57, New Marlborough.
Closed: Mon. year-round;
  Mon. & Tues. in winter.
Price: Moderate.
Cuisine: Continental.
Credit Cards: AE, MC, V.
Serving: Sun. lunch, 12– 2,
  D.
Reservations:
  Recommended.
Special Feature: Catering
  for parties up to 75
  people.

The Hillside, celebrating its 27th year in 1999, continues to excel in traditional Continental cuisine. No "nouvelle" dishes for chef/owner Giuseppe (Joe) Chighine. He knows how to cook classical dishes — and what a pleasure they are.

A modest but satisfactory wine list is available. Unfortunately the pâté maison wasn't served the night we were there, but we enjoyed a marvelous French onion soup and an avocado stuffed with real crabmeat. A fresh green salad accompanied the entrées, with a choice of dressing: Roquefort (creamy and delicious), Russian, Italian, or French. When a fine chef offers five different veal dishes, they are a sure bet. Our veal piccata was the best since that our old friend Roberto fixed years ago in south Florida. The filet of sole meunière was done to perfection. Other entrées included rigatoni puttanesca, entrecôte au poivre, chicken (or veal or filet of sole) Oscar, and roast duckling flambé.

The crème caramel was fine, but the coconut cream pie was insufficiently moist. Espresso, cappuccino, and a wide selection of international coffees were available. Well-prepared food, good service, and an attractive setting put the Hillside on our repeat list.

**OLD INN ON THE
  GREEN & GEDNEY
  FARM**
413-229-3131, 800-286-3139;
  fax 413-229-8236.
www.oldinn.com.

In a way it is too bad that the best food is more expensive; on the other hand, at least that gives us a destination, such as the Old Inn on the Green in New Marlborough (ca. 1760). Lighted entirely by candlelight and warmed by numerous fireplaces,

Rte. 57, New Marlborough.
6 mi. E. of Rte. 23.
Closed: Mon.-Wed.; Open
  six days in summer.
Price: Weekday: Moderate
  to Expensive. Saturday:
  Very Expensive (prix
  fixe).
Cuisine: French, American.
Serving: D.
Credit Cards: AE, MC, V.
Reservations: Required.
Special Features: Intimate
  candlelight dining
  rooms; Outdoor patio;
  Member, Berkshire
  Grown.

the atmosphere is truly welcoming. Food and service are excellent without stuffiness or pretension. The wine list is extensive and the waitstaff knowledgeable.

On weekdays, "Firesides à la carte" feature such appetizers as tavern salad with Rawson Brook Farm chèvre, wild mushroom bisque, and shrimp-and-escargot ragout. We asked chef to put together a vegetarian entrée of wild mushrooms and pasta, which was delicious. The house-cured pork loin was a treat. The pork reclined over a rising sun of sweet potato, with rays of asparagus and carrot. Saturday night's prix-fixe puts food enjoyment at $48 apiece, not including drinks.

Desserts are superbly presented. Crème brûlée was created by an artist. Presentation, not pretense; ambience, not ambivalence. Executive chef: Kristofer Rowe.

Sheffield

**STAGECOACH HILL
  INN**
413-229-8585.
Rte. 41, Sheffield.
N. of Lakeville, CT.
Price: Moderate to
  Expensive.
Cuisine: Regional
  American.
Serving: D Mon.–Sat., SB
  on porch.
Credit Cards: AE, MC, V.
Reservations:
  Recommended.
Special Features: Candlelit
  dining; Screened porch;
  Catering for groups &
  wedding receptions.

Proprietor Sandy MacDougall welcomed us into her lovely dining room and offered a tour of her inn, which has been a coach stop since 1829. She has operated the inn for five years. Chef Mark Guidi changes the dining room menu seasonally. It includes such delectables as sliced pan-roasted breast of duck over cabernet-braised root vegetables and red potatoes (the sauce was fabulous); and thyme-roasted boneless half chicken in herbed pan jus on potato pancakes and seared tomatoes (great flavors). Other entrée choices included New Zealand rack of lamb, filet mignon, and baked steak-and-mushroom pie.

Flaky, hot, freshly baked herb biscuits started us off. Appetizers chosen among many temptations were a delicious crab bisque and baked baby brie in toasted pecan crust with poached pear. A mixed greens and baby lettuces salad, tossed in lemon-garlic vinaigrette, followed. A short but varied wine list was available, as well as a number of excellent beers and ales on tap. Our wonderful meal ended with a crème brûlée and an *outrageous* lemon tart. We'll be back.

Stockbridge

**GLENDALE RIVER
GRILLE**
413-298-4711;
fax 413-298-4699.
www.ggrille.com.
14 Glendale Rd. (Rte. 183),
Glendale.
Closed: Mon. & Tues. off
season; Open seven days
July–Aug.
Price: Moderate.
Cuisine: American,
Continental, Universal
Eclectic.
Serving: D.
Credit Cards: AE, MC, V.
Reservations: Appreciated.
Special Feature: Catering
functions on and off
premises.

Proprietor Al Weinman has created a true foodlover's refuge on the banks of the Housatonic, just down the road from the Norman Rockwell Museum. The grill in question is a hot and versatile instrument, designed to turn out properly seared meat, fish, and fowl, with their own juices sealed in. The grilled offerings are accompanied by an excellent array of sauces and condiments of one's choice, all homemade and delicious. The balance of the menu offers an array of Continental selections, including several hearty and delicious vegetarian entrées. The lamb specialties feature delicious local Berkshire lamb. The wine list is predominantly American, and has a good selection of the increasingly appreciated wines of the Eastern United States. Al is a genial host; his staff are competent veterans. They make us feel welcome, well attended, and well fed.

RED LION INN
413-298-5545.
www.redlioninn.com.
30 Main St. (Rte. 7),
Stockbridge.
Price: Expensive.
Cuisine: Traditional
American.
Serving: B, L, D.
Credit Cards: AE, DC, MC,
V.
Reservations:
Recommended.
Handicap Access: Yes.
Special Feature: Member,
Berkshire Grown.

The Red Lion Inn is almost everyone's idea of a classic New England inn. Not surprising, as that is just what it has been since 1773. A hotbed of pre-Revolutionary fever then, it has been the focal point of the Stockbridge community ever since. Owned and operated by the Fitzpatrick family since 1968, the inn has grown and evolved with the times. While many things about it seem changeless — the wonderful collections of antiques, the festive holiday decorations, the 19th-century wire-cage elevator — the cuisine has made real advances in recent years. The classic favorites remain, from Red Lion clam chowder to carved native turkey to old-fashioned apple pie, but there are numerous contemporary New American–style selections as well, designed to tempt the palate of the more demanding diner. Complementing the newer menu selections, the inn has developed one of the most extensive and interesting wine lists in the region, and has earned a *Wine Spectator* magazine Award of Excellence for its efforts.

Both the handsome 19th-century main dining room and the adjoining Widow Bingham's Tavern offer the full menu. During the summer, so do the back porch and garden. Jackets are required at dinner in the dining room. The tavern, which has a wonderful rustic air, and the porch and garden are informal. A prime, and famous, place for cocktails or tea is the sweeping front porch, complete with wicker rocking chairs. The Lion's Den, in the basement of the inn, is a lion of a different color. Live music, a menu running to soups and sandwiches, and a busy bar make this one of the livelier nightspots in this quiet community. The Red Lion Inn is, deservedly, a very busy and popular place, especially during the summer months and the autumn leaf-peeping season, so reservations are always a good idea — and a day or two in advance during those times.

West Stockbridge

LA BRUSCHETTA
413-232-7141.
1 Harris St., W.
  Stockbridge.
Closed: Mon.–Thurs. in
  winter.
Price: Expensive.
Cuisine: Italian.
Serving: D.
Credit Cards: AE, D, DC,
  MC, V.
Reservations:
  Recommended.
Special Feature:
  Overlooking the
  Williams River.

This fine Italian restaurant makes a great excuse to visit a favorite Berkshire town, West Stockbridge. It sits right beside the often-rushing Williams River, tucked behind the town. The decor and design are simple and clean with a menu that combines classic and nouvelle Northern Italian cuisine.

We started with the butternut squash soup of the day. It was a thick, chunky purée, squashy-sweet and earthy with mushrooms and leeks.

Next came the pasta course: homemade tagliatelle with confit of duck, oven-roasted tomatoes, caramelized onions, and shiitake mushrooms. The pasta was perfectly cooked with caramelized whole pearl onions, baby spinach (nice and crisp, thrown in at the last minute), chewy shiitake mushrooms, and tender duck.

For the main course we tried the popular osso buco with saffron risotto. The dish was the classic Italian, bone-in veal shank, a meaty one, too, cooked until falling off the bone with garlic and oregano and chunks of lemon rind in a thick wine gravy, offered with a little fork to dig out the tasty marrow from inside the bone. It comes with a creamy risotto that, to our delight, did not skimp on saffron.

In classic Italian-restaurant style, La Bruschetta offers a thorough dessert-wine list to accompany the wide array of desserts. We finished our meal with espresso, homemade cinnamon-honey-almond biscotti, and the homemade gelati that came in flavors such as lemon–white chocolate, plum, and passion fruit that may be combined at will. The restaurant has a new chef since our last review; and though some say the restaurant has changed, our visit revealed a chef who is upholding this Berkshire fixture's excellent reputation.

CAFFE POMO D'ORO
413-232-4616.
6 Depot St., W. Stockbridge.
Closed: Tues. & Wed. in
winter.
Price: Inexpensive to
Expensive.
Cuisine: Tuscan Italian,
Continental.
Serving: B, L.
Credit Cards: None.
Special Features:
Vegetarian dishes;
Member, Berkshire
Grown.

Although the Caffe serves breakfast and lunch only, it is the gourmet's choice for those meals in the county and more expensive than the other establishments in our "Breakfast & Lunch" section. It is dining proof of the principle that good things come in small packages: eight smallish tables in a portion of the former West Stockbridge train station. The attractive decor consists largely of tastefully displayed gourmet packaged food offerings that make up the balance of Pomo d'Oro's business — pastas, exotic nonalcoholic beverages, cheeses, and sausages.

Scott Cole's tiny, Italian-inflected spot in West Stockbridge can be hard to get into on a Sunday morning. People often line up for his omelettes, French toast, bagels, and homemade breads. The lunch menu includes a soup and a pasta special, several salads, and about ten delicious sandwich offerings, a number of them vegetarian and largely of Italian persuasion in ingredients. Freshly brewed coffee from a large mug or caffe latte, the hot milk steaming up from the cup, superbly completes the meal. Well, perhaps there is room for the pear frangipani tartlet for dessert.

Judith Monachina

This shop is a recent additon to Trúc Orient Express, a Vietnamese restaurant in West Stockbrodge. It features many of the items, including food items and cooking gear, found in the restaurant.

TRÚC ORIENT EXPRESS
413-232-4204.
3 Harris St., W.
Stockbridge.
One block off Main St.
(Rte. 102), over Williams
River.

Trúc Orient Express, set behind Main Street and the Williams River, has been a West Stockbridge fixture for almost 20 years. The menu offers classic Vietnamese fare tailored to American tastes (to wit: none of the dishes are fiery hot; they don't serve much rice or greens with the entrées; all fish

Open: Year-round.
Price: Moderate to
 Expensive.
Cuisine: Vietnamese.
Serving: D.
Credit Cards: AE, D, MC,
 V.
Reservations:
 Recommended.
Special Features:
 Vegetarian dishes;
 Outdoor dining.

heads have been removed). For the less adventure-some, Trúc is a good place to begin exploring the flavors of Vietnam: a complex and sophisticated blend of sweet, sour, and piquant.

We started with the Trúc special shrimp rolls, a golden, crisp-fried, brown-rice-paper pocket densely filled with crabmeat, pork, shrimp, and cabbage: lots of flavor, lots of crunch; and the jumbo, battered honeycomb shrimp, coated in cellophane noodles and then quick-fried and served with a thick, soy-peanut sauce. The coating was slightly sweet and the thin, crisp, fried noodles made for a delightful and unexpected texture. Then came the Hanoi soup of sliced beef and thin rice noodles, in which the beef was only fair but the broth was superb, flavored with fish sauce, sprinkled with fresh cilantro and scallions, with just the right amount of after-heat.

For the main course, an excellent choice is the barbecued pork on rice noodles — thinly sliced, garlic-marinated broiled pork tenderloins served over thin rice noodles and sprinkled with peanuts, scallions, and a sweet-sour sauce — very flavorful, well marinated, and tender. The fried fish was a crisp, deep-fried whole flounder in a sweet-sour sauce with chilis. Though the fish was low on flavor, it was high on crisp and lots of fun to pull the meat from the bones. Also recommended are the happy pancake (a rice-flour crêpe studded with lots of meat and fresh vegetables) and the summer rolls (a cool, fresh summertime must). There is an entire page of vegetarian offerings. At lunch, everything is at least one-third off the evening price.

Coffee lovers should request the Vietnamese coffee, an espresso that slowly drips through a mini stainless steel contraption into a small cup, primed with sweetened condensed milk; great to soothe the digestion and beat the after-dinner drowse.

The interior of Trúc is light and spacious with wide wooden floorboards, a plant-filled balcony, Vietnamese art on the walls, and tinkling bamboo curtains to walk through, all signs of the owner's dedication to a quality dining experience. For postprandial browsing, the tasteful little adjoining shop is filled with imported Asian gifty items.

WILLIAMSVILLE INN
413-274-6118.
www.williamsvilleinn.com.
Rte. 41, W. Stockbridge.
About 10 mi. N. of Gt.
 Barrington, in the hamlet
 of Williamsville.
Closed: Mon.–Weds. in
 winter.

This 18th-century inn, furnished with antiques and Colonial art, is a most inviting place for a superb meal. The experience begins, in warm weather, with a glass of wine in the sculpture garden; in cool weather, in front of the fireplace.

The meal begins with fresh hot homemade popovers and focaccia. The menu changes regularly, yet the meals are excellent regardless of the

Price: Moderate.
Cuisine: American.
Serving: D.
Credit Cards: AE, MC, V.
Reservations: Requested.
Handicap Access: Partial.
Special Features: Smoking
   in bar only. Jan.–Apr.,
   storytelling with prix-fixe
   dinner. Member,
   Berkshire Grown.

season. For appetizers, we had salad of local organic greens, avocado, mango, and grapefruit with miso-citrus dressing; and scallops wrapped in bacon with a horseradish Dijon sauce. We chose roasted quail marinated in molasses and ginger with orange-chive sauce over walnut bulghur salad (a fantastic combination of flavors!), and pecan-crusted breast of free-range chicken stuffed with Monterey chèvre with Dijon sauce, both served with fresh vegetables. The famous Williamsville duck is worth a special trip.

Desserts included caramelized lemon tart, and rhubarb-and-ginger compote over house-made vanilla ice cream. Delicious!

RESTAURANTS CENTRAL COUNTY

Lenox

APPLE TREE INN
413-637-1477;
   fax 413-637-2528.
www.appletree-inn.com.
10 Richmond Mtn. Rd.,
   Lenox.
Off Rte. 183, S. of
   Tanglewood main gate.
Closed: Mon.–Weds. off
   season.
Price: Moderate to
   Expensive.
Cuisine: Continental.
Serving: SB, D.
Credit Cards: AE, D, DC,
   MC, V.
Reservations:
   Recommended.

While dinner at the Apple Tree Inn certainly leaves us satisfied, the real reason to visit this charming spot is the view. Located just south of Tanglewood high on a hill overlooking the Stockbridge Bowl, the inn's window-lined dining room takes full advantage of the spectacular scenery. Those who arrive after dark can still enjoy the octagonal room that has a carousel feeling down to the center post wrapped in vines and the white lightbulbs outlining the beams.

The menu is wildly varied, so the Apple Tree is good for a group with diverse tastes or those not sure what they are in a mood for. Entrées range from $8 to $28. For the less adventurous diner on a tight budget, the inn offers a burger or chili (the burger is accompanied by delicious sweet-potato fries). If pocketbook and palate allow, the wild-mushroom ravioli — rich, filling, and satisfying — beckons; or pecan-encrusted chicken with a sweet maple glaze. To accompany the meal the inn offers a fairly extensive and moderately priced wine list. Desserts are homemade. Anything à la mode is accompanied by Bev's ice cream, a special treat.

We are accustomed to no-smoking signs in restaurants, but a beacon of the times is a posted sign asking patrons to turn off their cellular telephones. The message folks on cell phones might miss: the Apple Tree Inn wants us to relax and enjoy. We embraced the spirit, drank in the view, and savored the wonderful food.

BLANTYRE

413-637-3556;
  fax 413-637-4282.
16 Blantyre Rd., Lenox.
Off Rte. 20, NW of Lee.
Closed: Nov. 8–May 8.
Price: Very Expensive (prix fixe).
Cuisine: French, Country House.
Serving: L July–Aug. by reservation only, D year-round.
Credit Cards: AE, MC, V.
Reservations: Required.
Handicap Access: Yes.
Special Features: Fireplaces; Private dining room; Excellent wine cellar; Member, Berkshire Grown.

Blantyre is the crown jewel of Berkshire innkeeping, a member of the world-renowned Relais et Châteaux association, and one of the very best dining venues in the region. Built as one of the grandest and most impressive of the Berkshire "cottages" of the Gilded Age, Blantyre was rescued and restored inside and out by the Fitzpatrick family. It has been developed to a high state of period excellence and seems to offer a true taste of the life of its original time. Manager Roderick Anderson directs it all with a sure hand and a light touch, sustaining an atmosphere of formal elegance without stiffness.

Before dinner, drinks are offered in the parlor from a handsome rolling bar. Champagne seems almost obligatory in the surroundings. Chef de cuisine Michael Roller generally offers six to eight appetizers and the same number of entrées on the prix-fixe menu. The cuisine is characterized as "country house" — utilizing contemporary French techniques to combine local, regional, and New England products. Offerings change seasonally. The food is exquisite — absolutely worth the lofty price — and the wine list is what one would expect from such an establishment, a *Wine Spectator* Award of Excellence winner, of course. Desserts are varied, generally rich, and worth the extra indulgence. The luncheon menu is a bit lighter, but still a major dining experience. A perfect setting for one of those "memorable occasion" celebrations. Though as many as a half dozen restaurants may have their adherents for "the best dining in the Berkshires," Blantyre and neighboring Wheatleigh stand alone in their combination of superlative dining with truly regal surroundings.

BISTRO ZINC

413-637-8800.
56 Church St., Lenox.
Closed: Tues.
Price: Moderate.
Cuisine: French Bistro.
Serving: L, D.
Credit Cards: AE, MC, V.
Reservations: Recommended.

Bistro Zinc is a bright new star in the Berkshire dining constellation. The site of the former Crosby's Catering has been handsomely redesigned by Lenox architect Frank Macioge to create a welcoming atmosphere — two of them, in fact. The dining room, with its perimeter banquettes and closely ranked tables in true bistro manner, is separated from the handsome, more open, bar/dining area by a glass wall, permitting everyone to see everything,

Seeing everyone twice at the Bistro Zinc in Lenox.

Judith Monachina

but the nonsmokers in the dining room to breathe undisturbed by the exhalations of the tobacco slaves in the bar.

The dinner menu, like the dining room, has a classic bistro look: mussels marinière, charcuterie, a number of delicious green salads, ten different grilled, roasted, or sautéed entrées, and desserts from selected cheeses to tarte tatin. The wine list is almost all French, moderately priced, and very well chosen. The lunch menu is a bit simpler and lighter, and one of the good dining bargains of the Berkshires. As a nice additional touch, not in the bistro tradition, Zinc offers a short but very good kids' menu, complete with kids' drinks and classic birthday cake with ice cream for dessert (adults can order it, too). All in all, it is not surprising that Bistro Zinc has been a dining hit from the happy day it opened, in 1999.

CAFÉ LUCIA
413-637-2640.
90 Church St., Lenox.
Closed: Mon. in summer;
    Mon. & Tues. in winter.
Price: Expensive.
Cuisine: Italian.
Serving: D.
Credit Cards: AE, D, DC,
    MC, V.
Reservations:
    Recommended.
Special Features: Outdoor
    dining; Member,
    Berkshire Grown.

Café owners Jim and Nadine Lucie continue to command the affections of a sophisticated clientele, who are made to feel like family in this elegant but cozy restaurant. The dress code is informal for guests and waitstaff alike, but the table settings, service, and other details are attractively formal and scrupulously correct.

The menu offers the Italian-modern favorites for which the restaurant has long been known, along with specials each evening. Appetizers include bruschetta alla pomodoro, peasant bread rubbed with garlic and baked with arugula, tomato, and sage blue cheese; or the antipasto della casa, thinly sliced prosciutto di Parma, house-roasted peppers with anchovies, mozzarella, tomato, and basil. Among the entrées, osso buco con risotto — veal shank braised in a veal sauce with vegetables and risotto — is the house specialty, but also wonderful are the chicken alla piccata, the pan-seared tuna, or any one of the pastas. (We enjoyed linguini and shrimp served in a seafoood velouté, with scallions and sundried tomatoes.) Desserts include tiramisú, bourbon pecan tart, a delicious Italian bocci (chocolate mousse cake in an extra-rich sauce, garnished with strawberries), and "tarta della nonna" (grandmother's lemon tart).

The first-class wine list is recipient of *Wine Spectator*'s coveted Award of Excellence.

CANDLELIGHT INN
413-637-1555, 800-428-0580.
www.candlightinn-
  lenox.com
35 Walker St. (Rte. 183),
  Lenox.
Closed: Tues.
Price: Moderate.
Cuisine: Continental
  American
Serving: L late June–Labor
  Day, D year-round.
Credit Cards: AE, MC, V.
Reservations:
  Recommended.
Special Feature: Fireplaces.

With exposed wood-beam ceiling, fireplace, lace-covered French doors, Victorian-styled windows, mirrored wall, flickering candles, dried flowers on every table, and soft background music, the Candlelight Inn provides an amiable atmosphere in which to enjoy its pleasing food. On one visit, the pasta puttanesca was spicy and satisfying as a good puttanesca should be, although a tomato-spinach pasta with garlic oil lacked flavor and substance. Desserts were plentiful and uniformly wonderful. Among the offerings: chocolate trifle; chocolate-chip pie with ice cream and hot fudge; cheesecake; spiced pear, cranberry, and apple crisp; crème brûlée; and an especially flavorful lemon tart, sweet and crisp just the way a tart should be.

In warmer weather, the Candlelight offers dining al fresco in their lovely backyard garden. This leaf-shaded glade is the catbird seat of Lenox. From this perch, diners can watch passersby on Church Street and music pilgrims on their way to Tanglewood.

CHURCH STREET CAFE
413-637-2745;
  fax 413-637-2050.
Churstcafe@aol.com.
65 Church St., Lenox.
Open: Daily in season;
  Tues–Sat. Oct–May.
Price: Moderate.
Cuisine: American,
  Regional Eclectic.
Serving: L, D.
Credit Cards: V.
Reservations:
  Recommended.

If the word *bistro* brings to mind a restaurant with a warm, friendly atmosphere where fine food and beverages are served, then an American bistro is an apt description of the Church Street Cafe. In mild weather, lunch is served on the spacious deck. Inside, each of the three cozy dining rooms is simply and tastefully decorated.

An outstanding offering on the autumn menu, one of the four pasta dishes, was a ragout of little-neck clams, roasted tomato and bacon, and garlic. One of eight entrées, the autumn vegetable platter consisted of a sumptuous roasted acorn squash, with five-grain pilaf, grilled endive, braised greens, and root-vegetable puree. This was a delectable

Special Features: Outdoor
dining; Member,
Berkshire Grown.

dish, with a green house salad and crusty, warm
rolls perfectly complementing the presentation.

And all that was followed by a tantalizing
dessert menu.

CRANWELL

413-637-1364, 800-272-6935;
fax 413-637-4364.
www.cranwell.com.
55 Lee Rd. (Rte. 20), Lenox.
Price: Expensive.
Cuisine: New American,
French with Asian
accents.
Serving: B, L, SB, D.
Credit Cards: AE, D, DC,
MC, V.
Reservations:
Recommended for SB, D.
Special Feature: Member,
Berkshire Grown.

On a lovely, mild autumn evening, under a hunter's moon, Wyndhurst —John Sloane's "cottage," a formal Tudor estate, with gardens by Frederick Law Olmsted — retains its charm. Now it's a condominium resort, conference center, and restaurant. The main dining room, with its cream-colored oval relief ceiling and damask curtains, has a kind of grandeur, albeit undercut by the pink chairs and the background music that plays inside the former mansion and out. Still, the fresh flowers and fireplace create the right atmosphere in which to enjoy executive chef Carl DeLuce's entrées, all beautifully prepared and artfully presented.

We enjoyed a bisque with enough texture left to say "pumpkin." The polenta wore a saucy tomato cap with bits of mushroom peeking from it. It was tasty, as was the breast of duckling, thoughtfully including slices to fork with ease as well as a drumstick with which to wrestle. It was perfectly cooked, the skin crispy, the meat moist. The delicate stuffing sailed its own rosemary banner. Although the elegant wine list is lengthy, a limited selection goes by the glass. We topped off with a fine crème brûlée, itself topped by a half dozen raspberries.

The menu makes the rounds from fish to steak to rack of lamb. Chef concentrates on the artistry of a few selections rather than squandering his talent on a multitude. Appetizers are imaginative, adding significantly to the variety of the menu. Desserts meet the basic, biological imperative for chocolate or cream.

GATEWAYS INN

413-637-2532, 888-492-9466.
www.gatewaysinn.com.
51 Walker St. (Rte. 183),
Lenox.
Closed: Mon. off season.
Price: Expensive.
Cuisine: New American.
Serving: L in season (off-
season for groups by
reserv. only), D year-
round.

This beautiful, stately Victorian inn — built by Ivory-soap magnate Harley Procter at the last turn of the century — houses an impressive winding mahogany staircase, designed by Stanford White, and impeccable service in hushed dining rooms with warm terra-cotta-colored walls on which hang the innkeepers' collection of vintage Italian prints. The restaurant's new chef, J. Steven Brockman, has changed the offerings considerably since the last review.

The soup of the moment, a seafood bisque, was

Credit Cards: AE, CB, D, DC, MC, V.
Reservations: Recommended.
Special Features: Vegetarian dishes; Outdoor dining; Private dining room; Member, Berkshire Grown.

nothing new, but the baby spinach salad was nicely dressed in a mellow pear-pecan vinaigrette and Gorgonzola crumble. The sharp Gorgonzola was an ideal complement to the sweet slices of pear. The baked oysters were fresh, very tasty, but hard to discern under a blanket of bacon, spinach, and Choron sauce. We followed up with a peppered, crusted filet of beef topped with a Hudson Valley foie gras. The meat was cooked to perfection, the consistency of butter; the grilled foie gras was like manna from heaven — one of the best filets we've had. The jumbo pumpkin gnocchi, on the other hand, was a disappointing, unsuccessful fusion of flavors. The gnocchi were doughy and flavored with pumpkin-pie spices, such as nutmeg and cloves: sweet and odd and then topped with an Asian-flavored vegetable medley.

For dessert we had the apple pie with cranberries and homemade vanilla ice cream. The crust was tough and the pie was a little too sweet; the house gelati were nicely textured. Overall, the meal was good and the service near perfect, but a few disappointments at such a fine establishment leave an indelible impression.

LENOX 218

413-637-4218;
    fax 413-232-4205.
www.lenox218.com.
218 Main St., (Rte. 7A), Lenox.
Price: Moderate.
Cuisine: New American, Continental, Northern Italian.
Serving: L, D.
Credit Cards: AE, D, DC, MC, V.
Handicap Access: Yes.

With its crackling fire, sleek bar, framed prints, spacious room, comfortable chairs, and art deco decor, Lenox 218 is a feast to the eyes as well as to the palate. The basket of breads and warm muffins were so irresistibly light and flavorful, they could have been meals in themselves. Wines are varied; service and presentation attentive and gracious.

Recent entrées by chef Jimmy DeMayo, teamed with chef Hugh Pecon Jr, included delectable salmon filets with red roasted pepper sauce; chicken Parmesan with penne pasta; and an interesting assortment of veal, chicken, duck, and fish. Several vegetarian selections are available as well.

Desserts such as the toll-house nut pie with chocolate sauce and ice cream, and deep dish fruit pies are delectable. Lenox 218 meets expectations.

PANDA HOUSE

413-499-0660.
506 Pittsfield–Lenox Rd. (Rtes. 7 & 20), Lenox.
N. of town.

Although they are all called "Panda," they are not created equal. This Panda, serving Szechuan, Mandarin, and Hunan cuisine, may be the best of the bunch. (Great Barrington and Pittsfield each have a good Panda, separately owned.)

Price: Inexpensive to
  Moderate.
Cuisine: Chinese.
Serving: L, D.
Credit Cards: AE, D, MC,
  V.

Though the decor feels something \ restaurant (aside from the extreme tained houseplants), the food makes an appetizer, the dumplings — so of ... a doughy, pasty disaster elsewhere — were a delicate delight here. The steamed vegetable version of minced carrot, spinach, mushroom, rice noodles, tofu, and garlic in a light, thin wrapper tempts the palate; and if the scallion cake is offered on the specials menu, it will be a very crisp, thin, layered, panfried cake, flavored simply with scallions, that is tasty, nicely browned, and not too greasy.

Next we had the hot-and-sour seafood soup, which was chock full of lobster, shrimp, scallops an assortment of fresh, chewy Chinese mushrooms, crisp, sweet snow peas, and silken tofu. The heat was right on, hitting us just after we finished saying it wasn't that hot. For entrées, the crisp deep-fried tangerine chicken (or beef) was very tender and moist with a thick, orange-sesame sauce that was a bit too sweet. The shrimp with chili sauce had a flavorful thick spicy onion sauce and the shrimp were generously sized and not overcooked. The chow fun was garlicky-good Chinese comfort food of flat, wide, slippery rice noodles pan fried with vegetables or meat that can be a very greasy dish, but thankfully was not.

The service at Panda house was good and the timing in the kitchen, like clockwork. Plenty of vegetarian choices and a great place for takeout.

TRATTORIA IL VESUVIO

413-637-4904.
242 Pittsfield Rd. (Rtes. 7 &
  20), Lenox.
Closed: Mon. in winter;
  Open daily in summer.
Price: Moderate to
  Expensive.
Cuisine: Italian.
Serving: D.
Credit cards: AE, D, MC, V.
Special features: Prix-fixe
  New Year's Eve dinner
  with special menu;
  Member, Berkshire
  Grown.

This Northern Italian outpost of carefully prepared, classic recipes is situated north of Lenox right in the heart of the Route 7 construction. Not the most appetizing of destinations but, rest assured, once inside this refurbished barn with its high ceilings and wood beams, friendly staff, and to-die-for smells, Northern Italian cooking at its finest replaces the traffic outside.

Though the menu offerings are not unusual for a good Italian restaurant, the preparation and service are what give it distinction. We started with the fried calamari appetizer, possibly the best in the Berkshires. It was not rubbery at all (a calamari pitfall), the breading was light and crisp, and it was served with a chunky homemade tomato filet sauce. Next came the mista di campo con formaggio: a mixed green salad with a fresh ricotta crumble, well-dressed in a super-garlicky-basil dressing. The arrosto di vitello is a rolled breast of veal, stuffed with prosciutto and spinach and slow-roasted for several hours in their mammoth brick oven until wonderfully tender and flavorful. And the frutti di mare

— a heaping dish of nice, fresh shrimp, scallops, New Zealand baby clams, Prince Edward Island mussels, and baked salmon in a pinot grigio–garlic-tomato broth — requires a refill of grandma's fresh, chewy homemade bread to get every last drop of that fine fish broth. Entrées come with a choice of pasta, homemade polenta, or mashed potatoes. We opted for the most comforting, creamy, corny little dish of polenta we've had in ages. For dessert, the homemade tiramisú was like floating in the sky and eating a cloud.

The staff raves about what comes out of the kitchen, and though they are not shy about sharing with customers the ingredients in the recipes, our waitress admitted that she has never been able to recreate a recipe at home. "It's magic," she claimed, which may very well be conjured in their giant brick baking oven, built by the owner himself and modeled after an ancient oven excavated from the ruins of Pompeii, buried under this talented culinary family's native home.

VILLAGE INN
413-637-0020, 800-253-0917.
www.villageinn-lenox.
  com.
16 Church St., Lenox.
Closed: Mon. for dinner.
Price: Moderate.
Cuisine: American, Italian.
Serving: B, SB, D.
Credit Cards: AE, DC, MC,
  V.
Reservations:
  Recommended.

For over 200 years, the Village Inn has been a beacon on Church St. In the soft amber light that pervades this Colonial way station, we can still bask in the luster of old-world attention. From a friendly greeting by owner Cliff Rudisill, to impeccable service, to carefully prepared food, not a detail is missed. Executive chef Frank Carnute prepared a creamy delight of broccoli soup recently, followed by penne pasta primavera. All the ingredients are listed on the menu, so that reading about the olive oil, garlic, fresh basil, onions, mushrooms, broccoli, zucchini, tomatoes, and Parmesan cheese is . . . well, not as much fun as the eating but certainly primes salivation — and assists those who have food allergies. Salad comes with the meal.

Also on the summer/fall menu was a variety of seafoods, veal, chicken, and prime rib. A fine merlot from a good wine list accompanied our meal. Available desserts were somewhat truncated our evening, but they normally range from pies to cake to torte, with Ben & Jerry's as a fallback or for à la mode.

WHEATLEIGH
413-637-0610.
www.wheatleigh.com.
Hawthorne Rd., Lenox.
Price: Very Expensive (prix
  fixe).
Cuisine: Contemporary
  French.
Serving: L, D; no L to
  nonguests in winter.

Proprietors Linfield and Susan Simon are uncompromising perfectionists. Wheatleigh is the product of their drive for excellence. The building, a Berkshire "cottage," has been handsomely restored to its Gilded Age splendor and made a perfect setting for the presentation of chef Peter Platt's superlative cuisine.

The prix-fixe menu changes nightly, but the structure is constant. Dinner is served in four courses

Elegance at Wheatleigh.

Judith Monachina

Credit Cards: AE, DC, MC, V.
Reservations: Required.
Special Features: Fireplaces; Private dining room; Member, Berkshire Grown.

courses, supplemented with several delicious small entremets between courses. There are generally three choices for each course. To this admiring reviewer, the cuisine evokes the best of classic French, although not given to heavy sauces; it is highly reliant on the development of natural flavors and full of imaginative and varied choices. The service is faultless and literally Continental, as many of the staff are European born, and trained in the rigorous schools of restaurant service there. The wine list has earned Wheatleigh a *Wine Spectator* Award of Excellence every year since 1989 — perhaps the longest run for that prestigious honor of any Berkshire restaurant. The wine selections are varied, running toward the finer and more expensive that Chef Platt's food deserves. During the summer season, Wheatleigh also opens its Grill Room, offering somewhat less fully structured meals and slightly more moderate prices, though still in the grand tradition.

Though as many as a half dozen restaurants may have their adherents for "the best dining in the Berkshires," Wheatleigh and its neighbor Blantyre stand alone in their combination of superlative dining with truly regal surroundings.

The Critics on Wheatleigh

"Sets a table fit for a prince."

— Marion Burros, *New York Times.*

"One of the finest tables in the United States."

— *Elle.*

Hancock

FOUNDERS GRILLE
413-738-5500.
37 Corey Rd, Hancock.
Betw. Rtes. 7 & 43.
At the Country Inn, Jiminy
　Peak.
Price: Moderate.
Cuisine: American.
Serving: B, D.
Credit Cards: AE, D, DC,
　MC, V.
Special Feature: Member,
　Berkshire Grown.

On the top floor of the Country Inn, Founders Grille functions as a convenience and amenity for the 96-room inn, Jiminy Peak condos, and the ski clientele. A polished bar and a row of wooden booths dominate the cavernous main dining room, decorated with iron chandeliers, wooden carts, and sleighs hung by chains from a cathedral ceiling. Dim lighting, dark green carpeting, exposed wood; walls covered with wooden sleds, toboggans, snowshoes, farm implements, and portraits — a male preserve, a barn in fact. In several smaller areas, tables and booths are decorated with 1960s ski photos and memorabilia, yielding a warmer feel.

The simple menu is limited to grilled or sautéed steaks, chops, fish, and game. The offerings include a chowder, a daily soup, three appetizers, salmon, shrimp, pork, or lamb chops, game hen, grilled chicken Caesar salad, filet mignon, or strip steak. A freshly baked, delicious loaf of sunflower seed bread arrived first, followed by an acceptable house salad with lots of veggies. The appetizer of baked, stuffed mushroom caps featured four overlarge, bouncy, flavorless 'shrooms filled with a soggy, tasteless stuffing, covered in melted Monterey jack cheese. The entrée of crisp and juicy grilled rock Cornish game hen, therefore, was a pleasant surprise, served glazed with a superior red wine and game hen reduction that brought fruit and fowl flavors to the charcoal of the grill. Brussels sprouts, an unusual vegetable of the day, were nicely done, while the wild rice was bland and overdone.

Despite a lovely coffee scent from a dusting of espresso powder and crunchy sugar sprinkled over whipped cream on the tiramisú, that light and well-balanced flavor was subdued by a waterfall of canned chocolate sauce, a dry cake, and rubbery custard; perhaps the dish, while gussied up for its viewing, had previously expired in the refrigerator.

It seems the best from Founders Grille comes right off the grill.

HANCOCK INN
413-738-5873;
　fax 413-738-5719.
hancockin@aol.com.
102 Main St. (Rte. 43),
　Hancock.
Price: Moderate.
Cuisine: American
　Regional.
Serving: D.

Built in the early 19th century as a private residence, the Hancock Inn is one of three or four quintessential New England inns we know of, offering cozy warmth and charm with rustic elegance. Joe and Gail Mullady, from Long Island, purchased the inn in the summer of 1998. Joe came to his role as chef from hospital engineering and enjoys the change. While the performance at our visit wasn't as polished as under the previous own-

Credit Cards: AE, D, MC, V.
Reservations: Appreciated.
Special Feature: Member,
   Berkshire Grown.

ers, he is learning. The tab has also gone down a bit.

In midwinter the salad, while adequate, was undistinguished. The tasty mustard shrimp contrasted nicely with the potato pancake over which it was served. Joe Mullady told us that, come summer, he would replace the potato with a sauce, to make it a bit lighter. The roasted pork loin was perfectly cooked and expressed a lovely flavor in its own right, somewhat overwhelmed by the Hancock apple-raisin chutney. A dollop of garlic mashed potatoes was a treat and the vegetables were refreshingly crisp. We practiced the philosophy of saving something for another time regarding the specialty, the filet mignon au poivre, twin four-ounce medallions of beef seared in cracked black pepper and served with a cognac cream sauce. For dessert we shared a piece of apple pie with an oatmeal top crust, a good idea that needed the oatmeal to be a bit crisper to work perfectly. The desserts listed are less lethal than old-time inn habitués might recall. The menu is evolving, however, and the good news is that the Mulladys plan to reinstate a Sunday brunch that used to be a feature.

Pittsfield

DAKOTA
413-499-7900;
   fax 413-499-8610.
www.dakotarestaurant.com.
1035 South St. (Rtes. 7 &
   20), Pittsfield.
Price: Inexpensive to
   Moderate.
Cuisine: American.
Serving: D, SB.
Credit Cards: AE, D, DC,
   MC, V.
Reservations:
   Recommended.
Special Feature: Fireplaces.

With its pine walls, raised fieldstone fireplaces, mounted deer and moose heads, and overhanging birch-bark canoes, Dakota successfully communicates the feeling of a grand hunting lodge. In addition, the restaurant fills its odd spaces and some of its walls with Native American artifacts, all of museum quality. The restaurant is vast, spacious, and comfortable. Well managed and conceived, it is likely the county's single most popular restaurant.

With good reason. The restaurant usually operates with clockwork precision, serving an imaginative, well-prepared menu that features Texas mesquite broiling and easily the best salad bar in the region. We chose from steak kebab and shrimp, salmon, swordfish, and chicken teriyaki, among others. A lobster pond up front offers lobster lovers their pick, with the day's price per pound clearly posted above.

All meals come with huge slabs of freshly baked whole-grain bread and privileges to the salad bar. The wine list offers two dozen popular varieties. Desserts are dandy, portions are bountiful, and prices are moderate, making Tony Perry's Dakota a Berkshire roadside delight.

DRAGON RESTAURANT
413-442-5594.
1231 W. Housatonic St. (Rte. 20), Pittsfield.
Closed: Tues. in winter; Otherwise open 7 days.
Price: Moderate.
Cuisine: Vietnamese.
Serving: D.
Credit cards: MC, V.
Reservations: Not accepted.

A friend described the best way to find Dragon is "just keep driving out Rte. 20 until past when you think you've missed it and you'll be there," but Kim Van Huynh's restaurant is worth the trip. Offering a variety of delicious Vietnamese cuisine fragrant with lemon grass and filled with delicious contrasts, Dragon is a great place to initiate a novice into the wonderful world of this French-inspired cuisine. The menu is in English, with clear descriptions of each dish. Portions are generous: a doggie bag will yield not just lunch for the next day but probably dinner as well.

Our favorites include pat thai (either vegetarian or shrimp), which is loaded with crispy vegetables; vegetable curry, a surprisingly spicy mélange of vegetables in red curry sauce; and shaken beef served on a bed of watercress and tomatoes. Dragon also offers a number of not-to-be-missed soups as starters.

Elegance, no (the tables are covered in plastic cloths); just great food. Kim urges that we allow an hour to eat, since he is preparing food to order. Just relax, enjoy some Vietnamese beer, and savor the flavor of this one-of-a-kind cuisine.

Table service, Elizabeth's style, at Elizabeth's Café, Pittsfield.

Jonathan Sternfield

ELIZABETH'S CAFE
413-448-8244.
1264 East St.
Price: Inexpensive.
Credit Cards: None.
Special Features: Specialty pizzas; No smoking.

Right in the heart of Pittsfield's industrial history, Elizabeth's stands like a tiny beacon to hominess. Its arty interior is a tip to the mix of the modern and the traditional here. Elizabeth's attracts such a loyal following that those who want one of the few dozen seats had better get there early.

Although Elizabeth's has been known for having some of the best pizza in the region, many travel from all over the county to experience the fresh, varied, and thoroughly delicious pasta dishes, many if not most of which are vegetarian. The salads are superior, for example, the insalata mista, chunked with delicious feta cheese, studded with old-world olives, striped with roasted pepper, crowned with slices of kiwi, and supported by a bed of the freshest, youngest, tenderest baby salad greens from the heart of the lettuce. The bread is also among the best available hereabouts.

As good as the soups, salads, sandwiches, and entrées are at Elizabeth's, it has always been their pizza for which the restaurant has justly been renowned. But times change, and as we go to press we have learned that Elizabeth's has discontinued the pizza in favor of a much expanded menu of their other delicious fare. We look forward to a future visit and an updated report. For the time being, you can rely on Elizabeth's to provide a delicious meal.

HOUSE OF INDIA
413-443-3262.
261 North St., Pittsfield.
Open: 7 days.
Price: Inexpensive.
Cuisine: Indian.
Serving: L, D.
Credit Cards: AE, D, MC, V.

For years folks in Berkshire County jonesing for Indian food had to drive at least an hour to Northampton or Albany. In the last half dozen years, the area has been lucky enough to see several Indian restaurants open. House of India, the least fancy, offers good Indian food at reasonable prices to please anyone in need of a fix or interested in sampling. Since it is located in a storefront on Pittsfield's main drag, a visit also supports a vital city center.

The appetizer sampler platter (offered in both vegetarian and nonveggie versions), is plenty for a table of two to four to share and offers a bevy of tastes. Outstanding in a recent visit were the samosas, pastry triangles stuffed with a variety of fillings. Indian food being known for its spiciness, one of the members of our party, a connoisseur of heat, pronounced his jalfreesi, ordered "hot," as "just right." House of India prepares dishes to suit the palate. The version of mild bharata featured the perfect amount of heat to keep this classic eggplant dish from being bland.

Low sitar music instills an Indian frame of mind, as do the several choices of Indian beer and wine by the glass. Service is prompt and friendly. Lunch is a steal at $5.95 for an all-you-can-eat buffet.

PANDA INN
413-445-5580, 413-443-0819.
795 Dalton Ave., Pittsfield.
Price: Inexpensive to
   Moderate.
Cuisine: Chinese.
Serving: L, D.
Cards: AE, MC, V.

See the review of Panda House in Lenox (page 108) for more information. Newest Panda on the block, this Coltsville outpost is one of the best, with a huge glassed-in atrium that's daylight-filled every day, rain or shine.

SANGEET
413-445-6700;
  fax 413-445-6789.
26 Cheshire Rd. (Rte. 8),
  Pittsfield.
Pittsfield Travelodge.
Closed: Mon.
Price: Moderate.
Cuisine: Indian.
Serving: L, D.
Credit Cards: AE, D, DC,
  MC, V.
Reservations:
  Recommended for D.
Special Feature: Off-
  premises catering.

Sangeet is on the east side of Rte. 8 at the junction with Rte. 9, the dreaded although much improved Coltsville intersection, in such a way that it's not clear that those going south on 8 can legally get there. Furthermore, "there" appears to be a typical motel restaurant, formerly a Pancake House as attested to by the Naugahyde booths. So, rated on ambience, the needle barely stirs, but for food and friendly service it flips far right. Where else does the waiter swish a napkin into a diner's lap?

No music, no frills, just authentic Indian cuisine, properly cooked and seasoned. For appetizers, the Sangeet special assorted platter, a combination of vegetable fritters and other items, with three sauces, is sufficient for two hungry adults. For entrées, from the clay oven (tandoor) arrived sizzling salmon cubes (fish tikka) with spices and herbs. Less spectacularly presented were chunks of lamb korma "in a delicate almond, cashew creamy sauce and spiced to taste." The sauce supported the lamb and converted the accompanying rice into rice dreams.

For dessert we shared gulab jamun, which tastes as good as its description, "milk puffs deep fried and soaked in honey and rose syrup." Indian as well as stateside beer available, and French wine by the glass.

TEO'S
413-447-9592.
1410 East St., Pittsfield
Price: Inexpensive.
Serving: L, D.
Cuisine: American
Credit Cards: None.

Teo's Family Restaurant is an institution and a local tradition — and home to the tastiest miniature (4") hot dogs smothered in chili sauce we've ever eaten. Friendly controversy rages as to who invented the sauce and when. We don't care; it is enough to know that Teo's is its present home. Go in for a plateful with "the works" (chili sauce, chopped onions, and mustard) and wash them down with the Genesee Cream Ale or Rolling Rock on tap. We stop at the takeout window for a bagful for the crowd at home. They all love'em!

RESTAURANTS NORTH COUNTY

Adams

BASCOM LODGE
At the summit of Mt.
  Greylock, Adams.

Whether we've climbed on foot, on a bike, or in our car, this mountaintop restaurant is worth the effort. Breakfasts and special dinners are the

413-743-1591
(winter 413-443-0011).
www.outdoors.org.
Off Rte. 7 to S. Main St.,
Lanesborough, then 7 mi.
up on Rockwell Rd. to
the top. Accessible via
Notch Road from N.
Adams also.
Season: Mid-May–late Oct..
Price: Inexpensive.
Cuisine: American.
Serving: B, L (snack bar), D.
Credit Cards: MC, V.
Reservations: Required B, D.
Handicap Access: Yes.
Special Feature: 70-mi.
view.

main events, served in the rustic stone-and-wood lodge. Berry-laden pancakes shine in the morning, the weekly barbecue buffets and New England dinners star Tuesday evenings, followed by informative programs. Whatever the hour, the views are breathtaking, the elevation heady. The "croo," mostly college age, some Appalachian Trail thruhikers working off their lodging, strives to please. Clearly, "the lowest price for the highest elevation in the state." No liquor license, but those who wish may B.Y.O.

Jonathan Sternfield

Mastering the art of French cuisine – Chef Maurice Champagne.

New Ashford

MILL ON THE FLOSS
413-458-9123.
www.members.tripd.com/
~themotf.
Rte. 7, New Ashford.
Closed: Mon.
Price: Moderate to
Expensive.
Cuisine: French.
Serving: D.
Credit Cards: AE, MC, V.

The food at chef Maurice Champagne's Mill on the Floss is dependably first rate; the atmosphere informal and warm, with massive rough-hewn beams overhead, candlelight, and firelight from the brick hearth in colder weather. The focus of the dining room is its open kitchen, where, behind a Dutch tile counter and a gleaming array of hanging copper pots, chef in his tall white hat prepares meals before our eyes.

We began with delicious crab cakes, also offered

Reservations:
  Recommended.
Special Feature: Member,
  Berkshire Grown.

as an entrée, and pea soup, vegetable with an aromatic, smoky flavor. Whether salads or escargot in garlic butter, the appetizers set us up without filling us up.

Entrées are uniformly excellent. The veal marsala lay in thin strips in a loving sauce; the special, halibut provençal, luxuriated in tomatoes with a few sly slices of mushroom. Those with dietary preferences should not be shy about asking to have a fish dish prepared in a lighter sauce.

Desserts range from a delicate crème caramel or chocolate mousse to the gâteau du jour. One evening we finished up with an apple turnover in a sauce anglaise. All the baked goods, including the dinner rolls, are perfection. The fulsome wine list begins with a page of by-the-glass selections, allowing the diner to mix and match.

SPRINGS
413-458-3465;
  fax 413-458-3957.
www.vgernet.net/timlitz.
Rte. 7, New Ashford.
Closed: Christmas.
Price: Moderate.
Cuisine: Eclectic.
Serving: L, D.
Credit Cards: AE, CB, DC,
  MC, V.
Handicap Access: Yes.
Reservations:
  Recommended.

A large, popular restaurant, owned and operated by the Grosso family from the 1930s, burned in the mid-1970s. Its replacement, now run by Doug and Dina Blair, has the appearance of a ski chalet, an impression amplified by the piped-in music. The food is satisfactory, however. The eclectic menu includes complimentary relishes, yummy cheese bread, baked stuffed clams, and a sherbet palate cleanser. An accent on veal, a variety of chicken, roasts, steaks, chops, and pasta are well prepared and presented. The Springs is an institution.

North Adams

DUE BACI
413-663-6500, 413-664-6581.
40 Main St. (Holiday Inn),
  N. Adams.
Jct. Rtes. 2 & 8.
Price: Moderate.
Cuisine: Italian.
Serving: B, L, D.
Credit cards: AE, D, MC, V.

To sit on the terrace, surrounded by the Berkshire mountains, overlooking the beautifully refurbished main street of this old mill town, while dining on a selection from the classical Italian menu — la dolce vita! Twice a month on summer evenings live music fills the air, a block under the overpass from Mass MoCA.

A sampling from the extensive menu includes veal saltimbocca with prosciutto and mozzarella, steak Firenze seasoned with garlic and mushrooms, pork medallions with hot peppers and onions, and succulent clams with linguine and flavorful sauces for pasta. An attractive salad served family style, and large and luscious desserts complete the meal.

The friendly, well-trained waitstaff manage to overcome the impersonality of the motel-modern dining room. The pleasant tone and good food provided by chef/owner John Moresi draws large crowds to the luncheon buffets on Wednesday through Friday, which feature a salad bar, meat platters, home-made entrées, and soups.

**FREIGHT YARD
RESTAURANT & PUB**
413-663-6547.
Western Gateway Heritage
State Park, N. Adams.
In Heritage State Park.
Price: Inexpensive.
Cuisine: American, Italian,
Mexican.
Serving: L, D.
Credit Cards: AE, MC, V.
Special Features: Fireplace;
Patio.

One of the few pubs in all of Berkshire (although the owners also own Water Street Grill; see under Williamstown), the Freight Yard is in a two-story former railroad building in a historic district — with patio seating in the summer. For lunch, a generous, well-stocked salad bar is an alternative to menu selections and blackboard specials.

A wide variety of enticing foods includes generously portioned hamburgers and steaks, a daily pasta special (second helping gratis), grilled Cajun chicken, and the best and most filling Mexican "sizzlin' fajita" in the area. Soups, salads, sandwiches (we like the grilled chicken breast with pub fries), desserts (from apple pie to "death by chocolate"), and popular appetizers (including spicy buffalo wings) go well with a good beer/drink selection.

Williamstown

CAPTAIN'S TABLE
413-458-2400.
505 Cold Spring Rd. (Rtes. 2
& 7), Williamstown.
Closed: Tuesdays.
Price: Moderate.
Cuisine: American.
Serving: D.
Credit cards: AE, D, MC, V.
Reservations:
Recommended.

For consistently good family dining, we like the Captain's Table. The generous salad bar, with perfectly cooked shrimp, makes appetizers seem unnecessary, although the selection includes escargots in mushroom caps, clams casino, and steamed littlenecks. Tots-in-tow keep busy with the salad course until dinner arrives (ordered from a children's menu).

Specializing in seafood and steak, the Captain serves the freshest and we daresay the largest lobsters 120 miles from the ocean. A 14-pounder looked big enough to take on Jabba the Hutt. We made quite a mess cracking the claws and sucking on the legs of some smaller ones, like true Yankees. As for the "petit" filet mignon, you will have enough left over for tomorrow's lunch. Prime rib, sirloin (including sirloin teriyaki), chicken parmigiana, baked scrod and halibut, shrimp scampi, fried oysters and clams, and various surf-and-turf combos — what's not to like?

For those whose stomachs have a chocolate compartment, the mud pie or fudge brownie à la mode should suffice.

1896 HOUSE
    RESTAURANT
413-458-1896 (of course).
910 Cold Spring Rd. (Rte.
    7), Williamstown.
Price: Moderate.
Cuisine: American.
Serving: L & SB Sun. only,
    D.
Credit Cards: AE, D, MC,
    V.
Special Feature: Member,
    Berkshire Grown.

A nice house merlot, tasty pork medallions, and pesto salmon, but the bugs continue. Too bad, because all Williamstown roots for Denise Richer and Sue Morelle, PanAm flight attendant and teacher, respectively, who first purchased the 1896 Motel (in 1985), then in 1993 the motel across the street (now 1896 Pondside), and then, fearing what would happen to the long-dormant barn-as-restaurant, purchased that as well, in 1994; opening it in 1996. They re-roofed and redecorated, including unusual but homey overstuffed dining chairs.

Yet when we arrived on time for our reservation recently, we were ushered into the smoky bar, in spite of numerous empty tables. Although we were not in any hurry, the hiatus between salad and entrée extended . . . and the fritter frittered its time away, never arriving. The apple crisp was apple soggy. In short it is still a new restaurant, still straightening out its miscues under the watchful eyes of its owners.

The '96 House aims to be straightforward and filling, with comfort food as well as more adventuresome fare as chef Robert Andrew expands his menu. We expect the 1896 House to regain the traditional place of old held in the hearts of locals, travelers, and Williams College alumni.

HOBSON'S CHOICE
413-458-9101.
159 St. (Rte. 43),
    Williamstown.
Price: Moderate.
Serving: D.
Credit Cards: MC, V.
Reservations:
    Recommended.
Special Feature: Member,
    Berkshire Grown.

L ocals know making Hobson's Choice is a good one in Williamstown for a quiet drink, dinner, or a late evening's snack. Hobson's is going to expand but probably won't return to serving lunch. Dark wooden booths line the walls of the restaurant's two rooms, creating a sense of intimacy (except for a few seconds when the outside door opens). Hobson's is a comfortable place to linger.

With owner Dan Campbell playfully holding court from the open kitchen behind the salad bar, one of the tastiest in northern Berkshire, the customer is likely to get a custom-cooked meal, just the way she likes it. We were delighted with a veal chop cooked in a light oil and seasoned just so. Hobson's offers a wide variety of chicken (grilled, blackened, barbecued, teriyaki, and Santa Fe style), beef, fish, pasta, and vegetarian specialties, all flavorfully prepared. It makes its own soups: an onion soup gratinée is especially good. The desserts are also excellent, especially the mud pie.

A comfortable, well-stocked bar includes a nice selection of imported beers and ales, plus a modest wine list. Espresso and cappuccino provide warmth and cheer for the abstemious.

LE JARDIN
413-458-8032.
777 Cold Spring Rd.,
  Williamstown.
S. of town.
Open: Thurs.–Sun..
Price: Moderate to
  Expensive.
Cuisine: French.
Serving: D.
Reservations:
  Recommended.
Special Features: Fireplace;
  Vegetarian dishes.

Le Jardin, a country inn in a lovely setting on a wooded hillside, has nine guest rooms and two dining rooms. Chef/owner Walter Hayne prepares a blackboard menu each evening in order to ensure freshness and to take advantage of seasonal local produce.

On our summer evening visit, start to finish we received a perfect restaurant meal. The vichyssoise was cool and silken, with rich potato flavor and a hint of fresh chive. Herring with red onion, sour cream, and tart apple was excellent; the house salads remarkably crisp and fresh. Grilled salmon and veal Marsala were served with delicate sauces and accompanied by brightly flavored fresh, steamed vegetables. A rich and smooth chocolate mousse arrived in stemmed glasses with whipped cream.

Such an inspired hand in the kitchen deserves a professional presence at the front of the house, yet the grounds seemed neglected, outdoor lighting fixtures were missing, and the interior decor was tired. The hostess could not find our reservation and, later, we overheard the clerk tell a honeymooning couple that their room reservation had been accidentally canceled.

MAIN STREET CAFE
413-458-3210
16 Water St. (Rte. 43),
  Williamstown.
Cor. Main St. (Rte. 2).
Price: Moderate.
Cuisine: Northern Italian
  Eclectic, Mediterranean.
Serving: L, D.
Credit Cards: AE, DC, MC,
  V.
Reservations:
  Recommended for D.
Special Features: Italian
  ambience in former
  general store with deck;
  Tapas bar.

Owner Jeff Bendavid takes seriously his invitation to diners to consult about their food rather than ordering from the menu. "I'll tell you what's in the kitchen, you tell me what you'd like to eat," he says, descending on a table from his post at the range. The light-filled space within exposed brick walks, the house wine waiting on the table, and the weighty tableware provide a gracious setting for a meal that is an experience.

We shared a three-mushroom appetizer, followed by a modest salad, rack of lamb, and swordfish with smoked salmon. None of them were on the menu. All provided delightful shades of color, texture, and flavor. The salmon did something to the swordfish that other fish would die for. While co-owner Peggy Apple teases Bendavid about massive helpings, we had no trouble disposing of the lamb, which rose imposingly over an elegant, delicate mint sauce and fresh, tender asparagus. An extensive wine list includes 20 labels by the glass, encouraging adventuresome mixing.

The restaurant is divided in three: the formal dining room, a tapas bar with brick oven serving appetizers and light fare until 1am, and a bar. Two ladies' rooms: the owners say they don't like to see women waiting in line. We'll drink to that. How about a gentle California dessert wine?

Decor du jour at Mezze, Williamstown.

Courtesy of Mezze

MEZZE
413-458-0123.
84 Water St. (Rte. 43),
   Williamstown.
Price: Inexpensive.
Cuisine: Global.
Serving: D, light dishes.
Credit Cards: AE, M, V.
Special Features:
   Specializes in appetizers;
   Deck overlooking Green
   River.

Nancy Thomas presides over this friendly bistro and bar, a welcome addition to the North County restaurant scene. Mezze's menu offers a creative variety, changing frequently. Guests are equally welcome whether interested in a light pre-theater snack, a full meal, or dessert and coffee. Year-round, the town influx of young Internet-connected hang out here. Well-known theatrical figures are apt to be found at the bar après theater in the summer.

Meat, fish, poultry, and several vegetarian offerings tempt the palate. We recommend creating a meal by ordering several appetizers. Couscous, chickpeas, lentils, Greek feta, olives, fresh fruits, and vegetables are woven into the dishes. Among entrées, the seared tuna steak with ginger is exceptional. Desserts are made on the premises.

ORCHARDS
413-458-9611.
222 Adams Rd.,
   Williamstown.
Price: Moderate to
   Expensive.
Cuisine: American, French.
Serving: B, L, SB, D.
Credit Cards: AE, DC, MC,
   V.
Reservations:
   Recommended.
Special Features: Table
   settings and linens;
   Member, Berkshire
   Grown.

Sayed Saleh's Orchards, in the midst of a major facelift, serves fine meals in a gracious setting. In its appointments and attention to tableware, the Orchards gets high marks. The tables are set with Irish linen, graceful stemware, and colorful fresh bouquets. The service is knowledgeable, efficient and friendly — in a discreet way. The restaurant feels like a club for people who live graciously. It is moving in the direction of small business conferences.

Our goat's cheese salad was beautifully presented and tasty, the bread warm and crusty. Items on the brief menu included a pasta, two fish, and three or four meat offerings. We chose a roast rack of young lamb, which crowned a small dome of mashed potato, onions, and peppers — lovely to look at and delightful to down. The preparation on all the food was exquisite. For dessert we chose the profiteroles, a delicate pastry with ice cream and chocolate sauce — and strawberries that suffered slightly for being out of season. The ample and imaginative wine list befits the club image.

The club atmosphere, impeccable service, smallish helpings, and pricey tab may not make everyone feel comfortable, but those whom that fits will much enjoy the Orchards.

**PAPPA CHARLIE'S DELI
   SANDWICH SHOP**
413-458-5969.
28 Spring St, Williamstown.
Price: Inexpensive.
Cuisine: American.
Serving: B, L, D.
Special Features: Open late.

Pappa Charlie's reigns supreme as a people's place and local hangout, convenient to the Images Cinema and the Williams College gymnasium. It serves sandwiches, chili, and mulled cider. The delicious overstuffed sandwiches and elaborately adorned, well-stuffed bagels are mostly named for actors at the Williamstown Theatre Festival, politicians, and other well-known personalities. Anyone for a bite of a Nikos? a nibble of Ralph Renzi? or a taste of Zonker Harris? Or an avocado smoothie — bagel of choice, spread of cream cheese, slices of avocado — all zapped in the steamer? The philosophical issue is whether or not the dishes are a commentary on their namesakes.

Fresh cider, root beer that traces its roots to the A&W where Charlie Nikitas began, exotic fruit juice combos like strawberry-banana-OJ. The cooler holds

Judith Monachina

Pappa Charlie's is a popular spot for studens and others in Williamstown.

one of North County's better arrays of domestic and imported cheeses. The ambience is created by the friendly service and plain wooden booths. The benches in the small park to the north are a fine alternative; the basement is reminiscent of a school lunchroom, however.

ROBIN'S
413-458-4489.
117 Latham, Williamstown.
Closed: Mon.–Thurs. in winter.
Price: Moderate.
Cuisine: Californian, Mediterranean, New England.
Serving: Summer: L Tues.–Sun., D Tues.–Sat.; Winter L Mon.–Sat., D Fri & Sat. only.
Credit Cards: AE, D, MC, V.
Reservations: Recommended in summer.

On a warm summer evening we come to sit under the tall pine trees that surround Robin's expansive deck at the end of Spring St., enjoying imaginatively prepared dishes featuring fine local organic produce. "A pleasure," said the *New York Times*, and we sigh "yes." The tables crowded together combine the lively atmosphere of urban cafe dining with the serenity of a nest. A recent menu featured a perfectly flavored gazpacho appetizer and mouth-watering entrées of lobster ravioli with pesto, braised curried rabbit, mixed grill, and penne pasta with spring vegetables.

A luscious lemon tart, chocolate torte with sweet sour cream and raspberry sauce, warm apple-blueberry crisp, or signature biscotti wrap up the meal. Robin Lenz, chef/owner, changes the menu daily to take advantage of seasonal specialties.

Special Features:
Wraparound deck under pine trees; Takeout service; Member, Berkshire Grown.

Robin winters over, offering satisfying soups and generous servings for a cold Berkshire evenings in a warm, cozy space. Enticing menu offerings include butternut sage ravioli, roasted vegetables with Robin's special polenta, and baby back ribs with black bean and garlic sauce.

TACONIC RESTAURANT
413-458-9499.
1161 Cold Spring Rd. (Rte. 7), Williamstown.
Jct. Rte. 2.
Price: Moderate.
Cuisine: New England.
Serving: L (Sun. only), D.
Credit Cards: AE, D, MC,V.
Reservations: Recommended.
Special Feature: Also home of Jimmy Dean's Catering; Member, Berkshire Grown.

Deborah Guiden, James Guiden, and Dean Grimes purchased the longtime restaurant that had been through uncertain days and now provides gracious space for banquets and dependably good food for the wayfarer. The menu, which features a half dozen veal dishes, revels in its New England environment, serving locally grown produce (Jimmy Guiden's brother farms). Dependable, fun, not exotic: a place to get a good baked potato with sour cream and string beans still crunchy. The main dining room provides an uninspiring view of the Rte. 7 traffic but a large fireplace to ward off the chill on a cool evening. The restaurant attracts local people and drivebys.

The soup du jour recently was homemade turkey, with a gravy-like cream sauce. The "original Vermont chicken" was a playful concoction with cinnamon apples and a maple syrup sauce. Among the other desserts, the Taconic pie is an extraordinary confection that tries even a chocolate-lover's capacity. The house wine by the glass, a cabernet sauvignon, played a subdued accompanying role.

WATER STREET GRILL
413-458-2175.
123 Water St. (Rte. 43), Williamstown.
Price: Inexpensive to Moderate.
Cuisine: Contemporary American.
Serving: L, D.
Credit Cards: AE, MC, V.
Reservations: Recommended.
Handicap Access: Yes.
Special Features: Tavern; Expanded menu in Grill, with fireplace.

The owners of the Freight Yard Pub in North Adams also own the former Savories as an upscale outlet. The Tavern is more like the FYP, with nachos, fajitas, burgers, and seafood. In the Grill we enjoyed Absolut chicken (with vodka) and the special, sirloin tips with mushrooms. The house chardonnay was above average. The house salad offered a great variety of dressings and the breadsticks receive a bonus for being served warm. Our waitperson seemed interested without hovering. All in all, a fine night out for the price.

One caution, or maybe it's an enticement: Overly live acoustics in this all-wood room can make innocent diners into eavesdroppers.

WILD AMBER GRILL
423-458-4000.
101 North St.,
  Williamstown.
Price: Moderate.
Cuisine: Contemporary.
Serving: D; L, D in
  summer.
Credit cards: AE, MC, V.
Special features: Terrace in
  summer.

Chef Sandy Smith prepares a truly fine meal at the restaurant owned by the three Smiths (brothers Alexander and Ned; unrelated Gerard) who also own the popular Cobble Cafe on Spring St. The menu is creative. The tasty sautéed Thai shrimp is the closest to Thai one can get in Berkshire. The filet mignon, with its delightful sliver of blue cheese, reclines attractively on a bed of mashed potatoes. The chef's salad gives a diner the choice of with or without (anchovies, that is); the field greens were just as crisp and tasty under a creamy house dressing. We enjoyed the sourdough bread and a forthright cabernet sauvignon from Chile. Several specials are offered, including fresh fish and pasta creations.

The exciting autumn dessert menu included a fine strudel with a drizzle of caramel over the plate, and a highly appreciated pair of chocolate cups with a white and dark chocolate mousse, respectively. Service and atmosphere were first rate.

In season the terrace grill opens, serving a separate menu featuring grilled foods. The terrace is also open for summer lunches.

Excellence in Wine Lists

Berkshire is a small county, especially in population, so that it is unusual that nine of its restaurants, out of 75 in Massachusetts, received awards of excellence from the *Wine Spectator* in its September 1999 issue. The awards are based on the strengths and pricing level of a restaurant's list. All the Berkshire establishments had "moderately priced" wine lists.

Blantyre, Lenox, wines from France and California.

Café Lucia, Lenox, wines from California and Italy.

Castle Street Café, Gt. Barrington, Bordeaux wines.

Church Street Cafe, Lenox, California wines.

1896 House, Williamstown, wines from France and California.

John Andrew's Restaurant, S. Egremont, California wines.

La Bruschetta, W. Stockbridge, wines from Italy and California.

Red Lion Inn, Stockbridge, wines from California and France.

Wheatleigh, Lenox, wines from California and France.

RESTAURANTS OUTSIDE THE COUNTY

Hillsdale, New York

AUBERGINE
518-325-3412.
www.aubergine.com.
Jct. Rtes. 22 & 23, Hillsdale.
Closed: Mon., Tues.
Price: Moderate to Very
  Expensive.
Cuisine: American with a
  French twist.
Serving: D.
Credit Cards: AE, MC, V.
Reservations:
  Recommended.
Special features: Vegetarian
  dishes; Member,
  Berkshire Grown.

Chef/owner David Lawson and his wife, Stacy, preside over Aubergine, offering fine food and lodging in a venue long renowned for both. It is housed in a handsome 1783 Dutch Colonial mansion just outside Berkshire County proper, but close enough for easy access, and well worth the trip. David offers "French-inspired country cooking" to a devoted clientele who followed him through several of the Berkshires' finest restaurants before he struck out on his own here several years ago. The atmosphere is not terribly formal; "high casual" is the suggested standard for attire, although most of their clients seem inclined to put on at least a jacket if not a tie out of respect for the food, wine, and atmosphere the Lawsons offer.

Like many of Berkshire's finest restaurants, Aubergine incorporates the best of locally produced foods into its menu. Selections are largely in the traditional French vein, imaginatively adapted by David to incorporate more cosmopolitan and contemporary elements, a couscous, a polenta, gnocchi, or shiitake mushrooms. The wine list draws on a cellar that has been there for many years and is one of the deepest and best in the region, featuring mostly fine French and California offerings. Desserts are rich and worth the calories. David's classic soufflés, which must be ordered at the outset of the meal, are themselves worth the visit here.

SWISS HÜTTE
413-528-6200, 518-325-3333;
  fax 413-528-6201.
www.swisshutte.com
Rte. 23, Hillsdale (on Mass.
  line).
Price: Expensive.
Cuisine: Continental.
Serving: D.
Credit Cards: MC, V.
Reservations:
  Recommended.
Special Features: View of
  ski slopes; Outdoor
  dining; Member,
  Berkshire Grown.

Ski enthusiast or not, a trip to Swiss Hütte is worth it. In the winter the views take in the Catamount ski slopes; in the spring, when we were last there, we enjoyed the crabapple trees in bloom and the well-kept gardens and grounds. We were tempted to move there for the weekend.

For appetizers we had two specials: oysters on the half shell, cold, crispy and salty; and a superb liver terrine with Armagnac and truffles. Our entrées were sautéed shrimps and scallops (perfectly cooked) served on a curry sauce with fresh fruit, berries, and almonds, and — ignoring the cholesterol — sweetbreads with chanterelle mushrooms and cream sauce. Rarely are sweetbreads this good. A moderately priced 1994 Robert Mondavi fumé blanc was a great accompaniment.

We overindulged with two great desserts, a crème de cassis parfait with ice cream, and chocolate remoulade with raspberry and chocolate mousse.

Cambridge, New York

CAMBRIDGE FARE
518-677-5626.
www.cambridgehotel.com.
4 W. Main St., Cambridge.
Price: Expensive
Cuisine: American.
Serving: B, L, D.
Closed: Mon.
Credit Cards: AE, MC, V.
Reservations:
  Recommended.
Special Feature: Passenger
  train stops at historic
  station across street.

Cambridge Fare Restaurant began when the Cambridge Hotel opened in the summer of 1999, after a year of total restoration. This national historic landmark, with upper and lower verandas, caters to tourists and an impressive number of local residents. Executive chef Jonathan Fine is dedicated to quality and variety. On one evening, entrées ranged from "the world's best chicken pot pie Maggie" (pronounced comforting if not exciting) to a char-grilled salmon, sun-dried tomato, and caper beurre blanc (pronounced succulent and satisfying). Chef constantly changes the menus.

Our potato leek soup was fetching, the salads both artistically displayed and tasty. We appreciated the bit of garlic nestled with the scoop of butter. Naturally at this hotel that in the mid-1890s invented pie à la mode, we sampled the new edition, a flavorful miniature apple pie with a crust that met all expectations and stood toe-to-toe with a chocolate trifle tower. The house wine, from Napa Valley, gracefully accompanied the food.

Cambridge Fare, which includes a bakery, is about three quarters of an hour from North Berkshire County, a lovely drive through eastern New York.

Charlemont, Massachusetts

WARFIELD HOUSE
413-339-6600;
  888-339-VIEW.
www.warfieldhouse.com.
200 Warfield Rd. (Rte. 2),
  Charlemont.
Closed: Mon.–Wed.
Price: Moderate.
Cuisine: European, New
  England.
Serving: L, D.
Credit Cards: AE, D, MC, V.
Reservations:
  Recommended.

From the outside, Warfield House looks like the barn that it was until 1997, but inside the high ceilings, spacious dining rooms, decades of Warfield family photographs, and a 20-mile view give one the feeling of having dropped in to an 1890s New England mountaintop hotel. The farm has been in owner John Warfield Glaze's family since 1868.

Windows in the main dining room give out on the Deerfield Valley and the slopes of Berkshire East, while a stone fireplace arises on another wall. The staff were country friendly, with both an easygoing charm and professional grace. On our evening they

Special Features: View; Function room.

had to cope with an unexpected dinner rush. The menu melds distinctive classical European cuisine with New England traditions: Wienerschnitzel and veal Milanese with liver and onions and grilled brook trout. Valley View Farm raises beef cattle, llamas, and emu, leading to emu au poivre. Our smoked trout appetizer was served with a crisp, sweet-and-spicy apple-horseradish relish. The soft liver pâté was earthy, strong, and satisfying. The vegetable medley that accompanied the pork rouladen was perfectly prepared, crisp and tender with bright flavors. Braised sweetbreads were nicely done, with a delicately balanced cream cherry sauce.

BREAKFAST & LUNCH

Of the many Berkshire eateries designed to gladden morning and noon, we have selected a handful. As is appropriate, all are on the inexpensive end of the scale.

ALLENTUCK'S NEW YORK DELICATESSEN (413-528-4500, 148 Main St., Rte. 7, Gt. Barrington)

For those who savor the tradition of a New York–style delicatessen, Allentuck's food should whet their appetites! Allentuck's staples are its steamed pastrami, corned beef, and braised brisket served hot daily, complemented by home-baked sourdough breads and H&H bagels. Vegetarians will find many fresh, wholesome dishes to choose from. There are tables for eat-in, but keep Allentuck's in mind for lunch and dinner takeout, a Tanglewood picnic, or a catered event.

GASLIGHT CAFE (413-528-0870; Rte. 23, S. Egremont)

Yankee Magazine loves the Gaslight. So do parents with kids and sentimentalists of all ages. The food is always fun — well-prepared sandwiches, burgers, omelettes, and pancakes. The ambience overflows to the patio and brook below. Member, Berkshire Grown.

DELI (413-528-1482; 345 Main St., Rte. 7, Gt. Barrington).

The best sandwich menu in Berkshire — the Jacques Cousteau, a seafood-filled marvel, for instance — two great soups every day, gobs of local color, and a loyal local following encompassing the whole social/commercial/artistic spectrum of the area make the Deli a treat for the eye and the tummy. Breakfasts start at 5:30am, with omelettes like the Cisco Kid, Eve Arden, and Miss Piggy rolling off Chef Frank's pan until 10am. The Deli shares space with Sip of Seattle, for espresso coffee drinks and panini straight out of Italy.

MARTIN'S (413-528-5455; 49 Railroad St., Gt. Barrington)

Martin's is bright and light, serving breakfast all day. Omelettes are varied and outstanding. Pancakes come standard plus the daily special, such as pumpkin. For lunch, burger styles include the Berkshire cheeseburger (mushrooms, onion, tomatoes, and peppers), sandwiches, salads, soups, and specials. Beer, plus the usual. Crayons at every table, so that artists can illustrate on their placemats, with true talent ending up on the wall. Member, Berkshire Grown.

MAIN STREET CAFE (413-298-5465; 40 Main St., Rte. 7, Stockbridge)

Not to be confused with Williamstown's upscale eatery of the same name, at Stockbridge's Theresa offers a full and diverse breakfast menu, from ham and eggs to breakfast burritos, and an extensive selection of luncheon choices. The roomy, rustic dining area with a large window facing onto Main Street is a pleasant setting for tasty fare. Member, Berkshire Grown.

MIDGE'S (413-298-3040; Elm St., Stockbridge)

Midge's offers a classic lunch counter, much favored by Stockbridge locals. A tasty chili and two good soups are offered every day. Sandwiches are filled as a hungry person wants them to be, or you might try one of Midge's hearty specials. In any case, the ice cream cones are super for strolling on warm days.

CAROL'S (413-637-8948; Franklin St., Lenox)

Serving in what was formerly an elder-services center, Carol's offers scant ambience but good and popular down-home food, including especially Carol's own homemade seven-grain and sourdough breads baked daily and offered for breakfast toast and sandwich wrappers. Breakfast is served all day, highlighted by imaginative pancake and omelette options, and justly famous home fries. Lunch features big and tasty sandwiches, and a good number of hearty vegetarian selections.

COURT SQUARE BREAKFAST & DELI (413-442-9896; 95 East St., Pittsfield)

Lawyers, judges, and politicians in the county seat mostly turn up at the Court Square for breakfast on a given day. And it's a good breakfast, too: eggs, French toast, omelettes — just about anything these folks need before sitting through a long day of weighty matters. They may be a bit more weighty, too, but satisfied.

COBBLE CAFE (413-458-5930; 27 Spring St., Williamstown)

The Cobble Cafe as a breakfast-and-lunch spot is rising from the ashes of a fire. Owner Gerard Smith advises us that it will reopen.

CHEF'S HAT (413-458-5120; 905 Simonds Rd., Rte. 7, Williamstown)

Packed every lunch; serving breakfast early, early; serving occasional weekend dinners, the Chef's Hat has a formula that clearly works. From truck drivers to Williams College academics, it has a truly eclectic clientele. Booths, tables, and counter . . . TCH serves solid, reliable, inexpensive breakfast and luncheon foods to regulars and even outsiders, without making them feel conspicuous.

JACK'S HOT DOGS (413-664-9006; 12 Eagle St., N. Adams)

Jack's Hot Dogs holds its historic position as the place to get hot dogs in North County. Continuing a 70-year family tradition, owner Jeff Levanos and manager Maria Carmain provide a continuous flow of hot dogs, plain and fancy, with rapid-fire conversation accompanying the bustle behind the counter. Whether pressed against the wall waiting for an order to go or wedged on one of the 12 stools along the counter munching hot dogs and fries, customers are experiencing a lively bit of history. Four of us ordered our dogs with the works: kraut, chili, and cheese. Together with French fries, fried onions, and beverages, the total tab came to less than $12.

MISS ADAMS DINER (413-743-5300; 53 Park St., Adams)

Although no longer under the care of Nancy Garton, Miss Adams remains the authentic streetcar diner in the middle of town. An Adams institution, it also attracts visitors from afar. The home-baked breads go down just so smoothly, the pies have distinctively flaky crusts, and the cream pies come with flavor and portions to satisfy even the truck driver farthest from home. Member, Berkshire Grown.

FOOD PURVEYORS

From the freshest sweet corn from the farmstand, raced from purchase to pot, to the latest imported gourmet specialty, appearing by candlelight on a Tanglewood picnic blanket, Berkshire supplies food that ranges from pure and simple to sophisticated and innovative. The food and beverage purveyors listed below are sources for baked goods, coffee and ice cream, produce and other farm products, picnic provisions, and health and gourmet food. The surprising array of unique food specialties created and produced in the Berkshires are listed at the end of the chapter.

BAKERIES

European pastries, New York bagels, French baguettes, and grandma's pies: breads and baked goods from Berkshire bakeries offer the staff of life and all its variations. Many of these bakeries also provide dining areas.

Bagel Smith (413-243-4041; 33 Park St., Lee) Tucked in the plaza behind Dunkin' Donuts, near Brooks Pharmacy, this spot offers bagels, sit-down breakfast and lunch, and more.

Bagels Too (413-499-0119; 166 North St., Pittsfield) Huge assortment of bagels and other pastries; coffee, too–to go or eat in. A favorite of people heading to work in downtown Pittsfield, this place bustles on a weekday morning.

Daily Bread (413-528-9610; 17 Railroad St., Gt. Barrington; also 413-298-0272; Main St., Stockbridge; Main St., Lenox) Give us our daily bread: real, crusty sourdough French baguettes fresh out of the oven, and almond crescent cookies, hazelnut torte, sticky buns, and other necessities of life. Closed Sun.

Neville's Doughnut Shop (413-663-5855; 149 Eagle St., N. Adams) This bakery exists to show that real doughnuts taste much better than simulated confections. Early hours; closed during parts of the day. Worth a call ahead.

Sweet Pea & Petunia (413-528-7786; 325 Stockbridge Rd., Rte. 7, Gt. Barrington) Baked goods, sandwiches and wraps made to order, and quiche. Also serves sit-down meals and homemade ice cream.

A sunny spot in front of the Appalachian Bean in North Adams.

Judith Monachina

COFFEE SPECIALISTS

Appalachian Bean (413-663-7543; 67 Main St., N. Adams) A pleasant spot for a quick sip or a leisurely drink, and there are chairs outside for people-watching or reading.

Barrington Coffee Roasting Co., Inc. (413-528-0998; 955 S. Main St., Rte. 7, Gt. Barrington) Coffees from all over the world, available at the touch of a faucet.

Berkshire Bistro (413-442-4226; 44 West St., Pittsfield) Offers coffee (Seattle's best) and light breakfast fare Mon.–Fri. from 7am; Sat. from 9am. Lunch is the main meal served Mon.–Sat., plus specialty sandwiches and desserts until 9pm. Takeout service and gourmet coffees to serve at home.

Berkshire Coffee Roasting Company (413-528-5505; 286 Main St., Rte. 7, Gt. Barrington; also 413-637-1606, 52 Main St., Lenox) A top choice for exceptional coffee in an unpretentiously funky setting, conducive to the related activities of conversation, relaxing, people-watching, reading, or admiring the latest art exhibit on the walls. The beans responsible for all this pleasure are imported green, then roasted here. Choose from a selection of coffee flavors, and cappuccino, espresso, hot chocolate, cookies, muffins, and biscotti (try the chocolate-covered variety). Bags of coffee beans are for sale. The popular coffee takeout set-up thoughtfully provides raised lids for preserving the foam on the cappuccino.

Deep in conversation at the Cold Spring Coffee Roasters in Williamstown.

Judith Monachina

Cold Spring Coffee Roasters, Ltd. (413-458-5010; 47 Spring St., Williamstown) More than 60 varieties of specialty coffees are roasted on the premises here (and there are 25 varieties of loose teas). Order cappuccino, latte, or espresso, and treat yourself to ice cream and other goodies in a cafe atmosphere. There's an array of tea- and coffee-making gear, too.

Juice n' Java (413-243-3131, 60 Main St., Lee; 413-499-6130, 216 Elm St., Pittsfield; 413-684-5080, 661 Main St., Dalton) Coffee, juices, plus salads and sandwiches to eat in or take out.

Sip of Seattle (413-528-6913; 343 Main St., Gt. Barrington) Shares space with the Deli; offers coffee and espresso drinks and great pannini (hot sandwiches made in a press).

FARM, ORCHARD, PRODUCE MARKETS

Fresh tomatoes right off the vine, crisp and juicy apples, enormous heads of organically grown lettuce — bounty from Berkshire fields and hills is available at area produce markets, farm and orchard outlets, seasonal farmstands, and farmers' markets, where area growers truck in their harvests to a central

---

Farmers' Markets

Farmers' markets, where local growers set up temporarily to offer this week's freshest harvest, have sprung up throughout the county. Held from June to the first frost, for the markets' days, times, and locations check a newspaper or the extension service (413-448-8285). In *Pittsfield*, the Allendale Shopping Center hosts a market on Weds. & Sat. mornings, and downtown Pittsfield sets up an open-air market on Columbus Ave. on Fri. In *Gt. Barrington*, the Farmer's Market is Sat. from 8:30am to 12:30pm in the yard of the old train station, with vegetables plus local cheeses and hand-crafted products related to farming. In *Lee*, Fri. 12–6, next to the Post Office, find fresh seafood (Vic's), herbs, veggies, flowers, and more. In *Williamstown*, on Sat. mornings, July through Sept., local farmers set up in the parking lot at the foot of Spring St.

---

outdoor location one or two days a week. Home-grown is potent, as in the restaurants that have enrolled in the Berkshire Grown program. Sources of non-Berkshire produce throughout the county, for those occasions when only kiwi fruit or bok choy will do, are listed as well.

The **Berkshire County Extension Service** (413-448-8285; 44 Bank Row, Pittsfield) can provide up-to-date information on seasonal farmstands and farmers' markets.

Bartlett's Orchard (413-698-2559; Swamp Rd., Richmond) "Buy 'em where they grow 'em." Apple varieties throughout the season include Empire, Mac, Delicious (Red and Golden), Cortland, Northern Spy, Macoun, Ida Red, Jonagold, and more. Each variety is labeled with a description of its distinct flavor and best use. Bartlett's own cider is all natural and preservative free. The shop also stocks an array of apple products and other country-gourmet condiments and preserves; the bakery offers doughnuts, turnovers, and pies.

Burgner's Farm Products (413-445-4704; Dalton Division Rd., Pittsfield) The turkey farm is a neighborhood gathering place for fresh produce, including Burgner's own, especially their corn in season, plus other fruits and vegetables from local farms and farther afield. Eggs, chicken, and turkey products are a specialty.

Chenail's Farmstand (413-458-4910; Luce Rd., Williamstown) Not easy to find since cornhuskers must follow Luce Rd. part way up to Mt. Greylock, but the corn and other vegetables Chenail's puts out are tastefully fresher than those at stands not on the farm. The farmstand should not be confused with Chenail's Farm Fresh Products (413-458-4737; 903 Simonds Rd., Rte. 7, Williamstown), which offers fresh fruit, vegetables (including corn), flowers, crafts, and seasonal decorations.

Corn Crib (413-528-4947; Rte. 7, Sheffield) Farm-raised produce, plus that of other local farmers: fresh fruit, veggies, plants, perennials. Carol's Cookery has homemade pastries, soup, and bread; Dolls & Dwellings offers dolls, supplies, doll houses, miniatures, dried flowers.

Guido's Fresh Marketplace (413-442-9909; 1020 South St., Rte. 7, Pittsfield; also 413-528- 9255; 760 S. Main St., Rte. 7, Gt. Barrington) A fine place to buy vegetables and fruit in the county, with local produce in season and a multicultural array of standards and exotics from all over the world year-round: baby carrots, cilantro, radicchio, endive, fresh herbs, oriental vegetables, tropical fruits, mushrooms. A true marketplace ambience, with distinct Guido touches: the signs posted at the carefully arranged but overflowing produce bins are polite and informative, and help carrying bags out to the car is available. Also at Guido's (Pittsfield) are Berger's Bakery and Deli, Mazzeo's Meat Center, Masse's Seafood, and Pasta Prima (described in the appropriate categories below), and all sorts of cooking supplies, health foods, earth-conscious cosmetics, gourmet items, candles, baskets, Guido's T-shirts. . . .

Jaeschke's Brothers Farms (413-743-3896; West Rd., Adams) In spite of a fire at the orchard, do-it-yourselfers can pick apples and pears at the orchard after the pro pickers have been through, or pick up apples and cider any time.The farm store is in Pittsfield, 736 Crane Ave. (Allendale area; 413-443-7180).

Taft Farms (413-528-1515; Rte. 183 & Division St., Gt. Barrington) Taft Farms' own delicious produce in season, including potatoes, tomatoes, peppers, broccoli, cucumbers, and their famous just-picked sweet corn. It's all grown according to the "integrated pest management" system, which minimizes or eliminates the use of pesticides. Taft also offers fruit and vegetables from other climes, such as radicchio, kiwi fruit, or pomegranates. Pasture-raised chicken, baked goods, jams and jellies, cider, Taft salsa, and seafood from the fish market (Thurs.–Sat.); flowers and plants from the greenhouse, too.

Picking Your Own Fruit

A berry- or apple-picking expedition is a great way to enjoy the Berkshire countryside, while gathering the makings for a special dessert, muffin, or pancake breakfast. Blueberries in particular are available wild throughout these hills, but few natives will reveal their special picking spots. Call ahead at the following farms and orchards for picking conditions.

Blueberries abound at *Blueberry Hill Farm,* which offers 320 acres for family picking from late July until frost (East St., 7 mi. up the Mt. Washington ridge; call 413-528-1479 for a recorded message about the status of picking). At *Strawberry Acres* (413-655-2672; off Rte. 8, Hinsdale) there are blueberries and Christmas trees, too.

Three acres of *strawberries* are at *Crooked Row Farm* (413-698-2608; Dublin Rd., Richmond). Strawberries can also be picked at *Ioka Valley Farm* (413-738-5915; 3475 Hancock Rd., Rte. 43, Hancock).

Apples at *Windy Hill Farm* (413-298-3217; Rte. 7, Gt. Barrington) are waiting to be picked in season; there's also a garden shop and nursery. Open Apr.–Oct.

GOURMET/DELI MARKETS, CATERERS

The small grocery markets and specialty food shops and caterers of the Berkshires will please the palates of just about everyone, from the classicist to the experimenter. These markets and food specialists combine the latest culinary styles with ethnic traditions and personal service, and also magnificently maintain the celebrated Berkshire custom of the gourmet picnic. There's an old-time country store or two thrown in, too.

Allentuck's New York Delicatessen (413-528-4500; 148 Main St., Rte. 7, Gt. Barrington) Spiffy New York-style deli with smoked fish, meats, rotisserie, prepared meals, H&H bagels, and unusual breads.

Berger's Specialty Foods (413-442-1898; 1020 South St., Rte. 7, Pittsfield, at Guido's) Some assert that the best baguettes to be found in the Berkshires are here; others avoid the controversy by selecting from the abundant variety of cheeses, crackers, condiments, pasta and other salads, and gourmet items from far and wide. Berger's also caters and does gift baskets.

Berkshire Hills Market (413-458-3356; 60 Spring St., Williamstown) Relatively new but old-fashioned in feeling, this market includes fresh meat and fish, plus smoked meat and sausage made on the premises. Gourmet items, including coffee and tea of the day, are to-go and by the pound. There's more: fresh produce, deli items, overstuffed sandwiches, gift baskets, and boxed meals. Call in your order or eat at the tables.

Caffe Pomo d'Oro (413-232-4616; 6 Depot St., W. Stockbridge) Gourmet provisions and a cafe in a sunny room in West Stockbridge's small-scale downtown. Cheese and deli items, bread, imported gourmet foods, even their own gourmet vinegar. Catering. Member, Berkshire Grown.

Cheesecake Charlie's (413-528-7790; 271 Main St., Gt. Barrington) Toasted almond, creamsicle, piña colada, peppermint patty — these are only a few of the cheesecake flavors that you can get here. Available in different sizes; the store ships too. Breakfast, lunch, dinner, or a break for a cappuccino or a healthy, refreshing blast from the well-stocked juice bar. Member, Berkshire Grown.

Chez Vous Catering (413-298-4278; P.O. Box 1162, Stockbridge) Elegant food, beautifully presented, including Oriental roast beef, Madeira chicken, lentil salad plates, and desserts.

Gorham & Norton (413-528-0900; 278 Main St., Rte. 7, Gt. Barrington) This authentically old-fashioned market has up-to-the-minute good things: groceries, gourmet items, imported cheese, an excellent wine selection.

Marketplace (413-528-5775; 760 S. Main St., Rte. 7, Gt. Barrington, at Guido's) Take out a complete fine restaurant meal, lunch or dinner. A variety of salads, hot and cold, fish, cold cuts, and more are also takeout ready. All explained and served up with enthusiasm and panache.

Monterey General Store (413-528-4437; Rte. 23, Monterey) Not necessarily a gourmet shop, but an established oasis in southeastern Berkshire, this old-time general store stocks fresh vegetables, cold cuts, preserves, and locally made maple syrup. It offers fresh-baked goods daily. With a lunchroom in the back and a front porch for people-watching, this spot is a perennial gathering place.

Samel's Deli & Catering (413-442-5927; 115 Elm St., Pittsfield) Bread, chicken, wine, cheese, pepperoni, legendary pickles, and much more in the deli and gourmet line. It delivers in the Pittsfield area.

Store at Five Corners (413-458-3176; jct. Rtes. 7 & 43, S. Williamstown) The upscale country store, with well-chosen wine and beer selections, juices and waters, imported and domestic cheeses, fresh-baked breads and treats, homemade fudge, picnic and gift baskets, gifts, fresh produce, deli items such as sandwiches and salads, fancy preserves, gourmet coffee and ice cream, and various international offerings. Breakfast and light fare here on the deck or inside. It will ship and cater. In a building that was a tavern in 1770; the Greek Revival façade was added in 1830.

Turner Farms Maple Syrup in Egremont.

Judith Monachina

Maple Sugar and Syrup

Maple sugaring and syrup-making is a Berkshire tradition. Watch the process or participate at the following places during the season (usually March), or just pick up some of the final product at any time of year. *Williams College's Hopkins Forest* (413-458-3080; Northwest Hill Rd., Williamstown) usually demonstrates sugaring off. *Sunset Farm Maple Products* (413- 243-3229; Tyringham Rd., Tyringham) has an open sugarhouse. *Turner Farms Maple Syrup* (413-528-9956; Phillips Rd., S. Egremont): the sugar shack operation is open to the public; groups of 15 or more should make an appointment for a tour. Other sources of local maple products include *Gould Farm's Roadside Store and Cafe* (413-528-2633; Rte. 23, Monterey); *Holiday Farm* (413-684-0444; Rte. 9, Windsor); and *Mill Brook Sugar House* (413-637-0474; 317 New Lenox Rd., Lenox).

Other area restaurants or markets with catering services include the **Castle Street Café, Harry's Supermarket, Robin's**, the **Silver Screen**, and the **Sweet Basil Grille**.

Picnic Provisions

The Berkshires are ideal picnic territory, whether the context for al fresco dining is a hike, an all-day canoe trip, or the prelude to an outdoor performance at The Mount or at Tanglewood. The picnic may start with turkey and end with ice cream, but the picnic specialists listed here also offer many other options. And, of course, the picnickers can provision the picnic themselves, at any of the markets and gourmet shops described in this section.

Cheesecake Charlie's (413-528-7790; 271 Main St., Gt. Barrington) makes a special New England Clambake Picnic for Two, which includes lobster, mussels, clams, shrimp, corn on the cob, melon, and bread. *Perfect Picnics* (413-637-3015; 72 Church St., Lenox) offers gourmet dishes and will deliver to Tanglewood. *Allentuck's New York Delicatessen* (413-528-4500; 148 Main St., Rte. 7, Gt. Barrington) prepares a variety of picnic-ready boxed meals or the buyer can select. The *Marketplace* (413-528-5775; 760 S. Main St., at Guido's, Gt. Barrington) will customize a gourmet picnic, with 24 hours' notice. The *Red Lion Inn* (413-298-5545; 30 Main St., Rte. 7), offers pick-up picnics, too. *Robin's* (413- 458-4489; 117 Latham, Williamstown) will pack up entrées and side dishes. *Samel's Deli & Catering* (413-442-5927; 115 Elm St., Pittsfield) has boxed meals ideal for portable dining. The *Store at Five Corners* (413-458-3176; jct. Rtes. 7 & 43, S. Williamstown) will pack a picnic from their deli.

HEALTH/NATURAL FOOD STORES

Berkshire Co-op Market (413-528-9697; 37 Rosseter St., Gt. Barrington) Open to the public, but co-op members get a 2 percent discount. Ingredients for healthy eating and living, including organic produce, much of it grown locally; and baked goods, macrobiotic foods, bulk pasta, beans, grains, and herbal remedies.

Clearwater Natural Foods (413-637-2721; 11 Housatonic St., Lenox) Fresh bread, sandwiches, a wide range of groceries, including macrobiotic and allergy-free selections; organic produce, nondairy and dairy ice cream. Look for monthly specials.

Locke, Stock & Barrel (413-528-0800; 265 Stockbridge Rd., Rte. 7, Gt. Barrington) Where health food meets gourmet food, artfully and abundantly arranged: a large selection of cheeses and cold cuts, fish, honey, teas, yogurt, juices, fresh tofu, flours, grains, rices, soy and tamari sauces, and more. There's a wall-length case of frozen health foods as well as vitamins, mineral supplements, and natural cosmetics.

Sprout House (413-528-5200; 284 Main St., P.O. Box 1100, Gt. Barrington) Steve Meyerowitz, the Sproutman, has sprouting kits and books, indoor vegetable kits and organic seeds; via mail order and wholesale.

Place for Pasta

Pasta Prima (413-499-7478; 1020 South St., Rte. 7, Pittsfield, at Guido's; also 413-528-3755; 740 Main St., Rte. 7, Gt. Barrington, at Guido's) Fresh pasta made on the premises. Cut to order or purchased in sheets for cutting at home. Selection of other pastas of the dried variety, sauces, and Parmesan and Romano cheese for grating.

Sunflowers Natural Foods (413-243-1775; 42 Park St., Rte. 20, Lee) Organic and natural items include bread, coffee, fat-free snacks, and natural personal care items; products are available here that are wheat free, gluten free, sugar free. Vitamins, books, health video club.

Wild Oats Community Market (413-458-8060; Rte. 2, Colonial Shopping Center, Williamstown) Organic and local produce, whole foods, gourmet and specialty items, vitamins, natural cosmetics, along with food and health books and magazines. Members get discounts but the public is welcome; the offerings have broadened to appeal to a wider audience.

ICE CREAM

Berkshire-made ice cream, plus that of those two guys from Vermont, can be found in strategic locations throughout the county. Reliably delicious, Massachusetts' own Friendly's ice cream, in cones, containers, and sundaes, is also available at any of the many Friendly's restaurants.

Ben & Jerry's Ice Cream (413-448-2250; 179 South St., Rte. 7, Pittsfield) Vermont's famous ice cream in cones, cakes, sundaes, and containers; frozen yogurt. Worth standing in line for.

Berkshire Ice Cream (413-232-4111; 4 Albany Rd., W. Stockbridge) The county's own premium is sold in specialty shops. Those wishing to own part of the Jersey herd should give 'em a call.

Bev's Homemade Ice Cream (413-637-0371; 38 Housatonic St., Lenox. Also: 413-528-6645; 5 Railroad St., Gt. Barrington) Bev's is made daily on the premises, and comes in traditional to exotic flavors; ice cream sodas and sundaes, malteds, and egg creams, plus coffee and baked treats. Stop here for great sandwiches and soups, too.

King Kone (413-496-9485; 133 First St., Pittsfield) A popular window-service source of soft ice cream and other treats in downtown, opposite First Lutheran Church.

Lickety Split (413-458-1818; 69 Spring St., Williamstown) With Herrell's Famous Ice Cream from Northampton, Lickety Split is a great day or evening treat; hot soup in the winter.

Utter Delight (413-644-9100; 684 Main St., Rte. 7, Gt. Barrington) Featuring Berkshire Ice Cream and other brands.

Berkshire Food and Beverage Specialties

Nurtured by Berkshire soil, or created by Berkshire entrepreneurs, this select group of food and beverage specialties includes condiments and sauces; breads and other baked goods; sweets and sweeteners; and dairy products, spring water, and soft drinks. Some are world famous; all are locally treasured. There's no individual retail outlet for many of these products, but look for them at Guido's, Bartlett's, the Store at Five Corners, Berkshire Cupboard, and most other gourmet shops, farm and produce markets, and many supermarkets. In some cases, you can also contact the food entrepreneur for more information. Or consider giving — or receiving — a gift basket or box with a selection of these unique items, cleverly packaged by Gifts of the Berkshires (800-BERKCTG) through Berkshire Cottage, the Great Barrington kitchen and gourmet store.

Beverages

Berkshire Spring Water (413-229-2086, 800-244-3212; Norfolk Rd., Southfield) Bottled daily at the spring, it's sodium, bacteria, and additive free. Or try *Sand Springs Spring Water Co.* (413-458-3412; 160 Sand Springs Rd., Williamstown) The American Indians liked it; why not you? Have either delivered, or buy it in gallon jugs in supermarkets. *Gilly's Hot Vanilla* (413- 637-1515) was created by Lenox resident Joanne Deutch as a hot-chocolate alternative; just add hot water to the vanilla-flavored powder. And there's no caffeine. Buy it by the bag locally, or have a cup at many local eateries.

Bread, Baked Goods

Look for some local goods made locally but not sold retail, such as *Berkshire Mountain Bakery*. Its traditional sourdough breads should be sought out at area natural food stores. The peasant bread and the raisin bread are particular favorites; try their crisp biscotti, too. *Cedars of Lebanon* makes pita bread that's in area supermarkets and groceries. It is pure, simple, and delicious. *Nejaime's Lavasch* is deliciously addictive: a Mideast specialty, lavasch is a crusty crackerlike bread. Nejaime's is made with a variety of flavorings, all good.

Condiments, Sauces

Bear Meadow Farm (413-663-9241) products from Florida, Massachusetts, include preserves, mustards, vinegars, chutneys, apple ketchup.

Dairy Products

Monterey chèvre is made from the milk of goats at *Rawson Brook Farm* (413-528-2138; P.O. Box 426, New Marlboro Rd., Monterey) and from acid starter from France. It's sold deliciously plain, or flavored with chives and garlic, or with a particularly tasty combination of wild thyme and olive oil. It is sold younger than imported chèvre and has a milder, more delicate flavor. Milk (with the cream on top) and light or heavy cream from **High Lawn Farm** (413-243-0672; high lawn@berkshire.net) is available at many grocery and convenience stores or can still be delivered to the door. The Jersey cows on the farm on Lenox Road in Lee are the source.

Afternoon milking time for High Lawn's Jersey Cows.

Jonathan Sternfield

Desserts, Sweets, Sweeteners

Baldwin's Extracts (413-232-7785; Depot St., W. Stockbridge) offers "since 1888, the best in vanilla." This manufacturer of flavoring extracts and maple table syrup uses only the best — the Bourbon vanilla bean from Madagascar — for their pure vanilla extract. It's made in a copper percolator (the "still") and aged in 100-year-old oak barrels, which can be seen in the small and fascinating retail outlet in a former carriage shop. Inhale essence of vanilla and admire the ranks of extract bottles — including lemon, orange, mint, and more — on the old-fashioned counter. Also available is **Baldwin's Table Syrup**, a blend of maple and cane sugar syrup from a recipe created in the 1920s.

Catherine's Chocolates (413-528-2510; Stockbridge Rd., Rte. 7, Gt. Barrington) are made on the premises from a century-old family recipe. These smooth and flavorful concoctions include chocolate truffles, a variety of hand-dipped candies, fudges, brittles, and barks. The nonpareils are, in fact, unequaled. By the piece, the pound, or in a boxed gift assortment. **David Rawson's honey** from Richmond is pretty close to nectar for the gods, who get it in 1-lb. jars at Bartlett's.

And . . .

The Delftree Corporation (413-664-4907; 234 Union St., N. Adams,) grows shiitake mushrooms on hardwood sawdust in a 19th-century textile mill building in North Adams. Shipped all over the world, they are available here.

MEAT, FISH, POULTRY

Burgner's Farm Products (413-445-4704; Dalton Division Rd., Pittsfield) Burgner's raises and sells turkeys and chickens; order them uncooked, roasted, or stuffed and roasted, in all sizes. Burgner's turkey pot pies are local favorites. The farm store also carries eggs, produce, and store-made bakery items and fresh homemade potato salad and coleslaw.

Masse's Seafood (413-499-3474; 1020 South St., Pittsfield, at Guido's) A variety of fresh and frozen former denizens of the sea.

Mazzeo's Meat Center Meat Concessions at Guido's Gt. Barrington (413-528-4488; 760 S. Main St., Rte. 7) and Pittsfield (413-442-2222; 1020 South St., Rte. 7).

Otis Poultry Farm (413-269-4438; Rte. 8, Otis) "Custom laid eggs" says the sign; eggs and chickens, geese, ducks, and capons, too. Their excellent frozen chicken and turkey pies are a staple of well-stocked Berkshire freezers. Various homemade goodies join sheepskin gloves and slippers and so forth in the country store.

Additional options for meat and fish include *Harry's Supermarket* (413-442-9084; 290 Wahconah St., Pittsfield) and (413-443-7247; 37 Elm St., Pittsfield), and *Vic's Seafood* at the Lee Farmer's Market, Fri. 12-6. *Other Brother Darryl's* (413-269-4235, 800-6FLOPPIN; Rte. 8, Otis) and *Other Brother Darryl's Too* (413-528-8088; 760 S. Main St., Rte. 7, Gt. Barrington, at Guido's) offer wholesale seafood to retail customers, and promise "still-floppin'" freshness.

WINE, BEER, LIQUOR

L iquor stores in Massachusetts are closed Sundays, except those within 10 miles of the Vermont or New Hampshire borders. In addition, at the discretion of individual towns liquor stores may be open Sundays between Thanksgiving and Christmas.

Domaney's Discount Liquors (413-528-0024; 66 Main St., Rte. 7, Gt. Barrington)

Gorham & Norton (413-528-0900; 278 Main St., Rte. 7, Gt. Barrington) Also deli and gourmet specialties.

Liquor Mart (413-663-3910; State Rd., Adams)

Liquors Inc. (413-443-4466; 485 Dalton Ave., Pittsfield) The biggest and best for discount wine, beer, and spirits.

Locke, Stock & Barrel (413-528-0800; Stockbridge Rd., Rte. 7, Gt. Barrington) A great wine selection.

Nejaime's Wine & Liquor (413-448-2274; 598 Pittsfield-Lenox Rd., Rte. 7), **Nejaime's Stockbridge Wine Cellar** (413-298-3454; Elm St.), and **Lenox Wine Cellar and Cheese Shop** (413-637-2221; 60 Main St., in the Village Center) In addition to wines, beers, and spirits, they offer gourmet and deli items, and helpful, knowledgeable assistance.

Pizza

Pizza cravings will be easily satisfied anywhere throughout Berkshire County, but all pizzas are not created equal. Top choices include the following:

Babalouie's Sour Dough Pizza Co. (413-528-8100; 286 Main St., Gt. Barrington) offers Italian-style pizzas (thin-crust, organic sourdough, or wheat-free crusts), cooked in a wood-fired oven with super fresh toppings and a full menu, too. *Manhattan Pizza Company* (413-528-2550; 490 Main St., Rte. 7, Gt. Barrington) Pizzas here are big, flat, oozing, and delicious. They reheat well, are available by the slice, and there is delivery service. *The East Side Cafe* (413-447-9405; 278 Newell St., Pittsfield), essentially a bar, makes pizza only on Thurs.–Sun. evenings from 5pm on; it's small, thin, crisp, and tasty. The unbeatable taste of a wood-fired brick-oven pizza is somewhere *Over the Rainbow* (413-445-6836; 109 First St., Pittsfield). Generous toppings and imaginative combinations include chicken pesto, spinach and broccoli, or the primavera (eggplant, black olives, broccoli, and more). Take out or eat in and watch the flames in the oven. *Hot Tomatoes* (413-458-2722; 100 Water St., Rte. 43, Williamstown) may be the best in town for those who prefer the thinner crust, while *Michael's Restaurant and Pizzeria* (413-458-2114; State Rd., Williamstown) is the dependable traditional; Michael's also has a heated truck for large orders.

Queensborough Spirits (413-232-8522; Main St., W. Stockbridge) Beer, liquor, and wine.

South Egremont Spirit Shoppe (413-528-1490; Rte. 23) "The wine shop of the Berkshires." Also a good selection of cigars.

Spirit Shop & Deli Station (413-458-3704; 280 Cole Ave., Williamstown) Beer, liquor, wine, and a deli.

Trotta's Discount Liquors (529-3490; Rtes. 23 & 7, Gt. Barrington) Beer, liquor, wine, and fine cigars.

Val's Pipe & Package Store (413-743-0962; 5 Columbia St., Adams) Beer, liquor, wine, groceries, milk, and lottery tickets.

West's Package & Variety Stores (413-663-6081; 367 State Rd., N. Adams) and West's Wines & Spirits (513-458-5948; 52 Spring St., Williamstown) Bob West is an authority on wine.

CHAPTER FIVE
What to See, What to Do
ARTS & PLEASURES

Judith Monachina

The Paul Taylor II company, part of Jacob Pillow's "Inside/Out" series, draws an overflow crowd on a rain-threatened night. In good weather, this series is held outdoors prior to mainstage productions.

To glorify God's grandeur by gracefully combining art and nature was the goal of the Stockbridge Laurel Hill Society, as expressed in 1853. Thinking such as this joined a new appreciation of the natural setting with a well-developed Berkshire cultural awareness that had roots in Colonial times when the earliest schools, churches, and newspapers were the centers of cultural activity. By the early 19th century, artists came to Berkshire to absorb the beauty and to teach its appreciation. By midcentury the tradition of a Berkshire cultural bounty had taken hold.

The county's artistic abundance is out of proportion to its size and population. In music, dance, theater, and other art forms, Berkshire has long had a cultural calendar of astonishing excellence and variety — especially for a mountainous area once thought of as remote. There are good reasons for this legacy. Summers in the crowded eastern cities were not only unpleasant but frequently unhealthy. Improvements in transportation opened this area, while other scenic spots some might now find more dramatic were still inaccessible. By the mid-1800s a few families of taste, talent, and money were setting the tone of cultural sophistication still found here today.

Of the local intelligentsia that developed around Stockbridge and Lenox in the early 19th century no single family was more dynamic than the convivial and civic-minded Sedgwicks of Stockbridge. Novelist Catherine Sedgwick shares honors with poet William Cullen Bryant as Berkshire's — and America's — first native-born published writers in their fields. The Sedgwick house and family still grace Stockbridge today.

Among writers, Herman Melville and Nathaniel Hawthorne cross-fertilized their fiction in Berkshire in the 1850s, along with the popular Oliver Wendell Holmes, the doctor/poet who returned to his roots by summering in Pittsfield. Henry David Thoreau beheld a transcendental technicolor sunrise on the summit of Mount Greylock. Edith Wharton moved here, creating an opulent European lifestyle while she skewered such a lifestyle in her fiction. The list of famous artistic residents is lengthy and impressive. Our bibliography (in Chapter Nine, *Information*) cites several engaging books that tell the story.

When the Berkshires became the "inland Newport" during the late 19th-century Gilded Age, culture rode into Berkshire along with big money: architectural indulgences, furnishings, musical instruments and people to play them, paintings, chefs with their foreign cuisines, and landscape gardeners. We are the beneficiaries of much inherited culture. Many of the family estates here have become cultural centers, such as Tanglewood, for music, and The Mount, for literature. And yet, as if to remind us that beauty need not be ornate or expensive, the Shaker Village at Hancock is also a Berkshire cultural legacy of remarkable value and vitality.

Furthermore, Berkshire families have been patrons of the art and the landscape. The Crane family of the Crane Paper Company of Dalton started the Berkshire Museum, Francine and Sterling Clark created the Art Institute in Williamstown, and the Tappan family gave Tanglewood to the Boston Symphony Orchestra. We owe them our thanks.

Many of the artists drawn to the Berkshires have lived here seasonally, like Wharton, or year-round, like Norman Rockwell. Thousands more have come just to perform or exhibit. Berkshire has left its mark on each. When asked what the Berkshires and Tanglewood mean to him, Seiji Ozawa, music director of the Boston Symphony Orchestra, replied: "Tanglewood has an absolutely special connotation for me. It was the first place I ever saw in America, since I came to Tanglewood as a student in 1960 at the invitation of Charles Munch. For me and the orchestra, Tanglewood represents an opportunity to appreciate both the beauty of the Berkshires, and of the music we make here."

Art combines with nature, from the fine woodwork in colonist John Ashley's study at Ashley Falls to the nation's four founding documents in Williams College's Chapin Library; from dioramas and Egyptian mummies at the Berkshire

Museum in Pittsfield to beautiful flowers and shrubs at the Berkshire Botanical Garden in Stockbridge. In performance halls, museums, libraries, theaters, nightclubs, and historic homes, Berkshire is rich in art and the pleasures it brings.

The following descriptions provide many ideas of where to go and what to do in Berkshire, but they cannot say what's currently playing or showing. Tanglewood issues its summer schedule around March 15; other arts organizations soon follow. For the larger seasonal schedules, such Jacob's Pillow, the museums, theaters, and other concert series, it's best to write or call for information. We provide addresses. That information helps to customize a personal Berkshire festival. Sold-out performances are not uncommon. Area newspapers provide information on cultural events as they happen. Especially comprehensive is the *Berkshire Eagle's* Thursday magazine supplement, "Berkshires Week."

ARCHITECTURE

The Congregational Church, Lee.

Judith Monachina

Those who enjoy roaming through New England in search of handsome buildings will find Berkshire County an inexhaustible delight. They will find styles popular in North America from Colonial times to the present. Few counties anywhere can claim this much architectural variety.

Berkshire is justly famous for the scores of mansions built during the opulent Gilded Age. Under "Historic Homes" in this chapter, in the chapters called *Restaurants* and *Lodging*, and elsewhere in this book, we describe several of the best surviving examples of these great "cottages," as they were called. Yet the saga of the sumptuous cottages isn't half the Berkshire building history.

Humbler examples include one-room schoolhouses or steepled churches, icons of America's simpler past. Still performing as designed in some Berkshire towns, adapted to alternative uses in others, these white clapboard structures are often handsome and always charming. Some of the best are the ones in Alford, Lenox, Lee, Washington, and Lanesborough (a stone structure, ca. 1800).

Berkshire villages seem architectural set pieces, so artfully coordinated are their building styles and locations. The villages of Alford, New Marlborough, Stockbridge, and Williamstown have this look. Conspicuously absent is neon and plastic commercial clutter. Feelings of space and grace predominate. Yet also in each town arises the clear sense of the heart of a community where religion (churches), education (schoolhouses), government (town hall), domestic life (private homes), and the honor due the dead (cemeteries) all naturally fit together. People who live in cities or suburbs will find the centralization of Berkshire villages intriguing as well as architecturally beautiful. New Marlborough bears all of this out with its archetypal village green, surrounded in part by the Colonial-style *Old Inn on the Green* (1760), a fine Federal-style house (1824), and a Greek Revival–style *Congregational Church* (1839).

Farms have formed the Berkshire landscape. Almost any country road leads past splendid examples of old farmhouses, with numerous outbuildings. Some of the barns date to times earlier than the homes. Good rides for farm viewing include Routes 57 (New Marlborough), 41 (south from South Egremont or north from West Stockbridge), and 7 (north from Lanesborough). Dramatic Tudor-style barns from the Gilded Age are still in use at High Lawn Farm (on Summer St. off Rte. 7, Lee), but the most famous barn in Berkshire is the round stone barn at *Hancock Shaker Village*, described under "Museums" in this chapter.

South County towns have many impressive buildings, among them several interesting industrial sites. Rising above them all is Fox River Paper's *Rising Paper Mill* building (ca. 1875; Rte. 183, Housatonic), with its handsome mansard slate roof. A similar mansard slate roof style is pushed to artful extremes on campus buildings at *Simon's Rock College of Bard* (Alford Rd., Gt. Barrington).

Crowning its *Congregational Church* the village of Lee boasts of having the tallest wood-framed steeple in the country. In South Lee (Rte. 102) the Federal-period building of the *Historic Merrell Inn* is exquisitely maintained by the Society for the Preservation of New England Antiquities.

Sheffield, architecturally lovely and filled with antique shops, appropriately prided itself on having preserved the *oldest covered bridge in Massachusetts* (1837) until it burned in 1994. The Massachusetts Highway Department has recently erected a duplicate. Otis, a Berkshire hilltown, is graced with *St. Paul's Church* (1829), a fine example of the Gothic Revival style.

Stockbridge dazzles. Architect Stanford White's turn-of-the-century work appears in impressive diversity here: a casino (now the *Berkshire Theatre Festival*, at Rte. 102 and Yale Hill Rd.), a mansion (*Naumkeag*, on Prospect Hill

Rd.), a former railroad station on Rte. 7 south of the village, and a church (*St. Paul's Episcopal*, in the center of town). Two other Stockbridge churches well worth a look are the red-brick *Congregational Church* (Main St., next to Town Hall); and the chapel at the *Marian Fathers Seminary* (on Eden Hill, off Prospect Hill Rd.). Whereas the interior of the Congregational Church has a powerful beauty in its plainness, the Marian Fathers' chapel is beautiful for its finely crafted stone, woodwork, painting, and fabrics — much of it done by transplanted European artists. We describe the *Mission House*, a Colonial historic home, later in this chapter.

Three outlying sites in Stockbridge are worth a drive. The district originally called Curtisville, now known as Interlaken (Rte. 183, north of Rte. 102), boasts several strikingly pretty 18th- and 19th-century homes and a remarkable former tavern-inn, as well as *Citizens Hall* with its Victorian-period Second Empire–style exterior details. Another building of note in rural Stockbridge is at Tanglewood's Lion's Gate (Hawthorne St., off Rte. 183), where the replica of Nathaniel Hawthorne's *Little Red House* overlooks Stockbridge Bowl and the distant mountains. The estate known as *Linwood* has opened to the public as the site of the *Norman Rockwell Museum*, a Robert A. M. Stern–designed New England town hall upscale. Charles E. Butler's unpolished marble cottage, *Linwood* (1859), remains the architectural highlight of this delightful Berkshire hilltop.

Finally, in South County, a ride out on the Tyringham Rd. (off Rte. 102, south of Lee) and then upland on Jerusalem Rd. will lead to *Jerusalem,* the remnants of a Shaker settlement dating from 1792. Five buildings remain, none open. Jerusalem Rd. begins in tiny Tyringham Village. Along the Tyringham Valley Rd. is the *Gingerbread House*, a thatched-roof English cottage built by sculptor Henry Hudson Kitson in the late 1800s and known presently as *Santarella*; see "Galleries" in this chapter.

The simplicity of Shaker design draws thousands each year to the Hancock Shaker Village.

Judith Monachina

<u>*Central County*</u> abounds with notable architecture. In Dalton, a ride along Main St. (Rte. 9) provides views of the *Crane Paper Mills* (the Old Stone Mill, dating to 1844, is open as a museum in season) and several Crane family estates. In addition to other fine papers, Crane manufactures U.S. currency paper in these venerable mills. In 1816, Zenas Crane, company founder, built a dignified Federal-style house that still stands. There are also three 19th-century Richardsonian Romanesque churches on Main St. in Dalton proper.

In the hilltown of Hinsdale on Rte. 8 are some architectural surprises, vestiges of more prosperous, populous times when various mills were alive and well in the Berkshire highlands. The oldest (1798) Federal-style church in Berkshire is here. A Greek Revival town hall was built in 1848. The public library is in the high Gothic style, designed in 1868 by architect Leopold Eidlitz, who did St. George's Church in New York City and the New York State Capitol in Albany.

The only stone early Gothic Revival church in the county is *St. Luke's Chapel*, in Lanesborough (on Rte. 7). Like many other buildings cited in this book, St. Luke's is on the National Register of Historic Places.

Equal to any other village in Berkshire as an impressive architectural set piece is stately Lenox, especially the historic center of the village including the *Lenox Academy* (Federal style, 1803); the irresistibly photogenic *Church on the Hill* (1805); and the *Lenox Library* (1815; see "Libraries" in this chapter). All three buildings are on Main St. (Rte. 7A). The *Curtis Hotel*, dominating the center of town, is now restored and converted to an apartment complex. From the Gilded Age to recent times, the Curtis was one of Berkshire's most fashionable addresses for travelers. Not far from Lenox village, on Rte. 20 heading toward Lee, is the *Cranwell*, once a Jesuit-run school, now a resort, golf club, and condominium complex.

Pittsfield's architectural record is distinguished although problematic. Preservation and restoration nowadays receive good attention, as a walk

By way of contrast, several Berkshire towns host a large number of Victorians.

Judith Monachina

around Park Square reveals. Several new buildings integrate quite well, with the ornate elegance of the old Venetian Gothic Athenaeum, with the two churches, with the bank buildings, and with the courthouse — all dating from the 19th century.

The former *Berkshire Eagle* newspaper building (on Eagle St., off North St.) is a fine example of the Art Deco style, set on a triangle like a miniature of Chicago's Flatiron Building. Another important business structure in Pittsfield is the General Electric Plastics House, a handsome and interesting experimental and display house in the Plastics Division's new world headquarters complex. Address? "Plastics Avenue," of course (between Merrill Rd. and Dalton Ave.).

North County provides stark contrasts in architecture and variety in the stories buildings tell about social history. The cities of Adams and North Adams owe their expansion to industrial times that are past. Revitalization proceeds, the most spectacular being the conversion of the idle Sprague Electric plant (formerly textile mills) into a mammoth museum of contemporary art (visual and performing), *Mass MoCA*. Although urban renewal hit the downtowns unkindly, Adams and North Adams have recently beautified their main streets. In North Adams, *Western Heritage Gateway State Park* celebrates a 19th-century architectural and engineering wonder, the *Hoosac Tunnel*. (See "Museums" in this chapter.) The spires of North Adams's many churches are a pretty sight when one descends into the city from the west on Rte. 2. In Adams, suffragettes will want to pass the *Susan B. Anthony Birthplace* (1814; a private home soon to be open near the corner of East Rd. and East St.); and the *Quaker Meeting House* (1782; near the end of Friends St.), another National Register of Historic Places building.

Williamstown contains homes from Colonial to contemporary, a college that has been adding buildings nearly since the country began, quaint shops, and

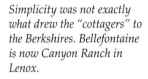

Simplicity was not exactly what drew the "cottagers" to the Berkshires. Bellefontaine is now Canyon Ranch in Lenox.

two masterfully designed art museums (the *Clark Art Institute* and the *Williams College Museum of Art,* both described under "Museums"). *West College* (1790), *Griffin Hall* (1828), the oldest (1838) extant college observatory in the United States, and the 1802 *President's House* at Williams are alone worth touring the campus (via a large map in front of the main administration building, Hopkins Hall, or pick up brochure maps at the Information Booth). The much-photographed *First Congregational Church* (1869) is a replica of a Colonial one that later burned in Old Lyme, Conn. The *Williamstown Public Library,* which houses the local history museum, faces the *1753 House,* built with authentic methods and materials for the town's bicentennial, on Field Park.

In Berkshire, a proud history still stands.

ARTS CLASSES

The world is turning interactive. Art in Berkshire is part of the trend. Not content with simply looking at fine art and craft work in the multitude of galleries and museums in the county, many residents and visitors want to create art as well. Opportunities grow apace. The Berkshire Museum, the Norman Rockwell Museum, and the YMCAs (call for their schedules) and several other local institutions have made education the mainspring of their business.

BERKSHIRE CENTER FOR CONTEMPORARY GLASS
413-232-4666.
6 Harris St., P.O. Box 377, W. Stockbridge, MA 01266.

Located just off Main St. opposite Trúc and La Bruschetta restaurants, BCCG is a gallery, a glassblowing studio, and a school for glassblowers from beginner through accomplished. Founded and run by artist/sculptors Edward and Judy Bates Merritt, it incorporates the *All Fired Up* gallery, offering fine glass and other art craft work by local professionals. The glassblowing studio is available to qualified glassblowers and their students. Best of all, the Merritts offer an array of well-structured glassblowing workshops and classes for beginners and intermediates. Students are offered a range from two-hour Saturday Workshops to a Glassblowing Getaway Weekend to a three-week course to a full beginner course.

INTERLAKEN SCHOOL OF ART
413-298-5252.
makeart@bcn.net.
13 Willard Hill Rd., P.O. Box 1400, Stockbridge, MA 01262.

Founded in 1992 by eminent handweaver and visionary Sam Kasten, Interlaken has developed into a full-scale, year-round school of arts. Located in historic Citizens Hall, on Hill Rd. just off Rte. 183 via Trask Lane, in Interlaken Village, it has something for everyone with artistic inclinations. With single classes, semester courses, half-day to weekend workshops, and lectures in painting, drawing, ceramics, sculpture, metal, jewelry, and textiles of several sorts, it offers programs for children and adults. Faculty members are drawn from the local artistic community and also include visiting teachers and lecturers. On "Lights & Socks" day in December, faculty art can be previewed for sale; continental breakfast and champagne are served and discounts are offered for enrollment in winter programs.

CINEMA

Cineasts should keep their eyes open for the *Williamstown Film Festival,* held in a preliminary way in June 1999. If the audience is there, the organizers have the will to make Berkshire's own Sundance, with performances in several North County theaters. Call 413-458-2700.

IMAGES CINEMA
413-458-5612.
www.imagescinema.org
50 Spring St., P.O. Box 283,
   Williamstown, MA
   01267.

North County's most dynamic movie house is flying high. Threatened by increasing rent and decreasing revenue, Images pulled itself together in the summer of 1989, with the help of Williamstown resident and actor Christopher Reeve. Then, in 1998, when its future was again uncertain, a small group of local residents organized a nonprofit organization to support the theater. So Images lives on in refurbished modernity, as the only year-round, single-screen, independent nonprofit house in the county. Eclectic, exciting films — the best from camp to classic. There are memberships, a printed film-schedule (mailed and e-mailed), and special programs — notably a breakfast club that meets once a month to view and discuss an important film.

LITTLE CINEMA
413-443-7171.
www.berkshiremuseum.org
39 South St., Pittsfield, MA
   01201.

This is *the* great little film festival in Berkshire, featuring state-of-the-art projection and sound. Films are shown through the summer, with special viewings throughout the year. Fine American and foreign films, downstairs in the Berkshire Museum.

THE MAHAIWE
413-528-0100.
14 Castle St., Gt.
   Barrington, MA 01230.

Reminiscent of how movie palaces used to look, the Mahaiwe's ornate elegance survives. Today the spruced-up theater (now operated by Hoyts) hosts special live concerts and occasional children's weekend movie matinees between conventional first-run movie offerings. More than the sum of its magnificent movies, the Mahaiwe is a local treasure.

OTHER CINEMA

South County

Simon's Rock College of Bard (413-528-7335; www.simons-rock.edu; 84 Alford Rd., Gt. Barrington) Occasional classics and fun films, open to the public.

Triplex Cinema (413-528-8885 info; 413-528-9841 office; fax 413-528-8889; www.thetriplex.com; 70 Railroad St., Gt. Barrington; Mail: P.O. Box 508, S. Egremont, MA 01258) An art venue as well as cinema with surround-sound.

Central County

Hoyts Berkshire Cinema 10 (413-499-2558; Berkshire Mall, Rte. 8 and Old State Rd., Lanesborough) Dolby stereo, action, adventure, drama, comedy, popcorn.

Pittsfield Cinema Center (413-443-9639; Rte. 20, W. Housatonic St., Pittsfield) Unlimited free parking and a choice of eleven (that's 11), different commercial flicks nightly.

North County

Hoyts North Adams Cinemas (413-663-5873; Rte. 8, Curran Hwy., N. Adams) North County's multiplex, with six screens.

Outside the County

Crandell Theatre (518-392-3331; Main St., Chatham, NY) One screen in a pleasant old-fashioned movie house, showing first-run films.

Movie House (518-789-3408; Main St., Millerton, NY) The best first-run films, three screens, espresso, and other refinements.

DANCE

JACOB'S PILLOW DANCE FESTIVAL
Box office 413-243-0745 (winter 413-637-1322). www.jacobspillow.org. P.O. Box 287, Lee, MA 01238.
Off Rte. 20, in Becket, 8 mi. E. of Lee.
Season: Summer, Tues.–Sun.
Tickets: $16–$50
Gift shop.

America's first and oldest summer dance festival, Jacob's Pillow keeps step with the times, presenting the best in classical, modern, postmodern, jazz, and ethnic dance. Its schedule of offerings creates the Who's Who of contemporary dance, featuring over the years Merce Cunningham, Dame Margot Fonteyn, Peter Martins, Alicia Markova, Twyla Tharp, Alexander Gudunov, Martha Graham, Paul Taylor, Alvin Ailey, Phildanceco, the Pilobolus troupe, Jane Comfort and Co., among many others.

Dancers in Studio One at Jacob's Pillow.

Gemma Comas, courtesy Jacob's Pillow
Dance Festival

High on a hillside in Becket is the farm that famed dancer Ted Shawn bought after successfully touring with his wife, Ruth St. Denis, and the Denishawn troupe in the 1920s. Here Shawn worked to establish dance as a legitimate profession for men, founding a world-class dance performance center and a school for dance. The school continues to flourish along with the festival, honoring its founder's heartfelt philosophy that the best dancers in the world make the most inspirational dance instructors. In addition to performing here, some of the Pillow's visiting dance luminaries stay on to teach masterclasses in the compound's rustic studios.

A visit is more memorable for those who drive to the Pillow early to stroll among those studios where works are in progress, dancers are in development. Through a window lithe figures create choreography. Down at the Pillow's natural outdoor theater, Inside/Out, avant-garde and experimental pieces are rehearsed and performed. And after savoring that dance hors d'oeuvre, strollers might wish to sup at the Pillow. Happily, here too there are several lovely options: Pillow Café, feasting under a brightly colored tent; or the picnic area, possibly glimpsing a dancer who will be performing later in the Ted Shawn Theatre. The Pillow's Studio/Theatre, seating 210, adds a separate 10-week schedule of new and emerging offbeat companies, complementing the Ted Shawn Theatre's exciting dance schedule.

ALBANY BERKSHIRE BALLET
413-445-5382.
www.berkshireballet.org.
51 North St., Pittsfield, MA 01201.
Season: Intermittently year-round.

New York Times dance critic Jennifer Dunning put it positively in her review: "Berkshire Ballet can be counted on for impressively clear classical technique and fresh performing." Said the influential *Dance Magazine*: "Berkshire Ballet displays solid training, a distinctly soft, lyrical style, and a wide choreographic range. In short, it is a company with integrity and taste."

Tickets: $15–$30; Discounts for seniors, children, groups.

The Albany Berkshire Ballet's summer season (July and August) takes place at Berkshire Community College's Robert Boland Theater, in the Koussevitzky Arts Center. Performances in other seasons are also given at the Consolati Art Center, at the Palace Theater in Albany, and at Symphony Hall in Springfield. Lavish productions of *Cinderella* and *Giselle* have highlighted past seasons. Fall and winter performances are capped with the traditional *Nutcracker*, staged at BCC and throughout New England in November and December.

OLGA DUNN DANCE CO., INC.
413-528-9674.
321 Main St., P.O. Box 157, Gt. Barrington, MA 01230.
Season: Year-round.
Tickets: $7–$25.

Since its founding in 1977, the Olga Dunn Dance Company has enjoyed such success that it spawned the Junior Company and the Olga Dunn Dance Ensemble. Performing a free mix of exuberant, witty jazz, modern, swing, and ballet, frequently with live musicians, the company has also toured area schools, exposing children to the creativity of dance and the excitement of movement. Annual performances at its own studio, at the Berkshire Museum, and at other theaters in the tristate area are highlights of the dance year. As Marge Champion, famed dancer and local Berkshire resident, put it: "The Olga Dunn Dance Company has become the radiating center of our experience in appreciating and participating in the art of dance."

OTHER DANCE

With Jacob's Pillow bringing the world's best dancers to the Berkshires, it's not surprising that quality dance troupes would spring up here and there throughout the county.

In **South County**, many of the most innovative performances take place at Simon's Rock's **Arts Center Theater**, known as "the ARC" — the school's barn-theater on Alford Rd. Simon's Rock (413-528-0771) has recently been offering two student-faculty dance programs during the school year, one in December, the other in May. These feature original music and choreography by members of the school's dance program. *Laurie McLeod* is a dancer and independent choreographer who, with her company, *Victory Girl Productions* (413-298-3006; www.victorygirl.com; P.O. Box 141, Stockbridge, MA 01262), presents innovative works at such places as Jacob's Pillow's Inside/Out Stage and Simon's Rock. Mass MoCA chose her as its first performing artist-in-residence, and her "Twelve Incantations" drew rave reviews and full houses. Modern dancer and choreographer *Dawn Lane* (413-637-0230; 326 Old Stockbridge Rd., Lenox, MA 01240) teaches for Jacob's Pillow, and is well known for her involvement with the community, particularly through her own "Round Pegs,

Square Whole Project." She performs at the Pillow, Simon's Rock, and throughout the county, including schools and nursing homes where her concerts are free. The *Barrington Ballet* (413-528-4963) gives classes and occasional performances. Eurhythmy performances are sometimes given by the *Rudolf Steiner School* (413-528-4015) on West Plain Rd. There is also a flourishing country and contra dance network in the Berkshires. Check the newspapers and bulletin boards for listings.

In *Central County*, *Susan Dibble* (413-637-3353; www.shakespeare.org) is resident choreographer for Shakespeare & Company. In addition to creating dances for the plays, she leads a company of eight members in presenting one or two weekends of dance at the Stable Theater at The Mount, Shakespeare & Company's present home.

In *North County*, the *Williams College Dance Department* (413-597-2410) sponsors an ongoing, energetic series with student and faculty choreography, and visiting notables. Chen & Dancers, a Chinese company, has been the artist-in-residence; the Chuck Davis African Dance Collective has also been seen and heard in Williamstown. Exciting Kusika, the college's own African dance company, which accompanies itself with drumming, often performs with the spirited Zambezi Marimba Band, usually inviting the audience to join in.

GALLERIES

Since the arrival in Berkshire of nationally recognized turn-of-the-last-century sculptors Daniel Chester French (who sculpted the statue for the Lincoln Memorial) and Sir Henry Hudson Kitson (who did the *Minute Man* at Lexington), the county has been home to an increasing number of talented visual artists.

Much of the art on display in local galleries reflects the uplifting reality of the Berkshire landscape. Many artists focus on the undulating hills and their ever-changing light. Local galleries also show other themes and styles as well, from traditional still-life sketches to intriguing mixed media works. Some galleries show Berkshire artists exclusively; others bring in works from artists the world over. Some are only regularly open in warm weather so, unless you're rambling, it's wise to call ahead.

South County

SOUTH EGREMONT

Moran-Dervan Gallery [formerly Barbara Moran Gallery] (413-528-0749; Main St.) All aspects of realism in painting; also, decorative arts — furniture and things for the home. Open weekends during summer and fall. Phone in NYC: 212-744-8945.

GREAT BARRINGTON

Anthony Nordoff Gallery (413-528-6063; 11 Railroad St., 2nd floor) The gallery offers the work of contemporary Berkshire artists and art classes.

Asian Arts (413-528-5091, 199 Stockbridge Rd., Rte. 7) Imported Asian furniture and art.

Berkshire Art Gallery (413-528-2690; Jenifer House Commons, Stockbridge Rd., Rte. 7) 19th-century and current Berkshire paintings; some sculpture.

Berkshire Dreams Gallery (413-528-9884; 177 Main St.) A small space containing fine art, furniture, and crafts. Thurs–Mon.

Birdhouse (413-528-0984; 87 Railroad St.) Contemporary American folk art and crafts. Thurs.–Mon. 10–6.

Clifford Roberts Handwovens (413-528-9789 or 877-299-6836; 70 Railroad St., P.O. Box 657) A fiber arts gallery of luxurious accessories for the home and body, masterfully hand-woven. Throws, blankets, wall installations, scarves, and more. Roberts' stunning work incorporates earthy hues, exquisite detail, texture and the effects of color. Winter: Fri.–Sat., 11–7; longer hours in season.

Geoffrey Young Gallery (413-528-6210; 40 Railroad St., 2nd floor) Contemporary Berkshire fine artists; changing exhibitions.

Habatat Galleries (413-528-9123, winter 561-241-4544; www.habatatgalleries.com; 117 State Rd.) The oldest gallery in the US to carry contemporary glass work, one of four locations. Shows the finest national and international artists working in the medium. Changing exhibitions. Seasonal at this location.

Kaolin & Co. Pottery (413-528-1531; 80 Rte. 71, near Gt. Barrington airport) Wheel-thrown and handbuilt ceramics, including sculptures of animals. Elegant home furnishings to whimsical conversation pieces. a richly colored palette; also specializing in black and white.

Mill River Studio (413-528-9433; 8 Railroad St.) Posters, hand-colored engravings, historic maps, and custom framing.

Simon's Rock of Bard College (413-528-0771; 84 Alford Rd.) Changing exhibits at various venues on campus.

HOUSATONIC

Front Street Gallery (413-274-6607; 129 Front St.) Co-op space is open on weekends and has the space to show large paintings.

S*A*S Gallery (413-274-0175, 1100 Main St., P.O. Box 519) Fine art, photography, some sculpture. Weekends and by appointment.

Tokonoma Gallery Framing Studio (413-274-1166, 401 Park St.) Contemporary arts and crafts, much of it by area artists and artisans. Also hand-built furniture, pottery, jewelry, accessories, framed original Edward Curtis American Indian photographs, sculpture, and much more. Changing fine art shows, too.

LEE

Warehouse Gallery – Council for Creative Projects (413-243-8030; www. ccpexhibits.org; 17 Main St.) Gallery for nonprofit museum service organization. Range of 20th-century intercultural work. Changing fine art shows, previews of museum exhibits, lectures, and performance pieces.

MONTEREY

Hayloft Art Studio (413-528-1806; Rte. 23, 4 mi. E. of Gt. Barrington) Berkshire prints and watercolors, including popular townscapes, by local artist Leonard Weber.

NEW MARLBOROUGH

Gedney Farm (413-229-3131; www.oldinn.com; Rte. 57) Gallery in the beautifully restored barn of an 18th-century inn. Open on an exhibit basis.

SHEFFIELD

Ann Shanks Photography (413-229-7766; 50 N. Undermountain Rd., Rte. 41) Great classic photographs. Weekends and by appointment.
Butler Sculpture Park (413-229-8924; 481 Shunpike Rd.) Open daily May–October and winter by appointment, the primary attraction is the outdoor exhibit of Robert Butler's welded sculpture — although smaller pieces are exhibited in his studio. New this year: an 18-acre section for monumental sculpture.
Fellerman & Raabe Glassworks (413-229-8533; www.fellerman-raabeglass. com; 534 S. Main St.) Glass artists Steve Fellerman and Claire Raabe have operated this working studio for ten years. They exhibit blown, sculpted, and cameo-carved glass of their own creation as well as that of 24 other fine artists throughout the U.S. The imagery includes cultural and primitive motifs, classical, fanciful flowers, sculpted figurative work, and art nouveau. Jewelry is also on display.
Loring Gallery (413-229-0110, winter 413-528-1242; Rte. 7, diagonal from Bradford's auction house) Fine art, sculpture, and turn-of-the-last-century posters. Open May till fall.

SOUTH LEE

House of Earth Studio (413-243-1575; Rte. 102 east of town center; P.O. Box 145, S. Lee, MA 01260) Contemporary oil, acrylic, and watercolor landscapes in a rammed-earth studio.

STOCKBRIDGE

Dolphin Studio (413-298-3735, 11 West Main St.) Creations by the ffrench family, including ceramics, collages, jewelry.

Holsten Galleries of Stockbridge (413-298-3044, www.holstengalleries.com; 3 Elm St.) Leading contemporary glass artists. Daily 10:30–5.

Image Gallery (413-298-5500; Main St., P.O. Box 111, Stockbridge, MA 01262) Modern arts (such as the intense and buoyant paintings of Stockbridge teacher Leo Garel) and photography (usually by gallery-owner and master photographer Clemens Kalischer).

Origins Gallery (413-298-0002; 36 Main St., The "Mews") Tribal and folk art of Africa and Asia collected since 1965 by Albert Gordon — from the Sahara to the Himalayas. Includes ceremonial sculpture, dance masks, antique jewelry, hand-woven textiles, pottery, beads, furniture, musical instruments, and folk collectibles.

Reuss Audubon Galleries (413-298-4074; Pine and Shamrock Sts.) This 19th-century house features a rotating exhibit of the "double elephant folio" bird prints from Audubon's *Birds of America*. (Sales outlet in Gt. Barrington; see under "Antiques" in Chapter Eight, *Shopping*.)

Ronrich (413-298-3556; Rte. 183, 2 mi. south of Tanglewood) Paintings and prints by American artists.

TYRINGHAM

Santarella Museum & Gardens (413-243-3260; 75 Main Rd., 3.5 mi. off Rte. 102, P.O. Box 414, Tyringham, MA 01264). This structure was designed and built by Sir Henry Hudson Kitson, sculptor of the Lexington *Minute Man*. The roof was hand-cut to resemble thatch and took three to five years to complete. Used as Kitson's last sculpting studio from 1916 to 1947, the building is now a museum of his work and a history of the structure. Outside are gardens, also designed by Kitson, with contemporary sculpture exhibited for sale. The museum exhibits works of over 40 artists. There is an artists-in-residence program. Museum shop.

WEST STOCKBRIDGE

All Fired Up Gallery — Berkshire Center for Contemporary Glass (413-232-4666; 6 Harris St., P.O. Box 377, W. Stockbridge, MA 01266) Hand-blown contemporary glass, workshops, demonstrations. See also under "Arts Classes," above.

Artifacts (413-232-9900; 5 Center St.) Architectural objects and related artworks, including miniatures, wooden objects, and intaglio.

Hotchkiss Mobiles (413-232-0200; fax 413-232-0210; www.artmobiles.com or www.hotchkissmobiles.com; e-mail: mobiles@bcn.net; 8 Center St., P.O. Box 373, W. Stockbridge, MA 01266) Original and colorful mobiles for moving art, both indoors and out. Museum quality at country prices. Another gallery in Lenox (see below).

Central County

BECKET

Becket Arts Center of the Hilltowns (413-623-6635; Rte. 8) Local shows and programs.

HANCOCK

Beaverpond Gallery (413-738-5895; 2993 Hancock Rd., Rte. 43) Berkshire watercolors by owner Richard Heyer and others, custom framing, art classes.

HINSDALE

John Stritch (413-655-8804; 526 Maple St.) Paintings, prints, and Tanglewood poster collection by popular Berkshire artist John Stritch, whose sculpture garden is open by appointment.

LENOX

Annee Goodchild American Primitive™ (413-637-0700; annee@anneegood child.com; 22 Walker St.) Paintings, painted furniture, rugs, stationery, fanciful objects d'art, all hand done or designed by the owner/artist.

Artworks Gallery (413-637-4433; 4 Housatonic St.) A rich collection by regional artists in an intimate space. Bruce MacDonald and a dozen others of the Berkshire art scene.

B.J. Faulkner (413-637-2958; www.bjfaulkner.com; 48 Main St.) Highlighting the watercolors, oils, and reproductions of the artist/owner's Berkshire scenes, musical themes, and European dreams.

Clark Whitney (413-637-2126; 25 Church St.) Contemporary art.

Concepts of Art (413-637-4845, fax 413-637-2723; www.lenoxjudaica.com; 65 Church St.) Crafts, including glass, jewelry, pottery, and wood. The Samuel Lauren Gallery offers realistic art and glass sculpture. The gallery's other speciality, Judaica, is now at a new gallery called **Judaica** (see below).

Lerner Gallery (413-637-3315; 17 Franklin St.) 18th-, 19th- and 20th-century paintings, American and European art in one of the area's oldest galleries.

Hado Studio (413-637-1088; 62 Church St.; summer only) Contemporary paintings and sculpture; also furniture and prints.

Hand of Man (413-637-0632; 5 Walker St. at the Curtis Shops) A wide range of appealing crafts, photographs, and paintings.

Hoadley Gallery: Contemporary Crafts (413-637-2814; 21 Church St.) Pottery by Tom Hoadley is one of this store's specialties. Functional and decorative objects in all media, including a collection of wearable art.

Hotchkiss Mobiles (413-637-4115 or 413-232-0200; www.artmobiles.com or www.hotchkissmobiles.com; 34 Church St.) The gallery's Lenox location features mobiles and artwork, jewelry, ceramics, and furniture.

Inspired Planet (413-637-2836; www.inspiredplanet.com; Brushwood Farms, Rte. 7) Photographs by the owner; paintings, furniture, and artifacts from Asia, Africa, and the Americas.

Judaica (413-637-4845; www.lenoxjudaica.com; 27 Church St.) Concepts of Art shows its Judaica in this space, and there's a tearoom serving pastries as well.

Lenox Gallery of Fine Art (413-637-2276; 69 Church St.) Two floors of paintings, watercolors, drawings, and sculpture by major Berkshire artists. Open daily year-round.

Michael Charles Cabinetmakers (413-637-3483; www.michaelcharles.com; 53 Church St.) A gallery of handmade custom furniture created by craftsmen using the finest American hardwoods and utilizing traditional 19th-century joinery techniques.

Nuovo Gallery (413-637-4141; 25 Franklin St.) Small gallery, primarily featuring works of local artists. Closed in winter except by appointment.

Stevens & Conron (413-637-0739; 5 Walker St. at the Curtis Shops) Watercolors and pastels, as well as traditional and contemporary crafts.

Towne Gallery (413-637-0053; www.townegallery.com; 68 Main St., below Villager Gifts) Regional paintings, graphics, sculptures, and crafts; framing.

Ute Stebich (413-637-3566; 69 Church St.) Contemporary art of museum quality including glass by Tom Patti; outstanding international collection of art and primitive African objects. Closed winter except by appointment.

PITTSFIELD

Berkshire Artisans (413-499-9348; www.berkart@taconic.net; 28 Renne Ave.; 1 block east of lower North St.) Exhibitions and workshops at the city's nonprofit municipal arts center.

Berkshire Community College, Koussevitzky Arts Center (413-499-4660; www.cc.berkshire.org; 1350 West St.) Changing exhibitions, 9am to 5pm., weekdays.

North County

ADAMS

Sylvia's (413-743-9250, 800-258-9078; 29 Park St., Rte. 8) Paintings, graphics, and drawings by modern artists.

NORTH ADAMS

Contemporary Artists Collaborative (413-663-9555; www.cacart.org; 189 Beaver St.) Contemporary art, open summer. Classes taught.
Dark Ride (413-663-6662; 189 Beaver St.) Ride the Sensory Integrator into creative space.
Day Six Gallery (413-664-9851; Western Gateway Heritage State Park) Gallery owner and artist Cheryl Lee Murphy's selection from the works of 30 artists, sculptors, and photographers, regional and national. Native American work. Closed Tuesday.

WILLIAMSTOWN

1/2 Dozen or So, Mount Greylock Regional High School (413-458-9582; 1781 Cold Spring Rd.) Changing exhibitions open during school hours.
Hip Pocket (413-458-2250; 181 Main St.) Changing exhibitions and archival custom picture framing. Shares space with Artists' Technical Services.
Wilson Wilde, Williams College (413-597-3578; Spencer Studio Building) Changing student exhibits.

HISTORIC HOMES

ARROWHEAD
413-442-1793.
www.mobydick.org.
780 Holmes Rd., Pittsfield, MA 01201.
About 1.5 mi. off Rte. 7, near Pittsfield–Lenox line.
Season: Memorial Day Weekend–Labor Day, open daily; Sept.–Oct., closed Tues.–Thurs.; Winter by appointment.
Fee: Admission charged.
Gift shop.

In 1850, seeking to escape what he later called "the Babylonish brick-kiln of New York," Herman Melville gave in to his yearning "to feel the grass" and moved with his family to the Berkshires. By the time he came here, Melville had already published two tales of his South Sea adventures, *Typee* and *Omoo,* and he earned a reputation as a man who "had lived among cannibals." Longing to be known as a great writer and fresh from a new "close acquaintance" with the "divine" writings of Shakespeare, here he took off on the grand literary whale hunt that was to be *Moby Dick*.

Drawing © Carol Wallace, 1998, the Preserve America™ Collection of Crane & Co.

Herman Melville's study at Arrowhead.

Arrowhead is the home of the Berkshire County Historical society, which offers excellent guided tours through the house. In the second-floor study Melville wrote his great novel looking northward at the Mount Greylock range, its rolling form reminiscent of a giant whale. He dedicated his next novel, *Pierre*, to "Greylock's most excellent majesty." The implements of the writer's trade and duplicates of many important books in his library are here.

The other thoroughly "Melville" room is the dining room, which is dominated by a grand stone hearth. His brother inscribed the mantel with the opening of Melville's story, "I and My Chimney." The house contains 19th-century period furnishings, fine arts, and textiles with Berkshire origins, several pieces of which belonged to Melville. The Ammi Phillips folk-art portraits are of particular interest.

Outside, the piazza is site of another story. The grounds include an extensive herb garden and a vintage cutting garden. Arrowhead is a lovely picnic spot.

The barn behind the house is the site of cultural programs such as literary readings and historical talks. A video about Berkshire literary figures and artists takes 20 minutes. Those hungry for more Melville can visit the Melville Room at the Berkshire Athenaeum on Wendell Ave., also in Pittsfield. (See the Berkshire Athenaeum entry under "Libraries" in this chapter.)

For a fee, Arrowhead will make its facilities and grounds available for functions such as weddings.

COLONEL ASHLEY HOUSE
413-229-8600.
www.thetrustees.org.
P.O. Box 128, Ashley Falls, MA 01222.
Cooper Hill Rd., Ashley Falls.
Off Rte. 7A.
Season: Sat. & Sun., Memorial Day through Oct. 14, Monday holidays, 1–5pm.
Fee: Admission charged.

In his military role as colonel and as a political radical, John Ashley was destined to become as prominent a citizen as the Revolution would produce in Berkshire. He began his Berkshire life as a surveyor, trudging through the woods and swamps of Sheffield and mapping the wilderness with compass and chain.

Ashley loved what he saw. By 1735 he had built a handsome home on the west bank of the Housatonic River, now the oldest extant house in Berkshire County. Framed of well-seasoned oak with chestnut rafters, it was the finest house in Sheffield. Woodworkers from across the colony came to carve paneling and to fashion the gracefully curved staircase. The craftsmanship of Ashley's study, with its broad fireplace and sunburst cupboard, inspires confidence. It was here that Ashley met with a group of his neighbors in early 1773 to draft the "Sheffield Declaration," stating to the world that all people were "equal, free and independent." In Ashley's study, they asserted their independence from Britain, some three years before Thomas Jefferson and associates did so in Philadelphia.

Thanks to an excellent restoration and relocation (a quarter mile from its original site) by the Trustees of Reservations, the Ashley House lives on. A herb garden flourishes outside while Colonial furnishings, a pottery collection, and the original wood paneling survive inside. A visit can complement viewing the extraordinary flowers at Bartholemew's Cobble or antique hunting in the Sheffield-Ashley Falls area.

The Sheffield Declaration, 1773

Resolved that Mankind in a state of Nature are equal, free and independent of each Other, and have a right to the undisturbed Enjoyment of there lives, there liberty and Property. . . .

Resolved that it is a well-nown and undoubted priviledge of the british Constitution that every Subject hath . . . a Right to the free and uncontroled injoyment use and Improvement of his estat or property. . . .

Resolved that the late acts of the parlement of Great Breton expres porpos of Rating and regulating the colecting a Revenew in the Colonies: are unconstitutional as thereby the Just earning of our labours and Industry without Any Regard to our own concent are by mere power revished from us. . . .

BIDWELL HOUSE
413-528-6888.
www.berkshireweb.com/
bidwell.house.
Art School Rd., Monterey,
MA 01245.
1 mi. off Tyringham Rd.
Season: Memorial
Day–Columbus Day,
Tues.–Sun., Holidays,
11–4.
Fee: Admission charged.

Bidwell is one of Berkshire's oldest homes, dating from 1750. Surrounded by 190 acres of pristine Monterey woodland, the house looks much as it might have back in the 18th century. We drive down Art School Road, then keep driving, back into the deep woods where the past still lingers. There rests the unassuming Bidwell House, simple, homey.

An active slate of lectures, workshops (among them, cider pressing), and hikes (in the fall along historical Royal Hemlock Road) take place at the former home of Adonijah Bidwell.

WILLIAM CULLEN BRYANT HOMESTEAD
413-634-2244.
www.thetrustees.org.
207 Bryant Rd.,
Cummington, MA 01026.
Off Rte. 9 on Rte. 112,
Cummington, MA 01026.
Season: Summer: Fri., Sat.,
Sun., Holidays; Labor
Day–Columbus Day:
Sat., Sun., Holidays;
1–5pm
Fee: Admission charged.

William Cullen Bryant was born in 1794 in a small gambrel-roofed cabin of rough-hewn lumber, two miles from the frontier village of Cummington, on a farm of 465 acres. He stayed at Williams College only eight months, shortly thereafter taking up the law. From 1816 on, Cullen, as he was called, practiced law in Great Barrington, where he wrote about 30 well-respected poems on such local themes as Monument Mountain's Indian legend, the Green River, and native waterfowl. With the influence of Catherine Sedgwick's brothers, Bryant became co-editor of the *New York Review* and *Athenaeum Magazine,* then editor at the *New York Evening Post* (one of America's oldest and most influential newspapers), and ultimately America's first popular and widely respected poet born in the States.

Bryant added substantially to his Cummington homestead; today it has 23 rooms. Visitors should read the poems first to capture the tour's fine points. Well managed by the Trustees of Reservations.

CHESTERWOOD
413-298-3579.
www.nationaltrust.org.
P.O. Box 827, Stockbridge,
MA 01262.
Off Rte. 183, in Glendale.
Season: May–Oct., daily
10–5.
Fee: Admission charged.
Gift shop.

At the age of 25, Daniel Chester French was commissioned by his home town of Concord, Massachusetts, to create his first public monument, the *Minute Man.* Its lifelike pose and exquisite sense of surface modeling won the artist national acclaim.

Years and scores of sculptures later, French sought a permanent country home to augment the New York City studio he maintained. In 1896, he and his wife, Mary, were shown the old Warner Farm and Boys School in the Glendale section of

Through the glass doors at Daniel Chester French's studio at Chesterwood.

Judith Monachina

Stockbridge. After taking in the magnificent vista southward, toward Monument Mountain, French pronounced it "the best dry view" he had ever seen and promptly arranged to buy the property. Thereafter, he and Mary spent half of each year in New York City, half in Glendale at Chesterwood. "[Glendale] is heaven," he said. "New York is — well, New York."

In Glendale he built a grand residence, studio, and garden complex, which are an enduring and eloquent tableau of his artistry. Here he created his masterpiece, the *Abraham Lincoln* that sits in the Lincoln Memorial in Washington. "What I wanted to convey," said French, "was the mental and physical strength of the great President." Visitors are invited to handle sculpting tools in his studio. Centerpieces are his marble *Andromeda,* an erotic work unknown to most Americans; and the "railway" to move his works-in-progress out into the revealing daylight.

French designed magnificent gardens, maintained today after his fashion by the property's managers, the National Trust for Historic Preservation. The grounds host special exhibits during the season.

FRELINGHUYSEN-MORRIS HOUSE & STUDIO
See under "Museums."

MERWIN HOUSE
413-298-4703.
www.spnea.org.
14 W. Main St., P.O. Box 72, Stockbridge, MA 01262.
Center of town.
Season: June 1–Oct. 15; Sat., Sun., 11–5.
Fee: Admission charged.

"Tranquility," a bit of 19th-century Berkshire refinement stopped in time, is the former home of Mrs. Vipont Merwin. This charming brick mansion, built about 1825, is filled with period antiques (mostly Victorian); both furnishings and collectibles reflect global travel and domestic dignity. Merwin House is maintained as a property of the

Society for the Preservation of New England Antiquities. For Stockbridge strollers, evening views through the multipaned front windows give an inviting glimpse of an elegant world gone by.

Paul Rocheleau

The Mission House.

MISSION HOUSE
413-298-3239.
www.thetrustees.org.
P.O. Box 792, Stockbridge, MA 01262.
Corner Main & Sergeant Sts.
Season: Memorial Day Weekend–Columbus Day, daily 10am–5pm
Fee: Admission charged.

In 1735 an earnest minister from Yale came to the Berkshire wilderness to preach to the Mahican Indians. John Sergeant learned the Indian language in which he preached two sermons every Sunday. In the springtime, he went out with the Indians to tap the sugar maples, writing the first account in English of this sugar production method. He frequently talked with the Indians in the back of his simple log cabin. Under Sergeant's leadership, the Stockbridge Mission flourished.

To please his wife, Abigail, the Reverend Sergeant built what is now called Mission House, high on Prospect Hill. The tall and ornate Connecticut Doorway — with panels representing the Ten Commandments, an open Bible, and St. Andrew's cross — was carved in Westfield, Connecticut, and dragged by oxen 50 miles over rugged terrain to Stockbridge. This front door and the front rooms were Abigail's domain; in the back, a separate entry and a long corridor allowed the Indians access to Sergeant's study.

When Sargeant died, in 1749, the days of the Stockbridge Mission were numbered too, although the eminent theologian Jonathan Edwards succeeded him. By 1785 the Indians had been displaced from Stockbridge, driven out for the most part by land speculators.

In 1927 Mabel Choate — the art collector and philanthropist who was heir to Naumkeag — acquired the Mission House. She moved it to its present Main St. position, close to the site of John Sergeant's first log cabin. Boston landscape architect Fletcher Steele, who had designed the gardens at Naumkeag, planted an orderly, symmetrical 18th-century herb, flower, and fruit garden beside the restored, relocated Mission House. There are today apple and quince trees; herbs such as lamb's ear, rue, and southernwood; bright flowers; a grape arbor; and a "salet garden" filled with garden greens.

The Trustees of Reservations maintains Mission House now. Tours of the house capture the 18th century's furnishings and kitchen implements and the feeling of humble domesticity around the dominant central hearth.

THE MOUNT

Edith Wharton Restoration, Inc.
413-637-1899; 888-637-1902.
www.edithwharton.org.
Plunkett St., P.O. Box 974, Lenox, MA 01240.
Near southern jct. of Rtes. 7 & 7A.
Season: May, Sat.–Sun., 9–2; Memorial Day Weekend through Oct., 9–2; last tour at 2pm.
Fee: Admission charged.
Book/gift shop.

In February 1901 writer and heiress Edith Wharton arrived at the Curtis Hotel in Lenox for a week in the country. She had summered in the area for the preceding two years, and now, having found the "watering place trivialities of Newport" all but intolerable, sought a new site on which to realize the design principles incorporated in her book, *The Decoration of Houses*.

The Georgian Revival house she built was modeled on Christopher Wren's Belton House in Lincolnshire, England. At first, Wharton retained as architect her old associate, Ogden Codman. When his design fees grew exorbitant, she called upon Francis V. L. Hoppin to complete the job.

Wharton supervised creation of the gardens, orchards, and buildings, while finishing her novel, *Disintegration,* writing as always in bed and tossing the pages on the floor for the staff to assemble. The Mount was elegant throughout, boasting marble floors and fireplaces, and requiring 12 resident servants. Besides the 14 horses in their stables, the Whartons owned one of the earliest motorcars, a convenience that thrilled the visiting Henry James. In the fall of 1904, James and Wharton motored through Berkshire's autumnal splendor every day, enjoying social afternoons and evenings with visiting sophisticates.

"The Mount was to give me country cares and joys," she wrote, "long happy rides, and drives through the wooded lanes of that loveliest region, the companionship of a few dear friends, and the freedom from trivial obligations which was necessary if I was to go on with my writing. The Mount was my first real home . . . and its blessed influence still lives in me."

Happily, its blessed influence lives on for all of us, as its physical and spiritual restoration continue. The National Trust for Historic Preservation bought The Mount to save it from commercial exploitation; today the house is run by Edith Wharton Restoration, Inc. (EWR), whose work was praised by Hillary Rodham Clinton during a visit to The Mount in July 1998.

In the summer, besides house and garden tours of The Mount, Shakespeare & Company offers plays centering on Shakespeare and on Wharton's life and writings. (See the entry on Shakespeare & Company under "Theater" in this chapter). The actors will soon move to a home of their own in Lenox, however.

A sculpture show in the garden at Naumkeag.

Judith Monachina

NAUMKEAG
413-298-3239.
www.thetrustees.org.
Prospect Hill Rd., P.O. Box 792, Stockbridge, MA 01262.
Season: Memorial Day–Columbus Day, daily 10am–5pm
Fee: Admission charged.
Gift shop.

During the Gilded Age of the late 19th century, men and women of power played out their fantasies in Berkshire, dotting the hillsides with dream houses. A most livable example is the mansion of illustrious lawyer Joseph H. Choate, the summer "cottage" the Choate family came to call "Naumkeag" (an American Indian name meaning "haven of peace"). Here Choate found both a retreat from New York City life and an enclave of great legal minds in Supreme Court justices Field, Brewer, and Brown, all Stockbridge residents!

In 1884, Choate bought the property from David Dudley Field and began construction. By the autumn of 1886, the 26-room shingled, gabled, and dormered Norman-style house was complete, with architectural design by Stanford White and imaginative gardens by the landscaping pioneer Nathaniel Barret.

The house eventually came into the hands of Choate's daughter, Mabel, who maintained it while adding extensively to the gardens, under the direction of landscape architect Fletcher Steele. The Fountain Steps, framed by birches; the Afternoon Garden, an outdoor room; further southward, the Chinese Pagoda and Linden Walk; uphill, the brick-walled Chinese Garden, where mosses and stone Buddhas gather with carved lions and dogs, all shaded by ginkgos; to the north, the topiary of the Evergreen Garden and the fragrance and color of the Rose Garden all reflect decades of inspired and distinctive garden design.

Now held by the Trustees of Reservations (www.thetrustees.org), Naumkeag still includes its gardens, furnishings, and an extraordinary porcelain collection, much of it from the Far East. The tours are excellent.

SEARLES CASTLE
413-528-9800.
389 Main St. (Rte. 7), Gt.
Barrington, MA 01230.

When Mark Hopkins, a founder and treasurer of the Central Pacific Railroad, died, his widow, Mary, consoled herself with the creation of a grand castle in Great Barrington. Stanford White designed this 40-room castle, which was constructed between 1882 and 1887 of locally cut blue dolomite stone. Upon its completion, Mary Hopkins married her interior decorator, Edward Searles, a man 20 years her junior. Searles had spared no expense on the castle's interior. Many of the major rooms feature massive carved wood or marble fireplaces, each one unique. More than 100 of the world's best artisans and craftsmen were brought on site to work with oak carvings, marble statues, atriums, columns, and pillars. The bills totaled $2.5 million.

With its Greek revival temple, indoor pool, golf course, and tennis court, the castle now serves as the home of the John Dewey Academy, a residential therapeutic high school. In 1982, Searles Castle was added to the National Register of Historic Places. Usually closed to the public, the building and grounds are visible to pedestrians walking along Main Street. Several times a year — for an Antiquarian Book Fair, for the Stockbridge Chamber Concerts, and at other special events — Searles Castle is open to the public, and well worth a visit.

Touring the Berkshire Mansions

For those who yearn to step back into Berkshire's Gilded Age, visits to Naumkeag, The Mount, and Tanglewood, described in this chapter, will make an excellent start. In the chapters on *Lodging* and *Restaurants,* other Gilded Age mansions are noted for their original beauty or their contemporary adaptations. In addition, local historical societies and garden clubs arrange visits to some of the best mansions, normally off limits because they are private homes.

Many Gilded Age "cottages" are visible from the road and are well worth a look. Their owners' privacy should be respected, of course. Carole Owens's book *The Berkshire Cottages* tells their stories in lively detail, bringing to life the business magnates, robber barons, philanthropists, architects and designers, artists-in-residence, and squadrons of domestic servants. Maps to guide the way are included. At most bookstores.

OTHER HISTORIC HOUSES

In *Tyringham,* there is *Santarella Museum & Gardens* (413-243-3260; 75 Main Rd., P.O. Box 414, Tyringham, MA 01264, 3.5 mi. off Rte. 102). This remarkable house, with its unique roof created to look like thatch, or the swirl of autumn leaves, was designed and built by Sir Henry Hudson Kitson, sculptor of the Lexington *Minute Man*. Used as Kitson's last sculpting studio from 1916 to 1947, the house is now a museum of his work. Outside are gardens, also designed by Kitson, with contemporary sculpture exhibited for sale.

In **Lenox**, starting in 2000, **Ventford House** (413-637-3206; 104 Walker St., Lenox MA 01240), one of the great summer "cottages" of the Berkshires, is open; tours are given by appointment.

LIBRARIES

BERKSHIRE ATHENAEUM
413-499-9480.
www.berkshire.net/Pittsfield
   Library.
1 Wendell Ave. Pittsfield,
   MA 01201.
Open: Sept–June:
   Mon.–Thurs. 9–9, Fri.
   9–5, Sat., 10–5; July &
   Aug.: Mon., Wed., Fri.
   9–5, Tues., Thurs. 9–9,
   Sat., 10–5. Closed
   holidays.

The former Berkshire Athenaeum is a 19th-century specimen of the Venetian Gothic style, constructed next to the courthouse on Pittsfield's handsome Park Square. Built of Berkshire deep blue dolomite (a limestone) from Great Barrington, along with red sandstone from Longmeadow, Massachusetts, and red granite from Missouri, this Athenaeum was once Berkshire's central library and now serves Pittsfield's courts and registry of deeds.

The new Athenaeum is a three-level brick and glass facility featuring a tall and airy reading room with natural clerestory lighting. One outdoor reading terrace serves adults and another serves children.

There is an outstanding dance collection, a Local Authors Room, and a Local History Room. The jewel of the Athenaeum is its Herman Melville Room: a trove of Melville memorabilia, from carved scrimshaw depicting the terror of the Great White Whale to first editions of the author's works. Here are *Moby-Dick* in Japanese, autograph letters from Melville, photos of his Pittsfield Farm, Arrowhead (see entry under "Historic Homes," in this chapter), and the desk on which he wrote his last haunting work, *Billy Budd*.

CHAPIN LIBRARY OF RARE BOOKS
413-597-2462.
P.O. Box 426, Williamstown, MA 01267.
On the 2nd fl. of Stetson
   Hall, on Williams College
   campus.
Open: 10–12, 1–5, exc.
   weekends & holidays.
   Open July 4. Call for
   summer hours.

Chapin Library has one of the most well-rounded collections of rare books and manuscripts anywhere. On permanent display are the four founding documents of this country: the *Declaration of Independence* owned by a member of the Continental Congress; the *Articles of Confederation and Perpetual Union*; the *Constitution of the United States* annotated by George Mason; and two copies of the *Bill of Rights*. The library owns General Greene's handwritten order for boats to cross the

Delaware; on loan is George Washington's copy of the *Federalist Papers*. Every July Fourth, actors from the Williamstown Theatre Festival read the Declaration and the British reply.

In 1923, Alfred Clark Chapin, Williams class of 1869, and mayor of Brooklyn, presented his alma mater with his magnificent library of first editions and manuscripts, specializing in historic literary and artistic master works. Other alumni have subsequently given their collections.

Among other literary holdings are a Shakespeare First Folio, and first editions of Pope, Swift, Fielding, Defoe, Richardson, Sterne, Johnson, Scott, Byron, Burns, Browning, Keats, Shelley, Thackeray, and Dickens. There is also a fine T. S. Eliot collection. Representing American literature are first editions by such writers as Crane, Melville, Whitman, and Faulkner. Scientific endeavor is represented by Tycho Brahe's *Astronomia* (1602), Harvey's *Anatomical Exercitations* (1653), Darwin's *Origin of Species* (1859), and a "double elephant folio" of Audubon's *Birds of America*. The Chapin frequently contributes documents to special exhibits at the Williams College Museum of Art and the Clark Art Institute.

LENOX LIBRARY
413-637-0197.
18 Main St., Lenox, MA 01240.
Open: Summer: Mon.–Sat. 10–5; rest of year, Tues–Sat. 10–5; Thurs. to 8.

Built in 1815 as the Berkshire County Courthouse, when Lenox was still the "shire town," this classic Greek Revival building became the Lenox Library Association in 1873. It is listed on the National Register of Historic Places. Those lucky enough to read there can enjoy the main reading room with its lofty illuminated ceiling and its amazing array of periodicals, or its outdoor reading park. This is Old World reading at its best. A solid collection of about 75,000 volumes plus a music room are available to the public. There is a closed collection of historical memorabilia, too, including the sled from the incident on which Edith Wharton based her novella *Ethan Frome*.

MILNE PUBLIC LIBRARY & HOUSE OF LOCAL HISTORY
413-458-5369; 413-458-2160 (HLH).
www.bcn.net/~willieb.
1095 Main St., Williamstown, MA 01267.
Open: Mon., Tues, Thurs., Fri. 10—5; Weds. to 8; Sat. to 1.

The town is proud that a treasured resource now has a much roomier home, with ample parking. It complements the Sawyer Library (below) with strong holdings of children's books, of fiction, local history, videos, and popular music. The House of Local History, open mornings, moved with the library, now having room enough to display much of its holdings. Library and HLH each offer frequent programs.

SAWYER LIBRARY
413-597-2501.
www.williams.edu/library.
Williams College, Williamstown, MA 01267.

At 834,755 volumes, 4,865 periodical subscriptions, 484,405 micro texts, 27,138 sound recordings including the Paul Whiteman Collection, 5,591 videos, and 407,689 Federal documents,

The Sled Ride

Though written after she completed her Berkshire life, Wharton's *Ethan Frome* is set in a Berkshire town that she calls Starkfield. In the climactic scene, soulmates Ethan and Mattie decide to take a suicidal sled ride rather than having to live apart, separated by Ethan's bitter wife, Zeena. The snowy downhill race toward obliteration was based on an actual sledding accident in turn-of-the-century Lenox.

She waited while he seated himself with crossed legs in the front of the sled; then she crouched quickly down at his back and clasped her arms about him. Her breath on his neck set him shuddering again, and he almost sprang from his seat. But in a flash he remembered the alternative. She was right: this was better than parting. He leaned back and drew her mouth to his. . .

Just as they started he heard the sorrel's whinny again, and the familiar wistful call, and all the confused images it brought with it, went with him down the first reach of the road. Half-way down there was a sudden drop, then a rise, and after that another long delirious descent. As they took wing for this it seemed to him that they were flying indeed, flying far up into the cloudy night, with Starkfield immeasurably below them, falling away like a speck in space. . . Then the big elm shot up ahead, lying in wait for them at the bend of the road, and he said between his teeth: "We can fetch it; I know we can fetch it —"

As they flew toward the tree Mattie pressed her arms tighter, and her blood seemed to be in his veins. Once or twice the sled swerved a little under them. He slanted his body to keep it headed for the elm, repeating to himself again and again: "I know we can fetch it"; and little phrases she had spoken ran through his head and danced before him on the air. The big tree loomed bigger and closer, and as they bore down on it he thought: "It's waiting for us: it seems to know." But suddenly his wife's face, with twisted monstrous lineament, thrust itself between him and his goal, and he made an instinctive movement to brush it aside. The sled swerved in response, but he righted it again, kept it straight, and drove down on the black projecting mass. There was a last instant when the air shot past him like millions of fiery wires; and then the elm. . . .

Center of Williams College campus.
Open: Except weekends when Williams is not in session.

SIMON'S ROCK LIBRARY
413-528-0771.

the Sawyer is a research resource unmatched within the county. Here we find a wide array of the latest periodicals, shelves of newly released books, and a library staff as helpful as they come. The public may use the facility, the stacks are open, Sawyer is a pleasant place in which to work. The Unified Science Center has its own library, as do other departments, but all works are listed in Sawyer.

The Simon's Rock Library is one of the best in South County, the staff always attentive to one's research needs. The college it serves may be

84 Alford Rd., Gt.
Barrington, MA 01230.
Open: Hours vary.

small, but this library's holdings are exceedingly well chosen. It is open to all visitors and to Berkshire County residents for borrowing. This is a library of half a dozen rooms, on two floors, in three interconnected pagoda-style buildings — all in a sylvan setting. With their big skylights, the reading rooms are highly recommended for naturally lighted, wet-weather browsing. And fascinating art exhibits almost always grace the library's skylit gallery.

**STOCKBRIDGE
LIBRARY &
HISTORICAL ROOM**
413-298-5501.
Main St. (Rte. 7), P.O. Box
119, Stockbridge, MA
01262.
Open: Mon.–Fri., 9–5; Sat.,
9–4; Mon. & Fri. eves,
7–9; closed Sun.
Historical Room:
Tues.–Fri., 9–5; Sat., 9–4

Parts of the Stockbridge Library date to 1864, and the reading room is one the most felicitous anywhere — tall, stately, and obviously from another era. The children's collection is also first-rate.

Called W-nahk-ta-kook ("Great Meadow") by the Mahican Indians who settled there, the town of Stockbridge was incorporated by the English in 1739. A Colonial charter not only made the town official, but made it Indian property as well, and thereafter it was known as "Indian Town." The history of this great meadow and its town is displayed and explained in the Stockbridge Historical Room, a small museum in the basement of the library. Here are Indian artifacts, photos from the mid-1800s onwards, memorabilia from many famous residents and visitors to the village, and other intriguing historical bits that illuminate Stockbridge present.

MUSEUMS

BERKSHIRE MUSEUM
413-443-7171;
fax 413-443-2135.
www.berkshiremuseum.
org.
39 South St., Pittsfield, MA
01201.
Open: Sept.–May, Tues.–
Sat. 10–5, Sun. 1–5;
June–Oct., daily 10–5.
Fee: Adults $6; seniors $5;
students $5; Members
and children under 3
free.
Gift shop.

Three museums in one, the Berkshire Museum presents strong collections of art, science, and regional history, as well as an exciting calendar of lectures, films, concerts, classes, and field trips.

Founded in 1903 by Dalton papermaker and philanthropist Zenas Crane, the museum shows the Hahn Collection of Early American Silver; the Gallatin Collection of Abstract Art; the Spalding Collection of Chinese Art; the Proctor Shell Collection; and the Cohn Collection of Minerals. The collections are far-ranging: 19th-century glass made in the towns of Berkshire and Cheshire and pre-Christian glass bottles from Egypt; exhibits of shells and aquatic life, fossils, mushrooms, reptiles and amphibians. The Bird Room has a special section on Berkshire birds; the owl exhibit especially captivates. The Berkshire Animal Room presents native mammal specimens. A collection of beautiful dioramas by Louis Paul Jonas Sr. shows the animals of the world in one-tenth scale. An aquarium holding more than 100 species features a hands-on children's exhibit called "Touch of the Sea."

That the museum is committed to families and community is demonstrated by past exhibits such as "Kid Stuff: Great Toys from Our Childhood," action toys, antique toys, and refurbished Alexander Calder toys. The life-sized stegosaurus on the museum's front lawn is a community landmark. The Museum Theater, a 300-seat facility, is site for lectures, plays, concerts, and the Little Cinema's admirable program of feature films.

Upstairs, works of Copley, Stuart, and Peale represent American portraiture. The Hudson River School appears in works by Cole, Inness, and others. Two European galleries are devoted to the work of such English portrait painters as West and Reynolds, and European works by masters from the 15th to the 18th century. In the museum's center is the lofty and skylit Ellen Crane Memorial Room, devoted to American and European sculpture from the 19th and 20th centuries. An ancient civilizations gallery includes Pa-hat, the ever-popular Egyptian mummy, who lies resplendent amidst a first-rate collection of ancient reliefs and artifacts.

Families and guide in the Clark's Impressionist gallery, in front of Monet's Cliff at Étretat.

Arthur Evans, courtesy Sterling & Francine Clark Art Institute

STERLING & FRANCINE CLARK ART INSTITUTE
413-458-2303, 413-458-9545.
www.clark.williams.edu.
225 South St., Williamstown, MA 01267.

Sterling Clark acquired his first Renoir in 1916. By the time he was finished he owned 36. He and his French wife, Francine, bought what they liked. Thus the basis of this fine collection reflects their personal taste. Included with Impressionists are galleries filled with 19th-century American

1 mi. S. of jct. Rtes. 7 & 2.
Open: Tues.–Sun., 10–5,
   incl. Presidents Day,
   Memorial Day, Labor
   Day, Columbus Day.
   Open Mon. July & Aug.
Fee: $5 July–Oct., exc.
   Tues.; free otherwise.
Gift shop; Cafe.

classics — by Winslow Homer, John Singer Sargent, and Frederick Remington — and a small but impressive collection of Old Masters. Traveling exhibits of Renoir, Degas, and Millet have recently attracted summer crowds.

The original 1950s building is elegant and efficient, a white Vermont marble neoclassic structure whose interior is finished in Italian marble, plaster, and natural-finish oak. The large red granite addition (1973) houses more galleries and a serious art library. Substantial remodeling in 1996 added more galleries, storage, and a cafe. The museum shop includes an extensive collection of art books.

For most visitors, the centerpiece of the museum's collection is its gathering of French Impressionists, the Clarks' greatest artistic love. Among the standouts, besides Renoir, are works by Monet and Degas, the latter in both his racehorse and ballet dancer series. There are also prints, drawing, antique furniture, and silver. Almost every gallery has some form of natural light; many galleries offer not only splendid art on the walls but peaceful views of the Berkshire Hills as well. A piano as artwork may be one of the Clark's most controversial acquisitions.

The Clark is more than a painting gallery, however. As we walk among its colorful masterworks and their accompanying drawings and prints, we see some of the collection's antique furniture and silver, masterpieces of craftsmanship. Also an important art education center, the Clark offers a broad spectrum of lectures open to the public, serving as classroom to a graduate program in art history run jointly with Williams College as well.

The Clark offers an extensive art lecture series, chamber music, and film programs. It hosts mimes, puppeteers, one-person shows, poets and storytellers, folk music, and the popular outdoor band concerts in the summer. Special exhibitions are offered throughout the year; the exhibit scheduled for summer 2000 was "Noble Dreams, Wicked Pleasures: Orientalism in America 1870–1930."

**CRANE PAPER
   MUSEUM**
413-684-2600.
www.crane.com.
30 South St., Dalton, MA
   01226.
Off Rte. 9, behind Crane
   office.
Open: Mid-June to Mid-
   Oct., Mon.–Fri., 2–5.
Fee: Free.

One of Berkshire's most important exports is money, not the finished product but the rag paper on which every U.S. bill is printed. The Crane Paper Company makes it; these treasured notes circulate from Berkshire County to the nation and then the world.

While the mills themselves are not open to the public, the Crane Paper Museum, established in 1929, is open and tells a fascinating industrial tale. This magical one-room brick museum — ivy covered and set in a garden — is really a restored 1844

paper mill building. The exhibits inside are scale models, historical photographs, and paper samples. Crane produces only rag paper (nothing from
wood pulp), and the exhibits show how the rags are soaked, softened, beaten
to a pulp, and dried into paper stock. A 20-minute video on papermaking
explains the process of water marking, surface finishing (hard or soft), and
anticounterfeiting techniques. Also on display are historic documents, White
House invitations, and U.S. and foreign currency, all printed on Crane paper.

**FRELINGHUYSEN-
MORRIS HOUSE &
STUDIO**
413-637-0166;
fax 413-637-9790.
92 Hawthorne St., Lenox,
MA 01240.
Open: July 4–Labor Day,
Thurs.–Sun. 10–4; June,
Sept.–Columbus Day,
Thurs.–Sat. 10–4 or by
appointment. Tours 10–4
(last tour begins at 3pm).
Fee: $8.
Limited items for sale.

Persons interested in art, architecture, and art
history might be intrigued by the home and
studio of George L. K. Morris and his wife, Suzy
Frelinghuysen, artists and advocates of the avant
garde. On exhibit are his and her framed works
and murals, along with those of Matisse, Degas,
Picasso, Braque, Léger, and Gris. A large earth
mother by Gaston Lachaise reclines among the
trees on the wooded 46 acres that stretch between
Hawthorne St. and Rte. 183, just like the neighboring Tanglewood.

Morris built his studio on the grounds in 1930,
then added the house in 1940. Combined, the Le
Corbusier–style building — with its flat roof, white
stucco, and glass blocks — made a stir when it was
plunked down in the midst of Berkshire's traditional residences. Today visitors can walk through the grounds and take a guided tour of the building. The
Barnes it is not, but the couple and their comrades were ahead of the rest of the
U.S. in espousing cubism. Visitors can see, particularly in his work, the move
from representational to abstract, together with the intentional humor that
made the art so much fun. Her blue, black, and chartreuse creations speak of
her lively spirit as well.

They were privileged. Morris was descended from Lewis Morris, a signer of
the Declaration of Independence. The artist died in an automobile accident
nearby, in 1975. Frelinghuysen was of the line of Dutch Reform clergymen, college presidents, and politicians, including president Chester A. Arthur's secretary of state. She survived the accident, although somewhat hobbled, living until
1988. They sold their New York City apartment to endow the property, which
has been open to the public since 1998 through the terms of their wills. Those
interested in architecture might like to compare their home with the American
Modern Style Field Farm (see Chapter Three, *Lodging*, under Williamstown),
built in 1948.

**HANCOCK SHAKER
VILLAGE**
413-443-0188.

The United Society of Believers in Christ's Second Appearing, later called Shakers, were
founded in England in 1747 as a small group of reli-

www.hancockshakervillage.
   org.
Rte. 20, P.O. Box 927,
   Pittsfield, MA 01202.
6 mi. W. of town.
Open: Mid-May–late Oct.
   9:30–5; late Oct.–mid May
   10–3; call ahead in winter.
   Closed Thanksgiving,
   Christmas, New Year's.
Fees: Main season, adult
   $13.50; 6–17 years, $5.50;
   5 and under free; family
   (two adults and children
   under 18 years), $33.
   Tour season, adult $10;
   6–17 years, $5; 5 and
   under free; family, $25.
Museum shops; Seasonal
   cafe; Walking tour
   brochures available in
   English, French, German,
   Spanish, Japanese, Braille.

gious nonconformists. Ann Lee, a young woman with strong religious convictions, became their spiritual leader. In 1774, a small group joined "Mother Ann" in sailing for the New World. They landed in New York, near Albany, where they later formed the Shaker community of Niskayuna.

Shaker religion was also a way of life. Members joined into distinct communities isolated from the outside world. Men and women held equal status in daily life and leadership positions, but the genders were separated to support the Shaker commitment to celibacy. Communities were organized into families. Members gave public confession of their sins. Ritual dancing gave rise to their name, originally used derisively but later adopted.

A community was established in 1790 at Hancock. Given the spiritual name of the City of Peace, it prospered for more than 150 years. Residents sought heavenly perfection, resulting in products that came to be known for their beauty. Design of clothing, furniture, implements, and buildings was strictly functional, without addition of deliberate ornaments. "'Tis a gift to be simple," goes an old Shaker hymn; and such simplicity was a primary aim of both inner and outer life. "Beauty rests on utility," said their credo. Of great beauty, then, is Hancock's symbol, the stunning Round Stone Barn. As splendid as the structure is to the eye, how much more splendid that with such an efficient architecture, one farm hand at the center could easily and quickly feed an entire herd of cattle.

When the sect was at its peak, in the mid-19th century, Hancock was one of 18 Shaker communities from Maine to Kentucky and had a population of about 300 members. The agricultural base of the village was augmented by cottage industries, offering such items as cooperware, flat brooms, agricultural seeds, and dairy products to sell to the world's people. But as religious ferment ceased, Shaker population at Hancock declined steadily until 1960, when the last of the Hancock Shakers moved away.

Since then, the village and its 1,200 acres of meadows and woodlands have been a living museum to accommodate visitors who want a taste of the Shaker ways. The City of Peace now acts as center of re-created Shaker activities, including workshops, candlelit dinners, and evening tours. The second weekend in July is the Americana artists and crafts show.

Visitors can tour 20 original Shaker buildings to see Shaker furniture and tools, some of them attended by craftspeople working in the Shaker way: the chairmaker, the blacksmith, basketmakers, spinners, and weavers. Hancock's workshops teach how to create Shaker chair seats, oval boxes, natural herb wreaths, and a variety of other crafts. From the gardens, both herbal and vegetable, and from any of the village workers, visitors absorb the power of Shaker simplicity.

The Hancock Shaker Village, always a destination for families, has been further enhanced for that purpose. There is now a replica of a one-room schoolhouse, ca. 1820, with presentations of authentic lessons of the time by a costumed Shaker teacher. The Discovery Room has been enlarged, offering a variety of hands-on Shaker crafts for children and adults. And starting in June 2000, a new Center of Shaker Studies both enhances facilities for visitors and researchers and provides gallery space for the village's rare gift-drawing collection.

For a fee, the village offers its facilities for special events such as weddings.

Photo by Nicholas Whitman, courtesy Mass MoCA.

At Mass MoCA. "The 1/2 Mile or 2 Furlong Piece" by Robert Rauschenberg. Mixed Media 1981–present.

MASS MoCA
413-664-4481;
    fax 413-663-8548.
www.massmoca.org.
87 Marshall St., N. Adams,
    MA 01247
Open: Nov.–May,
    Tues.–Sun. 10–4;
    June–Oct., Sun.–Thurs.
    10–5, Fri. & Sat. 10–7.
    Closed Thanksgiving,
    Christmas, New Year's.
Fees: Adults $8; 6–16 years
    $3; members free.
Museum shop, exhibits,
    and performances.

For 12 years the idea of a big museum in an old mill and director Joe Thompson hung on by their fingernails — until the Massachusetts Museum of Contemporary Art, or Mass MoCA as it's universally known, opened as a critical and public success in the summer of 1999. People in numbers beyond expectation streamed into the "supercollider for the best of today's visual, performing, and new media arts," as Thompson defines his 13-acre, 27-building factory campus. "Until now," he explains, "large complex art forms — exotic multimedia productions, for example, or monumental installations — have been without a public forum that is striking, properly scaled, and technically wired for cross-disciplinary collaborations."

Although perhaps not everyone has taken to the art works gigantic to minimalist by Rauschenberg, Rosenquist, Flavin, Nauman, and Morris, everyone has responded to the gorgeous retrofitting of the hangarlike spaces of what was once a textile mill and was more recently given over to the manufacture of capacitors. It was probably the accompanying variety of special events that made the opening summer and fall such a public success, however: "Swing Shift Dance Parties," "Film Factory" with outside projection, dance performances by the Paul Taylor Dance Company and others, concerts, and a musical, *Quark Victory*, put on by the Williamstown Theatre Festival. MoCA promises that, with the assistance of Jacob's Pillow, the Clark Art Institute, and WTF this kind of aggressive programing will continue.

North Adams, done up in banners and flowers, new street lights, and new signage, looks — improbable as it may seem — like a city being lifted up and uplifted by art. The city itself, with MoCA at its heart, may be the ultimate "large complex art form" on view to thousands of visitors from around the world. As it changes and evolves, we shall see what they shall see.

"Freedom of Worship," one of the famous "Four Freedoms" paintings by Norman Rockwell.

Courtesy © 2000 the Norman Rockwell Family Trust.

NORMAN ROCKWELL MUSEUM
413-298-4100,
  800-742-9450;
  fax 413-298-4142.
www.nrm.org.
Rte. 183, P.O. Box 308,
  Stockbridge, MA 01262.
0.6 mi. S. of jct. Rtes. 183 &
  102.

Whether we regard Norman Rockwell as illustrator or artist, the display of his life's work at the new Norman Rockwell Museum resonates. A visit to this grand monument to his talents and insight is worth the crush of bus passengers — or we can go off season.

Set on a gracious knoll overlooking the Housatonic River in the Glendale section of Stockbridge, the

Open: May–Oct., daily
10–5; Nov.–Apr.,
Mon.–Fri., 10–4;
Sat.–Sun., 10–5. Closed
Thanksgiving,
Christmas, New Year's.
Fee: Adults $9; Children
6–18, $2; under 5 free;
family rate $20.
Gift shop.

$4.4-million building designed by Robert A. M. Stern has a New England town hall look to it, with slate gables, clapboard siding, and fieldstone terraces. Inside, spacious well-lit galleries show permanent exhibits of Rockwell's paintings, while exhibits featuring Rockwell and other illustrators change thrice yearly.

At the core is the skylit gallery where Rockwell's *Four Freedoms* hang on permanent display. Created during the Second World War, they depict what we were fighting to uphold: freedom of speech, freedom from fear, freedom of worship, freedom from want. These four archetypal American images constitute a shrine to America's progressive image of itself.

Rockwell's 47-year relationship with the *Saturday Evening Post* is well known; in 1963 it ended and he signed on with *Look* and *McCall's*. His palette and his cast of characters broadened. Where once he depicted white boys running from a prohibited swimming hole, now federal marshals lead a young black girl to school in Little Rock. From lovers and gossips, he moved on to Peace Corps volunteers and astronauts on the moon.

Outside stands Rockwell's studio, with a bucolic view of the Housatonic. Inside the 19th-century carriage house, moved from the village to its present site in 1986, we understand the light in which he loved to paint, the curious assemblage of props with which he liked to surround himself, and the modest space he felt was his "best studio yet." The studio is open May through October.

The Rockwell Museum offers a variety of community-oriented programs beyond its public exhibitions, including lectures, performances, special events, and art classes.

WESTERN GATEWAY HERITAGE STATE PARK

413-663-6312.
9 Furnace St. Bypass, N.
Adams, MA 01247.
In freight-yard district.
Open: Daily, 10–5; closed
Thanksgiving,
Christmas, New Year's.
Fee: Donations accepted.
Gift shop; Restaurant.

Nestled between long glacial ridges, Berkshire had always been separated from the rest of Massachusetts. In 1854, engineers and construction workers began an assault, drilling and blasting a 4.75-mile-long tunnel through the northeastern ridge. This Hoosac Tunnel was the first major tunneling work in the United States. New methods were devised over the 20-year construction, at a cost of over $20 million and more than 195 lives. The building of the tunnel and related railroad development made North Adams the largest city in Berkshire in 1900. "We hold the Western Gateway," says the North Adams seal. At the turn of the century, more than half of Boston's freight came through the tunnel.

Western Gateway Heritage State Park now celebrates the former Boston and

Maine Freight House and the Hoosac Tunnel, both of which are on the National Register of Historic Places. Inside, films, slide shows, and written and visual histories of the railway and the tunnel are presented. Outside, there are shops, the restored freight yard, the Freight Yard Pub restaurant and the church-spired charm of North Adams.

WILLIAMS COLLEGE MUSEUM OF ART
413-597-2429.
www.williams.edu/
WCMA.
Main St. (Rte. 2),
Williamstown, MA 01267.
Set back from street across
from Gothic chapel.
Open: Tues.–Sat., 10–5,
Sun. 1–5, incl. Memorial
Day, Labor Day,
Columbus Day; closed
Mon., Thanksgiving,
Christmas, New Year's.
Fee: Free.
Gift shop.

One of the finest college art museums in the country, the Williams College Museum of Art is a 19th-century structure that has been strikingly revisited. Behind the original 1846 building, with its neoclassical octagonal rotunda, is an addition designed by Charles Moore, which opened in 1983. Combining wit and sophistication, Moore created a versatile multilevel exhibition space in both old and new buildings, retaining the brick wall of the former as the stunning backdrop for a multilevel stairwell. His design for the building's rear facade is a continuation of his lighthearted approach, featuring his "ironic columns," their nonfunctionality revealed by the gap near the top.

Inside, the museum's permanent collection contains some 11,000 objects. Complementing the Clark's collection of 19th-century European art, WCMA emphasizes early art, 20th-century art, and the art of Asia and other non-Western civilizations. Thanks to a $32-million gift by the widow of American impressionist Charles Prendergast, what was once a small regional museum now houses the finest collection by both Charles and his talented brother, Maurice, and is now the leading center in the world for study of the Prendergasts' work.

A lively education program includes school events and children's story/art hours. Several times a year, WCMA hosts popular, free "family days," when children can try a range of art projects thematically linked to the collection, guided by enthusiastic Williams students.

Frequent loan exhibitions focus on a wide range of provocative subjects. Visitors should expect to be engaged, not soothed.

BERKSHIRE SCENIC RAILWAY MUSEUM
413-637-2210.
www.regionnet.com/
colberk.
10 Willow Creek Rd., P.O.
Box 2195, Lenox, MA
01240.
At the end of Housatonic
St.

Penned in by red tape, Berkshire Scenic has had to cut its cross-county route to a short back-and-forth in front of Wood's Pond. Nevertheless, it's good family fun to take a ride in their shined-up 1920s-vintage Erie Lackawanna passenger coaches and diesel engine. You take the "short shuttle," a leisurely 15-minute ride along a 1,000-foot track, and hear a narration about the cars. Afterwards,

Open: Memorial Day–Oct.,
weekends & holidays,
10–4.
Short shuttle tickets: Adults
$2; children, seniors $1.
Museum & gift shop.

passengers can go forward and blow the train whistle and ring the bell, and also check out the model trains in the 1902 Lenox train station. A 70-year-old B&O coach is fitted out as a home for a Gilded Age exhibit.

OTHER MUSEUMS

Besides letting you delve into fine art and rare books, the many museums in Williamstown can take you in still other directions. You can go *out* at the *Hopkins Forest Museum* (413-597-2346; *Hopkins Memorial Forest*, the *Rosenberg Center*, and *Buxton Garden*; Northwest Hill Rd.), to such seasonal events as sheep shearing and maple sugaring, while the museum itself exhibits old photographs, farm machinery, and tools. And you can go *up* to the stars at the 19th-century fieldstone *Hopkins Observatory* (413-597-2188; Main St.) via the projected shows at the *Milham Planetarium* (evenings Tues. & Thurs. summer; Fri. during school year), and *out and up* to the real pulsars and quasars through the telescopes at Williams College.

Bennington Museum (802-447-1571), 15 miles north of Williamstown on Rte. 7 in Vermont; and *Historic Deerfield, Inc.* (413-774-5581), E. Rte. 2 and S. on Rte. 5, are fine day-trip destinations.

MUSIC

TANGLEWOOD
Box office 413-637-1600;
information 413-637-5165.
Off-season: 617-266-1492.
www.bso.org.
West St. (Rte. 183), Lenox,
MA 01240.
Mail: 301 Massachusetts
Ave., Boston, MA 02115.
Season: Summer.
Tickets: From $13.50
(lawn), then concert hall
and shed; different
events vary.
Gift shops; Restaurant.

Tanglewood remains *the* summer music festival in New England, an incomparable facility for all the world's musicians and music lovers. Whether we picnic on the lawn or sit closer to the Boston Symphony Orchestra in the Shed, hearing music at Tanglewood is an incomparable experience. The powerful positive feeling among musicians, students, and concertgoers alike, the sheer fun of seeing and hearing great music in the great outdoors makes Tanglewood the quintessential Berkshire entertainment.

Tanglewood began as the Berkshire Music Festival in the summer of 1934. Members of the New York Philharmonic were bused from Manhattan to the mountains and lodged in the area's hotels for the concert series. It was a rousing success and was repeated the following summer, but the New York orchestra withdrew. Then Serge Koussevitzky, Russian-born conductor of the Boston Symphony Orchestra, was wooed and

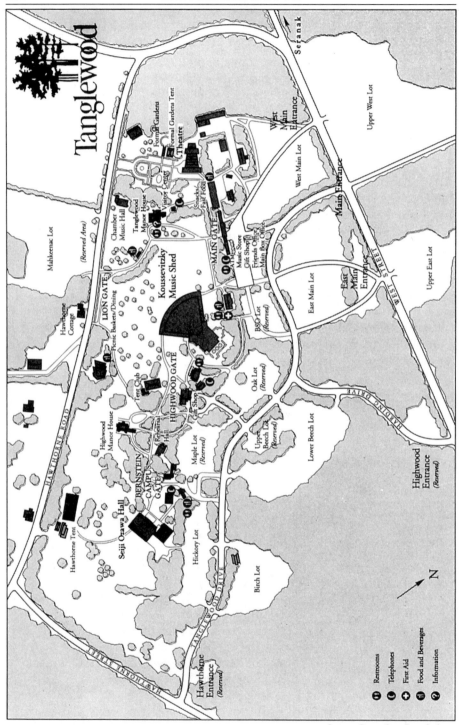

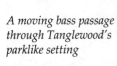

A moving bass passage through Tanglewood's parklike setting

won. The BSO signed on for a series of three concerts on a single August weekend in 1936.

The popularity of this series was immense, nearly 15,000 people attending. And in the fall of that year, the Tappan family gave their Tanglewood estate on the Stockbridge-Lenox border to the BSO for a permanent summer home in the Berkshires. For the first two summers, concerts were held in a large canvas tent but, during one 1937 program, a torrential thunderstorm drowned out Wagner's "Ride of the Valkyries" and dampened instruments, musicians, and audience alike. During intermission, an impromptu fund-raising drive raised pledges totaling $30,000 for the creation of a permanent "music pavilion." By the following summer, through the combined efforts of the distinguished architect Eliel Saarinen and Stockbridge engineer Joseph Franz the Shed was a reality.

Sensing the opportunity and the ideal setting, in 1940 Koussevitzky and the BSO added the Berkshire Music Center for advanced musicians, the only such school run by a major symphony orchestra. For the school's opening ceremony, Randall Thompson composed his haunting *Alleluia* for unaccompanied chorus, a work that made such a lasting impression that it has been performed as the school's opening music ever since.

Each summer the Tanglewood Music Center Orchestra is recreated from that year's crop of students; for their weekly concerts, this impressive group is usually led by a student conductor, but sometimes by the likes of Seiji Ozawa or Kurt Masur. So significant is this Tanglewood education that upwards of 20 percent of the members of America's major orchestras count themselves among Tanglewood Music Center alumni. Leonard Bernstein was a graduate, as are Seiji Ozawa and Zubin Mehta.

The $10-million arched Ozawa Hall opened in the summer of 1994. Accommodating 1,200 inside and an additional 700 on nearby lawns the hall has sides

---

Where to Sit at Tanglewood

Those planning to picnic at Tanglewood before a performance in the Shed should arrive an hour or so in advance of concert time. Besides allowing time to eat before listening, arriving early affords a greater choice of spaces on the lawn, an important factor if you're to hear the music clearly. Although Tanglewood's amplification system is excellent and facilitates good listening from almost any lawn position, places about 25 yards beyond the Shed-mounted speakers provide the best lawn listening.

Inside the Shed the last series of back rows are good only for saying you were there, allowing only the most distant orchestra views and suffering greatly from much-diminished sound. (Video screens were used in 1997 and 1998 but the experiment has not been repeated.) At the optimum speaker sites on the lawn the sound is far superior. Those who can afford to indulge (up to $74), should buy their way forward into the good seats where the sound is rich, sometimes robust and sometimes delicate, and where they can really see classical music in the making. (Food is not allowed in the shed, however.)

Ozawa Concert Hall has its own lawn with seating for several hundred.

All should allow time for a walk in Tanglewood's beautifully groomed boxwood gardens. As the sun sets on a clear day you can see the hills in three states.

---

that open, giving it flexibility and versatility as well as excellent acoustics. The hall is located on the Highwood section of Tanglewood, now designated as the Leonard Bernstein campus.

The Music Festival has evolved into a performance center of major proportions, with an annual attendance now of some 300,000 visitors. Pianists Emanuel Ax, Garrick Ohlsson, Peter Serkin, and Alicia de Larrocha; violinists Midori and Itzhak Perlman; and cellist Yo-Yo Ma return regularly. In addition to the regular BSO concerts, Tanglewood presents weekly chamber music concerts in the smaller sheds, Prelude Concerts on Friday nights, Open Rehearsals on Saturday mornings, the annual Festival of Contemporary Music, a Jazz Festival, and almost daily concerts by gifted young musicians at the Music Center. Some student concerts are free. The Boston Pops comes to play as well.

An annual favorite is Tanglewood on Parade, an amazingly varied musical

---

Festivals-within-the-Festival at Tanglewood

Not content to satisfy the classical music lover, Tanglewood offers mini-festivals and series featuring contemporary, jazz, and popular music.

Offerings in the Contemporary Music Festival are an appropriately eclectic mix, including a recent performance by puppets. When our free spirits are being kept too staid by our classicism, we require a dose of Tanglewood's Contemporary Music.

Artistry of an even jazzier sort is showcased during Tanglewood's annual Jazz Festival, with the likes of Branford Marsalis, Dave Brubeck, and the New Black Eagle Jazz band; and songs of a slightly different sort are featured during Tanglewood's Popular Artist Series, often including the ever-popular James Taylor.

day lasting some ten hours, climaxing with booming cannon shots and fireworks. But whatever the scale of the offerings, an evening at Tanglewood marks a high point in any summer.

SOUTH MOUNTAIN CONCERTS
413-442-2106.
Rtes. 7 & 20, P.O. Box 23, Pittsfield, MA 01202.
Ca. 1 mi. S. of Pittsfield Country Club.
Season: Mid-Aug.–early Oct.
Tickets: Prices vary.

South Mountain's Colonial-style Temple of Music, built in 1918, was the gift of Mrs. Elizabeth Sprague Coolidge, to house the concerts of the Berkshire String Quartet. The acoustically splendid 500-seat auditorium, listed on the National Register of Historic Places, is set gracefully on its wooded South Mountain slope.

Past standout performers at the Temple have included Leonard Bernstein, Alexander Schneider, Leontyne Price, and Rudolf Serkin. Currently, a typical season features concerts by leading American string quartets such as the Guarneri, the Juilliard, and the Emerson, as well as other types of ensembles. A popular highlight of every season is the concert by the Beaux Arts Trio.

South Mountain concerts almost always sell out in advance, so be sure to call ahead of time. Unlike Tanglewood, where watching the stars or basking in the sunshine may substitute for close listening to the music, South Mountain's more limited season and number of concerts are designed for the serious music lover.

ASTON MAGNA
413-528-3595; 800-875-7156.
www.astonmagna.org.
St. James Church, 352 Main St. (Rte. 7), P.O. Box 28, Gt. Barrington, MA 01230.
Just S. of Town Hall.
Season: July–Aug.
Tickets: Call for special prices.

Of historic preservation in the Berkshires, none is more artistic than the renaissance of Baroque, Classical, and early Romantic chamber music by Aston Magna. Offering unique cross-disciplinary educational programs for professional musicians and superb concerts both in the summer and at other times, Aston Magna has specialized in 17th-, 18th-, and early 19th-century music, always played on period instruments or reproductions. Hear Bach, Handel, Haydn, Mozart, Schubert, and their contemporaries as you might never have before, with festival director and virtuoso violinist Daniel Stepner leading a distinguished roster of singers and instrumentalists. Participants study the temperament and cultural milieu of the age and then make music that is imbued with the period's sensibility as well.

Andrew Porter, writing in the *New Yorker*, has given this festival several reviews, noting that the string players are "probably as good as any in the world. The winds are in tune. The old self-consciousness has been replaced by confidence, by character and, beyond that, by something one might almost describe as a philosophy intelligently and joyfully embraced. For there is more to Aston Magna than authentic instruments, stylistic insights, and technical ability."

BERKSHIRE CHORAL FESTIVAL
Box office 413-229-1800; administration 413-229-8526; fax 413-229-0109. www.choralfest.org. Concert Shed, Berkshire School, Rte. 41, Sheffield, MA 01257.
Mail: 257 N. Undermountain Rd., Sheffield, MA 01257.
Season: July–Aug.
Tickets: $20–$25.

An experiment in mixing amateur, semipro, and professional singers into a chorus culminated in a single concert. That success has led the Berkshire Choral Festival some 15 years later to evolve into a summer-long, professional quality chorus that can be counted on for stirring moments.

Each summer now brings a five-concert Berkshire celebration featuring 200 voices, powerful soloists and conductors, and the Springfield Symphony, at one of the loveliest preparatory schools in New England, the Berkshire School (Rte. 41, Sheffield; 413-229-8511). *Berkshire Eagle* critic Elsbet Wayne found the closing performance of a recent season "refreshingly boisterous," praising the chorus for its "beautiful diction." This is still something of a pick-up chorus, now being remade annually with a corps of 200 experienced amateurs and some professionals.

The Berkshire Opera's world premiere production of Summer. *From left: John Cheek as Lawyer Royall, Margaret Lattimore as Charity Royall, Michael Chioldi as Lucius Harney.*

**BERKSHIRE OPERA
COMPANY**
413-443-1234.
www.berkop.org.
297 North St., Pittsfield,
MA 01201.
Performances: Robert
Boland Theater, in
Koussevitzky Arts Ctr.,
Berkshire Community
College, 1350 West St.,
Pittsfield, MA 01201.
Season: May–Aug., Oct.
Tickets: $20–$60.

After a decade, first under founder-director Rex Hearn and now under conductor Joel Revzen, the Berkshire Opera seems stronger than ever. This talented group has won praise from audiences and serious critics alike for their English-language renditions of chamber opera.

There are discoveries to be made here. Among them recently was Stockbridge resident Maureen O'Flynn, whom Hearn initially heard singing at the First Congregational Church in Lee and who has since gone from the Berkshire Opera to the Metropolitan and a brilliant international career.

Recent offerings have included an adaptation commissioned jointly by the Berkshire Opera Company and by Edith Wharton Restoration, Inc., of Edith Wharton's novella "Summer." While critics' views on the success of the production varied, they united in praising Berkshire Opera Company for bringing the production into being and filling a needed role in the rich summer life of the region by offering artfully prepared chamber operas.

OTHER MUSIC

Courtesy Berkshire Bach Society

The winds of the Berkshire Bach Society, in rehearsal for the traditional New Year's Eve performance of the Bach Brandenburg Concertos.

In *South County*, the **Berkshire Bach Society** (413-528-9277; P.O. Box 553, S. Egremont, MA 01258) offers a fine series of concerts and lectures at various area churches, schools, and colleges. **Berkshire Friends of Music** (413-243-9744; www.friendsofmusic.org; P.O. Box 2397, Lenox, MA 01240) organizes chamber and orchestral concerts at Seiji Ozawa Hall, Tanglewood, and elsewhere, typically 5–7 concerts Sept.–June. **Simon's Rock College of Bard** (413-528-0771; Alford Rd., Gt. Barrington, MA 01230) is one of the liveliest promoters of professional music in South County. Under the artistic direction of Hilda Banks Shapiro, **Barrington Performing Arts** (413-528-4454) presents several concerts in Simon's Rock's Kellogg Hall. **Close Encounters With Music** (518-392-6677, 800-843-0778; P.O. Box 34, Gt. Barrington, MA 01230) offers beautiful music and intriguing commentary by artistic director Yehuda Hanani and guests at Gt. Barrington's St. James Church and elsewhere, with an annual community concert at the Berkshire Athenaeum. The **Curtisville Consortium** (413-698-2618; P.O. Box 140, W. Stockbridge, MA 01266) takes its name from the hamlet of Interlaken in Stockbridge, which was originally settled as Curtisville. The Consortium is a group of Boston Symphony musicians and guest artists who present a five-week-long series of concerts each summer at the Trinity Church in Lenox. **Music & More** (413-229-3126; HC 65, Box 123B, New Marlborough, MA 01230) presents late-summer Saturday programs at the Meeting House on New Marlborough Green.

In **Central County**, chamber music can also be enjoyed at the **Armstrong Chamber Concerts** (860-868-0522; www.acc.tsx.org; P.O. Box 367, Washington Depot, CT 06794), a Connecticut-based organization offering concerts at Springlawn in Lenox. More chamber music is featured at the **Richmond Performance Series** (413-698-2002; P.O. Box 199, Richmond, MA 01254). Each of these concerts — at Richmond Congregational Church (Rte. 41) and other venues — features professional symphony orchestra veterans, making intimate music in special settings. **Berkshire Community College** (413-499-4660; www.cc.berkshire.org; 1350 West St., Pittsfield, MA 01202) offers concerts year-round. **Stockbridge Summer Music** (413-443-1138; www.baygo.com/ssms) offers concerts on summer Mondays at Seven Hills Inn in Lenox. The **Berkshire Lyric Theatre** (413-499-0258; www.berkshirelyric.org; P.O. Box 347, Pittsfield, MA 01202) plays at Lenox Town Hall and in Central and South County churches. The **Berkshire Concert Choir** (413-442-1684; P.O. Box 174, Richmond, MA 01254), under the direction of John Cheney, presents sacred and secular music in two concerts each year, one in December, another in May.

In **North County**, **Williams College** alone offers enough music to keep anyone humming, with Thompson visiting performances, a world music series, and the Williams Chamber Players series — performances by Williams faculty. The **Berkshire Symphony**, part professional and part student, and the **Williams Choral Society**, under the auspices of the Williams Department of Music, generally present three concerts apiece during the academic year. The student **Jazz Ensemble**, **Kusika**, the **Zambezi Marimba Band**, and close harmony groups too numerous to name provide musical saturation of high quality. The *Griffin Hall* series presents harpsichord and organ music. (Concert manager's office: 413-597-2736; 24-hour Concertline: 413-597-3146; Griffin Hall Concerts: 413-597-2428.)

Elsewhere in Williamstown, the *Clark Art Institute* (413-458-2303; www. clark.williams.edu/concerts.htm; 225 South St., Williamstown, MA 01267) presents free band music outdoors in summer, and chamber music indoors, including several concerts offered by *Williamstown Chamber Concerts* (413-458-8273; P.O. Box 287, Williamstown, MA 01267). Over in North Adams, *Massachusetts College of Liberal Arts* (413-662-5000) sponsors the *Smith House Concert Series* (413-662-5201), usually professional musicians with local connections. MCLA helped with one of the six concerts put on in the May 1999 inaugural season of *Opus Berkshire* (413-663-3121, off-season 212-787-6262; 1391 Massachusetts Ave., N. Adams), a festival of performances by internationally renowned musicians organized by pianist Daniel Epstein of Blackinton.

Just *Outside the County*, in the Berkshire hilltown of Charlemont (Rte. 2, Franklin County), *Mohawk Trail Concerts* (413-625-9511, 888-MTC-MUSE; www.mohawktrail.org; P.O. Box 75, Shelburne Falls, MA 01370) presents a season of classical concerts at the Federated Church, as well as an annual holiday program. And in South Worthington, the Schrade family presents its famous summer *Sevenars Music Festival* (413-238-5854) at The Academy on Rte. 112.

Just over the state line in New Lebanon, NY, are the *Tannery Pond Concerts* (tickets 888-846-5848; information 888-820-1696; P.O. Box 446, New Lebanon, NY 12125). Tannery's season comprises five or six chamber performances between May and October. In adjacent Spencertown, NY, the *Spencertown Academy* concerts (518-392-3693; Rte. 203, P.O. Box 80, Spencertown, NY 12165) are among the Berkshire region's neatest.

Two highly regarded chamber music festivals in northwestern Connecticut enrich the greater Berkshire area. One is the *Norfolk Chamber Music Festival* (860-542-3000, fax 860-542-3004; www.yale.edu/norfolk; Ellen Battell Stoeckell Estate, Rtes. 44 & 272; P.O. Box 545, Norfolk, CT 06058; off-season 203-432-1966; P.O. Box 208246, New Haven, CT 06520). Norfolk presents visiting virtuosos such as the Tokyo String Quartet and the Vermeer Quartet, mid-June through mid-August, as a byproduct of the Yale Summer School of Music. The other major Connecticut festival is *Music Mountain* (860-824-7126, off-season 870-364-2080; www.musicmountain.org; Music Mountain Rd., off Rte. 7 opposite Housatonic Valley High School; P.O. Box 738, Lakeville, CT 06039). Here the Manhattan String Quartet and visiting artists perform mid-June to Labor Day. Founded in 1930 by Chicago Symphony concertmaster Jacques Gordon, Music Mountain is the oldest continuing chamber music festival in America.

NIGHTLIFE

The decor at the Celestial Bar, Castle Street Café in Gt. Barrington, contains the usual — and unusual — suspects.

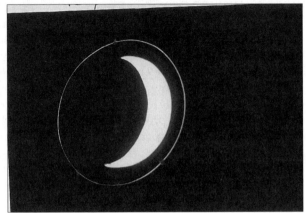

Judith Monachina

Although the Berkshires may be better known as home to great theater, visual art, and classical music, there is a longstanding, thriving tradition of popular nightlife in these parts, including top national and regional talent in jazz, folk, rock, and cabaret.

While new venues are always popping up and older ones occasionally fall by the wayside, there are several well-established nightclubs and restaurants that offer after-hours entertainment. Starting in _South County_, the **Old Egremont Club** (413-528-9712; 264 Hillsdale Rd., S. Egremont) is a venerable, honkytonk-style roadhouse boasting woody ambience and a regular schedule of rootsy rock and R&B bands every weekend. The newly renovated **Club Helsinki** (413-528-3394; 284 Main St., Rte. 7, Great Barrington) is an artsy hangout that features a mix of avant-garde jazz, blues, and world music — past artists include multi-instrumentalist Olu Dara, Cuban guitarist Juan-Carlos Formell, and New Orleans saxophonist Charles Neville. Berkshire's premier jazz venue is Castle Street Café's **Celestial Bar** (413-528-5244; 10 Castle St., Gt. Barrington), a traditional-style piano bar with featured performers most nights, including pianists, guitar and vocal trios, and the occasional swing group. Also in Great Barrington, folksingers occasionally get booked into **Sip of Seattle** (413-528-6913; 343 Main St., Rte. 7) and **Uncommon Grounds** (413-528-0858; 403 Stockbridge Rd., Rte. 7).

In Stockbridge, the **Lion's Den** at the Red Lion Inn (413-298-5545; 30 Main St., Rte. 7) is a cozy, coffeehouse-style nightclub featuring nightly entertainment — and no cover charge — drawing from the region's top talent, including the ever-popular David Grover. Well-known national performers such as

John Hall of Orleans, Tao Rodriguez-Seeger (Pete Seeger's grandson), and Berkshire's own Arlo Guthrie also occasionally drop by. During the summertime, the *Stockbridge Cabaret* (413-298-4032; Rte. 183), just down the road apiece from Tanglewood, is a popular late-night after-concert attraction, boasting top-flight cabaret artists such as K.T. Sullivan, Jeff Harnar, and Marian McPartland. Not to be overlooked — not to be missed, for that matter — is the *Dream Away Lodge* (413-623-8725; County Road), a sleepy little hideaway perched on a mountain road in Becket. For years the Dream Away has attracted the bohemian after-hours crowd from Tanglewood and Jacob's Pillow; after a period of hibernation, the rambling, off-the-beaten-path roadhouse, which has played host to everyone from Bob Dylan to Liberace, is under new management, which has revived the Wednesday night hootenanny and hosts music on weekends.

In *Central County*, blues and rock bands often hold forth on weekend nights at *Barkley's Pub* (413-637-4940; 36 Housatonic St., Lenox), where in the summer musicians from the Boston Symphony have been known to let their proverbial hair down and jam improvisationally. In Pittsfield, the *Crowne Plaza Hotel* (413-499-2000; 1 West Street) looms over the downtown architecturally and otherwise, and its ballroom is often the site of oldies concerts (featuring bands like the Drifters, the Coasters, and the Marvelettes) and blues shows (Magic Dick and J. Geils were recent headliners). Mexican restaurant *La Cocina* (413-499-6363; 140 Wahconah St.) is ground-zero for the local neo-hippie, jam-band set. Other Pittsfield nightspots include the *North End* (413-445-5325; 1331 North St.), an Italian restaurant featuring dinner music and the occasional blues artist, and the *Itam Lodge* (413-447-9492; 203 Newell St.), hosting an array of bar bands.

Sleepy *North County* has awoken over the last few years, in large part due to the opening of the Massachusetts Museum of Contemporary Art (413-662-2111; 87 Marshall St.) in North Adams. *Mass MoCA* itself has become a key venue for nightlife, with monthly dance parties featuring live bands playing swing, polka, zydeco, blues, and occasional concerts (Joan Armatrading, Guy Davis). North Adams seems to have felt a spillover effect from MoCA, with the *Appalachian Bean Café* (413-663-7543; 67 Main St.) and *Papyri Books* (413-662-2099; 49 Main St.) both now presenting bands and folksingers. The Contemporary Artists Center's *Loading Dock Café* (413-663-9555; 189 Beaver St.) heats up in the summer with DJ-dance parties sprinkled between readings and other artistic happenings. *Due Baci* (413-664-6581; 40 Main St.) at the downtown Holiday Inn often has a blues band entertaining on the outside deck in the summer.

Over in Williamstown, *Mezze* (413-458-0123; 84 Water St.) is the nexus for the 20-something hipster crowd that works down the block at one of several Internet companies that have garnered the area the nickname "Silicon Village."

The crowd at Mezze grooves to an eclectic menu of cutting-edge electronic music, avant-garde jazz bands, neo-punk, and psychobilly outfits. When the Williamstown Theatre Festival is up and running during the summer months, top stars of stage and film occasionally ham it up at the **WTF Cabaret** (413-597-3400). Over at the 1896 House (413-458-1896; 910 Cold Spring Rd.), Howie Levitz tickles the ivories on Saturday nights. On Friday nights you can catch Levitz accompanying guitarist Jim Bayliss at the **Williams Inn** (413-458-9371; 1090 Main St.), where the venerable Walt Lehman and his ensemble still swings the crowd on Saturdays.

Berkshirites think nothing of hopping in the car and driving to nearby Northampton for a fix of that college town's eclectic musical menu at one of several venues, including the recently restored **Calvin Theatre** to see the likes of Lyle Lovett or Sonny Rollins, **Pearl Street Nightclub** for hot rock, reggae, or hip-hop acts, or the venerable **Iron Horse Music Hall**, where the best in folk, jazz, country, rock, or comedy can be heard most any night of the year. Call the Northampton Box Office (413-586-8686) for schedules or reservations at any of these venues.

Festival Frenzy

Music moves outdoors in the summertime, when the Berkshire hills come alive with the sounds of bluegrass, blues, jazz, and cutting-edge rock music. The annual **Noppet Hill Bluegrass Festival** (413-499-2805; Bailey Road) on the rolling hills at Steele's Family Farm in Lanesborough might well lay claim to being the most idyllic site for an outdoor music festival. This family-friendly, weekend-long event attracts hundreds of campers among the thousands drawn to hear such top-notch fiddlers and pickers as Del McCoury, Laurie Lewis, and the Nashville Bluegrass Band in late July.

Neo-hippie jamming is the theme at the **Berkshire Mountain Music Festival** (888-245-7081) typically held in August at Butternut Basin ski area in Great Barrington. Past bands at the eclectic three-day event include Los Lobos, the Roots, and Soul Coughing. Butternut (413-528-2000; Rte. 23) also plays host to a one-day reggae festival each summer as well as performances by local bands.

Just a short drive over the New York State line gets you to two of the best summer music festivals in the nation. The venerable **Grey Fox Bluegrass Festival** (888-946-8495), formerly known as the **Winterhawk Bluegrass Festival**, takes place at the Rothvoss Farm in Ancramdale, NY. It's a must-stop on the summer bluegrass circuit for fans as well as top performers including Sam Bush, Tony Trischka, Ralph Stanley, Peter Rowan, Bill Keith, and Allison Krauss. And, after a decade, the Falcon Ridge Folk Festival (860-350-7472; Rte. 23) at the Long Hill Farm in Hillsdale, NY, rivals the Newport (RI) Folk Festival for crowds and top folk acts including Ani DiFranco, Patty Larkin, Dar Williams, Greg Brown, and John Gorka. Both festivals are in July, last for several days, and attract thousands of campers and families as well as day visitors.

THEATER

Kelli Rabke as Mabel Normand (left) and Jeff McCarthy as Mack Sennett (right) in Barrington Stage Company's production of Mack and Mabel, *directed by Barrington Stage Company's Artistic Director, Julianne Boyd.*

Richard Feldman, courtesy Barrington Stage Company

BARRINGTON STAGE COMPANY
413-528-8888;
  fax 413-528-8807.
www.barringtonstageco.org.
Consolati Performing Arts
  Center, Mount Everett
  Regional High School,
  P.O. Box 946, Gt.
  Barrington, MA 01230.
Season: Summer–Fall.
Tickets: Main stage,
  $10–$34; second stage,
  $12–$20; students half
  price.

BERKSHIRE THEATRE FESTIVAL
Box office 413-298-5576;
  administration
  413-298-5536.
www.berkshiretheatre.org.

Julianne Boyd, artistic director of the Barrington Stage Company, knows a good thing when she hears it. *Lady Day at Emerson's Bar & Grill*, starring Gail Nelson as blues singer Billie Holiday, launched Barrington in 1995, playing to sell-outs at restaurants. More recently *Mack and Mabel* had a highly successful run on the main stage, while *St. Nicholas* and *Grease* flourished on Stage II. Barrington runs KidsAct, training 10-to-17-year-olds, summer and fall.

In 1887 architect Stanford White completed his design for the Stockbridge Casino Company, created for the "establishment and maintenance of a place for a reading room, library and social meeting." Forty years later, when the structure had fallen into disuse, Mabel Choate, daughter of

The cast of Moby Dick —
Rehearsed, *by Orson*
Welles, directed by Eric
Hill on The Fitzpatrick
Main Stage of Berkshire
Music Festival.

Richard Feldman, courtesy Berkshire Theatre Festival

6 East Main St. (Rte. 102),
P.O. Box 797,
Stockbridge, MA 01262.
Season: Summer.
Tickets: Main Stage,
$27–$36; Unicorn
Theatre, $18; Children's
Theatre, $5–$7.50.
Gift shop.

Ambassador Joseph H. Choate of Stockbridge, gave the Casino to the Three Arts Society, which in turn moved it to its present site at the foot of Yale Hill, renting it to Alexander Kirkland and F. Cowles Strickland, who opened the Berkshire Playhouse in 1928.

Since that time the playhouse, later renamed Berkshire Theatre Festival, has been in the forefront of American summer theater. Major works by nearly every American playwright of note have been performed here, including Lillian Hellmann, Tennessee Williams, Eugene O'Neill, and Thornton Wilder. The playhouse produced Wilder's *Our Town* and *The Skin of Our Teeth,* with Wilder himself in featured roles.

Leading lights in the theater appear regularly, from a young Katharine Hepburn in 1930 to Joanne Woodward in 1996.

The last two decades have been a period of growth and refocusing for BTF. In the spring of 1976, the building was entered on the National Register of Historic Places. Since then, gradual refurbishment has continued, with a new paint job, and most noticeably, all new seats. The Theatre Festival has expanded its educational and rehearsal facilities, principally upon the gift of the Lavan Center, a few miles north of the playhouse. Interns and apprentices live at the center and rehearse there, while pursuing a program of classes in acting, voice, movement, and design.

BTF also features shows at its 100-seat Unicorn Theatre, a showcase for younger artists. These are becoming increasingly substantial, recently being highlighted by the painterly *Mississippi Nude,* by John Reaves, one artist's life in living color. The educational aspect, called "The BTF Plays," reaches out to local schools.

MUSIC-THEATRE GROUP
413-298-5504; off-season
212-366-5260.
During season: P.O. Box 42,
Glendale, MA 01229.
Off-season: Suite 1001, 30
W. 26th St., New York,
NY 10010.
Season: June & Aug. in the
Berkshires; year-round
performances.
Tickets: $15–$20.

For its innovative and penetrating explorations of music theatre, the Music-Theatre Group has won 20 Obie awards in New York. It brings to the Berkshires a world-class adventure for all lovers of music and drama. Under the leadership of producing director Lyn Austin, the group has tackled difficult, esoteric works and created ones that are close to sublime.

"The Music-Theatre Group blazes trails," raved the *Boston Globe*. Theater here is minimally staged; the emphasis is more on script and musical development as many of these works prepare for a New York run.

Said the *New York Times*: "The Music-Theatre Group has produced one of the most innovative and original bodies of work in American theatre."

Judith McSpadden as Jaques in the Shakespeare & Company Summer Performance Institute's production of As You Like It.

Ogden Gigli, courtesy Shakespeare &
Company

**SHAKESPEARE &
COMPANY**
Box office 413-637-3353;
off-season 413-637-1197.
www.shakespeare.org.
The Mount, 2 Plunkett St.,
P.O. Box 865, Lenox, MA
01240.
Near S. jct. Rtes. 7 & 7A.
Season: Summer, fall.
Tickets: $12.50–$33.50.

Shakespeare is revitalized onstage in Lenox, ending its run at Edith Wharton's palatial estate, The Mount, and moving uptown to Springlawn, formerly occupied by the National Music Center. Shakespeare & Company has made splendid use of The Mount's rolling lawn, performing most of their plays outdoors on a stage built in a glade, against the lovely stone wall of a rose garden. It will find more spacious and equally inspirational settings at its new site.

Under the powerful artistic guidance of English actor/director Tina Packer and her artistic associate, Jonathan Epstein, Shakespeare & Company has brought new light, feeling, and clarity to Shakespeare, making the works more accessible to many people. Shakespeare & Company works in area schools in the winter, spreading the wonder of the Bard even farther.

Part of the dramatic impact derives from the actors' ability to treat the audience as their alter ego, always privy to secrets of the drama. The plays are staged all around the seating area; intimacy with the action is inevitable, with stage and lighting design creating magical effects.

The company's inspired clowning is magical, too. Says Packer, "The function of the clowns is of the utmost importance in Shakespeare's plays. The influence of *commedia del l'arte* on Elizabethan theater, with its knockabout and improvised humor, cannot be overemphasized. Because of the inordinate amount of 'seriousness' that has been attached to 'the Bard,' much of the sheer joy and fun of Shakespeare has been lost for modern audiences." Not so at The Mount, where they're in for a good time.

Wrote *New York Times* critic Ben Brantley of the company's performance of *A Midsummer Night's Dream*: "The overall result is vulgar, over scaled and loud. And it works. . . . There are few productions of Shakespearean comedy in which the meaning of every joke (whether intended by Shakespeare or not) reads so clearly, and the audience was responsive to each one."

While Shakespeare & Company attends to its namesake, it has also produced Wharton-oriented plays, and other modern plays. The company has toured, for performances and workshops, to Denver, Toronto, and other cities and, under the aegis of Joe Papp's New York Shakespeare Festival, it has also taken productions from The Mount to Brooklyn's Prospect Park.

Shakespeare & Company is a must-see for locals and visitors alike.

WILLIAMSTOWN THEATRE FESTIVAL
Box office 413-597-3400;
administration
413-458-3200;
fax 413-458-3147.
www.WTFestival.org.
1000 Main St., P.O. Box 517,
Williamstown, MA
01267.
Season: Summer.
Tickets: Free–$35.

For WTF producer Michael Ritchie the challenge is not to be "the best summer theater but the best theater in America." Williamstown Theatre Festival took a giant step in that direction in the summer of 1999, exciting the theater world with Academy Award winner Gwyneth Paltrow in *As You Like It*, followed by an extraordinary production of Arthur Miller's *The Price*, which moved to Broadway in the fall. Meanwhile, in the place of the usual free theater, played outdoors, WTF mounted the new musical *Quark Victory at* Mass MoCA, where it was enthusiastically received by family audiences. WTF broke all records for attendance, for positive reviews, and for national attention.

In a previous year, *People Magazine* put it this way: "The showbiz capital of the U.S. may, for once, be on neither coast. The Williamstown Theatre Festival

Bebe Neuwirth as guess who in The Taming of the Shrew, *directed by Robert Rees, the Williamstown Theatre Festival.*

Richard Feldman, courtesy
Williamstown Theatre Festival

could boast the most powerful concentration of acting talent any place this summer."

Each summer, in addition to full-scale productions with first-rate sets and costumes on the Main Stage, WTF offers other more intimate theater experiences. There are the four productions of works-in-progress mounted at the Other Stage. Late-night musical cabarets provide surprise cameo appearances by Main Stage celebrities like Dick Cavett, inveterate songster and raconteur. There are Staged Readings; Museum Pieces at the Williams College Museum of Art; Act I Performance Projects by the WTF young actor training ensemble, at work in Goodrich Hall on the Williams Campus; and the Greylock Theatre Project, which connects economically disadvantaged young people from North Adams with professional theater artists.

It's no mistake, then, that *Newsweek* ranked WTF as "the best of all American summer theaters," with "the cream of America's acting crop." The best *theater* in America? It will be worth watching over the next few years.

OTHER THEATER

There are more than a dozen other theater companies in and about Berkshire.

In **South County**, the biggest little theater is **Mixed Company** (413-528-2320; at the Granary, 37 Rosseter St., Gt. Barrington, MA 01230), where fall-off-the-seat comedy alternates with moving drama. Under the direction of playwright Joan Ackermann, Mixed Company has built a solid following, often leading to competition for the theater's few dozen seats. Ackermann's award-winning *Zara Spook and Other Lures* premiered here, as did her droll *Bed and Breakfast,* in which she played an addled Mrs. Digby. The **DeSisto Estate Cabaret** (413-298-

4032; Rte. 183, Stockbridge, MA 01230) hosts dinner theater Tuesday through Thursday evenings in the summer, cabaret performances Friday and Saturday following dinner, and additional cabaret after some Friday and all Saturday Tanglewood concerts.

The *Central County* theater scene has never been livelier. The *Berkshire Community College Players* regularly appear at the Robert Boland Theater in the Koussevitzky Arts Center at BCC (413-499-0886 when performances are staged; 1350 West St., Pittsfield). *The Town Players* (413-443-9279) occasionally perform either at BCC or at the Berkshire Museum. In a recent season, they presented *Into the Woods*, by Stephen Sondheim. During the summer *The News in Revue* performs political satire at several locations.

North County is especially theatrical. Besides the Williamstown Theater Festival, Williamstown has the *Starlight Stage Youth Theatre* (413-458-4246), a hands-on theater experience for youth 8 to 18, which performs summers at the First Congregational Church. In the fall and winter, slack is picked up by *Williamstheatre*, the Williams College theater group (413-597-2342; www.williams.edu/acad-depts/theatre/; Adams Memorial Theatre), producing impressive revivals of plays by Shakespeare, Brecht, and Becket as well as contemporary plays. Also active in the academic year is the drama department at *Massachusetts College of Liberal Arts* (413-662-5000).

Outside the County, in neighboring Chatham, NY, the *Mac-Haydn Theatre* (518-392-9292; Rte. 204, P.O. Box 204, Chatham, NY 12037) has been offering 15-week-long summer seasons of robust Broadway musicals since 1969. Productions are staged in the round. Their high-energy casts are guaranteed to deliver a supercharge of musical theater, less than truly sophisticated perhaps, but usually a whole lot of fun. In New Lebanon, at the *Theater Barn* (518-794-8989; www.theaterbarn.com; Rte. 20; P.O. Box 39, New Lebanon, NY 12125), producers Joan and Abe Phelps zero in on musical comedy, with an occasional murderous dose of Agatha Christie thrown in. In the tri-city area, *Proctor's* in Schenectady (518-382-1083), and the *Egg* in Albany (518-473-1061; www.theegg. org; Empire State Plaza, P.O. Box 2065, Albany, NY 12220), both provide stages for national acts, shows, and dramas. Up in Bennington, VT, the *Oldcastle Theatre Company* (802-447-0564; Southern Vermont Arts Center; P.O. Box 1555, Bennington, VT 05201) can always be counted on for some fun, such as *Nunsense: The Second Coming*. Back in Massachusetts, the *Miniature Theatre of Chester* (413-354-7771; www.miniaturetheatre.org; in the Town Hall) hosts large-as-life drama.

SEASONAL EVENTS

Berkshire Bateria Scola de Samba plays at a spring street fair in Great Barrington.

Judith Monachina

There are a number of special Berkshire events tuned to the calendar. Somehow the Berkshire year wouldn't unfold properly without them. Leading the pack are Pittsfield's *Home Town Parade* on July 4 and North Adams's *Fall Foliage Parade* the Sunday before Columbus Day. For additional information, you can always try contacting the appropriate Chambers of Commerce; see the listings under "Tourist Information" in Chapter Nine, *Information*.

SPRING

Jazztown, Williamstown's salute to the authentic, takes place all around town in April, with Williams College and the town's chamber of commerce collaborating on a musical blowout. Performing are college big bands from the East, distinguished pros, and alumni groups.

Riverfest is North County's favorite outdoor event every May, celebrating the revitalized Hoosic River, which threads through Adams, North Adams, and Williamstown. Environmental art along the riverbanks, raft rides, food, and music at Cole Field, Williamstown. For information, call the Hoosic River Watershed Association, 413-458-2742.

SUMMER

Adams Agricultural Fair is the old-fashioned kind, with a midway of rides, noisy big trucks, and judging of produce and animals. For a weekend in mid-August it takes over the fairgrounds off the Curran Highway just south of the Adams-N. Adams line. Other notable fairs in the area include those of

Cummington, Schaghticoke, Altamont, and the **Eastern States Exposition** (the Big E), Springfield.

Berkshire Crafts Fair is a mid-August event, held at Monument Mountain Regional High School (413-528-3346; Rte. 7, between Stockbridge & Gt. Barrington). Top craftspeople offer their extraordinary creations, from handmade paper to handblown glass, from handwoven clothing to exotic wooden ware.

Best of the Berkshires Festival is Pittsfield's newest celebration of county-wide talents, in many fields, from music to dance, from food to drink. Held in mid-August, the festival has brought a jolt of life to North Street, luring thousands to the traffic-free party. The Berkshire Public Theatre Children's Ensemble has performed, as has acclaimed magician Timothy Wenk.

Fireworks over Stockbridge Bowl are spectacular because of echoes from the hills. The biggest bangs and most colorful starbursts come from Tanglewood, on the Fourth of July, and following the *1812 Overture* at the end of Tanglewood on Parade, a highlight of the BSO Berkshire season.

June Fest explodes annually in celebration of North Adams's Italian heritage. A true community effort, the festival features great food, top-name music, ethnic dance, a carnival, and children's activities. Profits go to North County schools.

Monument Mountain Author Climb is a literary event commemorating the August day in 1851 when Melville, Hawthorne, Holmes, and friends scaled the Gt. Barrington peak. They imbibed a good deal of champagne, weathered a thunderstorm, read William Cullen Bryant's poem about the Indian maiden who threw herself in sorrow from the top, and began a lasting friendship. Becoming a fixture is an annual recreation of Henry David **Thoreau's Climb up Mount Greylock**, on or about July 20. Watch the *Berkshire Eagle* for announcements.

Summerfest in Great Barrington has become a highlight on South County's early summer schedule. Held on a Saturday evening in mid-June, it has raised thousands of dollars for Hospice of South Berkshire and raised the spirits of thousands who attended. With the entire downtown closed off to motor traffic, locals and visitors have a grand old time listening to music, watching dance or magic, and grazing on various snack foods.

Susan B. Anthony Celebration & Adams Street Fair is held every July on Park Street, which is closed off for the event. Features are the "Pedal & Plod" (foot and bike race), food, and much more. For information, call the Adams Chamber of Commerce, 413-743-1881.

FALL

Great Josh Billings RunAground is Berkshire's greatest one-day party, an athletic extravaganza that involves thousands of participants and many more admiring, supportive spectators. This late-September biking-canoeing-running triathlon takes its name from Lanesborough's Henry Wheeler Shaw, an

inveterate 19th-century prankster humorist under the pen na
Billings. "If a fellow gets to going downhill, it seems as if every
greased for the occasion," wrote Billings (more or less); and every   _ the
RunAground the bike racers, shooting down that last hill on Rte. 183 to Stockbridge Bowl, prove how right old Josh was. After the race, there's a huge
party at Tanglewood with food, drink, dancing, and Berkshire camaraderie.

Greylock Ramble. On Columbus Day the Adams chamber celebrates the
height of fall foliage by inviting 3,000 people of every dimension to hike the
big hill. Often narrated by well-informed guides other hikes and climbs to
and around the lofty top of Mount Greylock in North County are sponsored
by the Appalachian Mountain Club, beginning at Greylock Glen in Adams,
the Visitors Center in Lanesborough, the Sperry Road Campground, or Bascom Lodge.

Harvest Festival at the Berkshire Botanical Garden, Stockbridge, is an early-
October event packed with cider and doughnuts, apples and pumpkins, hay
wagon and fire engine rides, plants and seeds, and mayhem of all sorts
appealing to children and grownups of every persuasion. A highlight of the
Berkshire calendar, this two-day event includes a live-performance tent featuring the likes of the Bluestars. Besides a great plant sale and flea market, a
book sale and second-hand clothes mart, the festival has also attracted a
greater number of crafts people, selling an increasingly refined collection of
handcrafts.

Lenox Apple Squeeze takes place in the week after the Tub Parade. Many
shops have major sales; there are crafts and food booths, plus demonstrations, live music, and more.

Octoberzest is a fall foliage festival of music and ballet, presented at Simon's
Rock by the Barrington Performing Arts. Mixing and matching poets with
musicians, dancers with actors into various ensemble pieces really does add
a zesty melange to the southern Berkshire fall.

Tub Parade is one of Berkshire's oldest annual events, dating back to the
Gilded Age. The late-September parade has been revived without a hitch.
Actually, there were plenty of hitches, but they were supposed to be there,
hitching show ponies to the ornate, flower-decked carts they pulled. Under
the auspices of the Lenox Village Association and the Colonial Carriage and
Driving Society, the Tub Parade gives a glimpse back into turn-of-the-previ-
ous-century Berkshire, when dogs with ruffled collars rode next to their
masters. Brief but brilliant.

WINTER

Chesterwood holds its Christmas open house from the first weekend in
November through Veterans' Day. Omitted in 1998 and 1999 due to renovations on the barn, the festival resumes in 2000. Tours of the house and studio, shops open, refreshments, demonstrations.

First Night is Pittsfield's salutation to the New Year, beginning around 7pm on New Year's Eve. Wearing an inexpensive tag, revelers are able to drop in on dozens of performances ranging from hardest rock to young ballerinas, playing in assorted sites in downtown. The same tag gets wearers a free ride on the B Bus, in case the walk gets burdensome. Noticeably absent are drunks and other bores. Recent years have featured a laser light show at Park Square. Fireworks announce the actual calendar change.

Holiday Walk in Williamstown opens Spring Street to horses and wagons, which carry spectators to shops where musical and dramatic groups perform. Nonprofit organizations present festive exhibits in the Williams College gymnasium and crafters exhibit in the Field House.

Holly-Days is Lenox's four-day celebration of the holiday season, with the arrival of Santa, a gingerbread-house contest, holiday entertainment (the Albany Berkshire Ballet and more), a pancake breakfast, and an ecumenical candlelight service on Sunday.

Naumkeag at Christmas is extra-special, because that's when the Choates's Christmas decorations are taken out and the house is made to look ever so festive. Looking in on a quiet turn-of-the-last-century Christmas can make the viewers merrier. The historic home in Stockbridge (described under "Historic Homes" in this chapter) offers this opportunity to the public on an irregular basis.

Stockbridge Main Street at Christmas, the first weekend in December, is Stockbridge's salute to Christmas and to Norman Rockwell. There are festive lights, arts and crafts, readings by actors from the Berkshire Theatre Festival, house tours, a "luminaria" walk by carolers, a gala concert, and a reenactment of Rockwell's famous painting "Stockbridge Main Street at Christmas" (1956), with antique cars on Main Street. For information call the Stockbridge Chamber of Commerce, 413-298-5200.

Tea Ceremony at Great Barrington Pottery is a moving meditation, a highly stylized form of social communion both for the Tea Mistress and for those she serves. Enter the Chashitsu (Japanese Ceremonial Teahouse and Formal Garden) at Richard Bennett's Great Barrington Pottery (described in Chapter Eight, *Shopping*) to return to 14th-century Japan.

VIDEO RENTALS

Here is a list of video rental outlets that stock the standard Hollywood movies; most also have a smattering of foreign art titles. (There may be others outlets in the county not listed here.) You can also borrow videos from public libraries throughout the county.

South County

AVC Video Showcase (413-229-2910; 231 Main St., Rte. 7, Sheffield, next to Sheffield Pub).
Alice in Videoland II (413-528-4451, fax 413-528-4451; 301A Stockbridge Rd., Rte. 7, Gt. Barrington).
Elm Street Market (413-298-3634; 4 Elm St., Stockbridge).
Housatonic Country Market (413-274-3500; 266 Pleasant St., N. Housatonic).
Impoco's (413-528-9162; 54 State Rd., Rte. 7, Gt. Barrington).
Lee Video (413-243-3636; 23 Park Plaza, Lee).
Millennium Video (413-528-5575; 740 Main St., Rte. 7, Gt. Barrington).
North Star Video of Great Barrington (413-528-1067; 224 State Rd., Rte. 23, Gt. Barrington).
West Stockbridge Video (413-232-7851; 20 Main St., W. Stockbridge).

Central County

Dalton Video (413-684-4480; 69 Depot St., Dalton).
East Street Video (413-443-2000; 10 Lyman St., Pittsfield).
First Run Video (413-442-6830; 1664 North St. Rte. 7, Lanesborough).
Hollywood Video (413-442-4805; 455 Dalton Ave., Pittsfield).
Melody House (413-442-5724; 307 North St., Pittsfield).
Patrick's Video (413-442-6666; 200 West St., Pittsfield).
Plaza Video (413-443-0943; 444 W. Housatonic St., Rte. 20, Pittsfield).
Stop & Shop Video Center (413-443-3548; 660 Merrill Rd., Pittsfield).
Variety Video (413-637-2046; 26 Housatonic St., Lenox).
Video Studio 12 (413-447-7595; 180A Elm St., Pittsfield).

North County

Dox (413-458-4420; 320 Main St., Williamstown).
Video Studio (413-743-7007; 1 Myrtle St., Adams).
Video Studio of North Adams (413-664-7880; N. Adams Plaza, N. Adams).

CHAPTER SIX
Spas & the Spiritual Life
BODY & SPIRIT

The green and blue of the Berkshire summer, turning to bright red, gold, and orange, and then the blue hills of winter, lavender at sunset, have long attracted the traveler in search of beauty. When one is driving along a Berkshire back road, and even Route 7 approaching Williamstown, the view suddenly opens up on each side, an enchanting scene of hills, mountains, farms, and farmhouses.

So, too, the feeling from the view from atop the Cobble in Tyringham, that gnarly hunk of land that some say was turned upside down once by a glacier and now sits in perpetual preservation — owned by the Trustees of Reservations. Just a 20-minute hike from bottom to the top transports pilgrims to the sky, maybe even heaven.

Courtesy Canyon Ranch

A quiet spot for relaxing at Canyon Ranch.

Sculptor Daniel Chester French called the Berkshires "heaven." The land is well known for attracting artists, such as French, and then those who like to be where the artists are. Here the connection of the land to the creative arts is long standing.

Less well known is the even longer attraction of this place to the various other kinds of seekers, those whose lifelong vocation was spiritual search, and more recently those who are looking for new ways, through the disciplines that begin with the body, to rejuvenate the mind and spirit. In the Berkshires the physical — the land and the health of the body and mind — has long been connected to the creative and the spiritual.

This mecca for music, dance, and art lovers also attracts yoga enthusiasts, macrobiotic and healing arts practitioners of all kinds. In many cases the homes of their organizations started as "cottages" during the Gilded Age — later becoming centers for the Jesuits, Carmelites, and Franciscans. Now visitors will find virtually all kinds of yoga practitioners, healing arts enthusiasts, and those who use the Chinese disciplines of Chi Kung and Tai Chi. A Franciscan monastery is now the Kushi Institute, a well-known macrobiotic center in Becket. On the site of the Kripalu Center for Yoga and Health once stood a massive 100-room home; the present building was constructed as a Jesuit seminary, and now people from all over the world come here to learn about yoga. Their international network of Kripalu-trained yoga teachers includes many countries, and the natural effect of this yoga center in the Berkshires means an abundance of classes in the various approaches to yoga.

The most luxurious of these health centers, Canyon Ranch in the Berkshires, was first an elegant house built on the model of Le Petit Trianon; then it too belonged to the Jesuits, and now people come from far and wide to learn to nurture their bodies and spirits. And a former Shaker settlement houses a Sufi community that opens its doors to visitors for workshops, classes, and services.

A WELLNESS CENTER WITH A FOCUS ON YOGA

KRIPALU CENTER FOR YOGA AND HEALTH (413-448-3400; Rte. 183 in Stockbridge, south of Tanglewood. Mailing address: Lenox, MA 01240).

One of the grandest of Berkshire's summer "cottages" was Shadowbrook, a 100-room Tudor mansion built by Anson Phelps Stokes. Later a Jesuit seminary, the original building burned to the ground and the Jesuit brothers built an equally large but much less ornamented building to replace it. Though modern and functional, the estate, with its breathtaking views of Stockbridge Bowl and the mountains beyond, continues to move its many guests.

It's hard to imagine a more complete line of yoga workshops and classes than can be found at Kripalu. The 70-page catalog includes listings for such classes as The Biomechanics of Yoga, Kripalu Yoga and Kripalu Yoga Teacher Training, Gentle Yoga Weekend, Advanced Viniyoga Therapy, Contact Yoga,

The Kripalu Center provides educational and spiritual seminars year-round.

Yoga for a Better Back, Women's Yoga Quest, Anusara Yoga, Chakra Yoga, A Kripalu Yoga Retreat, Meditation and Yoga, The Raja Yoga Intensive, Mindful Parenting, Raw Juice Fasting, Danskinetics and Haitian Dance, Letting Go of Fear — only a small fraction of the offerings at this center, which caters to beginners as well as those well advanced in their yoga training.

The offerings don't stop with yoga, however, and well-known experts such as Babatunde Olatunji and Susan Love are among those who have offered

Yoga at Kripalu.

weekend workshops in drumming and women's health throughout the year. Facilities include Danskinetics and yoga studios, saunas and whirlpools, 300 acres of forest, meadows, meditation gardens, miles of woodland trails, a private beach on Stockbridge Bowl, a bookstore and gift shop, special health services, and a natural-foods kitchen serving tasty, well-balanced vegetarian meals. Health services include various types of bodywork, including Aromatherapy Massage and Shiatsu Therapy, plus Dr. Hauschka Skin Care, Phoenix Rising Therapy, and Ayurvedic Body Treatments.

Kripalu's environment is nurturing. Clients sign on for short-term or longer term visits. Yoga teacher training and longer term professional training programs are available as well as opportunities for day guests. Prices are moderate.

A LUXURY SPA

CANYON RANCH IN THE BERKSHIRES (413-637-4400; 91 Kemble St., Lenox, MA 01240)

Canyon Ranch occupies a former Gilded Age "cottage," Bellefontaine.

Courtesy Canyon Ranch

Several years ago, health entrepreneurs Mel and Enid Zuckerman took their highly successful Tuscon, Arizona, Canyon Ranch formula and transferred it to the sculptured hills of Lenox. There they transformed and built upon Giraud Foster's splendid "cottage," Bellefontaine, a replica of the French Petit Trianon, to create a world-class spa.

It is a spectacular facility, smoothly run by a group of skilled and friendly professionals. Whether used for a short cool-out, a vacation, a chance to drop a few pounds, an invigorating change of pace, or a whole new start, Canyon

Ranch lives up to its billing as "the spa that never leaves you." With over 50 fitness classes to choose from daily, swimming, racquet sports of all kinds, and a state-of-the-art gymnasium, the three-level spa complex offers a customized physical workout. In addition, hiking, mountain biking, and cross-country skiing provide indoor and outdoor fitness possibilities unimaginable at the average spa. Besides Jacuzzis, steam rooms, and saunas Canyon Ranch offers inhalation rooms (combining steam and eucalyptus) and a range of personal services to pamper you. Massages include Reiki, to which can be added an herbal wrap, an aroma wrap, clay or salt treatment, or hydrotherapy. Each of these ancient, exotic treatments is performed by experts revitalizing inside and out. The healthful opportunities go on and on, from skin and beauty treatments to dietary education and stop-smoking hypnosis. Canyon Ranch visitors — unless they go out to Bev's Homemade for locally made ice cream — are on a low-fat, low-cholesterol regime that is as delicious as it is healthy.

Prices vary seasonally but are always substantial. Access to the facility is limited to guests. Says *Vogue* magazine: "Not a fitness factory or fat farm . . . you go to Canyon Ranch anticipating short-term results . . . and return with a long-term resolve." "A cross between boot camp and heaven," says *Self* magazine.

Cross-country skiing at Canyon Ranch.

Courtesy Canyon Ranch

MACROBIOTICS & HEALTH

KUSHI INSTITUTE (800-975-8744; store 800-645-8744; www.kushiinstitute. org; e-mail: programs@kushiinstitute.org. P.O. Box 7, Becket, MA 01223)

The quietest of the healthful learning places in the Berkshires lies just outside of the village of Becket, about five miles from Jacob's Pillow Dance Festival. The Kushi Institute now attracts people from all over the world who want to learn about this approach to health.

This 600-acre mountainside property overlooking the village of Becket was once a Franciscan monastery and is now home of the Kushi Institute. Michio and Aveline Kushi founded the Institute in 1978 in Brookline, Massachusetts, but gradually moved all programs out to Becket by 1990.

The internationally known macrobiotic center attracts people who wish to learn more about the macrobiotic way of life. The basic philosophy includes a whole-foods diet and an appreciation of other natural elements for a healthy lifestyle. These include exercise, body care, household products, and livelihood. Macrobiotics has been popularized through books and various media that have detailed its effects on health recovery from cancer. Many people choose the macrobiotic way of life as a natural approach to recovery and optimal health maintenance.

The basic institute program offered year-round is the weeklong Way to Health. It also offers a month-long macrobiotic career training program and an annual summer conference. The weeklong programs includes cooking classes every day plus menu planning workshops as well as lectures and question-and-answer sessions about how macrobiotics works. Participants gain skills and knowledge to practice macrobiotics after only one week.

The macrobiotic approach can be embraced by people of any philosophy or religion.

Accommodations include shared or private rooms, with shared or with private baths. Guests use walking trails on this mostly wooded property. They can patronize a retail and mail-order store on the property.

MONASTERIES & RETREAT CENTERS

MARIAN FATHERS (413-298-3931; Eden Hill, Stockbridge MA 01262)

Though they do not offer retreat facilities, the Marian Fathers do open their beautiful grounds and chapel to the public. They are a Catholic monastery, but invite anyone to use their candle shrines and chapels. The Eden Hill Recreation Center (see below) is owned by the Marians and is open to the public.

MOUNT CARMEL RETREAT CENTER (413-458-3164, fax 413-458-9420; Oblong Rd., P.O. Box 613, Williamstown, MA 01267)

One of the best views of Mount Greylock is through the window of a small chapel at Mount Carmel Retreat Center on Oblong Road in Williamstown. About 1000 visitors per year come to the center, which is run by the

Carmelites. They find a quiet beautiful landscape, two chapels, a library, and plenty of quiet. In addition, the Carmelites run family weekends and special retreats focusing on Carmelite spirituality. Groups are also welcome to make their own retreats.

The center sits on 700 rural acres that stretch up to the top of Berlin Mountain at the New York State border. Originally the site of a homestead, then a Georgian mansion, the property was owned by muckraking author Sinclair Lewis before it was purchased by the Carmelite Fathers of the New York province. To the mansion, a new building was added in 1955 that includes a chapel, gym, dining and recreation areas, and living quarters for about 25 people. The Carmelites strive to be "contemplatives in action," and as such are also involved in aspects of the community.

SISTERS OF THE VISITATION MONASTERY (413-243-3995; 14 Beach Rd., Tyringham, MA 01264)

In the beautiful Tyringham Valley this monastery is home to a small group of women who recently relocated here from Wilmington, Delaware. They built their new monastery at the end of Beach Road on a hill overlooking meadows and fields, and have cleared walking trails in the meadows. The sisters live in a cloister, and individual retreatants are invited into the cloister for private retreats of meditation and prayer. They are asked therefore to observe the silence of the monastery and the schedule, which includes a great silence after the 8pm service. There is room for two retreatants at any given time.

Retreatants are invited to attend the services at which the sisters sing the hours of the office five times per day. Visitors are not obligated to attend services or the morning mass but are invited to do so and are given assistance in using the various books for singing. The meadows and fields with walking trails are open to the retreatants once inside the cloister. Part of the chapel that is not in the cloister is open to the public all day from the morning mass on, and the public is invited to attend those services.

EAST MOUNTAIN RETREAT CENTER (Phone/fax 413-528-6617; 8 Lake Buel Rd., Gt. Barrington, MA 01230)

The center provides facilities and guidance to individuals and groups who wish to visit a quiet place for reflection and meditation. The director will help them find teachers or resources needed for a retreat, or just give them a place for their retreat. The center is open to any serious seeker regardless of faith.

While individual retreats are the primary activity of this center, groups are also welcome. Individual retreats are expected to be primarily silent, unless arrangements are made for such activities as instrument playing or chanting, for example.

The center is located on 90 acres of woodland on the side of East Mountain

State Forest in the town of Great Barrington. There are paths and logging trails and places to walk or sit in quiet and contemplation.

A minimum stay is two days and ordinarily two weeks would be the longest stay. Simple meals, bedding, and towels are provided. Kitchen facilities are available for guests to prepare their own breakfast and lunch. Vegetarian options for the hot evening meal, which is provided, are always available.

The director is a United Church of Christ minister and her advisory board is comprised of people from a variety of religious backgrounds. Fees are modest.

ABODE OF THE MESSAGE (518-794-8090; 5 Abode Rd., New Lebanon, NY 12125)

Just a stone's throw from the Massachusetts border, this former Shaker settlement is now home to a group of people who live in a Sufi community. They invite the public to attend their Sunday universal worship services and participate in various programs throughout the year.

This is a community whose members have embraced the ideas of Sufism, but all religions are respected and those who participate in programs and retreats could be from other paths.

The community puts on events, musical, artistic, and spiritual throughout the year from various traditions, including the Sufi, Buddhist, Zorastrian, and others. They have yoga, dance, and musical events and workshops as well.

Those who participate in the Abode and Breakfast program spend a night or two or a week, using that time to give themselves a spiritual retreat. There is also a retreat center, for those who wish to deepen their connection with God, whatever beliefs they hold. Universal worship service on Sunday morning is open to all, as are the monthly Dances of Universal Peace. Call for catalog.

OTHER YOGA, DAY SPAS, & RELATED OUTLETS

Here are some additional places to go for yoga, as well as some of the day spas and healing arts practitioners in Berkshire County. Related businesses continue to open, making it impossible to give a full listing here of the literally hundreds of private practices around the county. Also, many massage therapists, Reiki, acupuncture, and other practitioners operate solo businesses and can be found by looking at the various brochures and papers and the *Yellow Pages*. The *Advocate*, the *Women's Times*, and the *Shopper's Guide* (Great Barrington and surrounding area) are excellent sources of information about these professionals.

Berkshire Mountain Yoga (413-528-5333; 30 Elm Ct., Gt. Barrington, MA 01230) Yoga classes of various kinds, including Ashtanga, hatha, Kali Tri-Yoga, Power Yoga, Yoga for Men, Vinyasa Yoga, and other classes (such as

Acting for Non-Actors) throughout the year. Also offered here are Tai Chi and Qigong. Performing arts classes for children Sept. through May.

Body & Soul (413-528-6465. 42 Railroad Street, Gt. Barrington, MA 01230) Massage, Dr. Hauschka facials, body treatments, cosmetics, skincare, bath and body products.

Eden Hill Recreation Center (413-298-1106; Eden Hill, Stockbridge, MA 01230) Various types of recreational programming, yoga, African dance and drumming, programs for kids as well as adults are a small sampling of the kinds of classes offered here all year at this Marian monastery overlooking the town. The priests and brothers opened this center to the community years ago. Classes for kids and adults generally begin on a semester schedule.

Essencials Day Spa (413-443-6260; 439 Pittsfield-Lenox Rd., Lenox, MA 01240) Offers hair and body treatments, skin treatments, make-up, waxing, Swedish massage.

Kali Ray Tri-Yoga Center (413-229-3399; Rte. 7, Sheffield, MA 01257) This style of flowing Hatha yoga, which focuses on breath and posture, was founded 20 years ago. Kali Ray, its founder, lives in Malibu, California, and tours and teaches all over, visiting this center once or twice year. Classes are held several times daily.

Michele's Day Spa (413-528-9999; 54 Stockbridge Rd., Gt. Barrington, MA 01230) Full Day Escapes include such services as a salt glow or a massage, a starflower facial, manicure, spa pedicure, and healthy gourmet feasts. Any of these services and others by appointment.

Mind Your Body (413-458-2720; Williamstown, MA 01267) Massage, facials, pregnancy massage, infant massage, Kripalu Yoga, and many other treatments.

Phoenix Rising Yoga Therapy (800-288-9642; www.pryt.com; at Shaker Mill, 5 Albany Rd., Rte. 102, W. Stockbridge; Mail: P.O. Box 819, Housatonic, MA 01236) Michael Lee and Lori Bashour, who offer professional yoga training programs, recently purchased a West Stockbridge landmark restaurant/tavern, with the intention of turning one floor into a yoga center. Lee, founder of the modality of Phoenix Rising, describes it as a body/mind/health program based on yoga; thus it is spiritual as well as physical. Lee and Bashour will continue their professional training programs and offer yoga to the general public as well. They plan yoga weekend workshops and retreats.

Spanda Holistic Center (413-442-0123; www.spanda.com; 823 North St., Pittsfield, MA 01201) The philosophy of Spanda is "your health comes from the balanced flow of Chi (life force) in your mind, body and spirit." They offer acupuncture, herbal therapy, Chi Kung, Biomagnets, Chakra work, Reiki, Zen Shiatsu, Reflexology, Zero Balancing, Five Elements Therapies, and more.

The Healing Place (413-637-1980; www.thehealingplace.com; 1 West Street, Lenox, MA 01240). In the center of Lenox, a converted Colonial-style house is the site for this total-wellness center featuring massage and facials, yoga and spa treatments, and various classes. Therapies include Deep Tissue,

Swedish, Connective Tissue and Pregnancy Massage, Acupressure and Shiatsu, Cranial-Sacral Body Work, and Reiki. Treatments include Mud Body Treatments, Seaweed Body Wraps, Dr. Hauschka Facials, Dr. Hauschka Rhythmical Body Treatment, Raindrop Therapy, and Steam Therapy. Yoga and movement therapy are offered on a regular basis.

YMCAS & FITNESS CENTERS

Berkshire Nautilus (413-499-1217; 205 West St., Pittsfield MA 01201) Stationary bikes, rowing machines, treadmill, StairMaster, whirlpool, sauna, steam, and certified instruction.

Berkshire West (413-499-4600; Dan Fox Dr., Pittsfield; Mail: P.O. Box 2188, MA 01202) Nautilus and free weights, bikes. Also racquet sports facilities (tennis and racquetball), aerobics classes, saunas and steam room and hot tub, pool, and certified instruction. Nursery available.

Fitness Express (413-528-5600; 42 Bridge St., Gt. Barrington) Various classes including aerobics and dance, karate, and special instruction — e.g., tango lessons — held at different times of the year plus a weight room, rowing machines, stationary bikes, and treadmill. Pro shop on site.

Health Club (413-243-3500; Oak n' Spruce, 190 Meadow St., Lee, MA 01238) Universal and Nautilus Equipment, StairMasters, stationary bicycles, and free weights. Two indoor pools and one outdoor pool, water aerobics classes, hot tub, saunas, tennis, basketball, treadmills, rowing machine, and tanning beds.

Lenox Fitness Center (413-637-9893; 68 Main St., Lenox MA 01240) Nautilus, Liferower and Lifecycles, StairMasters, aerobics, eucalyptus steam rooms, tanning booths, free weights, yoga and certified instruction, group exercise classes, and a personal trainer is available as well.

Pittsfield YMCA (413-499-7650; 292 North St., Pittsfield, MA 01201) With its North Street facility and Ponterril Outdoor Recreation Center, Pittsfield's YMCA undoubtedly serves more public recreational needs than any other complex in the county. At the North Street Y, the range of fitness and sports is formidable. Here clients can enjoy aerobics, Aeoreflex (musical aerobics with hand-held weights); here too they can swim and scuba dive, both with instruction if desired, and play racquetball, handball, and squash. The racquetball program is particularly fine, even offering videotaped analysis. There are Nautilus machines and programs; special classes for kids in basketball, gymnastics, swimming, and Indian lore. To smooth things out, the Y has a sauna, a steam room, and sunlamps.

From Memorial Day through Labor Day, the **Ponterril Outdoor Recreation Center** (413-499-0640) comes to life, the facilities inviting, the programs enriching. On East Acres Rd. there's an Olympic-sized pool, a wading

Toning up at Canyon Ranch.

pool, and a tot's spray pool; swim lessons are also offered. Down at the lake, the Y has a marina with moorings for 50 boats and offers canoe, rowboat, and sailboat rentals; also sailing lessons, tennis camp and soccer camp, a day camp, and a preschool camp. And up at Ponterril's six fast-dry clay courts, some of the best tennis in the county is played. Other Y memberships are honored with a slight surcharge, and special short-term guest passes can be arranged.

Northern Berkshire YMCA (413-663-6529; 22 Brickyard Ct., N. Adams, MA 01247) North County's Y is another center of vitality, a facility that has continued to improve and upgrade its sports complex. There's a six-lane pool, a full gymnasium, a weight room and nautilus, a new gymnastics room for children, and two new handball-racquetball courts, all with programs to match. As with the Pittsfield Y, other Y memberships are honored with a slight surcharge, and special short-term guest passes can be arranged.

CHAPTER SEVEN
For the Fun of It
OUTDOOR RECREATION

Berkshire beckons its bikers, boaters, hikers, horseback riders, runners, skaters, skiers, swimmers, and lovers of nearly every other variety of sport to come outside. ` Although nature left the area shy of large bodies of water, the 19th-century industrialists dammed it well, to some degree making up the deficiency. Mountains and trails, lakes and rivers, and Berkshire valley air — which can be breathed without chewing — invigorate. The ski areas assure groomed winter sport with extensive snowmaking and, in warmer weather, Berkshire's golf courses and tennis courts draw sports people from all quarters.

Judith Monachina

Late afternoon at Stockbridge Bowl.

For the spectators amongst us, the high school and college sports — including downhill and Nordic skiing — are competitive and fun in fall, spring, and winter. The hills are alive with bouncing balls, from youth programs, to secondary school teams, to adult leagues. Three of the four Berkshire colleges — **Berkshire Community College** in Pittsfield, **Massachusetts College of Liberal Arts** in North Adams, and **Williams College** in Williamstown — field men's and women's teams in soccer, basketball, and baseball hard and soft. Williams perennially ranks among the best in the nation in Division III soccer, field hockey, football, cross country, basketball, ice hockey, track, tennis, squash, volleyball, swimming, lacrosse, and crew. In 1996, 1997, and 1999, Williams won the Sears Cup as the winningest small college in the nation. The athletic departments of the colleges can provide schedules.

SPORTING GOODS STORES

The following stores provide sporting goods for a range of activities. Additional listings are provided under individual sports (for example, bicycling, skiing).

South County

Appalachian Mountain Gear, 413-528-8811, fax 413-528-5054; www.amggear. com; 684 S. Main St., Rte. 7, Gt. Barrington.
Gerry Cosby & Co., 413-229-6600; www.cosbysports.com; 103 S. Undermountain Rd., Rte. 41, Sheffield.

Central County

Arcadian Shop, 413-637-3010, fax 413-637-4112; www.arcadian.com; 91 Pittsfield Rd. Rte. 7, P.O. Box 1637, Lenox.
Champ Sports, 413-448-2123; www.champsports.com; Berkshire Mall, Lanesborough (mail: Old State Rd., Rte. 8, Lanesborough, MA 01237).
Dave's Sporting Goods, 413-442-2960; 1164 North St., Pittsfield.
Dick Moon Sporting Goods, 413-442-8281, fax 413-448-2718; e-mail: pomeroy arm@aol.com; 114 Fenn St., Pittsfield.
Plaine's Bike Golf Ski, 413-499-0294; 55 W. Housatonic St., Rte. 20, Pittsfield.

North County

Berkshire Outfitters, 413-743-5900, fax 413-743-3359; www.berkshireoutfitters. com; Grove St., Rte. 8, Adams.
Goff's Sports, 413-458-3605, 800-424-3747; www.williams-shop.com; 15 Spring St., Williamstown.
Mountain Goat, 413-458-8445; 130 Water St., Williamstown.
Sports Corner, 413-664-8654; www.northadams.com; 61 Main St., N. Adams.

BASEBALL HARD & SOFT

The first collegiate baseball game ever was played in Pittsfield, July 1, 1859, Amherst defeating Williams 73–32 in a 26-inning marathon (the rules have changed since). Williams won a companion chess match.

Professional baseball in the Berkshires began later in the 19th century, but it wasn't till the Roaring Twenties that the hardball action was continuous. The Pittsfield Hillies played some admirable ball in the A-level Eastern League,

Jonathan Sternfield

Grounding out, at the Pittsfield Mets' Wahconah Park.

winning a couple of pennants. When the Depression came, baseball went. Through some of the 1940s, the Pittsfield Electrics played to large home crowds, finally being short-circuited by the advent of televised baseball. Then, in 1965, a Red Sox farm club came to play at Pittsfield's Wahconah Park. The Pittsfield-Berkshire Red Sox played in the AA Class of the Eastern League. Starring George "Boomer" Scott and Reggie Smith (both of whom went on to shine with the Sox), the club drew nearly 80,000 fans for the season. The Red Sox farm club moved from the Berkshires in 1976.

Now the **Pittsfield Mets** play in Wahconah. If they leave, as is likely after the 2000 season, the city will try to find another team, continuing the opportunity to watch budding big leaguers. The fast balls are wicked, homers are truly belted, and the playing field is real dirt (and grass). A moment straight Norman Rockwell happens when the setting sun shines directly in the batter's eyes, causing a brief game delay due to sunshine. (We hope Pittsfield can continue to host professional ball without building an entirely new park.)

Pittsfield Mets, 413-499-METS (6387); Wahconah Park, 105 Wahconah St., Pittsfield.

Women's softball is a feature of Berkshire colleges and secondary schools in the spring. Nowhere is the action thicker than at the Berkshire County Softball Complex, however; a three-field park that sees at least six games a night during the summer. The complex is home to the Berkshire County Slow Pitch Softball League, a 30-team men's league, sponsored by local businesses. To facilitate matters, the complex has a two-story clubhouse with bar and restaurant.

Berkshire County Softball Complex, 413-499-1491; 1789 East St., Pittsfield.

BICYCLING

A road race on Mt. Greylock.

John Hitchcock

How sweet the cycling! While dedicated bikeways in the county are still in the planning stage, for the views, the rolling terrain, and the variety of roadways, Berkshire is made for rider and derailleur. For racers, there's the ***Josh Billings RunAground*** in September, and an annual July race around Brodie Mountain. The ***Williams College*** cycling team holds a Criterion in the spring. The ***Greylock Cycling Club*** sponsors an annual Greylock Hill Climb, a 9.2-mile, decidedly uphill race.

For those who are touring, the back roads are tranquil and some main roads have wide shoulders. The varied terrain intrigues cyclists: stunning views are followed by exhilarating descents that call for wel-l-l-l-tuned equipment — especially brakes.

Mountain bikers thrive in these hills, 21-speeders rolling through the picturesque landscape, leaving the blacktop behind. Not too steep, not too tortuous, the Berkshire hills beckon those who have enough brawn, coupled with the right machine. Mountain bikers frequently gather at the ***Mountain Goat***, 130 Water St., Williamstown, taking to the hills en masse for some "undulating

all-terraining." Mountain bikers should remember that some hikir
not open to bikers.

Similarly, cyclists out on the roadways should remember that, until The
Revolution, motorists in their quaint way still claim the right-of-way. It seems
wise to oblige. So: right-hand riding, single file. After dark: a headlight, a red
rear reflector, as well as side and pedal reflectors. In traffic, turns require hand
signals with the left hand: extended for left turn, raised for right turn, held low
for stopping. Helmets help, in a crisis, to keep us from losing our heads. Bicycles should be registered at local P.D.s, so they can help you locate a lost one.
The fee: 25 cents.

An extremely detailed county map is available by mail from the Berkshire
County Commissioners (413-448-8424; Superior Court Building, 76 East St.,
Pittsfield 01201; $6.00, checks payable to "County of Berkshire"). Beware, how-
ever: the roads are coded to ownership, not condition.

Pittsfield resident Lewis Cuyler, avid bike rider and writer, sums it all up in
Bike Rides in the Berkshire Hills, available at book and sports stores. A major
push is underway to create a north-south bikeway through the county, one
segment of which would be the conversion of a former rail line between
Cheshire and Adams into the Ashuwillticook Bike Trail.

BICYCLE DEALERS

South County

Berkshire Bike & Blade, 413-528-5555, fax 413-528-1776; 326 Stockbridge Rd.,
Rte. 7, Gt. Barrington.
Harland B. Foster, 413-528-0546, fax 413-528-5474; 15 Bridge St., Gt. Barring-
ton.

Central County

Arcadian Shop, 413-637-3010, 800-239-3391; www.arcadian.com; 91 Pittsfield-
Lenox Rd., Rte. 7, P.O. Box 1637, Lenox.
Mean Wheels, 413-637-0644; 57A Housatonic St., Lenox.
Ordinary Cycles, 413-442-7225; www.ordinarycycles.com; 247 North St., Pitts-
field.
Plaine's Bike Golf Ski, 413-499-0294; 55 W. Housatonic St., Rte. 20, Pittsfield.

North County

Mountain Goat, 413-458-8445; 130 Water St., Williamstown.
Spoke Bicycles, 413-458-3456; www.sappy.com/the spoke; 620 Main St.,
Williamstown.
Sports Corner, 413-664-8654; 61 Main St., N. Adams.

BOATING

When Henry Ward Beecher called Berkshire the "American Lake District," he was comparing the number of writers settled here to England's home of the Romantic poets; nevertheless, while we have nothing the size of Lake Windermere, we have nearly 100 ponds and lakes and at least one "bowl." Big boats may wish to plow larger seas, but at 1,056 acres Otis Reservoir is the largest recreational freshwater body in the state. Mainly we have water bodies for small craft, from outboards down to inner tubes. Even shells: spring and fall we can watch the Williams College crews on Onota.

Berkshire Outfitters (413-743-5900, Rte. 8, on the Adams-Cheshire border) rents canoes and kayaks. Or we can row. Lew Cuyler founded *Berkshire Sculling Association* (413-496-9160; www.berkshiresculling.com), which provides rentals, lessons, or even purchase at Stockbridge Bowl, by appointment. Lew says: "It takes but an hour to learn the fundamentals. The rest is practice."

Lew Cuyler sculls on Onota Lake.

Lauren R. Stevens

South County

Benedict Pond, Beartown State Forest, 413-528-0904; Blue Hill Rd., Monterey. Sylvan pond suitable for canoe or rowboat only.

Lake Buel, Rte. 57, Monterey.

Lake Garfield, Kinne's Grove, Rte. 23, Monterey. Boat rentals.

Goose Pond, Tyringham Rd., Lee. Boat rentals.

Laurel Lake, Rte. 20, Lee. Boat rentals.

Otis Reservoir, Tolland State Forest, 413-528-0904; Reservoir Rd., off Rte. 8, Otis. The largest of Berkshire's lakes. Small fishing boats, canoes, sunfish, and sailboats for rent, and a small family restaurant at J&D Marina, 41\3 4839. Moorings, sales, and service, but no rentals at Miller Marine, 413-2 6358. Summer weekends the water is crowded.

Prospect Lake, 413-528-4158, fax 413-528-3666; e-mail: prospectlk@aol.com; Prospect Lake Rd., N. Egremont. Canoe, paddleboat, rowboat, and sailboard rental and instruction at a private-access family campground and lake.

Stockbridge Bowl, Rte. 183, Stockbridge. Public launching site on one of the county's prettiest lakes, just below Tanglewood.

York Pond, West Lake, Abbey Lake, Sandisfield State Forest, 413-258-4774; New Marlborough & Sandisfield.

Central County

Buckley-Dunton Pond, October Mountain State Forest, Yokum Road, Becket. An intriguingly remote spot.

Greenwater Pond, Pleasant Point, Becket. Boat rentals.

Onota Lake, Onota Blvd., Pittsfield. Free launching area for motorboats. Good windsurfing. Onota Boat Livery (413-442-1724; 455 Pecks Rd.) rents small powerboats.

Pontoosuc Lake, Rte. 7, Pittsfield. The YMCA's Ponterril (413-499-0640) offers sailboat and canoe rentals. U-Drive Boat Rentals (413-442-7020) on Rte. 7 features ski boats and jet skis.

Richmond Pond, Swamp Rd., Richmond. Boat rentals.

North County

Mausert's Pond, Clarksburg State Forest, 413-664-8345; Middle Rd., Clarksburg.

Cheshire Reservoir (Hoosac Lake), Rte. 8, Cheshire. Launching site. Heavy weeds.

North Pond, Savoy Mountain State Forest, 413-663-8469 (summer only); for camping reservations call 877-422-6762; off Rte. 2 in Florida, in Savoy. North Pond and South Pond are two jewels in the hills, quite remote, rarely busy.

CAMPING

See " Walking, Camping, Cross-Country Skiing."

CANOEING, KAYAKING

Besides all of Berkshire's lovely lakes to canoe and kayak, the paddler has four rivers to choose from, with stretches varying from lazy flat water to rushing rapids. The Housatonic River rises in Washington and the lakes near Pittsfield, flowing southward between the Taconic Range and the Berkshire Plateau, heading for Long Island Sound near Stratford, Connecticut. Four Berkshire trips down the Housatonic are recommended by the Appalachian Mountain Club: Dalton to Lenox (19 mi.); Lenox to Stockbridge (12 mi.); Stockbridge to Gt. Barrington (13 mi.); and Gt. Barrington to Falls Village, CT (25 mi.). Send for *The AMC River Guide to Massachusetts, Connecticut and Rhode Island* ($9.95, from AMC, 5 Joy St., Boston, MA 02108) or ask local booksellers.

A Canoe Guide to the Housatonic River: Berkshire County, a nifty little booklet published jointly by Housatonic supporters and the Berkshire Regional Planning Commission, contains line drawings, a history of the river and its flora and fauna, and dozens of access points. Highly recommended for Housy paddling; see local booksellers.

In *South County*, the stretch on the Housatonic from Gt. Barrington to Bartholomew's Cobble in Ashley Falls is classic, lazy river paddling. Canoes can be purchased and rented in Sheffield at *Gaffer's Canoe Service* (413-229-0063; Rte. 7) or *South County Paddling* (413-229-2541; 10 Miller Ave.).

For lovely lake paddling, canoes can be rented at *Prospect Lake* (413-528-4158; Prospect Lake Rd., N. Egremont) and *Lake Garfield* (413-528-5417; www.kinnes.com; Rte. 23, Monterey).

In the fall, when the dam on Otis Reservoir is opened, the West Branch of the Farmington River swells. The stretch south of Rte. 23, along Rte. 8 in Otis and Sandisfield, is the site of an annual Olympic kayak racing event. In early spring, this stretch is a Class Three rapids, making for exciting whitewater paddling and great viewing. The Westfield offers whitewater racing in the spring.

Up in *North County*, the Hoosic River flows northwards, and in those parts, *Berkshire Outfitters* (413-743-5900; www.berkshireoutfitters.com; Grove St., Rte. 8, Adams), canoe and kayak specialists, rent craft and offers sound advice on the best in area boating. The Hoosic River Watershed Association has put out a recreational map of the river to the Hudson, available at sports stores.

CROQUET

In the Berkshires, croquet has had a small but tenacious group of followers, willing to risk the indignity of their ball being sent to the periphery of the lawns at the Lenox Club. The town of Lenox has more courts than any other town in the state. Blantyre, in Lenox, offers resident guests the use of imported equipment and lessons by a certified professional, during a season from July to September. See Chapter Three, *Lodging*, for more information on Blantyre.

The Lenox Club and Blantyre each host a tournament in this wicket sport once a year, duly noted in the newspapers.

CROSS-COUNTRY SKIING

See "Walking, Camping, Cross-Country Skiing."

DOWNHILL SKIING

Berkshire downhill ski areas go back to the 1930s. Evidence suggests that three significant advances in modern skiing had their origins here: the surface ski lift, snowmaking, and the ski bar. Berkshire ski areas continue to be innovative, always questing for better, more consistent conditions over a longer season.

But it's not the technology that makes Berkshire skiing so appealing, so popular. The Berkshire hills are challenging yet picturesque, without being imposing. From the summits of the area's ski mountains, the vistas are splendid — mountains on the horizon (like the Catskills, seen from atop Butternut) and skinny bands of civilization below. With seven major ski areas in the region to choose from, skiers in the Berkshires can pick their mountain for a week or tour the hills and ski a different area each day. Each ski mountain has its own character, each caters to a slightly different skier yet always welcomes all. Jiminy Peak and Berkshire East have the highest proportion of trails suited to advanced skiers only; but Butternut, Catamount, and even Bousquet have dicey runs, demanding enough for many experts. And for the best deal for the dollar, the Mt. Greylock Ski Club shines. Every Berkshire ski area offers instruction; Bousquet with its ski school and Otis Ridge with its ski camp emphasize youth instruction.

Snowboarding has become a familiar and accepted fixture on Berkshire slopes. Popular especially with younger enthusiasts, snowboards offer both thrilling sport and a challenge to one's skills and coordination. Most Berkshire ski areas can rent or sell a board and follow up with instruction. Some areas segregate snowboarders from skiers; all require courtesy and safety from everyone descending the slopes.

BERKSHIRE SKI INFORMATION

From *outside* Massachusetts: 800-237-5747.

Berkshire Ski Conditions: 413-499-7669. New England Ski Council reports are broadcast twice daily from radio station **WBEC-AM (1420)** and **FM (105.5)** on the dial, Pittsfield.

WHERE TO BUY & RENT SKI EQUIPMENT

Besides the ski areas themselves, all of which have fully stocked ski shops renting and selling equipment, the following specialty shops sell skis and related paraphernalia. Price-conscious skiers should keep their eyes open in the fall for ski-and-skate sales of used equipment such as the one at Jiminy Peak that benefits the Hancock Fire Department and the one at Pine Cobble School.

South County

Kenver Ltd., 413-528-2330, fax 413-528-2396; www.kenverltd.com; Rte. 23, S. Egremont.

Central County

Arcadian Shop, 413-637-3010; www.arcadian.com; 91 Pittsfield Rd., P.O. Box 1637, Lenox.

Klein's All Sports, 413-443-3531; Berkshire Mall, Lanesborough.

Plaine's Bike Golf Ski Center 413-499-0294; 55 W. Housatonic St., Pittsfield.

Ski Fanatics 413-443-3023; 20 Williamstown Rd., Lanesborough; and at Brodie Mtn.

Snowboards Unlimited 413-637-4337; Lenox.

North County

Berkshire Outfitters, 413-743-5900, fax 413-743-3359; www.berkshireoutfitters. com; Grove St., Rte. 8, Adams.

Goff's Sports, 413-458-3605, 800-424-3747; www.williams-shop.com; 15 Spring St., Williamstown.

Mountain Goat 413-458-8445; 130 Water St., Williamstown.

Sports Corner 413-664-8654; www.northadams.com; 61 Main St., N. Adams.

Bearing in mind that Berkshire areas are less expensive than those in northern Vermont, New Hampshire, and Maine, we call our top price category, $35 to $45 for an adult, weekend and holiday pass, in 1999,"Moderate." Below $35 we call "Inexpensive." Skiers should contact ski areas for a more elaborate breakdown, which often includes lower rates for weekdays, for night skiing, for junior and seniors. Bousquet's offers free skiing to those 65 years and older.

South County

BUTTERNUT BASIN
413-528-2000.
Ski conditions:
  800-438-SNOW.
www.skibutternut.com.
Rte. 23, Gt. Barrington, MA
  01230.
2 mi. E. of town, toward
  Monterey.
Trails: 22 (20% novice, 40%
  intermediate, 30% expert);
  also x-c trails (8 km.).
Lifts: 6 Chairs (quad, triple,
  4 doubles); Puma; Rope
  tow.
Vertical drop: 1,000 ft.
Snowmaking: 100% of area.
Tickets: Moderate.
Open: Weekdays 9–4;
  Weekends 8:15–4.
Ski School Pro: Einar Aas.

Ski-resort developer Channing Murdoch was lucky. Few entrepreneurs can realize their business dreams in their own backyards, as he did. His son, Jeff, now carries on the business.

Murdoch designed and built Butternut Basin Ski Area right there on a site that has become one of the Berkshires' premier winter recreation meccas. At Butternut, challenging downhill runs, a separate beginner's slope, and extensive cross-country ski trails offer ideal options for every kind of skier — from first-timer to serious racer.

But Butternut is more than terrific trails and the welcoming charm of its two lovely lodges. From the top of Warner Mountain extend extraordinary views of the distant Catskills in the west and of Mt. Greylock at the northern end of Berkshire County. The mountain's timed slalom course is open to everyone, making a potential Olympic-class racer — at least in fantasy — even out of a beginner. Butternut's personable ski pro, Einar Aas, and his team of expert ski instructors, can aid advanced skiers or those on the slopes for their debuts. Two snowboard parks have been opened. Butternut's ski shop is one of the most extensive and stylish at any Berkshire mountain.

Butternut's quadruple, fixed-grip lift; food facilities at the base, including an area exclusively devoted to their Ski Wee kid's program; and outside "Cruiser" barbecue deck show that the resort remains at the skiing edge. From the mogul fields of the expert run, Downspout, to the meandering path of the novice Pied Piper's Trail, Butternut is a delight to the eye as well as a refreshing test of athletic skill.

CATAMOUNT
413-528-1262, 518-325-3200.
www.catamountski.com
Rte. 23, S. Egremont, MA
  01258.
On New York State border.
Trails: 26 (novice to expert).
Lifts: 4 Chairs; T-bar; J-bar.
Vertical drop: 1,152 ft.
Snowmaking: 96% of area.
Tickets: Moderate.

On the cutting edge of Berkshire ski country," as *Skiing Magazine* put it, Catamount straddles two states and offers magnificent views of four: Massachusetts, New York, Connecticut, and Vermont. The slopes are primarily novice and intermediate, but seasoned skiers can find quite a bit of challenge through the glades near the summit, and down on through the Flipper and Dipper trails.

Called by some a vestpocket Killington, Cata-

Open: Weekends/holidays 8:30–4; Midweek/nonholidays, 9–4; Night skiing, Wed.–Sat., 5–10.
Ski School Pro: Shy Reeves.

mount is convenient, especially to New Yorkers. Not the trendiest, competition-minded ski resort, it cultivates a pleasant quaintness, right down to the Swiss Hütte restaurant at the mountain's base. Snowmaking capacity at Catamount has been over-hauled and expanded, firing state-of-the-art equip-ment at virtually all trails and slopes. Catamount has installed an additional 22 airless snowmakers mounted on towers. Night skiing is also an attraction at Catamount. An area for kids has opened.

A 1,200-foot extension of Ridge Run, one of the region's more splendid trails, now connects Esplanade to Promenade. For borderline skiing in the Berkshires, there's no better.

OTIS RIDGE
413-269-4444.
www.otisridge.com.
Rte. 23, Otis, MA 01253.
Trails: 11 (3 novice, 5 intermediate, 3 expert).
Lifts: Double chair; T-bar; J-bar; Pony-bar; 2 Rope tows.
Vertical drop: 400 ft.
Snowmaking: 90% of area.
Tickets: Inexpensive.
Open: 7 days, 6 nights.

Otis Ridge is the molehill among the mountains, but few slopes do so much to cater to beginners and youngsters, with Bob Demairio head of the ski school. Famous for its winter ski camp, the area takes on a special character on frosty weekends and holiday periods when camp's in session, starting the day after Christmas.

Central County

BOUSQUET
413-442-8316.

In 1932 a group of winter enthusiasts approached Clarence Bousquet about using the slopes of

R. Courtland "Court" McDermott was Bousquet's ski school instructor for 39 years, until he retired in 1999.

John Hitchcock

www.bousquets.com.
101 Dan Fox Dr., Pittsfield,
  MA 01201.
Access off South St. (Rte. 7)
Trails: 21 (novice to expert);
  All-terrain area.
Lifts: 2 Chairs; 2 Rope tows;
  Snowboarding halfpipe.
Vertical drop: 750 ft.
Snowmaking: 98% of area.
Tickets: Inexpensive.
Open: Weekdays 10am–
  10pm; Weekends 9am–
  10pm; Sun. 9–4; Night
  skiing, Mon.–Sat. 4–10.
Ski & Snowboard School
  Pro: Vickie Wilder.

JIMINY PEAK
413-738-5500.
www.jiminypeak.com.
Corey Rd., Hancock, MA
  01237.
Access from Rte. 7,
  Lanesborough, or Rte. 43,
  Hancock, via Brodie Mt.
  Rd.
Trails: 40 (novice to expert).
Lifts: 5 Chairs; Rope tow
  for snowboard park.
Vertical drop: 1,140 ft.
Snowmaking: 95% of area.
Tickets: Moderate.
Open: Weekdays
  9am–10:30pm;
  Weekends,
  8:30am–10:30pm.
Ski School Pro: Jay
  Barranger.

Bousquet Farm for skiing. Three years later, the fledgling Bousquet Ski Area put together one of Berkshire's great travel promotions: ski trains from New York to Pittsfield (with bus connector to Bousquet) for $2 round trip.

Now, over 60 years later, Berkshire's oldest ski area continues to provide friendly slopes, primarily for novice and intermediate skiers. There are, however, several very demanding runs. As a plus, from the summit of Bousquet, a skier has a fine view of Mt. Greylock's whale-like profile (nearly the same view that so inspired Melville; see "Arrowhead" in Chapter Five, *Arts & Pleasures*). Bousquet is well known for its effective ski school, a corps of some 50 teachers.

Jiminy is committed to long seasons of well-groomed slopes. To that end, it goes to extraordinary lengths, frequently opening early in November and staying open well into March, utilizing advanced snowmaking equipment. It is also in the first stage of an $8- to $109-million expansion program. A new mountain, Widow White's Peak, opened in 1998–1999, and a cluster of five new buildings, Bentley Brook, is set for completion in 2000.

This is one of the area's most demanding mountains, with 30 percent of its trails suitable for advanced skiers only. Those with such talents will greatly enjoy the North Glade, Upper Lift Line, and Whirlaway. For intermediates, there's the 360, the WestWay, and the Ace of Spades. These last two trails reveal a magnificent vista of the Jericho Valley, northwards toward Vermont. New are two expert glades, an expanded beginners' area with a triple-chair, a midmountain rope tow to service a snowboard park, and improved snowmaking.

In addition to a full calendar of ski events (races, clinics, and demonstrations), Jiminy also runs a race team just for children, a more serious tri-state race team, a freestyle team, a night adult program, and a ski school. Those who ski at Jiminy spend most of their time actually skiing: lift lines are carefully monitored so that skiers rarely have to wait more than 12 minutes. Jiminy closes the parking lots when the area nears its capacity of 3,500 skiers.

Jiminy offers facilities and activities to compete with any resort in Vermont, and it is continually adding more: more beds (ski-in, ski-out accessible), new lifts, and snowmaking improved to operate at higher temperatures.

North County

BERKSHIRE EAST
413-339-6617.
www.berkshireeast.com.
Rte. 2, P.O. Box 727,
 Charlemont, MA 01339.
Trails: 38 (9 novice, 13
 intermediate, 16 expert).
Lifts: 2 Double chairs,
 Triple chair; J-bar; Rope
 tow; Snowboarding
 halfpipe.
Vertical drop: 1,180 ft.
Snowmaking: 100% of area.
Tickets: Moderate.
Open: Sun.–Tues. 9–4:30;
 Wed.–Sat. 9am–10pm.

Billing itself as "southern New England's most challenging ski area," Berkshire East's steep terrain lives up to that claim. With more than 40% of its trails suited to experts, this mountain is demanding, especially down the steep Flying Cloud and Lift Line trails, both of which are over 4,000 feet long. For beginners, three separate open slopes around the west lodge provide plenty of room to learn the basics.

From the summit of Berkshire East, amid the pines, skiers can get a fine view of the steep-sided Deerfield River valley (to the east). The area offers day and night skiing, accompanied by a rustic lodge with a bar upstairs.

BRODIE MOUNTAIN
413-443-4752.
Rte. 7, New Ashford, MA
 01237.
Trails: 40 (novice to expert);
 snowboard park with
 halfpipe; also x-c (25
 km.).
Lifts: 4 Chairs; 2 Surface
 lifts.
Vertical drop: 1,250 ft.
Snowmaking: 95% of area.
Tickets: Moderate.
Open: 8:30–11; Twilight
 skiing 3–11; Night skiing,
 7–11.
Ski School Pro: John Koch.

One of the oldest ski areas in the Berkshires, Brodie Mountain started out under the direction of Gregory Makeroff, acquiring a different flavor under the guidance of the Kelly clan. It became "Kelly's Irish Alps," right down to the occasional staff leprechaun dressed in green and schussing downhill. In the fall of 1999, Jiminy Peak purchased Brodie, to be run as "separate but cooperative operations." Brodie will continue to be a fun area, and has always had tremendous appeal to singles and younger skiers.

Three-quarters of Brodie's 40 trails and slopes are geared to novice and intermediate skiers, and one slope (Tipperary) offers a not-too-demanding 2.25-mi. glide, the longest trail in southern New England. For experts, there's Mickie's Chute, Gilhooley's Glade, Danny Boy's Trail, and three glade trails. Brodie is committed to its snowmaking, pioneering large-scale snowmaking in 1965 and now covering 95% of its slopes. It utilizes state-of-the-art equipment, employing various systems and a super arsenal of Hedco Snow Cannons. In addition, Brodie invented its own Master Blaster snowgun.

At sundown especially, the views from Brodie across the Rte. 7 valley are stunning. Of particular note is the view northward to Mt. Greylock. But the skiing doesn't stop at sundown at Brodie; for Kelly's Irish Alps is one of the largest night-skiing areas anywhere, with over 17 mi. of trails and four chairlifts fully illuminated.

And after skiing, off the slopes, Brodie keeps the fun going, with five indoor tennis courts, five racquetball courts (racquets and sneakers can be rented for both), and a sauna. After sports, there's the Blarney Room and Kelly's Irish Pub.

MT. GREYLOCK SKI CLUB
413-458-3060; ski conditions 413-445-7887.
Roaring Brook Road, Williamstown, MA 01267. In south Williamstown, turn east on Roaring Brook Road, beside the Rte. 7 state DPW garage. Continue up gravel road which, in season, is one way up until 2:30pm.
Trails: 16 (4 novice, 9 intermediate, 3 expert); also x-c.
Lifts: 2 Rope tows.
Vertical drop: 500 ft.
Tickets: By very inexpensive membership.
Open: Weekends & holidays when snow permits (no snowmaking).
Lodge, outhouses, ski lessons available.

Mount Greylock Ski Club is a cooperative, which means that in exchange for low rates (family membership at about $100 for a season, including children up to 21 years), everyone works. Jobs range from helping take care of the wood-heated lodge to cutting brush on the trail to running the antique Ford and GMC engines that power the lifts. It is a fine place for a family, because the adults look out for all the kids. The very young amuse themselves by the hour sliding near the lodge while parents ski. Members ski patrol and members teach.

The area, which has a base altitude of 1,200 ft, faces north and holds snow well, but if the snow doesn't fall . . . well then, members get to enjoy the social events and work parties the club sponsors. If the one-way traffic is daunting, the alternative is a pleasant 0.5 mile walk.

FOOTBALL

High school teams and pick-up touch football games carry on throughout the county, but only in Williamstown can one see collegiate gridiron action, as presented by the Williams College Ephmen (named after their school founder, Ephraim Williams). This is football at its sweetest: No athletic scholarships, studies really do come first, and competition with the likes of Amherst is even and spirited.

Williams College Football, Weston Field, Williamstown: 413-597-2344.
Berkshire Mountaineers, a professional team in the Empire League, can be located through the sports pages in season.

GOLF

On the green at Waubeeka, Williamstown.

John Hitchcock

In 1895, Joseph Choate Jr., son of the prominent Stockbridge lawyer, returned from a Canadian trip with three rudimentary golf clubs. Using tomato cans for holes, he made a course in his backyard at Naumkeag, establishing golf in the Berkshires. Three years later, having perfected his swing, Choate won the National Championships with a record low score. (A variation on the tomato can tale cites the Taconic as the first course in the county.)

Nowadays hardy sports folk tee up on more than a dozen courses county-wide from March through November. Every course and club runs tournaments. A call or visit will provide exact dates. Long-distance driving options have expanded, too. First there were wood woods, then metal woods, and now — developed from Pittsfield-GE engineered resins — Lexan woods, by Thermo Par. And for those who just have to hit some in the dark of night, *Baker's Driving Range & Miniature Golf* (413-443-6102; e-mail: dstorie4@ aol.com; Rte. 7, Lanesborough) keeps its driving range open from 10am till 10:30pm. Possibilities in the miniature division: *Par 4 Family Fun Center* (413-499-0051; Rte. 7, Lanesborough), *Jiminy Peak* (413-738-5500; Hancock), with 18 holes, and in South County there's *Rainbow's End Miniature Golf* (413-528-1220; Rte. 7, Gt. Barrington) inside Cove Bowling Lanes.

GOLF CLUBS

Price Code — Greens Fees
Inexpensive   Up to $20
Moderate $20 to $35
Expensive   Over $35

South County

Egremont Country Club, Pro: Marc Levesque; 413-528-4222; Rte. 23, S. Egremont; 18 holes; Par 71; 5,900 yds.; Price: Moderate.

Greenock Country Club, Pro: Michael Bechard; 413-243-3323; W. Park St., Lee; 9 holes; Par 35; 5,990 yds.; Price: Moderate.

Stockbridge Golf Club, Pro: Jim Walker; 413-298-3423; Main St., P.O. Box 233, Stockbridge; 18 holes; Par 71; 6,294 yds.; Price: Expensive; Must be introduced by a member.

Wyantenuck Country Club, Pro: Tom Sullivan; 413-528-3229; Sheffield Rd., Gt. Barrington; 18 holes; Par 70; 6,137 yds.; Price: Expensive; Private club.

Central County

Bas-Ridge Golf Course, 413-655-2605; 151 Plunkett Ave., Hinsdale; 18 holes; Par 70; 5,164 yds.; Price: Inexpensive.

Berkshire Hills Country Club, Pro: Bob Meheran; 413-442-1451; Benedict Rd., Pittsfield; 18 holes; Par 72; 6,606 yds.; Price: Moderate; Must be introduced by a member.

Country Club of Pittsfield, Pro: Brad Benson; 413-447-8504; 639 South St., Pittsfield; 18 holes; Par 71; 6,100 yds.; Price: Expensive; Must be introduced by a member.

Cranwell Golf Course, Pro: David Strawn; 413-637-1364; www.cranwell.com; 55 Lee Rd., Rte. 20, Lenox; 18 holes; Par 70; 6,387 yds.; Price: Expensive.

General Electric Athletic Association, Pro: Ed Rossi; 413-443-5746; 303 Crane Ave., Pittsfield; 9 holes; Par 72; 6,205 yds.; Price: Inexpensive.

Pontoosuc Lake Country Club, Pro: Bob Dastoli; 413-445-4217; Ridge Ave., Pittsfield; 18 holes; Par 70; 6,305 yds.; Price: Inexpensive.

Skyline Country Club, Pro: Jim Mitus; 413-445-5584; 405 S. Main St., Lanesborough; 18 holes; Par 72; 6,643 yds.; Price: Moderate.

Wahconah Country Club, Pro: Paul Daniels; 413-684-1333; Orchard Rd., Dalton; 18 holes; Par 71; 6,541 yds.; Price: Expensive; Public restricted on weekends.

North County

Forest Park Country Club, 413-743-3311; Forest Park Ave., Adams; 9 holes; Par 68; 5,100 yds.; Price: Inexpensive.

N. Adams Country Club, Pro: Jack Tosone; 413-664-9011; River Rd., P.O. Box 241, Clarksburg; 9 holes; Par 72; 6,070 yds.; Price: Inexpensive.

Taconic Golf Club, Pro: Rick Pohle; 413-458-3997; Meacham St., P.O. Box 193, Williamstown; 18 holes; Par 71; 6,640 yds.; Price: Expensive.

Waubeeka Springs Golf Links Pro: Jeff Gazaille; 413-458-8355; New Ashford Rd., Rte. 7, Williamstown; 18 holes; Par 72; 6,296 yds.; Price: Moderate.

Golfers live in anticipation of the reopening of an 18-hole course at **Greylock Glen,** Adams, judged one of the most lovely and challenging around during a brief, earlier incarnation.

HIKING

S ee "Walking, Camping, Cross-Country Skiing."

HORSEBACK RIDING

Learning to groom at Jeanette Rotondo's Windy Knoll Farm in Lee.

Judith Monachina

O ver meade and under mountain, there's a slew of riding academies and stables in and around Berkshire County. A quick look in the Yellow Pages opens the barn door to information on horse breeders, dealers, trainers, farriers, and saddle shops. The following is a partial list.

Bonnie Lea Farm, 413-458-3149; 511 North St., Rte. 7, Williamstown; Private & group lessons; English, Western; Indoor & outdoor rings; Guided trail rides; Year-round.

Horsesense at Golden Hill Farm, 413-637-1999; 87 Golden Hill Rd., Lenox; Private & group lessons; English; Indoor & outdoor rings; Year-round.

Oakhollow, 413-458-9278; 651 Henderson Rd., Williamstown; English lessons; Trails; Indoor & outdoor rings; Special therapeutic riding program; Year-round.

Overmeade School of Horsemanship, 413-499-2850; 940 East St., Lenox; English private & group lessons; Year-round.

Riverbank Farm, 413-684-3200; 619 East St., Dalton; Summer riding program; Year-round English & Western lessons.

Undermountain Farm 413-637-3365; 400 Undermountain Rd., Lenox; English lessons; English & Western trail rides; Spring through fall.

Windy Knoll Farm, 413-243-0989; 40 Stringer Ave., Lee; Stable management and riding lessons (weather permitting) for beginners; May 1–Dec. 1. Also horse-drawn wagon rides.

HUNTING & FISHING

Fly fishing South County's Green River

Jonathan Sternfield

The first settlers found Berkshire teeming with fish and game; now the wildlife is more plentiful than it has been in 150 years. Deer visit town to devour ornamental shrubbery; wild turkey and beaver have been successfully reintroduced; bear, pheasant, quail, rabbit, raccoon, fox, coyote, and gray squirrel are sufficient to satisfy nearly every hunter's aim. In Berkshire's waters, large- and smallmouth bass, northern pike, white and yellow perch, horned pout, and trout of all persuasions swim in abundance. Numerous brooks, rivers, ponds, and lakes are stocked with trout each year.

Essential equipment for any hunting or fishing is a pamphlet containing abstracts of the *Massachusetts Fish & Wildlife Laws,* available free at local sporting goods shops; from the **Division of Fisheries & Wildlife** (617-727-3151; www.state.ma.us/dfwele/dfw; 100 Cambridge St., Boston 02202); or from the **Western Wildlife District Manager,** Tom Keefe (413-447-9789; Hubbard Ave., Pittsfield 01201). This pamphlet carefully outlines the rules and regulations of Massachusetts fishing and hunting. Also essential is a license, which can be obtained either through city or town clerks, or through the Division of Fisheries & Wildlife at the Boston address above, or through many local sporting goods stores (see the list at the beginning of this chapter).

A license permits hunting, fishing, or trapping on property that is not posted, although some towns also require owner permission. State lands are open with a few exceptions, such as a three-quarter-mile radius around the tower on Mount Greylock. No hunting is allowed on Greylock during the summer and early fall. While deer season varies by a few weeks between Massachusetts and neighboring states, hunters are responsible for knowing which state they are in.

A LIST OF TROUT-STOCKED BERKSHIRE WATERS

South County

Alford Green River, Seekonk Brook.

Egremont Green River, Hubbard Brook.

Gt. Barrington Green River, Lake Mansfield, Thomas & Palmer Brook, West Brook, Williams River.

Lee Beartown Brook (west branch), Goose Pond, Greenwater Brook, Hop Brook, Laurel Lake, Washington Mt. Brook.

Monterey Lake Buel, Lake Garfield, Konkapot River, Rawson Brook.

New Marlborough Konkapot River, Umpachene Brook, York Pond.

Otis Big Benton Pond, Little Benton Pond, Dimock Brook, Farmington River, Otis Reservoir.

Sandisfield Buck River, Clam River, Farmington River.

Sheffield Hubbard Brook, Konkapot River.

Stockbridge Marsh Brook, Stockbridge Bowl.

Tyringham Goose Pond, Goose Pond Brook, Hop Brook.

West Stockbridge Cone Brook, Flat Brook, Williams River.

Central County

Becket Greenwater Pond, Shaker Mill Brook, Shaw Pond, Walker Brook, Westfield River (west branch), Yokum Brook.

Dalton Housatonic River (east branch), Sackett Brook, Wahconah Falls Brook.

Hancock Berry Pond, Kinderhook Creek.

Hinsdale Bennet Brook, Housatonic River (east branch), Plunkett Reservoir.

Lanesborough Pontoosuc Lake, Sachem Brook, Town Brook.

Lenox Laurel Lake, Marsh Brook, Sawmill Brook, Yokum Brook.

Peru Trout Brook.

Pittsfield Daniel Brook, Housatonic River (southwest branch), Jacoby Brook, Lulu Cascade Brook, Onota Lake, Lake Pontoosuc, Sackett Brook, Smith Brook.

Richmond Cone Brook, Furnace Brook, Mt. Lebanon Brook, Richmond Pond.

Washington Depot Brook.

FISH, EXCLUSIVE OF TROUT, IN BERSKHIRE WATERS

TOWN	WATER	NP	LMB	SMB	CP	WP	YP	BB
South County								
Egremont	Prospect lake				✔		✔	✔
Lee	Goose Pond		✔	✔	✔		✔	✔
Lee	Laurel Lake		✔		✔	✔	✔	✔
Monterey	Benedict Pond		✔				✔	✔
New Marlborough	Thousand Acre Swamp			✔	✔		✔	✔
Otis	Benton Pond			✔	✔	✔	✔	✔
Otis	East Otis Reservoir	✔	✔	✔	✔	✔	✔	✔
Stockbridge	Stockbridge Bowl		✔	✔	✔		✔	✔
Central County								
Becket	Center Pond		✔	✔	✔	✔	✔	✔
Becket	Yokum Pond		✔				✔	✔
Hinsdale	Ashmere Lake		✔	✔			✔	
Pittsfield	Onota Lake	✔	✔		✔		✔	✔
Pittsfield	Pontoosuc Lake		✔		✔		✔	✔
Pittsfield	Richmond Pond		✔	✔	✔		✔	✔
Windsor	Windsor Pond		✔		✔		✔	✔
North County								
Cheshire	Cheshire Reservoir	✔	✔		✔		✔	✔
Clarksburg	Mauserts Pond					✔		✔

Symbols
NP— Northern Pike
LMB— Largemouth Bass
SMB— Smallmouth Bass
CP— Chain Pickerel
WP— White Perch
YP— Yellow Perch
BB— Brown Bullhealds
(Horn Pout)

Windsor Westfield Brook, Westfield River (east branch), Windsor Brook, Windsor Jambs Brook, Windsor Pond.

North County
Adams Anthony Brook, Hoosic River (south branch), Southwick Brook, Tophet Brook.
Cheshire Dry Brook, Hoosac Lake, Hoosic River (south branch), Kitchen Brook, Penniman Brook, South Brook, Thunder Brook.
Clarksburg Hoosic River (north branch), Hudson Brook.
Florida Deerfield River, North Pond.
N. Adams Notch Brook, Windsor Lake.
Savoy Center Brook, Chickley River, Cold River, Westfield River (east branch).
Williamstown Broad Brook, Green River, Green River (west branch), Hemlock Brook, Roaring Brook.

KIDS ONLY

Taking a break near the skateboard park in Great Barrington.

Judith Monachina

A s far as most kids are concerned, Berkshire is cool. Besides the dozens of children's camps here, most of the ski slopes operate children's ski schools. In between the summer camping and the winter skiing dozens of little events are happening on a child's scale all over the county. Most local libraries have story hours, most of the museums and playgrounds have kids' programs, and many of the local theaters have innovative children's productions. In addition, bulletin boards and signs at all kinds of locations — inns, local stores, libraries, post offices, and the like — keep you up to date on unfolding events. Finally, web sites for the various local museums and other institutions are valuable resources, particularly since they are updated often, as new events come along.

South County

At the Cove Bowling Lanes, on Rte. 7, is the **Rainbow's End Miniature Golf Course** (413-528-1220, 800-352-4398; fax 413-528-5295), an indoor extravaganza to test even the deftest little putter. In West Stockbridge, **Clay Forms Studio** (413-232-4349; Austerlitz Rd., Rtes. 102 & 41) offers private classes, workshops, and other activities for kids 8 and up (including those with special needs) who like to work in clay. Out in New Marlboro, **Four Colors Company** presents theater workshops for kids of all ages at the Flying Cloud Summer Camp (413-528-5614).

The **Stockbridge Library** (413-298-5501; Main St., Rte. 7, Stockbridge) has a large and cozy children's section, with story hours as a regular event. During the summer the **Berkshire Theatre Festival** (413-298-5536; Rte. 102, just east of the junction of Rte. 7, Stockbridge) gives Children's Theatre performances of plays written by local kids. It also offers an acting class for students age 12–14. The **Norman Rockwell Museum** (413-298-4100) offers a variety of activities geared to kids, one of the best being their Family Day on the last Sunday of every month. Admission prices are lowered and special guides are provided to inform both parents and kids. The **Berkshire Botanical Garden** (413-298-3926) holds a wonder-filled day camp for kids in summer, offering children in grades 1–6 the opportunity to explore the world of nature. Their early October Harvest Festival has lots of kids' activities, too. Art classes are a part of the **Interlaken School of Arts** (413-298-5252) program, with classes as young as 3 and special courses for kids 8–17.

Central County

Pittsfield is a mecca for undercover entertainment. **Blue Skies & Rainbows** (413-445-7777) has moved to Dalton Ave., teaming up with Buster's Family Fun Center (see below). The **Arena** (413-442-3347) provides for skating (that's wheels). Located at the corner of East & Lyman Sts., it offers laser tag, rollerblading (with a street course), skateboarding, and batting cages. It also hosts specific events, such bicycle days and birthday parties and, for adults, indoor soccer. More on the arcade line is **Buster's Family Fun Center** (413-499-7500), 457 Dalton Ave., and **Galaxy** (413-499-3919) on Rte. 20, which also features the Discovery Zone, bumper cars, and go-carts.

The **Lenox Library** (413-637-0197; 18 Main St., Rte. 7A) has a terrific children's room, which always seems to be brimming with kid energy. **Pleasant Valley Wildlife Sanctuary** (413-637-0320; www.massaudubon.org; e-mail: berkshires@massaudubon.org; 472 W. Mountain Rd., Lenox) runs a Natural History Day Camp, offered in 1- and 2-week sessions, featuring exciting educational outdoor activities for boys and girls grades 1–12.

Central County's other Massachusetts Audubon Society property, **Canoe Meadows Wildlife Sanctuary** (413-637-0320; www.massaudubon.org; e-mail: berkshires@massaudubon.org; Holmes Rd., Pittsfield; mail: 472 W. Mountain Rd., Lenox), in conjunction with the Berkshire Museum, runs a 1-week Native

American camp for boys and girls in grades 3, 4, and 5. During the summer, *Hancock Shaker Village* (413-443-0188, 800-817-1137; www.hancockshaker village.org; Rte. 20, P.O. Box 927, Pittsfield) offers a hands-on experience in its Discovery Room, where children may try on Shaker-style clothes and participate in such facets of 19th-century life as spinning wool, weaving, or writing with a quill pen at a Shaker desk. Outside, children can see the farm animals and demonstrations of sheep shearing or sheep-herding trials. In February and April, Hancock Shaker Village also conducts school vacation crafts workshops in basket making, cooking, and textiles.

The *Robbins-Zust Family Marionettes* often perform a full range of "classic tales for children of all ages." Bringing out the heavyweight dramas such as "Three Little Pigs," "Rumpelstiltskin," and "The Emperor's New Clothes," the Robbins-Zust troupe often performs in Lenox and Pittsfield. For more information, call the Marionettes themselves (413-698-2591; www.berkshireweb. com/zust). They are the "smallest established permanent floating repertory company in America."

In downtown Pittsfield, the children's library at the *Berkshire Athenaeum* (413-499-9483; www.berkshire.net/PittsfieldLibrary; Wendell Ave. at East St.) has a wide range of programs, from story hours to films. The *Berkshire Museum* (413-443-7171; www.berkshiremuseum.org; 39 South St., Rte. 7) also has an extensive series of educational children's events: theater, dance, and storytelling for the whole family.

At *Dalton Community House* (413-684-0260; 400 Main St., Dalton) kids will find a positive plethora of fun activities. There's miniature golf in Lanesborough to keep little hands busy at *Baker's Driving Range & Miniature Golf* (413-442-6102; Rte. 7) and the *Par 4 Family Fun Center* (413-499-0051; Rte. 7). Upcounty a ways, at *Jiminy Peak* (413-738-5500; Rte. 43, Hancock), the fun goes right into summer with the *Alpine Slide*, a scenic 15-minute ride up, and an exhilarating 5-minute slide down. Jiminy also has a miniature golf course, trout fishing, and a separate tennis program.

North County

Over in N. Adams, at the *Western Gateway Heritage State Park* (413-663-6312; 9 Furnace St. Bypass) a recent feature was a Kid's Korner craft workshop. In Williamstown, there's an extensive summer playground program at the public schools, along with swimming lessons and a nature program at *Margaret Lindley Park*. Information can be had by calling the *Youth Center* (413-458-5925; Cole Ave.). A summer playground program and a score of winter recreational programs are also offered through the Youth Center. The *Appalachian Mountain Club* (413-443-0011; Greylock Visitors Center, Bascom Lodge, Greylock Glen) and the *Massachusetts Department of Environmental Management* (413-442-8928) offer scores of children's programs at several sites on Mount Greylock. And treasure hunts, along with children's workshops on various artists, are a few of the *Clark Art Institute's* (413-458-8109; South St.) offerings for kids. The *Williams College Museum of Art* frequently has imaginative children's programs. Brand new is *Kidspace@MassMoCA* , a combined effort of the Clark, WCMA, and MoCA to provide a program for children and families who have had little exposure to art. The *Williamstown Public Library* offers read-alouds and a summer reading program. Children's tennis and soccer camps are available on the *Williams College* campus in the summer; call the Conference Office (413-458-2229). The *Williamstown Theatre Festival* (413-458-3200) runs a program for N. Adams youth.

CAMPS

There's a colorful list of overnight resident summer camps in the Berkshires — some specializing in sports, some tuned to the arts, some with other enthusiasms. Whether your youngsters are interested in dance or theater, hiking or canoeing, tennis or gymnastics, dressmaking or computers, Berkshire has a camp for them. Most camps take advantage of the beauty of their natural setting, which for many includes lakes and mountains. Warm days and cool nights make for season-long aquatics and sound sleeping. Berkshire cultural life also enriches campers' time here, with Tanglewood and Jacob's Pillow being two of the more popular side trips.

The Indians were the first campers in the Berkshires, and many of its camps bear Indian names. Following is a list of addresses and telephone numbers. "Full program" indicates availability of both arts and sports activities.

South County

Camp Ashmere, 413-655-2650, summer; 413-663-3780, winter; Hinsdale 01235.

Camp Half Moon, 413-528-0940; www.camphalfmoon.com; 400 Main St., P.O. Box 188, Gt. Barrington, MA 01230; Day & resident camp; Coed; Full program.

Camp High Rock, 413-528-1227; www.camphirock.com; RD 3 Box 49, Mt. Washington, MA 01258; Sessions for coed groups & adults; Full program.

Camp Kingsmont, 413-232-8518; RFD 2, W. Stockbridge, MA 01266; Coed; Nutrition & dietary education program; Physical fitness.

Camp Lenox, 413-243-2223, summer; 413-269-6036, winter; Rte. 8, Lee, MA 01238; Coed; Sports.

Camp Nawaka, 413-269-4296; Reservoir Rd., Otis, MA 01253.

Crane Lake Camp, 413-232-4257, summer, 212-362-1462, winter; State Line, W. Stockbridge, MA 01266; Coed; Full program.

Eisner Camp, 413-528-1652 summer, 212-650-4130 winter; Brookside Rd., Gt. Barrington, MA 01230; Coed children's & adult retreats; Full program & Jewish education.

Central County

Belvoir Terrace, 413-637-0555 summer; Belvoir Terrace, Lenox, MA 01240; 212-580-3398 winter, 145 Central Park West, New York, NY 10023; Girls; Fine & performing arts.

Camp Becket, 413-623-8972; Becket, MA 01223; Boys; Full program; Operated by Two-State YMCA.

Camp Emerson, 413-655-8123 summer, 914-779-9406 winter; Long View Ave., Hinsdale, MA 01235; Coed 7-15, Full program.

Camp Greylock, 413-623-8921 summer, Rte. 8, Becket, MA 01233; 212-582-1042 winter, 200 W. 57th St., Ste. 307, New York, NY 10019; Boys; Full program.

Camp Mah-Kee-Nac, 413-637-0781 summer, 201-429-8522 winter; Lenox, MA 01240; Boys; Sports.

Camp Mohawk, 413-443-9843; 300 Old Cheshire Rd., Lanesborough, MA 01237; Day camp; Coed.

Camp Romaca, 413-655-2715 summer, 800-779-2070 winter; Long View Ave., Hinsdale, MA 01235; Girls; Full program.

Camp Stevenson Witawentin, 413-445-5850; Churchill Rd., Pittsfield, MA 01201; Day camp; Girls; Sports; Through Girls Inc..

Camp Taconic, 413-655-2717 summer; 914-762-2820 winter; Hinsdale, MA 01235; Coed; Full program.

Camp Watitoh, 413-623-8951 summer; 914-428-1894 winter; Center Lake, Becket, MA 01223; Coed; Full program.

Camp Winadu, 413-447-8900 summer; 407-994-5500 winter; Churchill St., Pittsfield, MA 01201; Boys; Full program.

Chimney Corners, 413-623-8991; Becket, MA 01223; Girls; Full program; Operated by Two-State YMCA.

RACQUET SPORTS

RACQUETBALL

There's a lively racquetball scene in Berkshire, with courts in Lenox, Pittsfield, New Ashford, N. Adams, and at Williams College. The *N. Adams YMCA* (413-663-6529; www.bcn.net/~nbymca; 22 Brickyard Court), has two fine courts. At the *Brodie Mtn. Racquet Club* (413-458-4677; Rte. 7) in New Ashford, there are five courts, open 8:30am–10pm (Sat., Sun. 9am–5pm). The *Pittsfield YMCA* (413-499-7650; 292 North St.) has four courts, and *Berkshire West* (413-499-4600; www.ultranet.com/~berk; Dan Fox Dr., P.O. Box 2188, Pittsfield) offers 5 indoor courts and 7 outdoor courts — 3 hardcore and 4 clay. Both Pittsfield facilities offer topflight teaching programs. Williams College's court is located at the football field.

SQUASH

Squash in Berkshire? Yes, but it's mostly the garden variety. As for the sporting type, many squash courts do exist, but, alas, most are open only to people associated with the private schools maintaining them. Memberships are available at Williams College, which has increased the size of its courts. For travelers: the Pittsfield YMCA (413-499-7650; 292 North St.). Luckily the Y's court is also new, well built, and lively.

TENNIS

In the Berkshires' Gilded Age, at the close of the 19th century, tennis was played on lawns, close-cropped and lined with lime. Wheatleigh was an especially favored site, and the lawn tennis parties there featured men in long white linen trousers and ladies in ankle-length tennis dresses. Most of the grass courts are front lawns now, and though a few Berkshire connoisseurs still play on turf, tennis — here as elsewhere — is now played principally on clay, composites, and hard courts.

Several tournaments are annual events and can be counted on to test the best skills or provide exciting viewing. Starting in late summer, tournaments are run by the *YMCA's Ponterril* (413-499-0687 or 413-499-0640; Rte. 7, Pontoosuc Lake, Pittsfield).

Southern Berkshire has traditionally been lacking in public tennis courts. But *Monument Mountain High School* (413-528-2410) and the Berkshire Hills Tennis Association have created seven hard courts at the school, for both scholastic and community play. The courts are open to the public, with priority given to the school's tennis teams' needs.

TENNIS FACILITIES

South County

Egremont Country Club, 413-528-4222; Rte. 23, S. Egremont (mail: P.O. Box 547, Gt. Barrington); 2 hard-surface courts; Fee.

Monument Mtn. Regional High School, Rte. 7, Gt. Barrington; 7 hard courts, used by school students on weekdays from 3pm.

Monument Mtn. Motel, 413-528-3272, fax 413-528-3132; 249 Stockbridge Rd., Rte. 7, Gt. Barrington (opposite Friendly's); Lighted all-weather court; Fee; Call for reservation.

Greenock Country Club, 413-243-3323; W. Park St., Lee; 2 clay courts; Fee.

Oak N' Spruce Resort, 413-243-3500; off Rte. 102, P.O. Box 237, S. Lee; 2 clay courts; Fee.

Prospect Lake Park, 413-528-4158; e-mail: prospectlk@aol.com; 50 Prospect Lake Rd., P.O. Box 78, N. Egremont; 2 courts; Fee.

Simon's Rock College of Bard, 413-528-0771; 84 Alford Rd., Gt. Barrington; 4 hard courts plus backboard; Summer memberships available.

Stockbridge Golf Club, 413-298-3838; Main St., Stockbridge (behind Town Hall); 3 clay, 2 hard-surface courts; Nonmembers may arrange for lessons only.

Stockbridge Public Courts, For town residents and registered hotel guests.

> **Pine St.,** 2 hard courts.
>
> **Plain School,** Main St., Rte. 7; 2 hard courts.

Central County

Berkshire West, 413-449-4600; Dan Fox Dr., Pittsfield; 7 outdoor courts, 5 indoor hard courts; Memberships available.

Cranwell Resort, 413-637-1364; www.cranwell.com; Rte. 20, Lenox (mail: 55 Lee Rd, Lenox); 4 Har-Tru courts; Fee.

Jiminy Peak, 413-738-5500; Hancock; 5 outdoor courts; Fee.

Pittsfield Public Courts, Free to the public when school not in session; all courts are asphalt.

Herberg Middle School, Pomeroy Ave.; 4 courts.

Lakewood Park, Newell St.; 2 courts.

Pittsfield High School, East St.; 4 courts.

Taconic High School, Valentine Rd.; 4 courts.

Ponterril/YMCA, 413-499-0687; Pontoosuc Lake, Rte. 7, Pittsfield; 6 outdoor clay courts; Members only, but when courts are free, nonmembers may use them for a fee; Summer memberships available.

North County

Brodie Mountain Tennis & Racquetball Club, 413-458-4677; www.skibrodie. com; Rte. 7, New Ashford; 5 indoor courts; Memberships available.

N. Adams Public Courts, Free to the public; all courts are asphalt.

Greylock Recreation Field, Protection Ave., off Rte. 2; 2 courts.

Noel Field, State St., Rte. 8A, in back of Child Care of the Berkshires; 2 courts.

Williams College, 413-597-3131; Linde Lane (betw. Park St. & Cole Ave.), Williamstown; 24 clay & hard-surface courts; Summer memberships available: apply to Buildings & Grounds Dept. The town maintains a court off Main St., first come, first serve (ah!).

RUNNING

Runners have run into the right neck of the woods in the Berkshires. With terrain and roadways of all types, clean mountain air, and inspiring vistas, Berkshire draws out the relaxed runner, that meditative runner who can run almost forever. Most back roads and byways have little traffic. Running may be even more pleasant on trails. For the rugged cross-country runner some of the trails outlined under "Walking, Camping, Cross-Country Skiing" are suitable. For racers or wannabes, many towns and organizations across the county run road races; exact dates and entry information for these can be obtained from local chambers of commerce.

SKATING

For ice skaters, there are many smooth and slippery possibilities in the Berkshires, most of them framed by the hills. There are three rinks open to the public: one at the *Pittsfield Boys Club* (448-8258; 16 Melville St.), open Sat. & Sun. 2–3:45pm; another at *Lansing Chapman Rink* (413-597-2433) in Williamstown (*Williams College*); and the third in N. Adams at the *Vietnam Veterans Memorial Skating Rink* (413-664-9474; S. Church St.). All the rinks offer low-priced children's programs. Outdoor skating on flooded fields is a Berkshire tradition. During the colder months, public works crews groom ice at the Common in Pittsfield, by the Dalton Community House, and on the Stockbridge Town Field at Rte. 7 & Park St. Lake and pond skating is exquisite in Berkshire when it freezes before the snow flies.

For those who prefer their skating on wheels, many of the county's smoother back roads make for ideal blacktop cruising. Rollerblading, or inline skating, has taken off. Bladers can now be seen skating the hills three seasons a year. Some towns have developed skateboard parks, while others bother about how to keep skateboarders off the sidewalks. Many skiers now tune up during the warmer weather on roller skis.

SOARING

Altitude controls speed, which is ideally 51 mph. In this unearthly quiet, half a mile high, the Berkshires seem like a Swiss landscape, all rolling patterns of farm and woodland.

The *Mohawk Soaring Club* operates out of Harriman West Airport, N. Adams (413-458-8650). Those wishing to soar should hang out with the glider pilots at the far edge of the airstrip on weekends. Those who watch and ask a few questions could end up floating on air.

Should an aircraft seem an encumbrance to soaring, people with wings regularly jump off the top of Mt. Greylock in Adams, and just as often off the Taconic Range, on Rte. 2, west of Williamstown, or at the Western Summit of the Mohawk Trail, in Florida. They rely on lightweight *hang gliders* to support their flight. We take no position on Icarian activity.

SWIMMING

Berkshire is blessed with countless magical swimming spots, some secluded and known only to the likes of otter, and some quite public. There are sizable lakes and ponds, rushing green rivers, and deep, chilly quarries. For wintertime, and for those who prefer their water sport in a more controlled setting, there are numerous swimming pools, both indoor and out. Most state and municipal ponds have day use and inexpensive season passes available to residents and nonresidents.

South County

Benedict Pond, Beartown State Forest, 413-528-0904; Gt. Barrington; Follow signs from Rte. 23 or from Rte. 102 in S. Lee.

Egremont Country Club, 413-528-4222; Rte. 23, S. Egremont; Outdoor pool.

Green River, Off Rte. 23, 1 mi. W. of Gt. Barrington. Clearest of the clear, greenest of the green, purest of the pure — a summer treat not to be missed.

Lake Garfield, Kinne's Grove, Rte. 23, Monterey.

Lake Mansfield, 413-528-6080; off Christian Hill Rd., Gt. Barrington.

Oak n' Spruce Resort, 413-243-3500; off Rte. 102, S. Lee; Heated outdoor & indoor pools, saunas, whirlpool bath, physical fitness room; By membership only.

Otis Reservoir, Tolland State Forest, 413-269-6002 or 413-269-7268; off Rte. 23, Otis; Camping, fishing, picnicking, boating.

Prospect Lake, 413-528-4158; Prospect Lake Rd. (0.75 mi. W. off Rte. 71), N. Egremont; Camping, day picnics, adult lounge; Open to 6pm daily.

Spectacle Pond, Cold Spring Rd., Sandisfield.

York Lake, Sandisfield State Forest, 413-258-4774 or 413-229-8212; off Rte. 57, New Marlborough; Picnicking, fishing, hiking.

Central County

Ashmere Lake, Ashmere Beach, Rte. 143, Hinsdale.

Berkshire West, 413-499-4600; Dan Fox Drive, Pittsfield; Indoor/outdoor pool, bath house, snack bar, showers; Memberships available.

Boy's & Girls Club, 448-8258; 16 Melville St., Pittsfield; Under 18; Indoor pool open to members only; Memberships available; Free swimming early evenings, weekdays; Sat. 1–3.

Onota Lake, Onota Blvd., Pittsfield; Free municipal beaches, supervised, 12–8pm daily.

Pontoosuc Lake, Rte. 7, Pittsfield; Free municipal beach.

Pittsfield Girls Club, 413-442-5174; 165 East St., Pittsfield; Indoor pool open for recreational swimming evenings Mon.-Fri.; Sat. 1–2:15.

Pittsfield State Forest, 413-442-8992; Cascade St., Pittsfield; Swimmir guards on duty 10–6), picnicking, hiking, nature trails.

Pittsfield YMCA, 413-499-7650; 292 North St., Pittsfield.

Plunkett Lake Lion's Club Beach, Church St., Hinsdale.

Ponterril, 413-499-0647; Pontoosuc Lake, Rte. 7, N. of Pittsfield; Operated by the Pittsfield YMCA; Pool open to members only; Season memberships available.

Windsor State Forest, 413-684-0948; Windsor; Follow signs from Rte. 9 in W. Cummington or Rte. 116 in Savoy.

North County

Cheshire Reservoir, Farnam's Road, Cheshire. Look out for the weeds.

Clarksburg State Park, Rte. 8, Clarksburg, near Vermont line; Camping, picnicking.

Hoosic Valley High School, 413-743-5200; Rte 116, Cheshire; Indoor pool open Sept.–June.

Jiminy Peak, 413-738-5500; Corey Rd., off Rte. 7, Hancock; Outdoor pool.

Margaret Lindley Park, Rte. 2 at Rte 7, Williamstown; Swimming pond open during school summer vacation.

North Pond, Savoy Mountain State Forest, Florida; Follow signs from Rte. 2 in Florida or Rte. 116 in Savoy.

Northern Berkshire YMCA, 413-663-6529; Brickyard Ct., N. Adams. Indoor pool.

Sand Springs Pool & Spa, 413-458-5205; off Rte. 7, near Vermont line, Williamstown; 50x75-ft. mineral pool (year-round temperature of the spring is 74 degrees); 2 mineral whirlpools (102 degrees), mineral showers, sauna, shuffleboard, picnic area, beach; Pavilion for private party use.

Windsor Lake, 413-662-3047; N. Adams; Access via Bradley St. from Mass. College or via Kemp Ave. from E. Main St.; Municipal swimming area; Supervised daily.

WALKING, CAMPING, CROSS-COUNTRY SKIING

If you would be happy in Berkshire, you must carry mountains in your brain.

— Oliver Wendell Holmes

It is possible to approximate the opportunities with numbers. Massachusetts may be the sixth smallest state in the union, but its forest and park system is the sixth largest. And of the state's quarter-million protected acres, nearly 150,000 are in Berkshire County. Of the 606,000 total county acres, those owned publicly include 97,000 managed by the state Forests & Parks and 12,500 by

Fisheries & Wildlife. There are 21 state parks in the county, all of which have interesting tales and trails. Berkshire nature centers each have scenic paths. In addition, 86 miles of the Appalachian Trail run up Berkshire County, entering near Bartholomew's Cobble in Ashley Falls and exiting from Clarksburg.

The real pleasures are qualitative, however. With trails along lake and riverside, up hills and steep mountains, the Berkshires offer all types of terrain for "anyfling" from an afternoon's jaunt to a full-fledged pack trip.

Now some enthusiasm. No place else exists with the variety of trails from light walks to heavy hikes, suiting any available amount of time, convenient from anywhere in the county, and open to the public. These trails are marked and maintained by volunteers, who give of their time because they love this remarkable place and want visitors to like it, too.

Although a compass and maps are advisable for any deep-woods hiking, it's comforting to note that in Berkshire County, no matter how wild the surroundings, hikers are never more than five miles from a road. Nevertheless, for walks of any length, and especially for those taken alone, hikers should notify a friend of plans, including estimated hour of return. Carry water.

PROPERTIES WITH MAINTAINED TRAILS

State campgrounds are marked with an asterisk (*). For camping reservations call 877-422-6762 or visit www.park-net.com on the Web. Type-1 campgrounds have running water, Type-2 campgrounds do not. For more properties, see under Trustees of Reservations, below.

South County

STATE OWNED

*Beartown & East Mtn. State Forest, 413-528-0904; Blue Hill Rd., Monterey; 10,879 acres. Benedict Pond. 12 Type-1 campsites; Mountain bicycling, non-motorized boating, boat ramp, fishing, hunting, horseback riding trails, picnicking, x-c skiing, snowmobiling, swimming.

Campbell Falls State Park, Campbell Falls Rd. leaves Norfolk Rd. at the Connecticut line in New Marlborough. A lovely little falls in a two-state park.

*Mt. Washington State Forest, 413-528-0330; East St., Mt. Washington; 4,169 acres. 15 Type-2 wilderness campsites; Mountain bicycling, fishing, horseback riding trails, hunting, x-c skiing, snowmobiling. **Bash Bish Falls** on Bash Bish Falls Rd. are 0.5 miles from the lower parking lot. Celebrated by painters of the Hudson River School and poets, these falls say their name to those who listen carefully. Nearby **Mt. Everett State Reservation** includes three-state views, Appalachian Trail, and a road that approaches the summit.

*October Mtn. State Forest, 413-243-1778, 413-243-9735; Woodland Rd., Lee; 16,127 acres. Appalachian Trail. 50 Type 1-campsites; Mountain bicycling, nonmotorized boating, fishing, hiking, horseback riding trails, hunting, x-c skiing. Some campsites handicapped accessible.

Sandisfield & Cookson State Forest, 413-258-4774; West St., Sandisfield (New Marlboro); 7,785 acres. Day use only. Nonmotorized boating, fishing, hunting, x-c skiing, snowmobiling, swimming.

*Tolland State Forest, 413-269-6002, 413-269-7268; Rte. 8, Otis; 9,795 acres. 93 Type-1 campsites, some overlooking Otis Reservoir; Mountain bicycling, boating, fishing, hunting, picnicking, x-c skiing, snowmobiling, swimming.

OTHER NATURAL PLACES WITH TRAILS

Bartholomew's Cobble, 413-229-8600; Weatogue Rd., Rte. 7A, Ashley Falls (Sheffield). Bartholomew's Cobble, a National Natural Landmark, is a 277-

---

History of the Trustees of Reservations

In 1890, before the present national interest in the environment, a young landscape architect returned from study in Europe with a deepening concern for the need to preserve the natural beauty and historic sites of his community.

Charles Eliot (1859-1897), just 31 years old, the son of Charles W. Eliot, then president of Harvard University, proposed the establishment of an organization "empowered to hold small and well-distributed parcels of land . . . just as the Public Library holds books and the Art Museum pictures for the use and enjoyment of the public."

The Trustees of Reservations was incorporated by the Massachusetts General Court a year later, 1891, the first independent organization in the United States established for the purpose of preserving land.

The Trustees of Reservations, 413-298-3239; www.thetrustees.org; e-mail: westregion@ttor.org; 1 Sargeant St., Stockbridge 01262.

Many of the properties are listed under "Historic Homes" in Chapter Five, *Arts & Pleasures.* Excellent hiking opportunities await you at the following properties of the Trustees of Reservations in the county or nearby.

Bartholomew's Cobble, 413-229-8600; Weatogue Rd., Rte. 7A, Ashley Falls (Sheffield).

Chapelbrook, Williamsburg Rd., Ashfield.

Chesterfield Gorge, River Rd., Chesterfield.

Field Farm, 413-458-3144; Sloan Rd., off Rte. 7 at Five Corners, Williamstown.

Glendale Falls, Clark Wright Rd., Middlefield.

McLenan Reservoir, Sun Rd., Tyringham & Otis.

Monument Mtn., Stockbridge Rd., Rte. 7, Gt. Barrington.

Mountain Meadow Preserve, off Rte. 7, N. of Williamstown center.

Notchview Reservation, 413-684-0148; Rte. 9, Windsor.

Questing, New Marlborough Hill Rd., New Marlborough.

Tyringham Cobble, 413-298-3239; Jerusalem Rd., Tyringham.

acre sanctuary with limestone outcroppings about 500-million years old. The terrain supports wildflowers, trees, and ferns in great variety and number. It's a fine place to view the Housatonic River and its surrounding valley. On the site is the Bailey Museum of Natural History (closed Mon., Tues.). Group tours on request; picnic privileges available. Season: Apr. 15–Oct. 15; Fee; The Trustees of Reservations.

Berkshire Botanical Garden, 413-298-3926; www.berkshirebotanical.org; e-mail: info@berkshirebotanical.org; jct. Rtes. 102 & 183, P.O. Box 826, Stockbridge. The foremost botanical complex in the county for more than 50 years spreads over 15 acres of gently rolling land. The magnificent plantings include primroses, conifers, daylilies, perennials, and shrubs. A terraced herb garden, a rose garden, raised-bed vegetable gardens, and exotic flowers abound. The greenhouses (one of them passive solar) grow seedlings, cuttings, and plants of all sorts. Visitor Center, Garden Gift Shop, and Herb Products Shop offer information, practical garden items, and invigorating odors. The Botanical Garden runs a full schedule of activities year-round, ranging from flower shows and herb symposiums to lectures on flower arranging and on English country gardens. Its fine reference library offers books, magazines, and the latest seed catalogs. The Botanical Garden calendar culminates with the Harvest Festival in early October, offering fun and food for children and adults — and bargains on used clothes.

Ice Glen, Ice Glen Rd., Stockbridge. Cross the footbridge over the Housatonic River, follow the trail southward to walk a primeval path of glacial boulders — not recommended for the weak-kneed.

Race Brook Falls, Rte. 41, Sheffield. The pullover at the side of the road is marked and usually full of cars. A couple miles of hiking leads to cascades or, farther on, the Appalachian Trail.

Central County

STATE OWNED

*Mt. Greylock State Reservation, 413-499-4263, 413-499-4262; Visitors Center, Rockwell Rd., Lanesborough; also accessible from Notch Road, N. Adams; 12,500 acres. *La crème de la crème* of Berkshire hiking, with the state's highest peak, the Appalachian Trail, a 100-mile-view from the War Memorial Tower. (For **Bascom Lodge,** see Chapter Three, *Lodging*). 35 Type-2 campsites, 45 miles of trails; Hunting, x-c skiing, picnicking, interpretive programs, snowmobiling.

*Pittsfield State Forest, 413-442-8992; www.park-net.com; Cascade St., Pittsfield; 10,000 acres. Streams, waterfalls, views. 31 Type-1 & type-2 campsites. Bicycling, nonmotorized boating, canoeing, fishing, hunting, picnicking, interpretive programs, ski lodge, x-c skiing, snowmobiling, swimming; Wheelchair accessible picnic area, trails. Includes **Balance Rock** on Balance

Rock Rd. Of the county's glacial erratics, apparently about to tip off their small bases, the most dramatic.

Wahconah Falls, Rte. 9, Dalton. One of the county's largest cascades.

***Windsor State Forest,** 413-698-0948; winter 413-442-8928; River Rd., Windsor; 1,743 acres. 24 Type-2 campsites; Mountain bicycling, hunting, picnicking, snowmobiling, x-c skiing, swimming. Includes **Windsor Jambs**, a spectacular gorge.

OTHER NATURAL PLACES WITH TRAILS

Canoe Meadows Wildlife Sanctuary, 413-637-0320; www.massaudubon.org; Holmes Rd., Pittsfield; 262-acre preserve of forest, ponds, streams, the Housatonic River banks and flood plain; Owned and managed by the Massachusetts Audubon Society; Fee.

Dorothy Francis Rice Sanctuary, South Rd., off Rte. 143, Peru; 300-acre preserve of woodland trails, owned and managed by the New England Forestry Foundation.

Notchview Reservation, 413-684-0148; Rte. 9, Windsor; 3,000 acres of forest, crossed by miles of trails; owned and managed by the Trustees of Reservations; Fee.

Pleasant Valley Wildlife Sanctuary, 413-637-0320; www.massaudubon.org; 472 W. Mountain Rd., off Rte. 7, opposite the Quality Inn, Lenox; 1,400 acres of forest, field, ponds (beaver dams with real beaver), and streams with 7 miles of trails; Educational programs; Owned and managed by the Massachusetts Audubon Society; Fee.

North County

STATE OWNED

***Clarksburg State Park,** 413-664-8345 summer, 413-442-8928 winter; Middle Rd., Clarksburg; 346 acres. Mausert's Pond for swimming. 47 Type-2 campsites; Bicycling, boating (electric motors only), canoeing, fishing, hiking, hunting, picnicking, x-c skiing, snowmobiling.

Natural Bridge State Park, 413-663-6392; Natural Bridge Road, N. Adams (just N. of downtown on Rte. 8). Waters tumble over a marble dam and then course beneath a natural marble bridge.

***Savoy Mtn. State Forest,** 413-663-8469; Central Shaft Rd. off Rte 2, Florida or Rte. 116, Savoy; 11,000 acres. 45 Type-1 campsites and 3 cabins with fireplaces on South Pond. North Pond for swimming, boating, fishing. Tannery Falls. Bicycling, canoeing, picnicking, interpretive programs, x-c skiing, snowmobiling.

Taconic Trail State Forest, 413-499-4263, Williamstown.

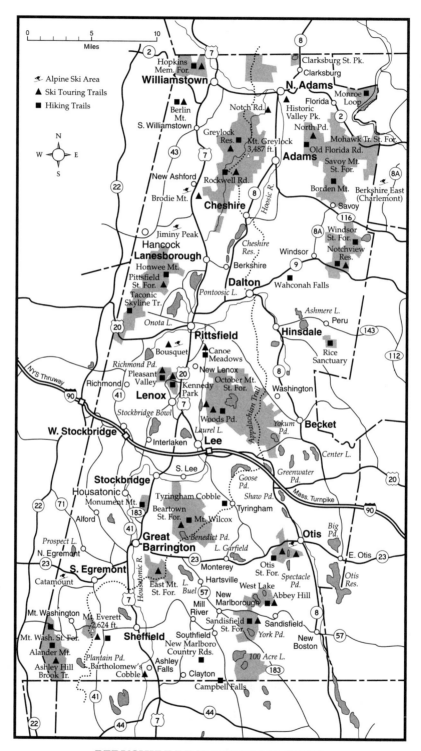

BERKSHIRE RECREATIONAL SITES

Berkshire County Land Trust

The Berkshire County Land Trust and Conservation Fund is an offshoot of Berkshire Natural Resources Council, a private, not-for-profit environmental advocacy group, established in 1967. Led by President George S. Wislocki and Director Tad Ames, this group believes that the wealth of Berkshire lies in its quality of life, in its natural environment, and in its cultural heritage. The council works with state and local agencies to ensure that those lands are protected from abuse.

There are about 200 land trusts in America, many of them in New England. By all counts, BNRC and its offspring in several Berkshire towns are some of the more successful. In Pittsfield, the Trust was responsible for increasing the Pittsfield State Forest by 1,800 acres. Along the Housatonic, south of Pittsfield, the Resources Council is coordinating the creation of a 12-mile-long river park, reaching to Woods Pond in Lenox. The Land Trust facilitated the preservation of Gould Meadows, that gorgeous 95-acre pasture reaching from Tanglewood to Stockbridge Bowl. The Stockbridge-Yokum Ridge Reserve is another land corridor the Trust is assembling to remain forever wild, an 8-mile-long, 6,300-acre spread of Berkshire park.

Berkshire County Land Trust and **Berkshire Natural Resources Council**, Inc. President: George Wislocki; 413-499-0596; 20 Bank Row, Pittsfield, MA 01201. E-mail for Berkshire Natural Resources Council: bnrc@bcn.net.

OTHER NATURAL PLACES WITH TRAILS

Bear Swamp Hydroelectric Project, 413-424-5213; River Rd., Florida. A stop at the visitors center reveals how pumped storage works; a call ahead can result in a tour of the works deep in the mountain.

Duvall Nature Trail, Rte. 116 (at Hoosac Valley High School), Adams; two miles of nature trails overlooking the Greylock Range.

Hopkins Memorial Forest, 413-597-2346; www.williams.edu/ces; Bulkley St., off Rte. 7, P.O. Box 637, Williams College, Williamstown; 2,500 woodland acres on the slopes of the Taconic Range with miles of hiking trails. No camping, fires, hunting, wheeled vehicles; Leashed dogs only. Forest includes rare plants, historical relics: barn, sugarshack, carriage house with exhibits on past use of the land. Guided walks by appointment (413-597-4353).

For more detailed information on the county's state parks, write: *Massachusetts Dept. of Environmental Management*, Division of Forests & Parks, (617-727-9800; www.state.ma.us/dem/; 100 Cambridge St., Boston, MA 02202) or its Region Five office (413-442-8928; Box 1433, Pittsfield, MA 01202).

There are several hiking clubs in the Berkshires. Among them, the *Appalachian Mountain Club* (413-443-0011), the *Taconic Hiking Club* (Troy, NY), and the *Williams (College) Outing Club* (413-597-2317) are the most active. Each organizes hikes through the county. The map on the facing page shows the entire length of the Appalachian Trail in Berkshire County.

Greylock Discovery Tours (413-637-4442; 800-877-9656; www.greylock

tours.com; P.O. Box 2231, Lenox, MA 01240), formerly Berkshire Hiking Holidays, will guide preformed groups of eight or more along the Appalachian and Taconic Range trails in half- or whole-day hikes, while arranging tickets to a Tanglewood concert, perhaps, and a sumptuous dinner and comfortable lodging to follow. From a long, vigorous hike up a mountain to a slow meander through a birch-shaded path, Greylock will help the urbanite back to nature. Trail snacks and lunches are included, as are stopovers at scenic vistas and cascading waterfalls. Packages vary from a weekend to 10 days in length: for those who like meeting nature while maintaining their comfort quotient.

Cogent books on Berkshire hiking are available: *Hikes & Walks in the Berkshire Hills* by Lauren R. Stevens and, for the Williamstown environs, *The Williams College Outing Club Northern Berkshire Outdoor Guide*, first published in 1927 and completely new in 1999. Stevens's book covers not only a wide variety of challenging hikes for the energetic and ambitious, but also a large number of easy strolls for those with less time or gumption. A section outlines walks for the blind and the physically handicapped. A foldout map provides an overview of public lands throughout Berkshire. In addition to its vast forests, Berkshire is blessed with many interesting outdoor sites, each of which shows off natural features such as waterfalls, unusual geology, or plant life. For a listing of *Natural Places* in the county, see the book of that name by René Laubach, and *Nature Walks in the Berkshire Hills* by Charles W.G. Smith.

CAMPING

For camping reservations in *state parks* call 877-422-6762 or visit the website at www.park-net.com. As well, some of the sites at each property are available first come, first serve. For further information but *not* reservations: *Massachusetts Dept. of Environmental Management*, Region Five Headquarters, 413-442-8928; P.O. Box 1433, Pittsfield, MA 01201.

Fees are as follows at all state parks and forests: *Day use* per car $2 per day; season pass $15 for day use; *Camping:* wilderness, per night: free; unimproved toilets $5 for Massachusetts residents, $6 for out-of-state visitors; flush toilets with showers $10 for Massachusetts residents, $12 for out-of-state visitors; group camping $25; one-room log cabins $25. Public campgrounds are designated with an asterisk (*) above; private campgrounds follow.

Private Campgrounds

South County

Camp Overflow, 413-269-4036; on Otis Reservoir, 5 mi. off Rte. 8, P.O. Box 645, Otis, MA 01253; 100 sites; Electric hookups, dumping station, camp store, fishing, swimming, boating; Seasonal rates.

Klondike Campground, 413-269-6010; Rte. 8, Otis, MA 01029.

In the 1860s and 1870s Williams College professor Albert Hopkins organized summer-long Camp Fern at what's now the Sperry Road Campground on Mount Greylock. Borrowing up to 10 tents from a Methodist meeting and hiring a local Irish girl to cook, families stayed there as they could, with members returning to town as necessary. The boys descended to the Bacon farm in the Hopper early in the morning for milk, eggs, and other perishables. Most of the time Fern campers explored the mountain; other adventures included organized games, skits, poetry, painting, journal writing, berrying, fishing, singing around the campfire, and, oh yes, courting in the hills. Did people know how to have more fun 100 years ago?

Laurel Ridge Camping Area, 413-269-4804; Old Blandford Rd., E. Otis, MA 01029; Electric & water sites.

Maple Glade Campground, 413-243-1548; 165 Woodland Rd., across from October Mtn. State Forest, Lee, MA 01238; 70 sites; hook-ups available. $15 for tents, $17 with water. Small store; Swimming pool.

Prospect Lake Park, 413-528-4158; Prospect Lake Rd., N. Egremont, MA 01252; 140 sites; Basketball court, boat rentals, swimming, tennis, volleyball; Snack bar, playground.

Central County

Bissellville Estate & Campground, 413-655-8396; Washington Rd., Rte. 8, Hinsdale, MA 01235; 13 campsites with sewer hookups; 18 with water, electricity; 13 with all three. Closed Labor Day–May 15.

Bonnie Brae Cabins & Campsites, 413-442-3754, 108 Broadway, Pittsfield, MA 01201); 3 mi. N. of downtown Pittsfield, off Rte. 7 at Pontoosuc Lake; Full hookups. Free showers, trailer rentals, new pool, cabin rentals May 1–Oct. 31. Closed Nov.–Apr. 30.

Bonnie Rigg Campground, 413-623-5366; jct. Rtes. 8 & 20 in Becket (mail: P.O. Box 14, Chester, MA 01011); 200 campsites, by owner/membership only (call for information). Adult lounge, playground, swimming pool, sauna, Jacuzzi.

Bucksteep Manor, 413-623-5535; Washington Mtn. Rd., Washington, MA 01223; 10 mi. E. of Pittsfield, across from October Mtn. State Forest; 15 sites, 9 cabins; Showers. Swimming pool, tennis, hiking, x-c skiing.

Fernwood Forest Campground, 413-655-2292; 41 Plunkett Reservoir Rd., Hinsdale, 1 mi. from Appalachian trail; 30 campsites with water, toilets, showers, electricity; Recreation field. Closed mid-Oct.–May 1.

Ponterril, Pittsfield YMCA; 413-499-0640; North St., Rte. 7, Pittsfield, MA 01201; off E. Acres Rd. at Pontoosuc Lake N. of town; 12 campsites; Sailing & sailing instructions, tennis; Swimming pool.

Summit Hill Campground, 413-623-5761; Summit Hill Rd., Washington, MA 01235; 110 campsites for tents & trailers, 83 sites with electricity & water. Adult lounge, swimming pool, recreation hall. Closed in winter; reopens May 1.

Brodie Campgrounds, 413-443-4754; www.skibrodie.com; Brodie Mtn. Ski Resort, New Ashford, MA 01237; off Rte. 7, just N. of Lanesborough town line; 120 campsites for tents & trailers, rented seasonally; Tennis; Heated swimming pool, recreation hall.

Historic Valley Park Campground, 413-662-3198; on Windsor Lake, Box 751, N. Adams, MA 01247; 100 campsites with electric, water hookups; Laundry, camp store, recreation hall, hiking trails; Public, private beaches with life-guards.

Privacy Campground, 413-458-3125; Hancock Rd., Rte. 43, N. Hancock, MA 01267, 5 mi. S. of Rte. 35 sites on 475 acres, 10 mi. of hiking trails, 4 small cabins. Waterfall, pond; badminton, basketball, campfires, horseshoes, paddleboats, tetherball, volleyball, water wheel; Windmill, trolley car, playground, sauna. Hydroelectric plant provides electricity for campground. Tours given.

CROSS-COUNTRY SKIING

Several of the resorts listed above under "Downhill Skiing" also offer cross-country skiing.

Berkshire is made for cross-country skiers — from flat runs along the Housatonic to steep trails up Mt. Greylock; from tours in town, such as Kennedy Park in Lenox and Historic Valley Campground in N. Adams, to wilderness paths like the one around North Pond in Savoy Mountain State Forest.

With no lines, no chair lifts, and no fees, generally, Berkshire cross-country skiing depends only on the whims of the weather. Since Nordic skiing has gained in popularity, however, private touring centers have multiplied in the Berkshires. For a small fee, trails are groomed, waxing huts warm, at half a dozen such places to cross-country ski. Cranwell and the to-be-opened Greylock Center offer snowmaking

It's best to ski accompanied, especially in a wilderness area. Those skiing in a state forest should check in at forest headquarters first. Maps and helpful hints are available; besides, it's a good precaution for staff to know a skier's out there. Skiers should carry a compass and extra clothes. Snacks and drinks are well-advised equipment on the trail. The well prepared also carry a first-aid kit, knife, whistle, flashlight, and space blanket. Hypothermia is the greatest danger; if 20 minutes of exercise doesn't warm the blood, it's time to head home.

Although many cross-country skiers profess to dislike snowmobiles because of their growl and their tendency to prowl in packs, the going is easier if those creatures have packed the trail. And sometime a cross-country skier in trouble might appreciate a snowmobiler's assistance. We recommend friendly relations with snowmobilers and, on their part, courtesy to skiers.

Most of the properties listed above are available to skiers. A selection of trails are described below, with sufficient directions for a short tour. More detailed descriptions for some of these tours, including maps, can be found in *Skiing in the Berkshire Hills*, by Lauren R. Stevens. Skiers should know that if snow is not good in Berkshire, just over the line in Vermont a natural snowbelt provides some of the best cover in the East. **Prospect Mountain** (802-442-2575; Rte. 9, 8 mi. E. of Bennington) benefits from nature's largess. Trails are groomed. Snowshoeing is also available. Rentals & retail. The food offered at the base lodge ranges from vegetarian to burgers. Fee.

Many trails in the **Mt. Washington State Forest** offer quintessential Berkshire ski touring. No snowmobiles are allowed, so the whistle of the wind will be the loudest noise. From the forest headquarters (East St.), the Ashley Hill Brook Trail runs south along the brook toward New York State, a four-mile, slightly uphill trip suitable for intermediate skiers. Nearby, from the parking lot just outside the Mt. Everett Reservation, you can ski up that 2,600-foot-tall mountain, the Dome of the Taconics. The climb up is gentle, passing Guilder Pond; the run down is long and exhilarating with plenty of room to maneuver.

Bartholomew's Cobble in Ashley Falls (Sheffield) has an interesting system of trails, with the runs on the far side of Weatogue Rd. being the best. Some spots are wet in marginal weather. A map is posted in the parking lot. Donation box: $3 per person.

Beartown State Forest in Monterey has some lovely trails, starting at Benedict Pond and circling through the 14,000 acres of forest preserve. Maps are available at the **State Forest Headquarters** (413-528-0904; Blue Hill Rd., off Rte. 23). Triangular red blazes or wooden markers designate the ski-touring trail in Beartown, with a blue-blazed trail circling Benedict Pond, the white-blazed Appalachian Trail passing through, and the orange-blazed trails for snowmobilers.

The West Lake area of the **Sandisfield State Forest** is a fine site for Nordic skiing. No snowmobiles are allowed on the Abbey Hill Foot Trail (marked with blue blazes). From the state forest headquarters and parking area, just off West St., a beautiful tour of about two hours circles around Abbey Lake, up Abbey Hill (1,810 ft.) and then down past West Lake.

Skiers can follow the Knox Trail in the **Otis State Forest**. Take Rte. 23 to Nash Rd. in Otis. Where Nash joins Webb Rd. is a good place to wax up. Skiers should watch for red Ks and red blazes marking the trail.

In Gt. Barrington, **Butternut Basin** (413-528-2000; Rte. 23) has 8 km. of groomed novice and intermediate trails, lovely lodges, and a pondside warming hut. **Otis Ridge** (413-269-4444; www.otisridge.com; Rte. 23, Otis), open 7 days, 6 nights, has more than 6 km. of packed, but not tracked, trails. And *Oak n' Spruce Resort* (413-243-3500; off Rte. 102, S. Lee) has 6 km. of Nordic trails.

Lenox is graced with beautiful ski-touring areas, the most popular of which is **Kennedy Park**. Its 500 acres were once the site of the grand old Aspinwall Hotel (which burned to the ground in 1931). Now its long, rising driveway and its bridle paths are used for ski-touring. The Main Trail (white blazes) is the widest and simplest, with Lookout Trail (red blazes) being more of a challenge. Stately oaks dot this pretty highland, with access either at the Church on the Hill (Main St., Rte. 7A) or behind the Lenox House Restaurant (north of town on Rte. 7). Equipment available from the Arcadian Shop.

Pleasant Valley Wildlife Sanctuary, also in Lenox, has a trail system laid out by the Massachusetts Audubon Society. For $3 ($2 for kids; members less), skiers go out on the trail marked with blue blazes and back on the one marked in yellow. There's also Yokum Brook Trail, Nature Trail, and others. Maps are free at the office next to the parking area (closed Mon.). The *Woods Pond* area in Lee and Lenox has a pretty, mostly flat trail running along the southern shore of Woods Pond, then north along the eastern bank of the Housatonic River for just over 2 miles. A footbridge now spans the Housatonic River. Enter via Woodland St. in Lee. The trail is best skied on weekdays, as weekend snowmobile traffic is apt to be heavy. *Canoe Meadows* is another Massachusetts Audubon Society area, and it too has some lovely trails, open on weekends only. The $2 fee includes a map.

For more advanced Nordic skiers, the *Honwee Mtn.-Turner Trail* circuit is a challenge. Park just off Cascade Rd. in Pittsfield State Forest. Check in at forest headquarters, get oriented, then start up the Mountain Trail, initially marked in orange, then in white. This trail has some great views, tough climbs, and steep descents. Closer to the center of the city, in *Sackett Brook Park* (Williams St.), there are 4 miles of marked trails.

On Rte. 9 lies *Notchview Reservation*, in the town of Windsor. Generally here can be found the best snow in Berkshire. Trails are well marked and maintained; there is a modest charge for touring. Maps are available for 50 cents. The Budd Visitor Center is open daily as a warming and waxing shelter. Notchview is owned by the Trustees of Reservations.

South of Lenox on Rte. 20, *Cranwell* (413-637-1364; 55 Lee Rd.) has a network of trails, crisscrossing their golf course. It ventured into snowmaking in the winter of 1996–97. Open to the public; fee charged.

In the hilltown of Washington, *Bucksteep Manor* (413-623-5535; Washington Mt. Rd.) operates a long ski-touring season. Set on over 250 acres, at 1,900 ft., Bucksteep has 25 km. of looped, interconnecting trails. There's a waxing room, a ski shop that sells and rents, as well as on-site lodging and dining. Nearby in Becket, *Canterbury Farm* (413-623-8765; Fred Snow Rd.) grooms 11 mi. of trails for its inn guests and daily cross-country ski guests. Ski shop for rentals; lessons available; ski fee.

Up at 2,000 ft., where the snows come early and stay late, *Savoy State Forest* has miles of cross-country trails, best navigated with a map obtainable at *State Forest Headquarters* (413-663-8469). Enter the forest from Rte. 2 (Florida) or Rte. 116 (Savoy). A 2.5-mi.-long trail (blue blazes) makes a challenging circuit around North Pond and then South Pond. In N. Adams, *Historic Valley Park* offers ski touring quite close to downtown. The trail starts at the parking area next to Windsor Lake and is well marked by blue blazes and signs that even describe the degree of difficulty of the next stretch of trail. The *Greylock Glen*, a public-private development, proposes to offer cross-country skiing on its golf course in Adams. It will have snowmaking; a fee will undoubtedly be charged.

John Hitchcock

Cross-country at Brodie Mountain, New Ashford.

On *Mt. Greylock*, many opportunities for fine ski touring exist. Here again though, it's best to ski during the week, because weekends tend to draw heavy snowmobile traffic. (The snowmobiles are supposed to stick to the roads.) Check in at the Visitor Center on Rockwell Rd., off Rte. 7, Lanesborough. Depending on skills and fitness, there's an 8-mi. round trip up Rockwell Rd. to Jones Nose and back, a 15-mi. round trip to Stony Ledge, or a 17-mi. round trip to the summit. The views are breathtaking, the skiing sometimes testing, and the weather more dramatic than expected from below. Take extra warm clothing and some snacks.

The area in and around *Williamstown* is striped with trails, ranging from novice or intermediate to demanding, like the *RRR Brooks Trail*. For Brooks, and the *Taconic Crest Trail* attached to it, begin either at Bee Hill Rd., W. of Rte. 2, or Petersburgh Pass, at the top of Rte. 2 W. of town. The *Taconic Golf Club* course, which Williams College grooms, and the 4-mi. *Stone Hill* loop in

Williamstown are the area's most popular: relatively easy while offering all the splendor of the best ski touring. The golf course trail begins at the clubhouse on Meacham St. Stone Hill starts and finishes in the Clark Art Museum parking lot (South St.), circling the 1,100-ft. Stone Hill, with its wonderful views. At *Hopkins Forest*, Williams College maintains a network of trails just off Northwest Hill Rd. The trails are sometimes groomed and maps are available at the forest Carriage House. Many other trails exist, the best of which are described in the *Williams Outing Club's* *Northern Berkshire Outdoor Guide.*

In New Ashford, *Brodie Mountain Ski Area* (Rte. 7) maintains a 25-km. trail network, of which 10 km. are groomed daily. A ski center provides equipment rental and warmth. Training site of the Williams College cross-country ski team, Brodie's trails were laid out by ski coach Bud Fisher. Many of the trails are double-tracked and wind through field and wood. For those adventurous enough for a guided ski tour to the summit of Mt. Greylock, Brodie can arrange it (413-443-4752; call well in advance). See also the *Mount Greylock Ski Club*, under downhill skiing.

CHAPTER EIGHT
Fancy Goods
SHOPPING

Even the shops that were closed offered, through wide expanses of plate-glass, hints of hidden riches. In some, waves of silk and ribbon broke over shores of imitation moss from which ravishing hats rose like tropical orchids. In others, the pink throats of gramophones opened their giant convolutions in a soundless chorus; or bicycles shining in neat ranks seemed to await the signal of an invisible starter; or tiers of fancy-goods in leatherette and paste dangled their insidious graces; and, in one vast bay that seemed to project them into exciting contact with the public, wax ladies in daring dresses chatted elegantly, or, with gestures intimate yet blameless, pointed to their pink corsets and transparent hosiery.

A description of shop windows on the main street of "Nettleton," the fictional name for Pittsfield in *Summer*, by Edith Wharton, 1917.

Mistral's on Railroad Street in Great Barrington has every luxurious item a kitchen or dining room would need.

Judith Monachina

Antiques, books, clothing, handcrafts, home furnishings — shoppers for the necessities and the accessories of life will find ample scope in the Berkshires, on still-vital downtown streets and at a variety of retail destinations. They'll find an ever-changing mix of the latest trends and styles, the genuinely old, and the timeless — sometimes all in one shop. They'll also find imaginative wares designed and made in the Berkshires, as well as goods from the farthest corners of the world. There are some chain stores, and outlets and discount centers, too. Note: many Berkshire shops have been in place for generations; others sprang up last week and will have moved on by next Monday; it's helpful to call ahead before making a special trip.

ANTIQUES

From formal 18th-century furniture to bold Art Deco tableware, with country primitive carvings and High Victorian accessories in between, antiques in the Berkshires are varied and abundant. Whether you hanker after museumquality pieces of a specific style and period or whether you simply enjoy exploring for unique home furnishings, you'll find plenty to choose from. The antiques scene here includes furniture large and small; vintage clothing, textiles, and jewelry; prints, paper, and other ephemera; trunks and lamps, kitchenalia and militaria, clocks and rugs, baskets and wicker. European and Asian antiques specialists have also found their way to the Berkshires. And a number of antiques shops also include new furnishings and accent pieces that complement their antiques, and custom decorating services, too.

South County in particular is an antiques center, with Rte. 7 the main artery for an array of multidealer shops, specialists, and generalists. They know their merchandise, and their prices reflect their knowledge. In Central and North County, prices are more flexible, but finding a bargain takes some looking.

Those who extend antiques hunting to auctions or — the sign of the true diehard — to yard sales and flea markets, should check listings in the helpful free weekly shoppers' guides (such as the Berkshire *Penny Saver*), which are stacked up at supermarket entrances and newsstands around the county. The *Berkshire Eagle*, the largest daily paper in the county, also carries classified listings for antiques, tag sales, and auctions. A list of auctioneers is also given below. The annual brochure of the *Berkshire County Antique Dealer's Association* lists dealers and locations, with business hours, telephone numbers, and a brief description of what they offer. Members of this association "take pride in their merchandise and guarantee its authenticity." Their brochure is available in member shops or by mail (send a SASE to BCADA Directory, P.O. Box 95, Sheffield MA 01257).

Several rare-book specialists also make their home here; they're listed in the following section, "Books."

South County

GREAT BARRINGTON

Asian Antiques (413-528-5091, phone/fax; 199 Stockbridge Rd. Rte 7) High quality Asian, Korean, Japanese, and Indonesian antiques, furniture for home or garden, handcrafts, art, and gifts. If you've always wanted an opium bed or a temple gong, this is the place to find it.

Bygone Days (413-528-1870; 969 S. Main St., Rte. 7) Country and formal furniture, large and small, especially for bedrooms and dining rooms; tables and chairs, armoires, nightstands, hutches and china closets, and more. Open 12–5 daily.

Carriage House Antiques (413-528-6045; 389 Stockbridge Rd.) Tables, chairs, furniture, even sets of doors. Antique furniture restoration, repair, stripping, refinishing, and custom cabinetry by Eric Schutz.

Coffmans' Country Antiques Market (413-528-9282; Jenifer House Commons, Stockbridge Rd.) Three floors of high-quality wares, pre-1949, from 100 New England and regional dealers, in the yellow house with two green doors. The large assortment is appealingly arranged in cases and room settings, and includes ephemera and prints, kitchenware, primitives, wood, pottery, furniture, tools, quilts, rugs, baskets, folk art, stoneware, glassware, and tin, brass, and copper. Books on antiques and collectibles are also sold here, and there's a lounge with coffee, tea, and hot chocolate for customers and dealers.

Corashire Antiques (413-528-0014; Rte. 7 & 23, at Belcher Square) In the red barn: American country furniture and accessories.

Country Dining Room & Tea Garden Antiques (413-528-5050; 178 Main St., Rte. 7) Complete accouterments for dining in style, formal or country. In lavishly coordinated rooms, dining tables boast elaborate place settings of china, silver, glass, crystal, porcelain — down to the matching damask napkins with silk rose napkin rings. Chairs, rugs, paintings, and other furnishings and accessories complete the look. For a less formal but still elegant approach, Tea Garden Antiques, upstairs, offers more place settings, linens, and other accents. Country Dining Room's own Sheila Chafetz wrote the stunning books that show you how to put it all together, *Antiques for the Table* and *Modern Antiques for the Table.*

Elise Abrams Antiques (413-528-3201; 11 Stockbridge Rd. Rte. 7) Large selection of antique china and stemware, plus decorative accessories and fine linens, silver, art, and dining room furniture.

Emporium Antique Center (413-528-1660; 319 Main St.) A variety of dealers here offer estate and costume jewelry, crystal, silver, accessories, furniture, furnishings, linens. June–Dec., open daily; Jan.–May, closed Tues., Weds.

Great Barrington Antiques Center (413 644-8848; 964 S. Main St., Rte. 7) A group shop featuring quality country furniture and oriental rugs. Look for the opening of a big new addition in the Spring of 2000.

The Kahns' Antique & Estate Jewelry (413-528-9550; 38 Railroad St.) Antique jewelry is their specialty; appraisals, diamond grading, gem identification, repairs, and custom work.

Le Perigord (413 528-6777; 964 South Main St., Rte. 7) A great source for French furniture, pottery, and garden and architectural accents from the 18th century to Art Deco. If you want to create a Gallic ambience in your home, this is the place to shop.

Donald McGrory Oriental Rugs (413-528-9594; 12 Castle St.) Antique and decorative Oriental rugs. 11–5 daily, closed Tues.

Mullin-Jones Antiquities (413-528-4871; 525 S. Main St., Rte. 7) The fragrance of lavender pervades this importer of 18th- and 19th-century country French furniture and accessories, including large-scale farmhouse pieces, garden accents. Closed Tues.; call ahead in winter.

Olde — An Antiques Market (413-528-1840; Jenifer House Commons, Stockbridge Rd.) Jam-packed with potential treasures. Over 85 dealers in a two-story red barn, offering collectibles, dishes, china, glass, porcelain, silver, games, books, jewelry, decorative items.

Paul & Susan Kleinwald, Inc. (413-528-4252; 578 S. Main St.) 18th- and 19th-century American and English antique furniture, fine art, accessories; appraisals. Closed Tues.

Phil Watson Antiques & Vintage Lighting (413 528-2677; 183 State Rd., Rte. 7 at Rte. 23) Interesting collection of 19th- and 20th-century light fixtures and lamps, from funky to fabulous.

Reeves Antiques (413 528-5877; Jenifer House Commons, Stockbridge Rd.) Old trunks and blanket boxes, restored shoe racks. and old workbenches are their speciality. They fit in both traditional and contemporary decors.

Reuss Audubon Galleries (413 528-8484; Jenifer House Commons, Stockbridge Rd.) Specializing in Audubon and Gould prints and artful adornments for the home.

Snyder's Store (413-528-1441; 945 Main St.) What's inside: funky furniture and accessories, with rustic pieces, wicker, tramp art, jewelry, linens, garden accents, and architectural elements. Open most weekends 12–5; weekdays by whim.

LEE

Aardenburg Antiques (413-243-0001; 144 W. Park St.) Early 19th-century furniture and accessories; restoration and refinishing. Weekends by chance; any time by appointment.

Antiquely Lee (413 243-2151; 77 Main St., Lee) Not just antiques from Lee, but country pieces and collectibles from all over.

Henry B. Holt (413-243-3184; P.O. Box 699) Specialist in 19th- and early 20th-century American paintings. Call for appointment regarding appraisal, purchase, sale, or restoration.

SHEFFIELD/ASHLEY FALLS

Note: The following antique shops are in the township of Sheffield where there are two villages — Ashley Falls and Sheffield proper.

Ashley Falls

Don Abarbanel (413-229-3330; E. Main St., at Lewis & Wilson.) Formal furniture of the 17th through 19th centuries, and needlework, brass and other metalwork, English pottery, English and Dutch delft, Chinese export porcelain. Open daily, but in winter it is advised to call ahead.

Ashley Falls Antiques (413-229-8759; Rte. 7A) American country and formal furniture, accessories, antique buttons, and authenticated antique jewelry.

Circa (413-229-2990; Rte. 7A) Good collections of Majolica and Canton; 18th- and 19th- century furniture, accessories, and "sophisticated oddments."

Lewis & Wilson (413-229-3330; E. Main St.) English, American, and Continental 18th- and 19th-century furniture and appropriate accessories; Oriental porcelains. Call ahead in winter.

The Vollmers (413-229-3463; Rte. 7A) 18th- and 19th-century furniture, formal and country, firearms, period accessories, and wine-related antiques. Open weekends; weekdays by chance or appointment.

Sheffield

Berkshire Gilders Antiques (413 229-0113; 15 Main St., Rte. 7) Period French, English, and American gold-leaf mirrors. Upholstered furniture, dining tables, decorative pieces, and tableware. Often closed Tues., Weds.

Carriage Trade Antiques Country furniture, blanket chests, kitchen items, jewelry, out-of-the-ordinary collectibles now located in "Olde" in Gt. Barrington and the "Buggy Whip" group shops in Southfield.

Centuryhurst Antiques and Bed And Breakfast (413-229-8131, 3277; Main St., Rte. 7.) Specializing in antique clocks and Wedgwood; with 18th- and 19th-century furniture, glass, china, paintings, prints, toys and accessories.

Classic Images Art & Antiques (413 229-0033; 527 Sheffield Plain) Antique prints and reprints concentrating on natural and sporting subjects. Some Southwestern country furniture, fine art photography and 19th- and 20th-century color-plate books. Call ahead.

Corner House Antiques (413-229-6627; corner of Rte. 7 & Old Mill Pond Rd.) Specialists in antique wicker furniture, including whole sets; with a variety of styles and finishes. A well-chosen selection of American country furnishings and accessories as well.

Cupboards & Roses Antiques (413-229-3070; Rte. 7) Beautifully displayed antique and reproduction paint-decorated 18th- and 19th-century furniture, featuring capacious armoires and chests from Denmark, Sweden, Germany,

Austria, and France. Decorative accessories, old and new, including wedding baskets, paint decorated bride boxes, textiles, and ceramics. Closed Tues.

Darr Antiques & Interiors (413-229-7773; S. Main St., Rte. 7) Two buildings of elegant room settings displaying formal 18th- and 19th-century American, English, Continental, and Oriental furniture and accessories, with a focus on dining room furnishings. June–Oct., open Weds.–Mon. ; Nov.– May., open Thurs.–Mon., or by appointment.

Dovetail Antiques (413-229-2628; Rte. 7) A select collection of American clocks, country furniture, including pieces with original paint or finish, and spongeware, stoneware, and redware. Open daily; Tues. by chance.

Falcon Antiques (413-229-7745; 176 S. Undermountain Rd., Rte. 41) Country furniture and accessories, with a good selection of brass, copper, pewter, woodworking tools, and treen (small wooden pieces).

Frederick Hatfield Antiques (413-229-7986; S. Main St., Rte. 7) Antiques and collectibles from the 18th through 20th centuries, with country and formal furniture, paintings, silver, paper items, jewelry, architectural elements, and other treasures from New England homes.

Good & Hutchinson Associates, Inc. (413-229-8832, -4555; Main St., Rte. 7, on the Green) Specialists in fine antiques and decorative arts from the 18th and 19th century, with American, English, and Continental furniture, Chinese export porcelain, paintings, brass, lamps; for collectors and antiquarians. June–Oct., open 10:30–4, Sun. 11–4; closed Tues. Open Nov.–May by chance.

John Sideli Art & Antiques (413 229-8424; 139 S. Main St., Sheffield) Stylish objects from the 18th, 19th, and 20th centuries. A gallery specializing in American folk art including weathervanes, trade signs, painted furniture, etc. in a sophisticated setting. Hours by appointment or chance.

Kuttner Antiques (413-229-2955; N. Main St., Rte. 7) Formal and high country American and English furniture and decorative accessories from the 18th and 19th centuries. Closed Tues.

Le Trianon (413 528-3940; 1854 N. Main St.) 17th-, 18th-, and 19th-century French and Continental furniture, carpets, tapestries, and accessories.

Lois W. Spring Antiques (413-229-2542; Ashley Falls Rd., Rte. 7A) 18th- and 19th-century furniture and accessories, country and formal. Original painted finishes as far as possible. Open by chance or appointment.

Madison Arts & Antiques (413 229-3949; 1695 N. Main St.) A shop filled with architectural elements. Closed Tues., Weds.

May's Everything Shop (413 229-2037; Rte. 7) A range of items from kitsch to collectible. You never know what you will find. They also buy.

Ole T.J.'s Antique Barn (413-229-8382; Rte. 7) Antiques and collectibles on two floors from all over, some of it gathered by the owners on their travels in the Far East and Africa, also early American and European furniture, jewelry, paintings, rugs, lamps, and other accessories. Thurs.–Mon. or by chance or appointment.

Robert Thayer American Antiques (413 229-2965; 197 Main St.) 18th- and early 19th-century country antique furniture and decorative arts, and folk art. By chance or appointment.

1750 House Antiques (413-229-6635; S. Main St., Rte. 7) Specialists in the sale and repair of American, French, and European clocks. Also offering music boxes, phonographs, glass, china, and other accessories, and furniture.

665 North Main Street (413-229-9029; 665 N. Main St.) Group shop with an eclectic mix of collectibles and antiques at good prices.

Saturday Sweets Antiques & Design (413-229-0026; 755A N.. Main St.) 20th-century decorative arts with an emphasis on Art Deco, including furniture, accessories, and vintage costume jewelry. Closed Tues.; in winter call ahead.

Susan Silver Antiques (413-229-8169; N. Main St., Rte. 7, P.O. Box 621) English and American furnishings from the 18th and 19th centuries. Specializing in library furniture. Closed Tues.

Twin Fires Antiques (413-229-8307; Berkshire School Rd. & Rte. 41) Hand-made imported country pine furniture, stained and painted, antique and reproduction. Armoires, cupboards, dressers, tables, beds from the British Isles and Europe — all attractively and abundantly displayed, along with other furniture and home accessories. Closed Tues.

David M. Weiss Antiques (413-229-2716; e-mail: weissjas@vgernet.net; N. Main St., Rte. 7) 18th- and 19th-century American furniture, paintings of the Hudson River School, and decorative accessories. Open by chance or by appointment

SOUTH EGREMONT

Douglas Antiques (413-528-1810; Rte. 23 at the Weathervane Inn, P.O. Box 571) Victorian and turn-of-the-century furniture in oak and walnut, with tables, chairs, desks, bookcases, dressers, and chests, and accessories, including lamps and quilts. Open 10–5:30 daily; Tues. by chance.

Geffner/Schatzky Antiques & Varieties (413-528-0057; Rte. 23, at the sign of the Juggler) 19th century to '50s furniture and accessories, jewelry, architectural elements. Open May–Aug., daily 10:30–5; Sept.–Apr., Fri.–Sun. 10:30–5, during the week by chance or appointment.

Howard's Antiques (413-528-1232; Rte. 23, P.O. Box 472) Specialists in American country furniture and lighting. Antique lighting fixtures from the late 1890s to the 1930s have been wired for the 1990s. 19th-century dining room tables and chairs are also offered, as well as other country-style antique furniture. Closed Tues.

Red Barn Antiques (413-528-3230; Main St., Rte. 23, P.O. Box 25) Restored antique lighting from the early 19th century and onward, including kerosene, gas, and early electric fixtures. Repair and restoration of antique lamps on site; refinished furniture.

Elliot & Grace Snyder (413-528-3581; Undermountain Rd., Rte. 41, 0.5 mi. south of Rte. 23) By appointment. 18th- and 19th-century American furniture and accessories, with an emphasis on textiles: needlework, rugs, and quilts.

Splendid Peasant (413-528-5755; Rte. 23 & Old Sheffield Rd.) 18th- and 19th-century painted country furniture and folk art, all stunningly displayed in a fascinating series of galleries and niches. Original paint a specialty.

SOUTHFIELD

Buggy Whip Factory Antique Market Place (413 229-3576; Main St.) An antiques market of 100 dealers featuring country to formal furniture, architectural pieces, kitchenware, tools, china, sterling, glassware, jewelry, and books. Cafe on premises. Closed Tues., Weds.

Kettering Antiques (413 229-2859; Main St.) Formal English and American 18th- and 19th-century furniture and decorative porcelain and brass. Cabinet restoration and polishing available. Winter hours vary.

WEST STOCKBRIDGE

Sawyer Antiques (232-7062; Depot St.) In a Shaker-built grist mill, early American furniture and accessories, in a variety of styles: formal, Shaker, country. Open Fri.–Sun; otherwise call ahead.

Ebenezer II Antiques & Gifts (413 232-7017; 2 Main St.) Eclectic assortment of antiques and collectibles; also Turkish rugs and copper.

Central County

LANESBOROUGH

Amber Springs Antiques (413-442-1237; 29 S. Main St., Rte. 7) Country American furnishings "from as early as we can find to as late as we can stand." That description includes tools, pottery, country store items, trivia. The alternate motto, according to owner Gae Elfenbein, is "we have it but we can't find it." Open daily; weekends in winter, or call ahead.

LENOX

Charles L. Flint Antiques Inc. (413-637-1634, -1242; 2 Kemble St., P.O. Box 971) Furniture, painting, accessories, folk art, Shaker items. The owner is a noted local historian who has a genuine knowledge of and enthusiasm for his wares.

La Vie En Rose (413-637-3662; 67 Church St.) Painted furniture (French Canadian), vintage jewelry, contemporary museum-quality art prints, and gifts in a cottage-like setting.

Past & Future (413 637-2225; 63 Church St.) 19th- and 20th-century silver and small antiques and collectibles; including scales, inkwells, perfumes, sewing items, and sporting antiques.

Stone's Throw Antiques (413-637-2733; 57 Church St.) American, French, English, and Oriental 19th- and early 20th-century furniture, accessories, and collector's items, including china, glass, silver, prints,

PITTSFIELD

Berkshire Hills Coins & Antiques (413-499-1400; 111 South St.) Specializing in collectible coins, estate gold and costume jewelry, sterling items, pocket watches, oak furniture, and a variety of antique decorative accessories.

Bargain Shop (413-499-0927; 1 Reed St., off South St.) Unprepossessing though it may seem, there are treasures here: past finds included a Czech pitcher, an ironstone bowl, and interesting tin molds. Also used Levis and vintage fabrics. Closed Tues., Sun.

Memory Lane Antiques (413-499-2718; 446 Tyler St.) A recommended source for useful and decorative pieces: furniture, rugs, mirrors, lamps, accessories, china and glass, ephemera, other collectibles. Owner Bev Martin is helpful, friendly, and enthusiastic about her merchandise. Look for the mannequin in a vintage dress on the sidewalk outside. Closed Tues., Sun.

RICHMOND

Wynn A. Sayman (413-698-2272) A by-appointment-only specialist in English pottery of the 18th and early 19th century, for collectors and museums; including saltglaze, redware, tortoiseshell ware, cream ware, pearl ware, and Staffordshire bocage figures.

North County

CHESHIRE

Cheshire Antiques (413-743-7703; 80 Willow Cove Rd.) An eclectic offering of china and glassware and furniture.

Winterbrook Farm Antiques (413 743-2177; Rte. 8) Late 19th- and 20th-century restored and refinished furniture and accessories. Howard's refinishing products and replacement hardware in stock. Weds.–Sat., 9–5, or by appointment.

WILLIAMSTOWN

Collector's Warehouse (413-458-9686; 105 North St., Rte. 7) Antiques; collectibles, including glassware, jewelry, frames, dolls, linen, furniture. Tues.–Sat., 10–3, or call ahead. In the McClelland Press Building.

Library Antiques (413-458-3436; 70 Spring St.) Old and new items in a series of rooms, artfully displayed, including jewelry, furniture, writing supplies, housewares, pillows, prints, books, international decor pieces, silver, dishes, pottery, fabrics, and textiles. They welcome browsers. A great place for gifts or for yourself.

Saddleback Antiques (413-458-5852; 1395 Cold Spring Rd., Rte. 7) Furniture, glass, pottery, prints, posters. A group shop in an old schoolhouse with a bell tower whose inventory changes weekly and includes a fine selection of pieces at realistic prices. Mon.–Sat., 10–5, Sun. 12–5.

Auctioneers

Beaver Auctions & Appraisers (413 243-8208; 1455 Cape St., Lee)

William Bradford Auction Galleries (413-229-6667 or -8737 evenings; Rte. 7, Sheffield)

Roy C. Burdick (413-664-6055; 24 S. County Rd., Florida)

John & Dina Fontaine (413-448-8922, 1485 West Housatonic St., Pittsfield)

Ralph Fontaine & Heritage Auctions (413 442-2537; 94 Dawes Ave., Pittsfield)

T. A. Gage (413-528-0076, 413-528-4771; Rte. 23, S. Egremont)

LuJohn's Auctioneers (413 243-4660; Cape St., Lee)

BOOKS

The Berkshires' literary traditions are upheld by several excellent bookstores, new and used, each with its own distinct character. Specialists, rare-book, and antique-book dealers are also listed.

South County

GREAT BARRINGTON

Bookloft (413-528-1521; Barrington Plaza, Stockbridge Rd., Rte. 7) A thoughtfully chosen selection of books and tapes, both music and books. It's also a good source for Berkshire-related titles. With its wooden bookcases and pleasant atmosphere, one of the nicest places in South County for browsing and consulting with fellow book-lovers, particularly owner Eric Wilska.

Farshaw's Books (413-528-1890; www.bibliofind.com; 13 Railroad St.) A select offering of antique and used or out-of-print titles, for the reader, collector, and bibliophile, in a well-organized, browser-friendly shop. The owners, Helen and Michael Selzer, established *bibliofind*, the largest inventory of old, used, and rare books, from an international list of booksellers, on the Internet. In 1997, it was the number one site on Yahoo.

Yellow House Books (413-528-8227; 252 Main St.) Bob and Bonnie Benson offer a fine selection of used and rare books in three rooms of a house that is more than 100 years old. Specialities include photography, Native American, literature, art, music, children's illustrated books, cooking, metaphysical.

LEE

Media Merchant (413 243-3359; 50 Water St., Lee, at Prime Outlets) This is a discount book and media outlet. Can be a good source for bargain books.

SHEFFIELD

Berkshire Book Co. (413-229-0122, 800-828-5565; 510 S. Main St., Rte. 7) The ideal used-book store for the reader, with an extensive and well-organized collection. Co-proprietor Esther Kininmonth truly knows and loves her stock and its authors, and it's a pleasure to consult with her about various writers and editions. Categories include literature, travel, biography, children's, art, and antiques.

SOUTH EGREMONT

B&S Gventer Books (413-528-2327; Tyrrell Rd. & Rte. 23, P.O. Box 298) "Tons of books" from the 15th century to the 19th. Medieval manuscript and Renaissance pages on vellum, and various pages from books published from 1300 to 1600; 19th-century hand-colored engravings. Knowledgeable owner Bruce Gventer can tell you their stories. June–Oct., Weds.–Sun.; occasional weekends in winter.

Central County

LANESBOROUGH

Waldenbooks (413-499-0115; Berkshire Mall) Berkshire County's entry for this well-known chain, stocking current hardcover and softcover best sellers, as well as representative collections in various categories, including children's books and books of local interest. Books, tapes; magazine section.

The Bookstore in Lenox.

Judith Monachina

LENOX

The Bookstore (413-637-3390; 9 Housatonic St.) A literate and imaginative selection of new fiction, old fiction, and nonfiction. There are collections of small-press titles and books by local and regional authors, and well-chosen children's and young-adult titles. The Bookstore is a community center, too, presided over by owner Matt Tannenbaum with grace and humor. Matt and his assistants know their books and are happy to converse with you about them; they organize book-signing parties and special events, too. "The world's oldest, permanent literary establishment, serving the community since last Tuesday."

PITTSFIELD

Barnes & Noble (413-496-9051; Berkshire Crossing Mall) This chain "super-store" has a large selection of the most popular titles, along with book tapes and some musical scores. The in-store cafe features Starbucks coffee and other goodies.

North County

NORTH ADAMS

Crystal Unicorn Bookstore (413-664-7377; 59 Main St.) New and used paper-backs and hardcovers; gifts, handmade jewelry, and a small selection of old and rare books.
Papyri Books (413-662-2099; 49 Main St.) Mostly used, some new; regular pro-grams of music and readings.

Book Dealers

These specialist book dealers do business by catalog or appointment.

Adler Children's Books (413-298-3559; Stockbridge) Out of print, old and rare children's books; search services.

Howard S. Mott (413-229-2019; Rte. 7, Sheffield) First editions; books from the 16th to the 20th centuries, autographs.

J&J Lubrano (413-528-5799; 39 Hollenbeck Ave., Gt. Barrington) Specialist in old and rare music books and autographs.

John R. Sanderson Antiquarian Bookseller (413-298-5322; P.O. Box 844, Stockbridge) Rare and fine books.

North Star Rare Books and Manuscripts (413 644-9595; 684 S. Main St., Gt. Barrington, Rte. 7) Specializing in 18th- to 19th-century historical literary manuscripts and rare volumnes.

WILLIAMSTOWN

Water Street Books (413-458-8071; 26 Water St.) A large selection in just about every category displayed on classy architectural shelving. The help is hip and friendly. There are sale books, children's books, and the Williams College bookstore is in the back. A booklover's paradise.

Farther afield, but a destination for a good browse: *Librarium* (518-392-5209; off Rte. 295, 1 mi. E. of East Chatham) More than 25,000 second-hand, out-of-print books "for all interests and ages." Sat. & Sun. 10–5; by chance or appointment otherwise.

CLOTHING & ACCESSORIES

You can outfit yourself in just about any style of your choice in the Berkshires: classic, traditional, designer, funky, all-natural, English country squire, buckaroo — it's all here. Some boutiques also feature designs and concepts created in the Berkshires. For clothing factory outlets, and there are a number of them, check the listings below plus the "Shopping Streets, Mews, & Malls" section.

South County

GREAT BARRINGTON

Barrington Outfitters (413 528-0021; 289 Main St.) A good selection of shoes for men, women, and kids along with casual clothes for men and women.

Byzantium (413-528-9496; 32 Railroad St.) The sweaters in chenille, wool, and cotton will catch your eye first, but don't stop there. Stylish and easy women's dresses, blouses, skirts, and ensembles, casual to dressy; lots of lovely lingerie and sleepwear; jewelry, throws, and other accessories.

Drygoods (413-528-2950; 42 Railroad St.) Contemporary women's clothes, hats, jewelry, accessories, and shoes. **Body and Soul** is now sharing space in this cheerful shop offering a wide variety of body care products.

Gatsby's (413-528-9455; 25 Railroad St.) Useful and funky stuff, including cotton nightgowns, Doc Martins, Teva sandals, Birkenstocks, denim, socks and turtlenecks, and housewares. Gatsby's covers the territory with shops in Williamstown (413-458-5407; 31 Spring St.) and Lee (413-243-3412; 62 Main St.).

Hildi B (413-528-0331; 320 Main St.) Natural fiber clothes, including batik sweaters, skirts, blouses, dresses; handcrafted jewelry and other crafts, leather items, oils and soaps. A friendly atmosphere created by helpful sales people.

Jack's Country Squire (413-528-1390; 316 Main St., Main St.) Family clothing and shoes, including Nike, Woolrich, Reebok, Levi.

LEE

Ben's (413-243-0242; 68 Main St.) A friendly store packed with clothing and footwear for the whole family.

A Change of Art (413-243-4800; 61 Center St.) An energetic mix of American designers featuring cotton, linen, and other natural fibers that complement hand-painted and hand-sewn pieces.

Zabian's Ltd. (413 243-0136; 19 Main St.) Clothing for men with an emphasis on personal service.

Prime Outlets (413 243-8186; 50 Water St. Exit 2 off the Mass Turnpike at Rte. 20) Over 60 discount and factory outlet stores featuring women's clothing (Jones New York and Liz Claiborne), pocketbooks (Coach), sporting goods, menswear and shoes (Johnson & Murphy, Haggar), Polo, and Brooks Brothers.

STOCKBRIDGE

Greystone Gardens (413-298-0113; In the Mews, Main St.) Antique clothing for men and women. See the description under Pittsfield.

Katherine Meagher (413-298-3329; 10 Elm St.) Women's clothing, casual and dressy, classically fashionable; sportswear, separates, dresses, accessories, jewelry.

Sweaters Etc. (413-298-4287; South St., Rte 7) The third house behind the Red Lion Inn contains a veritable feast of sweaters in wool and cotton. Some are high fashion, while others are more casual. Many are hand-knit and all sweaters are discounted.

Especially for Children

Gifted Child (413-637-1191; 80 Church St., Lenox) Children's clothing, newborns to pre-teens, with a contemporary flair; high-quality toys and gifts. Camp care packages — what a great idea. And don't miss the sale barn. Also in Gt. Barrington at 23 Railroad St.; 413 528-1395, featuring clothes from newborn to size 6x.

kids and kin. . . (413-528-1188; Rte. 23, S. Egremont) Bright unusual children's clothing and accessories, along with quilts and gifts for adults. Closed Tues., Weds.

M. Lacey (413 528-5991; 12 Railroad St., Gt. Barrington) A beautiful selection of children's clothing for infants and children, much of it imported. The whimsical designs are sure to delight both wearer and buyer.

Matruska (413 528-6911; 252 Main St., Gt. Barrington) Toys and books chosen to enhance a child's imagination and sense of beauty. Wonderful dolls from Holland that do nothing but absorb a child's love.

Tom's Toys (413 528-3331; 307 Main St., Gt. Barrington) A happening place for kids that carries all the most popular toys and a great selection of inexpensive trinkets to amuse the most bored young traveler.

What Kids Want (413-743-7842; 31 Park St., Adams) Children's clothing, sizes newborn to size 16 at less than retail prices.

Other spots for clothes, toys, and gifts for children include *Hodge Podge* in Stockbridge and *Mary Stuart* in Lenox (for exquisite clothes designed for grandmothers to give); and several area museums and galleries, particularly the *Berkshire Museum* in Pittsfield, have gift shops with sections devoted to educational items disguised as toys.

Vlada Boutique (413-298-3656; Elm St.) Retail therapy for sure. Sophisticated women's clothing with an emphasis on comfort. Witty gifts and accessories, lovely and outrageous cards, and clever contemporary jewelry.

Central County

LANESBOROUGH

Berkshire Pendleton Store (413 443-6822; Rte. 7 between Pittsfield and Williamstown) Classic wool clothes and accessories for the complete look. Men's sport shirts and sweaters, too, and a large selection of Indian trade blankets and robes.

Berkshire Mall comprises many and varied clothes-shopping options for men, women, teens, and children: the Gap, American Eagle Outfitters, Weathervane, Jonathan Reid Ltd., Lerner's, Eddie Bauer, and Filene's (413-445-4400; Old State Rd., Rte 8).

LENOX

Casablanca (413-637-2680; 27 Housatonic St.) Men's and women's clothes, stylishly displayed in a gallery setting.

Chase Ballou (413-637-2133; 25 Pittsfield-Lenox Rd., Rte. 7) Women's clothing, dressy to casual with a large selection of bridal and special-occasion dresses; and shoes, lingerie, sleepwear, and accessories. A large selection, frequent sales, and personable salespeople, too.

Fabrics and Weavers

Skilled hands and tools of the trade, at Undermountain Weavers, Housatonic.

Jonathan Sternfield

For your home or for yourself, four sources of special textiles and fabrics:

Maplewood Fabrics (413-229-8767; Rte. 7A, Ashley Falls) Liberty of London, Scalamandré, Schumacher, and other fine fabrics in a low-key setting.

Clifford Roberts Textiles (413-528-9789; 70 Railroad St., Gt. Barrington) A relatively new source for handwoven scarves in luscious fibers including silk and chenille, plus wonderful pillows and throws. The jewel-like colors of the works on display provide a visual feast.

Sam Kasten (413 528-3300; 46 Castle St. in the Train Station, Gt. Barrington) The old Great Barrington Train Station houses the looms of Sam Kasten's nationally renowned architectural fabrics firm. Wall coverings, upholstery fabrics, and carpeting almost too fine to tread upon are the mainstay of his business, but shawls and wraps in exotic and unusual yarns are available, too. Call for hours.

Undermountain Weavers (413-274-6565; Rte. 41, W. Stockbridge, RR1, Box 26, Housatonic) In a restored barn, on century-old hand looms, traditional Shetland Island patterns are taking shape. Purchase by the yard, or tailoring can be arranged.

Evviva (413-637-9875; 22 Walker St.) Sophisticated dresses, separates, and accessories by designers "well known and undiscovered."

Glad Rags (413-637-0088; 76 Church St.) Clothes with an emphasis on easy fit and easy care in a variety of fabulous fabrics. Wonderful hats, scarves, and other accessories and jewelry. Also a source for *Berkshire Humane Society* T-shirts and sweatshirts.

K's Coats (413-443-5358; 450 Pittsfield-Lenox Rd., Rte. 7) Ladies' coats, dress and casual, in a variety of styles, with designer labels like Forcaster, Bromley, and Jones New York. Across from **Michael's Shoes** (413-442-3464), with footwear for men and women, handbags.

Purple Plume (413-637-3442; 35 Church St.) A large selection of fun and unusual clothing, some batiked or hand-painted, featuring the latest looks and natural fibers. The amazing array of accessories includes jewelry, headbands, and scarves. Gifts and cards, too.

Talbot's (413-637-3576; 46 Walker St.) Classic women's clothing and accessories, and a special Petites section.

Tanglewool, Inc. (413-637-0900; 28 Walker St.) Sophisticated clothing, shoes, gorgeous sweaters (from *Patricia Roberts* and other well-known designers), for the fashion-conscious.

Weaver's Fancy (413-637-2013; 69 Church St.) One-of-a-kind clothing and hats in hand-created fabrics. Beautiful hand-painted silks and luscious rayon chenille. Don't miss the whimsical hats that provide both warmth and wit.

PITTSFIELD

Champion Factory Outlet (413-442-1332; 456 W. Housatonic St., Pittsfield Plaza) Sweatshirts and turtlenecks at discount prices, and other athletic apparel.

Cosmetic Design Center & Color Accents (413-443-0872, 137 North St.) Designer scarves, hats, belts, jewelry, lingerie, and various accessories for the boudoir, including English toiletries and other cosmetics. Instruction in make-up; color analysis; wardrobe planning. Also, in Lenox at 38 Church St.

The Cottage (413-447-9643; 31 South St.) A popular shop where women's clothing shares space with home and gift items.

Greystone Gardens (413-442-9291; 436 North St.) An emporium of timeless treasures. Victorian and vintage clothing, accessories, jewelry, and linens, for men and women. The long, high-ceilinged shop has floral carpeting, curtained dressing rooms with antique mirrors, stacks of hat boxes, swanky fashion prints, and vintage songs being crooned in the background — the perfect setting for '40s evening gowns, sporty rayon dresses, lacy camisoles, vintage tuxedos, top hats, tweed jackets and coats, bowling shirts, fringed scarves, and more, all eminently wearable. Owner Carla Lund, creator of this outpost of nostalgia, is a genius at putting it all together. Cards, soaps, and other niceties, too. Don't miss it or the shop in the Mews in Stockbridge.

Stock Room (413-445-5500; Allendale Shopping Center) Liquidators offer clothing from upscale department stores at a discount, from blue jeans to evening wear. You never know what you might find. They have some non-clothing items, too. The outlet for *Crane* and *Caspari* paper products.

Steven Valenti (413-443-2569; 157 North St.) Menswear for the '90s in a well-appointed store, with up-to-date styles by Perry Ellis, Jhane Barnes, and other contemporary designers. Shirts, sweaters, suits, jackets, and coats here feature fine fabrics and colors ranging from traditional to fashion-forward styles. An outstanding collection of silk ties.

North County

WILLIAMSTOWN

The Cottage (413-458-4304; 24 Water St.) Specialty fabrics and apparel from designers like April Cornell, Vera Bradley, Putumayo, and Crabtree & Evelyn (nightwear).

House of Walsh (413-458-8088; 39 Spring St.) Classic clothes for men and women in a classic setting, with sportswear, accessories, gifts, and Williams College items, too.

Williams Shop (413-4583605; 15 Spring St.) A large selection of items bearing the Williams College logo, as well as athletic and sporting goods.

Zanna (413-458-9858; 41 Spring St.) Contemporary women's clothes and accessories, featuring natural fibers and up-to-the-minute looks. Also there is a selection of sophisticated but comfortable shoes from *Arche* and *Aerosoles*.

GIFT & SPECIALTY SHOPS

South County

ASHLEY FALLS

Primrose Cottage (413-229-8401; Rte. 7A) In a cottage setting with soft lighting are lovely dried flowers everywhere, hanging in bunches from the beams overhead, spilling forth from baskets, artfully arranged in swags, topiaries and other imaginative forms. They're from local gardens and from the wild. They have their own signature potpourri, "Berkshire Woods," and are also the source for Berkshire Twig furniture. Well worth a trip. Call ahead for information about classes or to order special arrangements.

GREAT BARRINGTON

Berkshire Botanika, Inc. (413 528-5112; 389 Stockbridge Rd., Rte. 7) A wonderful melange of plants, pots, gardening tools, candles, garden urns and accents, books on gardening, and seed packets fill this bright attractive new building next to the Gingham Rabbit shop.

Church Street Trading Company (413-528-6120; 4 Railroad St.) A trendy mix of antiques, natural-fiber clothes, nature-oriented cosmetics, pottery, crafts, and various lifestyle accessories, attractively arranged.

Crystal Essence (413-528-2595; 39 Railroad St.) Geodes, jewelry, gemstones, ceramics, clothes, books, and other items for enhancing a New Age lifestyle.

Gingham Rabbit (413-528-0048; 389 Stockbridge Rd.) A pastel palette predominates in this two-story shop that sells wonderful cards, pillows, gift items, infant clothing, lingerie, and bath products. They have a delivery service to area hospitals to facilitate congratulating a new mother or cheering up a sick friend.

La Pace (413 528-1888; 313 Main St.) A beautifully conceived and decorated store full of luxurious bath items imported from all over Europe with an emphasis on Italy. Linen handtowels, chic shower curtains, bath pillow — even rubber duckies for the tub.

Mama's Earth: The Environmental General Store (413-644-8996; 87 Railroad St.) A store dedicated to saving the environment by selling recycled, organic, or environmentally friendly products. Clothes from 100% organic cotton, toys, books, etc.

Mistral's (413-528-1618; 7 Railroad St.) "Provence in the Berkshires" is the way the owners describe their shop. You can find French wire baskets, lamps, and vases here, as well as jacquard-patterned napkins, provençal olive oil, faience plates, cutlery, and serving pieces all guaranteed to win a Francophile's heart. Upstairs are bath and bedroom products.

Red Door (413-528-1899; 3 Railroad St.) Behind the red door is a tiny shop carrying a variety of gift items both old and new.

Sappa (413 528-9592; 308 Main St.) An elegant new store on the Gt. Barrington scene. The very charming young owner has a great sense of design and eye for the unusual. Gifts and accessories from Europe join American antiques and interesting art works in an ever-changing display of beautiful objects.

Seeds & Co., Inc. (413 528-8122; 34 Railroad St.) Simplicity and sophistication of design are the hallmarks of this store. Home and bath accessories with wit and charm share space with those having a 21st-century edge.

Talavera (413-528-2423; 9 Railroad St.) Handcrafted items from tiny pitchers to grand serving bowls. Fanciful carved wooden items and colorful textiles.

T.P. Saddle Blanket & Trading Co. (413-528-6500; 304 Main St.) An outpost for the Southwest look, from cowboy-motif pajamas to saddleblankets for your living room, with a colorful abundance of boots, belts, pillows, books, candles, bedding, dishware, shirts, vests, and furniture accents.

LEE

Essential Body (413 243-3550; 40 Main St.) Occupying the former Pamela Loring space is a new shop dedicated to aromatherapy, bath, and body products. They carry Caswell-Massey products among other lines.

Pamela Loring Gifts & Interiors (413-243-2689; 151 Main St.) Tastefully decorated shop in a renovated Victorian house. Each room is filled with carefully chosen merchandise. There's an emphasis on seasonal gifts and decorations. Besides household decorative items there are candles, bath oils, soaps, potpourri, and charming gifts for children.

SHEFFIELD

Campo de Fiori (413 528-9180; Rte. 7) A wonderful source for garden ornaments, pots, botanical prints, interesting soaps, plants, and containers. A very sophisticated touch of Tuscany in the Berkshires.

STOCKBRIDGE

Pink Kitty (413-298-3134; at the Red Lion Inn) A lovely shop with gifts, cards, and accessories, featuring Berkshire items.

Seven Arts (413-298-5101; Main St.) A concentration of items with Rockwell motifs, also T- shirts, jewelry, and gifts.

Williams & Son Country Store (413-298-3016; Main St.) A Stockbridge institution, with jams and jellies, soaps, candy, gourmet foods, glassware, gifts, cards, and various nostalgia items. You'll enjoy the old tins displayed behind the counter.

Yankee Candle (413-298-3004; Main St.) A huge selection of candles in a variety of shapes, colors and scents.

SOUTH LEE

Woman of Wands (413 243-4036; Rte. 102) This tiny shop contains books and products dedicated to New Age spirituality.

WEST STOCKBRIDGE

Charles H. Baldwin & Sons (413 232-7785; 1 Center St.) Not only is this an outlet for Baldwin's flavoring extracts along with table and maple syrup, it is also a general store with seasonal gifts, cards, candy, and inexpensive toys for children. Recently featured in *Martha Stewart Living* magazine.

Hotchkiss Mobiles Gallery (232-0200; 8 Center St.) Open Sat.–Sun.; or call for an appointment. Contemporary mobiles for your home or office.

Central County

LENOX

B. Mango & Bird (413-637-2611; 48 Main St.) An eclectic mix of home furnishings and accessories in a bright new location.

Colorful Stitches (413-637-8207; 48 Main St.) A rainbow of yarns in wools, silks, cottons, and blends would tempt even the most novice knitter. Wonderful patterns, buttons, and all the necessary needles, etc. There are even regular weekend instruction sessions.

Mary Stuart (413-637-0340; 69 Church St.) Accessories for gracious country living, including china, glassware, linen, needlepoint, and toiletries; lingerie and sleepwear; books and cards. Beautiful clothing for infants and toddlers.

Miranda's Secret Garden (413 637-8061; 12 Housatonic St.) This seasonal shop concentrates on garden-related gifts, birdhouses, and decorative items.

Naomi's Herbs (413-637-0616; 11 Housatonic St.) Dried herbs and flowers fill the rafters of this charming shop. There's an assortment of potpourri fragrances, essential oils, and medicinal herbs. Teas, bath blends, massage oil, and floral arrangements are also offered here as "resources for a healthy and beautiful life."

Silver Sleigh (413-637-3522; Lenox House Country Shops, Pittsfield-Lenox Rd., Rte. 7) Complete and imaginative Christmas accessorizing, plus gifts for all season.

The Soap Box Factory (1 800 880-SOAP; 38 Church St.) This is an outlet for the 100% olive oil soap made by the owners. They sell the soap individually and will also make up gift packages with bath accessories and bath essentials.

Villager Gifts (413-637-9866; 68 Main St.) An engaging variety of gifts and collectibles, featuring jewelry, pottery, stationery, candles, and cards. They are the largest area dealer for the *Cats' Meow Village* houses and custom pieces.

Yankee Candle (413-499-3626; 639 Pittsfield-Lenox Rd., Rte. 7) Candles, gifts, bath accessories. Also on Main St. in Stockbridge.

PITTSFIELD

The Cottage (413-447-9643; 31 South St.) Attractive tableware, including glasses, vases, dinnerware, table linens, baskets, frames, soaps, along with clothes and jewelry.

Pasko Frame & Gift Center (413-442-2680; 243 North St.) Berkshire landscapes by Walter Pasko, the Berkshire map, superb custom framing, prints and posters, and gifts and handcrafts from around the world. Largest area dealer of *P. Buckley Moss* prints.

North County

DALTON

Goddess's Gifts (413-684-1167; 2 Depot St.) This shop carries homemade beauty and skin-care products: soaps, lotions, shampoos, essential oils, and massage oils. There is a small section devoted to vitamins and bulk herbs. Consignment craft items and paintings by local artists round out its offerings.

ADAMS

Crafter's Cottage (413 743-2640; 23 Park St.) Unique handcrafted gifts and seasonal offerings in a range of prices. An outlet for crafters whose work is often only seen at craft fairs or holiday boutiques.

WILLIAMSTOWN

The Cottage (413-458-4305; 24 Water St.) A variety of gift items including tableware and table linens, cards, children's gifts, photo frames, toiletries from Crabtree & Evelyn, and women's clothes from designers like Putumayo.
Mulbury & Co. (413-458-1999; 125 Water St.) Jewelry, linens, bed & bath, gourmet food items, and gifts.
Where'd You Get That (413-458-2206; 20A Spring St.) This is a fun store that aims to provide gifts and toys to tickle your fancy, your brain, and your funnybone — and succeeds.

HANDCRAFTS

S ee Chapter Five, *Arts & Pleasures*, for additional listings of galleries with handcrafted art.

South County

GREAT BARRINGTON

Evergreen (413-528-0511; 291 Main St.) Contemporary American crafts include vases, tableware, pottery, clocks, and handcrafted jewelry.
October Mountain Stained Glass (413-528-6681; 343 Main St.) A vivid array of lampshades, window panels, and glass accessories. Custom design work is a specialty, including commissions for home owners, builders, architects. Beveling, sandblasting, repairs, and supplies are also offered. Closed Mon.
Wonderful Things (413-528-2473; 232 Stockbridge Rd.) Handcrafted gifts, or

make your own with yarn, needlework accessories, beads, feathers, stencils, paint, other craft supplies. Largest needlework store in the county.

Richard Bennett, master potter, working the clay at Great Barrington Pottery.

Jonathan Sternfield

HOUSATONIC

Great Barrington Pottery (413-274-6259; Rte. 41) Potter Richard Bennett uses a Japanese woodburning kiln for firing pottery designs that combine East and West. In a beautiful garden setting, visit the pottery showroom or participate in an ancient tea ceremony. (See "Seasonal Events" in Chapter Five, *Arts & Pleasures*.)

MONTEREY

Joyous Spring Pottery (413-528-4115; Art School Rd.) Potter Michael Marcus fires his climbing kiln once a year for a 10-day period for his Japanese-inspired unglazed ceramics.

SHEFFIELD

Fellerman & Raabe Glass Works (413-229-8533; 534 S. Main St., Rte 7) Glass art here includes perfume bottles, jewelry, vases, and paperweights — try one of these on a small light-box for a glowing miniature universe. Large glass bowls in organic shapes and glass sculpture, too. Call to find out when you can watch glass artists at work. Closed Mon.

Sheffield Pottery (413-229-7700; Rte. 7) New England potters' ware, including mugs, tea pots, platters, tureens; terra cotta items. Supplies and equipment.

WEST STOCKBRIDGE

Berkshire Center for Contemporary Glass (413 232-4666; 6 Harris St.) Iridescent bowls, glassware, paperweights and gift items, clever Christmas tree ornaments. Public viewing area. Glassblowing instruction, demonstrations, and classes offered.

Hoffman Pottery (232-4646; 103 Rte. 41, Gt. Barrington Rd.) Hand-thrown, hand-painted functional works that dance with energy.

New England Stained Glass Studios (232-7181; 5 Center St., P.O. Box 381) A specialist in Tiffany-style lamps. Admire the giant mushrooms and flowers in the windows next to the showroom, and a lion set in a door, on the way to the main entrance. Hundreds of lampshades; windows and other items, too. Custom work on a limited basis.

Central County

LENOX

Inspired Planet (413-637-2836; Brushwood Farm Shops, Pittsfield-Lenox Rd., Rte. 7) This abundant collection of distinctive "cross-cultural art" includes high-quality paintings, jewelry, primitives, rugs, icons, textiles, masks, pottery, carved wooden animals, and other sculpture. These handcrafted items with symbolic meaning are "gifts that connect." Call ahead for hours.

Concepts of Art (413-637-4845; 67 Church St.) Fine crafts and local artisans, with lamps and other glass, wood sculpture, jewelry, throws. There is an emphasis on Judaica.

Stevens & Conron Gallery (413-637-0739; Curtis Shops, 5 Walker St.) Fine art and rugs, handhooked and handwoven.

Wall Quilts (413-637-2286; 30 Cliffwood St.) Contemporary and imaginative wall hangings, in a variety of techniques: quilted, appliquéd, embroidered. Daily 1–5 in July, Aug.; closed Weds.; Sun. 10–2, and by appointment. Call to confirm hours.

North County

WLLIAMSTOWN

Amber Fox (413 458-8519; 622A Main St., Rte. 2) Antiques and collectibles, unusual gifts, and special treasures. Open Thurs.–Sat. 10–5, Sun. 12–5; Mon.–Weds. by appointment.

HOME & KITCHEN

South County

GREAT BARRINGTON

Chef's Shop (formerly **Berkshire Cottage Kitchen**) (413-528-0135; 290 Main St.) A hardware store for serious cooks, featuring innovative kitchen equipment including top-of-the-line cookware and knives. From garlic peelers to pasta pots, they have it all. Also pottery serving pieces and cookbooks.

Gatsby's (413-528-9455; 25 Railroad St.) In addition to wearables, you'll find futons, wicker and other furniture, bedclothes, and housewares.

Out Of Hand (413-528-3791; 81 Main St.) Every size, shape, and color of basket you could ever need or imagine — one upstairs room is full of them — plus rugs, throws, pillows, glassware in a rainbow of colors, toys, candlesticks, clothing. A great place for accessorizing your kitchen or sun porch. Or dining room or bedroom. Or . . . .

Lamplighter (413-528-3448; 162 Main St.) An exceptional lighting store with a wide selection and knowledgeable staff. Chandeliers, floor and table lamps, and outdoor lighting in all shapes, sizes, and styles, from Colonial to Art Deco to contemporary. Shades and other accessories.

STOCKBRIDGE

Berkshire Furniture Arts (413 298-3799; 6 Elm St.) Hand-painted furniture and custom-designed items. Also, the location for Carol Levison's "Once Upon A Table" collection of kitchen and tableware, which has been featured in several national magazines including *Country Living* and *Victoria*.

Country Curtains (413-298-5565; at the Red Lion Inn) Curtains and matching bedding are displayed in a series of bountifully accessorized room settings. You can select from a variety of styles and fabrics.

WEST STOCKBRIDGE

Anderson & Sons' Shaker Tree (232-7072; Rte. 41 in downtown W. Stockbridge) Exquisite Shaker reproduction furniture, with quilts, herbs, and other wares. The craftsmanship is so highly regarded that the Andersons were entrusted with permission to measure the Shaker pieces in the noted Andrews collection at the Metropolitan Museum of Art. The showroom is not always open; call ahead.

Central County

HANCOCK

Hancock Union Store (413-738-5072; Main St, P.O. Box 1009) Fine reproductions of American cabinet furniture, and tables, chairs, sofas, beds, in Queen Anne, Shaker, Federal, and Chippendale styles. Michael Boulay, cabinetmaker. Call for appointments.

LENOX

Different Drummer's Kitchen (413-637-0606; 568 Pittsfield-Lenox Rd., Rte. 7) All manner of equipment and accessories for kitchen and table, from coffee pots to measuring spoons.

Kaoud Oriental Rugs (413-499-5405; 598 Pittsfield-Lenox Rd., Rte. 7) Antique dhurries and kilims and "semi-antique" rugs, hand-knotted 100% wool.

Michael Charles Cabinetmakers (413-637-3483) Fine hand-crafted furniture in a variety of finishes, all beautiful in their stylish simplicity.

Tassels (413-637-2400, fax 413-637-1836; Brushwood Farm Shops, Pittsfield-Lenox Rd., Rte. 7) Fine furniture and accessories in room settings in a variety of styles. A division of Designers Furniture Showcase, Ltd.

PITTSFIELD

Haddad's Rug Company (413-443-4747; 32 Bank Row, Park Square) Specialists in Oriental and Oriental-style rugs, new and antique, plus carpeting and other types of rugs.

Homegoods (413 236-6996; 676 Merrill Rd.) A huge discount emporium with everything for the home including furniture on occasion.

Paul Rich & Sons Home Furnishings (413-443-6467, 800-723-7424); 242 North St.) A large and well-chosen selection of traditional, contemporary, and country furniture and accent pieces.

North County

ADAMS

Interior Alternative (413-743-1986; 5 Hoosac St.) A home-furnishings center with seconds and discontinued famous-brand upholstery and curtain fabric, wallpaper, Oriental carpets, hooked rugs, area rugs, bedspreads, comforters, pillows. Two huge floors in this old mill.

Old Stone Mill (413-743-1042; Rte. 8) Factory outlet for famous brands of wallpaper, fabric for upholstery and drapes. Wallpaper is hand-printed and machine printed. Over-runs, seconds, close-outs up to 70% off.

NORTH ADAMS

International Outlet (413-664-4580; 115 State St., Western Gateway Heritage State Park) A good source for imported crystal, glassware, dinnerware, kitchen utensils, wicker furniture, rugs, brass, table and kitchen linen, candles, pottery, cookware, and terra cotta pots.

JEWELRY

For additional jewelry options, check the listings in "Antiques," "Gift & Specialty Shops," and "Handcrafts."

Heirlooms Classic Jewelry (413-298-4436; The Mews, Stockbridge) A glittering treasure-box of a shop, offering affordable, elegant jewelry. Truly an international selection.

L'Artisanat (232-7187; Main St., W. Stockbridge) Elegant one-of-a-kind custom jewelry pieces; artisan's shop on premises.

McTeigue and McClelland (413 528-6263; 597 S. Main St., Gt. Barrington) This little gem in a tiny, renovated Victorian house emphasizes estate and consignment jewelry.

R. W. Wise Goldsmiths (413-637-1589; 81 Church St., Lenox) Richard Wise finds gemstones from all over the world — traveling recently in Brazil, Africa, and Tahiti — and offers them superbly crafted in contemporary fine art jewelry. Imaginative and unique combinations of gems and precious metals. Custom design service. Closed Mon. in winter.

Sienna Gallery (413 637-8386; 80 Main St., Lenox) A very contemporary decor provides the appropriate setting for stunning and expensive jewelry from the most talented new designers. The owner's father is a well-known glass artist and the artistic eye is very much in evidence here.

SHOPPING STREETS, MEWS, MALLS

Many of the shops described in this chapter are, happily, on Berkshire downtown Main Streets, where real people actually walk along the sidewalks, go to the hardware store and post office, get books at the library, pick up a few groceries, run into friends, and stop for lunch or coffee or ice cream, against a backdrop of mostly 19th-century civic architecture, highlighted by a few notable historic buildings. For beyond-the-downtown shopping experiences, short, usually scenic, drives will take you to clusters of destination shops, some in genuinely venerable buildings, others where the quaintness is of more recent vintage. And yes, there are even some malls. Following is a

*Downtowns are still
shopping places in
Berkshire County.*

Rich Beaty

roundup of where to find your favorite shops and shopping settings. More detailed listings of many of the establishments in these centers may be found in relevant sections of Chapters Four, Five, Seven, and Eight — *Restaurants & Food Purveyors, Arts & Pleasures, Outdoor Recreation,* and *Shopping.*

South County

Southfield's Buggy Whip Factory (Main St., Rte. 272) The drive there takes you through classic New England scenery. The huge, two-century-old building houses a large antiques center and a cafe.

Downtown Great Barrington is a happening place, with a true Main Street atmosphere created by a combination of several shops and boutiques, antiques stores, bookstores, an outstanding selection of eateries, a first-rate coffee place, and the grand old Mahaiwe Theatre and new Mahaiwe Triplex for current movies and special live performances. The action centers around Railroad St. and Main St., and takes in other side streets, too. Great Barrington hosts downtown food and music events throughout the year.

Jenifer House Commons (Rte. 7, Stockbridge Rd., Gt. Barrington) is just north of Great Barrington's center. This cluster of multilevel barns and buildings — some old and some new — houses an extensive group of antiques dealers' wares, a consignment clothing shop, art galleries, and a restaurant/brewery. Do lunch there or nearby. Open daily.

Main St., Stockbridge still looks like — and is — Norman Rockwell territory, even though the Rockwell Museum has moved (but not far; see Chapter Five, *Arts & Pleasures*). The welcoming expanse of the Red Lion Inn shares the scene with the gracious library, an excellent market, and several stores. Connected to Main St. is *The Mews,* a cozy cul-de-sac of shops offering clothes, jewelry, and gifts. Many Stockbridge shops offer Rockwelliana in one form or another, from T-shirts to signed prints. Also around the corner from Main St. is Elm St., with more shops, eateries, and the post office. Note: Main St. and The Mews can seem overrun on high-season weekends; come during the week, then, if you can.

A side trip to the small downtown of **West Stockbridge** will reward you with several galleries, good restaurants and cafes, and antiques — not to mention a hardware store and a shop devoted to flavoring extracts. The gallery scene offers outdoor sculptures on display, hand-crafted jewelry, mobiles, stained glass, and reproduction Shaker furniture, and many other options for contemporary art and craft work. A vintage depot houses a cafe and studios; a Shaker mill building is home to antiques. A small concentration of excellent restaurants will please everybody from the hamburger-and-pizza crowd to the international gourmet.

A relatively new offering on the Berkshire shopping scene is *Prime Outlets* (formerly known as the Berkshire Outlet Village). These shops are all stocked with discounted (and, some say, last year's) merchandise. Shoes, clothing, leather goods, cards, gourmet food, and watches are all available from top-of-the-line manufacturers to those more trendy and inexpensive. New to the complex is Brooks Bros. Conveniently located near Exit 2 of the Mass Pike in *Lee*, the Village's visibility attracts out-of-town shoppers, as well as locals. Local controversy over the design notwithstanding, it is an attractive, well-landscaped area. Shops include *Coach, Liz Claiborne, Jones New York, Tommy Hilfiger, Ralph Lauren, Harry&David, Mikasa, Gap*, and *Carter's* among others.

Recordings, Classical and Jazz

Compact discs, cassette tapes, and even those dinosaurs, records, are available throughout the county, in various chain stores and other retail outlets. Most places here with CDs and tapes have a small classical music selection, but if you're looking for more than the Three Tenors or the Four Seasons, visit the *Tanglewood Music Store*, at Tanglewood in Lenox, open for Tanglewood audiences, and featuring the music and performing artists of that week, plus much more. The *Berkshire Record Outlet* (413-243-4080; Rte. 102, Lee) has classical remainders listed in a catalog — send for one for $2 — from which you can select from thousands of classical CDs, tapes, and LPs, at closeout prices. On Saturdays, you can also browse through an eclectic selection of recordings in the small retail room, and you will be sure to turn up something you always wanted.

A well-chosen selection of classical, jazz, and blues is available at *Tune St.* (413 528- 4999; 294 Main St., Gt. Barrington) along with pop, folk, New Age, and world music recordings. They also sell electronic gear (stereo equipment, etc.) and do custom home installations. A low-key but vital business since 1979, *White Knight Records* (413 528-9466; 288 Main St., Gt. Barrington) carries a broad range of CDs and tapes. They have been complimented by out-of-towners for their collection of classical music and will do special orders.

Jazz enthusiasts in particular will enjoy *Toonerville Trolley Records* (413-458-5229; 131 Water St., Williamstown) and its array of current CDs, tapes, and out-of-print LPs. In addition to jazz, there's rock, folk, and reggae.

Central County

Downtown Lenox still maintains a "real" downtown flavor, though the boutique and gallery contingent seems to be in the ascendancy. The appealing variety of architecture — neoclassic and Victorian-cottage predominate — is home to inns and taverns, several dining options, an exceptional library and bookstore, and those shops and galleries: a number of clothing shops, mostly for women, covers the style territory from fine to funky, from classic to casual; art and handcraft galleries offer Berkshire scenes and world-renowned jewelry and other creations. The Curtis Shops — in an imposing hotel building, *the* place to stay in the 19th century — also is home to a mix of fine shops and galleries.

Just north of Lenox on the Pittsfield-Lenox Rd., Rte. 7, are the **Brushwood Farm Shops** and the **Lenox House Country Shops** (currently awaiting revitalization when Rte. 7 road work is completed). *Brushwood Farm* is a complex of barn buildings housing an interior decorating and design firm and a craft and painting gallery featuring Asian pieces.

Downtown Pittsfield was once the commercial and civic hub of the Berkshires, and though the glory of its main thoroughfare, North Street, has somewhat faded, it still hosts a number of services and shops. The downtown area includes several large churches and buildings that will interest the architecture buff, plus the Berkshire Museum and the Berkshire Athenaeum (the public library). You might catch a free concert downtown in the summer.

Berkshire Crossing Mall is the newest addition to the mall scene in the Berkshires. Located on Rte. 9 in Pittsfield, it has a Barnes & Noble store, a Pier One, and the ubiquitous Wal-Mart along with craft, grocery, and clothing stores.

Lanesborough's Berkshire Mall can supply your basic mall needs, with a multiscreen cinema complex, clothing and shoe stores, dozens of places to eat, a bookstore, and so forth.

North County

Spring Street and *Water Street* in *Williamstown* roughly parallel each other and are across from the main Williams College campus. Both easily walkable, they offer handcrafts, clothing, books, tapes and CDs, places to eat, antiques and accessories, sports gear, and all the Williams memorabilia you'll ever need.

Outside the County

A recommended destination just outside the county is **Chatham, New York**. Main Street shops include the **Dakota** for clothes; the **Chatham Bookstore**; *American Pie*, a contemporary general store; the **Handcrafters** for fine crafts; and the **Warm Ewe** for knitting supplies.

Cultural Shopping

Many Berkshire museums, and other institutions devoted to the arts and culture or to historical preservation, fund and publicize their operations with their own gift and book shops. They are excellent sources for unique Berkshire gifts, books about a wide range of historical subjects and the visual and performing arts, and fun and educational items for children. Institution members often get discounts at the shop.

Berkshire Museum Shop (413-443-7469; 39 South St., Pittsfield) An excellent array of items reflecting the scope of the museum's collections: books, cards, plates (including the reproduction Spode blue and white "Pittsfield" plate) and other home accessories, international crafts, and jewelry. There is a treasure-trove of small and creative items for children, from the artistic to the scientific reflecting the Museum's natural history collection. Shop staff, mostly volunteers, are helpful and personable.

Museum Store at the Clark Art Institute (413-458-9545; 225 South St., Williamstown) features items based on the Clark's collection and those of museums and art galleries around the world: cards, posters, and prints, matted and framed; fine art books; jewelry; and great toys from basic to upscale. The selection of books has been greatly enlarged, in the past few years, to include a more extensive collection of art books and regional titles.

Ex Libris: The Lenox Library Shop (413-637-0197; 18 Main St., Lenox) This pocket-sized shop offers cards, postcards, toys, T-shirts, bookplates, bookmarks, games, tote bags, sealing wax, and various Berkshire-related items.

Hancock Shaker Village Shop (413-443-0188; Rte. 20, Pittsfield) The spacious gift shop offers books, clocks, Shaker reproduction furniture and other items, in kits or assembled — even the Shaker cloak. Prints of drawings of the Hancock Shaker community and of Shaker "spirit drawings," too. Wonderful children's toys and kits. Open April through November and for school vacation week in February. Soon to relocate to a new and enlarged Visitor's Center.

Norman Rockwell Museum Store (413-298-4100, Rte. 183, Stockbridge) A well-designed center for books, prints, and cards; the children's section has books and toys and art-related things to do. There are limited-edition artist's proofs signed by Rockwell; and other items related to current exhibits and programs.

Additional cultural shopping options include the shop at the Massachusetts Audubon Sanctuary, *Pleasant Valley*; *Chesterwood,* particularly for their selection of National Trust publications; *Tanglewood*'s gift shop, with lots of Tanglewood-logo wearables and other items; the *Arrowhead Museum* shop, with books about Melville and county history, and cards, gifts; the *Garden Gift Shop* at the *Berkshire Botanical Garden*; *The Mount* (former home of Edith Wharton and current home of Shakespeare & Company); *Williams College Museum of Art*; *Mass MoCA*; the *Berkshire Theater Festival*; and even the *Berkshire Scenic Railway Museum* (books, toys, T-shirts).

CHAPTER NINE
Practical Matters
INFORMATION

Waiting for a bus near the Lee Information Booth

Judith Monachina

We offer here a small encyclopedia of useful information to help facilitate everyday life for residents and visitors in the Berkshires.

AMBULANCE, FIRE, POLICE

The general emergency number for Pittsfield and most Berkshire communities is 911. This "enhanced-911" service is part of a statewide system. Consult an up-to-date phone book for details.

In an emergency situation anywhere in the county, dial "0" and the operator will connect you directly to the correct agency.

Another county-wide set of emergency numbers is:

Ambulance, Fire, Police	911
Poison Control	800-682-9211
Rape Crisis Hotline	413-664-9642 (South County)
	413-443-0089 (Central County)
	413-663-7459 (North County)
	413-663-5807 (North County)

AREA CODES, TELEPHONE EXCHANGES, ZIP CODES, TOWN HALLS/LOCAL GOVERNMENT

AREA CODES

The area code for all of Berkshire County is **413**. Area codes for adjacent counties are as follows.

Massachusetts
Franklin (most towns), Hampshire, and Hampden counties — **413**.

Connecticut
Litchfield County — **860**.

New York
Columbia and Rensselaer Counties — **518**.

Vermont
Bennington County — **802**.

TOWN HALLS

All Berkshire communities have a town or city hall as the seat of local government. Most townships are governed by a Board of Selectmen; several also have a town manager. For general information, call the town offices at the following numbers or write to the Town Clerk, c/o Town Hall in the village in question.

Town	Telephone Exchange	Zip Code	Town Hall Office
Adams	743	01220	413-743-8320
Alford	528	01230	413-528-4536
Ashley Falls	229	01222	413-229-8752 (Sheffield)
Becket	623	01223	413-623-8934
Berkshire County Commissioners	Pittsfield	01201	413-448-8424
Cheshire	743	01225	413-743-1690
Clarksburg	663	01247	413-663-5282
Dalton	684	01226	413-684-6111
Egremont	528	01258	413-528-0182
Florida	662	01247	413-662-2448

Glendale	298	01229	413-298-4714 (Stockbridge)
Gt. Barrington	528	01230	413-528-3140
Hancock	458	01237	413-738-5225
Hinsdale	655	01235	413-655-2301
Housatonic	274	01236	413-528-3140 (Gt. Barrington)
Lanesborough	442, 443, 447, 499	01237	413-442-1167
Lee	243, 823	01238	413-243-5505
Lenox	637	01240	413-637-5506
Lenox Dale	637	01242	413-637-5506 (Lenox)
Middlefield	623	01243	413-623-8966
Mill River	229	01244	413-229-8116 (New Marlborough)
Monterey	528	01245	413-528-1443
Mt. Washington	528	01258	413-528-2839
New Ashford	458	01267	413-458-5461
New Marlborough	229	01244	413-229-8116
N. Adams	662, 663, 664	01247	413-662-3011
N. Egremont	528	01252	413-528-0182 (Egremont)
Otis	269	01253	413-269-0101
Peru	655	01235	413-655-8027
Pittsfield	442, 443, 445 446, 447, 448 494, 499	01201 01202 (Post Office)	413-499-9361
Richmond	698	01254	413-698-3882
Sandisfield	258	01255	413-258-4771
Savoy	743	01256	413-743-4290
Sheffield	229	01257	413-229-8752
S. Egremont	528	01258	413-528-0182 (Egremont)
S. Lee	243	01260	413-243-5505 (Lee)
Southfield	229	01259	413-229-8116 (New Marlborough)
Stockbridge	298	01262	413-298-4714
Tyringham	243	01264	413-243-1749
Washington	623	01223	413-623-8878
W. Stockbridge	232, 274	01266	413-232-0300
Williamstown	458, 597	01267	413-458-9341
Windsor	684	01270	413-684-3811

BANKS & CREDIT UNIONS

S everal Berkshire County banks are linked electronically to banking systems elsewhere in the United States. If you are visiting here, you may find these options quite helpful, especially if you need extra cash or traveler's checks. It's best to inquire with your home bank to see which system you can use and which Berkshire bank can serve you.

Phone numbers below connect you to the main office, or — in the case of some 800 numbers — to all offices or to special services.

Adams Co-operative Bank
93 Park St., Adams, 413-743-0001. Branches: Lanesborough, N. Adams.

First Massachusetts
Main office: 99 West St., Pittsfield, 413-499-3000; also in Pittsfield: 200 Elm St.; 1 Dan Fox Dr. Other branches: Adams, Dalton, Gt. Barrington, N. Adams, Williamstown.

BerkshireBank
Main office: 24 North (cor. Park Sq. & North St.), Pittsfield, 413-443-5601; also in Pittsfield: Old Town Hall, Park Sq.; 66 West St.; Allendale Shopping Ctr. (39 & 75 Cheshire Rd.); 165 Elm St. Other branches: Gt. Barrington, Lee, N. Adams, Sheffield, Stockbridge, W. Stockbridge. Toll-free to all branches: 800-773-5601.

City Savings Bank
Main office: 116 North St., Pittsfield, 413-443-4421; also in Pittsfield: 734 Williams St. (Bradlees Plaza). Other branches: Gt. Barrington, Lee, N. Adams, Otis. Toll-free in MA: 800-292-6634.

Fleet Bank
69 Veterans' Memorial Dr., N. Adams; 800-841-4000.

Greylock Federal Credit Union
Main office: 150 West St., Pittsfield, 413-256-4000; also in Pittsfield: 75 Kellogg, 413-443-5114; 660 Merrill Rd., 413-445-5555. Other branches: Adams, Gt. Barrington, Lee.

Hoosac Bank
Main office: 93 Main St., N. Adams, 413-663-5353. Branch: 296 Main St., Williamstown, 413-458-9503.

Lee Bank
Main office: 75 Park St., Lee, 413-243-0117. Branch: Elm St., Stockbridge, 413-298-3611.

Lenox Bank
Main office: 7 Main St., Lenox, 413-637-0017. Branch: Pittsfield-Lenox Rd., Lenox, 413-499-0717.

Lenox Savings Bank
Main office: 25 Main St., Lenox, 413-637-0147. Branch: 2 Holmes Rd. (at Rte. 7), Lenox, 413-443-4433.

Pittsfield Co-operative Bank
Main office: 70 South St., Pittsfield, 413-442-6501. Branches: 488 Main St., Dalton, 413-684-5115; 325 Main St., Gt. Barrington, 413-528-2840.

Pittsfield Municipal Federal Credit Union
70 Allen St., Pittsfield, 413-442-6501.

S. Adams Savings Bank
Main office: 2 Center St., Adams, 413-743-0040. Branches: 273 Main St., Williamstown, 413-458-2141; State Rd., Cheshire, 413-743-0270.

Williamstown Savings Bank
795 Main St., Williamstown, 413-458-8191.

BIBLIOGRAPHY

Here are two lists of books about the Berkshires, many of which we used in researching this book.

"Books You Can Buy" shows titles available either through Berkshire bookshops, bookstores elsewhere or from the publishers. For information on Berkshire booksellers, see "Bookstores" in Chapter Eight, *Shopping.*

"Books You Can Borrow" suggests a wealth of other reading in earlier publications now no longer for sale. Some of the more rarefied material on this list does not circulate outside the libraries, and its use may be restricted to those with professional credentials. Several popular items here will especially interest history buffs. The best sources for book borrowing are described under "Libraries" in Chapter Five, *Arts & Pleasures.*

Books You Can Buy

COOKBOOKS

Chase, Suzi Forbes. *The New Red Lion Inn Cookbook.* Lee, MA: Berkshire House Publishers, 2000. 272 pp., photos; $23.95.

Conway, Linda Glick. *Country Inns and Back Roads Cookbook.* Lee, MA: Berkshire House Publishers, 1995. 256 pp., illus., $17.95. Collection of recipes from inns around the nation, including Blantyre (Lenox), the Red Lion Inn (Stockbridge), and the Village Inn (Lenox).

Cook, Janet, ed. *Berkshire Victuals.* Stockbridge, MA: Berkshire County Historical Society, 1993. 208 pages, illus., $19.95. Historical and contemporary recipes.

Jacobs, Miriam. *Best Recipes of Berkshire Chefs.* Lee, MA: Berkshire House Publishers, 1993. 208 pp., illus., $12.95 pap.

Levitt, Atma Jo Ann. *The Kripalu Cookbook.* Lee, MA: Berkshire House Publishers. 1995. 448 pp., $16.95. Recipes featured at the Kripalu Center in Lenox, tailored for home use.

Shortt, C. Vincent. *The Innkeepers Collection Cookbook.* Lee, MA: Berkshire House Publishers, 1993. 272 pp., illus., $16.95. Collection of recipes from inns around the nation, including the Inn at Stockbridge and the Red Lion Inn.

Williamstown Theatre Festival. *As You Like It.* Williamstown, MA: Williamstown Theatre Festival Guild, 1993. 222 pp., illus, $15.00. Recipes from the festival's stars, directors, writers, and associates.

LITERARY WORKS

The Berkshire Review. Pittsfield, MA: The Berkshire Writers Room. Literary annual devoted to poetry, fiction, plays, and essays by Berkshire authors.

Howard, Walter. *Sisyphus in the Hayfield: Views of a Berkshire Farmer.* Tyringham, MA: Cobble Press, 1988. 128 pp., photos, $14.00.

Melville, Herman. *Great Short Works of Herman Melville.* New York, NY: Harper & Row, 1969. 507 pp., bibliog., $18.50.

Metcalf, Paul, ed. *October Mountain: An Anthology of Berkshire Writers.* Williamstown, MA: Mountain Press, 1992. 163 pp., $11.95 pap.

Nunley, Richard, ed. *The Berkshire Reader.* Lee, MA: Berkshire House Publishers, 1992. 544 pp., illus., $29.95 hardcover; $16.95 pap.

Wharton, Edith. *A Backward Glance.* New York, NY: Charles Scribner's Sons, 1985 reprint. 379 pp., index, $13.95 pap.

———. *Ethan Frome.* New York, NY: Scribner's, 1988 reprint. $5.95 pap.

———. *Summer.* New York, NY: Scribner's, 1998 reprint. $10.00 pap.

LOCAL HISTORY & CULTURE

Babcock, Richard, and Lauren R. Stevens. *Old Barns in the New World.* Lee, MA: Berkshire House Publishers, 1996. 192 pp., photos, $21.95.

Burns, Deborah E. *Shaker Cities of Peace, Love, and Union: A History of the Hancock Bishopric.* Hanover, NH: University Press of New England, 1993, 246pp., $45.00; $19.95 pap.

————, and Lauren R. Stevens. *Most Excellent Majesty: A History of Mount Grey-lock*. Lee, MA: Berkshire House Publishers, 128 pp., photos, $8.95 pap.

Cahill, Timothy, Mae G. Banner, Richard Nunley, Fred Sokol. *Muses in Arcadia: Cultural Life in the Berkshires*. Lee, MA: Berkshire House Publishers, 2000. 272 pp., illus., $19.95 pap.

Chapman, Gerard. *Eminent Berkshire Women*. Gt. Barrington, MA: Attic Revivals Press, 1988. 32 pp., $5.00.

————.*Great Barrington*. Gt. Barrington, MA: Gt. Barrington Historical Society, 1999. illus. $49.95.

————. *A History of the Red Lion Inn in Stockbridge, Massachusetts*. Stockbridge, MA: Red Lion Inn, 1987. 54 pp., illus., $12.00.

Consolati, Florence. *See All the People: Or, Life in Lee*. Lee, MA: The Author, 1978. Colorful, quaint history of the town and its citizens. 442 pp., photos, bibliog., index, $25.00; $15.00 pap.

Drew, Bernard A. *Berkshire Further Off the Trail*. Gt. Barrington, MA: Attic Revivals Press, 1992. 56 pp., illus., $7.50 pap.

————. *A History of Notchview Reservation: The Arthur D. Budd Estate in Windsor, Massachusetts*. Gt. Barrington, MA: Attic Revivals Press, 1986. 48 pp., illus., maps, $5.00.

————. *History of The Mahaiwe Theatre in Great Barrington, Massachusetts*. Gt. Barrington, MA: Attic Revivals Press, 1989, 48 pp., illus., $5.00.

————. *Spanning Berkshire Waterways*. Gt. Barrington, MA: Attic Revivals Press, 1990. 32 pp., photos, maps, $5.00.

————. *William Cullen Bryant's "A Border Tradition."* Gt. Barrington, MA: Attic Revivals Press, 1988. 32 pp., bibliog., $6.50.

————, and Donna M. Bernard. *Mapping the Berkshires*. Gt. Barrington, MA: Attic Revivals Press, 1985. 48 pp., illus., maps, $5.00.

Lee, Laura. *Arlo, Alice & Anglicans: The Lives of a New England Church*. Lee, MA: Berkshire House Publishers, 2000. 240 pp. illus., $16.95 pap.

Miller, Amy Bess. *Hancock Shaker Village/The City of Peace: An Effort to Restore a Vision 1960–1985*. Hancock, MA: Hancock Shaker Village, 1984. 170 pp., illus., photos, appendices, bibliog., index, $19.95; $12.00 pap.

Murray, Stuart, and James McCabe. *Norman Rockwell's Four Freedoms*. Lee, MA: Berkshire House Publishers, 1993. 176 pp., illus., $24.95; $14.95 pap.

Owens, Carole. *The Berkshire Cottages: A Vanishing Era*. Stockbridge, MA: Cottage Press, 1984. 240 pp., photos, illus., index, $29.95 pap.

Pincus, Andrew L. *Scenes from Tanglewood*. Boston, MA: Northeastern University Press, 1989. 287 pp., photos, $14.95, pap.

————, and Phyllis Curtin. *Tanglewood: The Clash Between Tradition and Change*. Boston, MA: Northeastern University Press, 1998. 192pp, $24.95.

The Stockbridge Story: 1739-1989. Stockbridge, MA: Town of Stockbridge, 1989. 209 pp., illus., photos, index, $25.00.

PHOTOGRAPHIC STUDIES

Bazan, John. *Rails across the Berkshire Hills. Railroad Photography, 1890-1984.* Pittsfield, MA: The Author, 1984. Photos, $9.95 pap.

Binzen, Bill. *The Berkshires.* Lee, MA: Berkshire House Publishers, 1995. 90 color photos, $24.95.

Chefetz, Sheila. *Antiques for the Table.* New York, NY: Viking-Penguin, 1993. 232 pp., 275 color photos, bibliog., Berkshire resource directory, index. Many photographs of Berkshire summer "cottages."

Gilder, Cornelia Brooke. *Views of the Valley: Tyringham 1739-1989.* Tyringham, MA: Hopbrook Community Club, 1989. 142 pp., photos, $15.00 pap.

Resch, Tyler, ed. *Images of America: Bill Tague's Berkshires.* Intro. by George A. Wislocki. Dover, NH: Arcadia Publishing, 1996. 128 pp., map., photos, $16.99. Berkshire landscapes and people from the 1950s to the 1980s, as seen in 178 black-and-white photos by a noted Berkshire Eagle photographer, editor, and reporter.

———. *Images of America: Bill Tague's Berkshires, Volume II.* Intro. by Ted Giddings. Dover, NH: Arcadia Publishing, 1998, 128 pp., photos, $16.99. More of Bill Tague's nostalgic photographs.

Scott, Walter. *The Norman Rockwell Bicycle Tours of Stockbridge.* Stockbridge, MA: SnO Publications, 1980. 32 postcards, $10.95.

RECREATION & NATURE

A Canoe Guide to the Housatonic River, Berkshire County. Pittsfield, MA: Berkshire County Regional Planning Commission. Illus., maps. Updated in 1994.

Appalachian Trail Guide to Massachusetts-Connecticut. Harpers Ferry, WV: Appalachian Trail Conference, 1990. 189 pp., maps, $18.95.

Cuyler, Lewis C. *Bike Rides in the Berkshire Hills,* Revised and Updated Edition. Lee, MA: Berkshire House Publishers, 1995. 200 pp., illus., maps, $9.95 pap.

Laubach, René,. *A Guide to Natural Places in the Berkshire Hills,* Second Edition. Lee, MA: Berkshire House Publishers, 1997. 288 pp., illus., maps, $12.95 pap.

Lyon, Steve. *Bicyclist's Guide to the Southern Berkshires.* Lenox, MA: Freewheel Publications, 1993. 256 pp., $16.95 pap.

Stevens, Lauren R. *Hikes & Walks in the Berkshire Hills,* Revised Edition. Lee, MA: Berkshire House Publishers, 1998. 224 pp., maps, $14.95 pap.

———. *Skiing in the Berkshire Hills.* Lee, MA: Berkshire House Publishers, 1991. 232 pp., maps, $8.95 pap.

Strauch, Joseph G., Jr., *Wildflowers of the Berkshire & Taconic Hills.* Lee, MA: Berkshire House Publishers, 1995. 160 pp., maps, illus. $12.95 pap.

TRAVEL

The Berkshire Hills: A WPA Guide, with a new foreword by Roger Linscott. Boston, MA: Northeastern University Press, 1987. 390 pp., illus., photos, maps, lore, history, $14.95 pap.

Bryan, Clark, W. *The Book of Berkshire*. N. Egremont, MA: Past Perfect Books, 1993 reprint. 304 pp., engravings, index, large color map of county, $24.95. A splendid reprint of the first guide to the Berkshires.

Davenport, John. *Berkshire-Bennington Locator*. Madison, WI: First Impressions, 1988. 112 pp., maps, $10.95 pap.

Whitman, Herbert S. *Exploring the Berkshires*. New York, NY: Hippocrene, 1991. 240 pp., illus., $9.95 pap.

Books You Can Borrow

Annin, Katherine Huntington. *Richmond, Massachusetts: The Story of a Berkshire Town and Its People, 1765–1965*. Richmond, MA: Richmond Civic Association, 1964. 214 pp., photos, illus., index. The only complete readable history of the town.

Birdsall, Richard. *Berkshire County, A Cultural History*. New York, NY: Greenwood Press, 1978 reprint. 401 pp., notes, bibliog., index. The only cultural study of the region; the emphasis is on the first half of the 19th century. Chapters cover the development of law, newspapers, education, religion. Special attention to the literary heritage.

Bittman, Sam, and Steven A. Satullo, eds. *Berkshire: Seasons of Celebration*. Pittsfield, MA: Either/Or Press, 1982. 112 pp., photos.

Boltwood, Edward. *The History of Pittsfield, Massachusetts, from the Year 1876 to the Year 1916*. Pittsfield, MA: The City, 1916. Covers the history of the most important county communities to the early 20th century.

Brook, Robert R.R., ed. *Williamstown: The First Two Hundred Years*. Williamstown, 1953. 458 pp., 69 illus.

Bulkeley, Morgan. *Mountain Farm: Poems from the Berkshire Hills*. Chester, MA: Hollow Springs Press, 1984. 95 pp., illus.

Collections of the Berkshire Historical and Scientific Society. Pittsfield, MA: Sun Printing Co., 1892–1899. Papers on historical topics read at Society meetings. Often composed by local authorities; subjects range from Berkshire geology to glass manufacture in Berkshire. Often unique and usually reliable.

Consolati, Florence. *See All the People: Or, Life in Lee*. Lee, MA: The Author, 1978. Colorful, quaint history of the town and its citizens. 442 pp., photos, bibliog., index.

Coxey, Willard D. *Ghosts of Old Berkshire*. Gt. Barrington, MA: The Berkshire Courier, 1934. Legends and folktales of Berkshire people and places.

Drew, Bernard A. *Berkshire between Covers: A Literary History*. Gt. Barrington, MA: Attic Revivals Press, 1985. 32 pp., illus., bibliog. Brief biographical sketches of deceased fiction writers with significant connections to the Berkshires.

————. *Berkshire Off the Trail*. Gt. Barrington, MA: Attic Revival Press, 1982. 96 pp., illus., index. Informal history of less traditional subjects.

Emblidge, David, ed. *The Third Berkshire Anthology: A Collection of Literature and Art*. Lenox, MA: Berkshire Writers, Inc., 1982. 185 pp., illus.

Field, Stephen, ed. *A History of the County of Berkshire, Massachusetts.* Pittsfield, MA: Samuel W. Bush, 1829. Perhaps the first history of the Berkshires, sponsored by the Berkshire Association of Congregational Ministers. A general history of the county, followed by accounts of individual towns, each written by its minister.

Jones, Electa F. *Stockbridge, Past and Present: Or, Records of an Old Mission Station.* Springfield, MA: Samuel Bowles & Co., 1854. History of the Indian mission and the Stockbridge Indians.

Kupferberg, Herbert. *Tanglewood.* New York, NY: McGraw-Hill, 1976. 280 pp., photos, bibliog., index. Most thorough history of the Berkshire Music Festival.

Lewis, Joseph W. *Berkshire Men of Worth.* 4 Vols. Scrapbook of newspaper articles. From 1933 until well after Lewis' death in 1938, over 300 columns on Berkshire notables were published in the Berkshire Evening Eagle. The series featured penetrating biographical sketches of men whom Lewis regarded as important historical figures. Perhaps the most comprehensive biographical treatment of historical Berkshire figures.

Oakes, Donald, ed. *A Pride of Palaces: Lenox Summer Cottages, 1883–1933.* Lenox, MA: Lenox Library, 1981. 83 pp., illus., photos.

Perry, Arthur L. *Origins in Williamstown.* New York, NY: Charles Scribner's Sons, 1896. Detailed, well-researched history of early Williamstown and other segments of northern Berkshire.

Preiss, Lillian E. *Sheffield, Frontier Town.* Sheffield, MA: Sheffield Bicentennial Commission, 1976. 188 pp., photos, illus., bibliog., index. Good, traditional town history.

Resch, Tyler, ed. *Berkshire, The First Three Hundred Years 1676–1976.* Pittsfield, MA: Eagle Publishing Co., 1976. 163 pp., photos, illus., maps, bibliog., index. Photographs and illustrations of significant and interesting historical events and people, with concise captions.

Sedgwick, Sarah Cabot, and Christina Sedgwick Marquand. *Stockbridge, 1739–1939: A Chronicle.* Stockbridge, MA: The Authors, 1939. 306 pp., photos, illus., bibliog. Popular, readable history.

Smith, J.E.A., ed. *The History of Berkshire County, Massachusetts, With Biographical Sketches of Its Prominent Men.* 2 Vols. NY: J.B. Beers & Co., 1885. Wide-ranging history covering every aspect of Berkshire life. Nine chapters on individual towns. The most comprehensive, reliable history of the first 200 years of Berkshire development.

Smith, J.E.A., ed. *The History of Pittsfield (Berkshire County), Massachusetts, From the Year 1734 to the Year 1800.* Boston, MA: Lee, Shepard, 1869. *The History of Pittsfield (Berkshire County), Massachusetts, From the Year 1800 to the Year 1876.* Springfield, MA: C.W. Bryan & Co., 1876. The most detailed, thorough town histories for the county. Smith had access to much material since lost; covers surrounding communities as well.

Taylor, Charles J. *History of Great Barrington (Berkshire), Massachusetts*

1676–1882. Part II, Extension 1882-1922 by George Edwin MacLean. Gt. Barrington, MA: 1928. Detailed, accurate history of the town, particularly the Taylor segment.

Wood, David H. *Lenox, Massachusetts Shire Town.* Lenox, MA: 1968. Similar to Sedgwick history of Stockbridge but more detailed.

Bridge along the Housatonic River. The river winds through South County and provides many opportunities for sport and relaxation.

Judith Monachina

WEATHER REPORTS

CLIMATE

How the Berkshire climate strikes you depends on what you're used to. People visiting from outside the region may be helped by the following information.

In general, while summers are blessedly mild because of the elevation of the Berkshire hills, winters can be cold and snowy with tricky driving conditions. Of course, what someone who doesn't ski finds annoying in a New England winter greases the skids for another who does ski. Summer visitors should remember that nights can be cool; bring sweaters and even light coats or jackets. And those in search of great snow should note that spring comes to South County well before it does up north and up higher. One morning we cross-country skied in the morning on good snow at Notchview in Windsor and rototilled the garden in Great Barrington the same afternoon.

TEMPERATURE AND PRECIPITATION

Average Temperature	October	48.4° F.
	January	20.4°
	April	43.4°
	July	68.3°

Average Annual Total Precipitation

Rainfall plus water content of snow	44.15"
Snow	75.7"

For people who are really into statistics or are interested for business or investment purposes, the source for this information and a great deal more, *The Berkshire County Data Book,* is available (for $100) from the **Berkshire Regional Planning Commission** (413-442-1521; Dunham Mall, Pittsfield, MA 01201).

WEATHER REPORTS

Gt. Barrington	413-528-1118
Pittsfield	413-499-2627
N. Adams	413-663-6264

GUIDED TOURS

If you want to be bused directly to Berkshire's high spots by an informed guide, there are hosts of possibilities, some based here in the hills, some coming from New York and Boston. From the big cities, there are fall-foliage tours, Tanglewood tours, and ski tours, all of which provide transport, tickets, meals, and lodging plus background on the sites. For an individual, these tours offer a taste of the area's delights in a perfectly packaged form. For groups, the tours turn a possible logistical nightmare into a fun-filled holiday.

Should you be coming from New York or Boston, a travel agent may be helpful in choosing the right tour. The best of the commercial tour companies belong to the National Tour Association. The best of the charter bus companies belong to the American Bus Association. Here are a few of the most experienced Berkshire guided-tour companies operating from New York and Boston.

NEW YORK

Parker Tours, 516-349-0575, 800-833-9600; 255 Executive Dr., Plainview, NY 11803.

Tauck Tours, 203-226-6911, 800-468-2825; 276 Post Rd. W., Westport, CT 06880.

BOSTON

Berkshire Tour Company, See "Within the Berkshires," below.
Collette Tours, 401-728-3805, 800-752-2655 (in New England except Maine), 800-832-4656; 162 Middle St., Pawtucket, RI 02860.

WITHIN THE BERKSHIRES

Within Berkshire, there are also a number of guided-tour options. For something relatively brief and informal, a local cab driver can usually be persuaded to drive you around, adding colorful histories that only a cabbie might know. For more organized, detailed tours, consider the following.

Berkshire Tour Company, 413-443-5778; 86 Samson Pkwy, Pittsfield, MA 01201 (In Boston: 781-438-2056.) Berkshire native Nancy C. Hickey provides a wide range of tour services, including group tours of Berkshire County sites (a favorite is the Berkshire Cottages tour), plus walking tours of the Main Streets of Stockbridge, Lenox, and Williamstown. She also provides customized tours including lunch or dinner at local restaurants, excursions to Tanglewood and other music and theater festivals, and combinations of tours for any size group. Phone for prices and schedules.
Greylock Discovery Tours, See "Walking, Camping, Cross-Country Skiing" in Chapter Seven, *Outdoor Recreation.*

HANDICAPPED SERVICES

Although Berkshire is a region with lots of rough terrain, handicapped people will find access quite easy to most cultural sites and events, to many lodgings and restaurants, and to most shops. In Chapter Three, *Lodging*, we specify those places where we know handicapped access is either feasible or not. Elsewhere, to confirm the situation, use the phone numbers we provide to get information.

The *Berkshire Visitors Bureau* (413-443-9186; Berkshire Common, Pittsfield, MA 01201) publishes an annual guide listing many Berkshire services and attractions, in many cases specifying access to handicapped people.

The *AAA Tour Guide*, available through *AAA Berkshire County* (413-445-5635; 196 South St., Pittsfield, MA 01201) also designates restaurants, lodging, etc. with handicapped access.

As for transportation, the *Berkshire Regional Transit Authority* (413-499-2782 or in county 800-292-2782) runs the public bus system throughout the major towns in the county and has buses equipped with wheelchair lifts. See Chapter Two, *Transportation*, "Getting Around the Berkshires" for more information.

HOSPITALS

GREAT BARRINGTON

Fairview Hospital, 413-528-0790; 29 Lewis Ave.

PITTSFIELD

Berkshire Medical Center, 413-447-2000; 725 North St.
Hillcrest Hospital, 413-443-4761; 165 Tor Court.

NORTH ADAMS

N. Adams Regional Hospital, 413-663-3701; Hospital Ave.

LATE NIGHT FOOD & FUEL

Berkshire Truck Plaza (food); open all night except restaurant is closed Sat. 11pm–Sun. 7am.: Rte. 102, W. Stockbridge, 413-232-4233.

Christy's (food and fuel); open all night: 223 Columbia St., N. Adams, 413-743-0322; 41 Housatonic St., Lee, 413-243-2088.

Convenience Plus (food and fuel); open all night: 90 Tyler St., Pittsfield, 413-499-1741; 241 Main St., Lee, 413-243-2399. Open till 11pm: South St., Stockbridge. 413-298-4036.

Cumberland Farms (food and fuel); open all night: 140 Main St., Gt. Barrington, 413-528-9852; 594 Mohawk Tr., N. Adams, 413-662-2721 and 413-664-9150; 446 Main St., Williamstown, 413-458-9170. Open till midnight: 70 Ashland St., N. Adams.

Dakota Restaurant (food); open till 11pm Fri.–Sat.: Pittsfield-Lenox Rd., Rte. 7, Pittsfield, 413-499-7900.

Fillin' Station, at **Lee Travel Plaza** (food and fuel); restaurant open daily 24 hrs., including New Year's Day, Easter, Thanksgiving, Christmas. Pumps open all night, exc. Fri. till midnight: Rte. 102, Lee, 413-243-4411.

Dunkin' Donuts (food); open all night: 5 Union St., N. Adams, 413-662-2274; 18 First St., Pittsfield, 413-499-0371. Open till 11pm: Main St., Lee, 413-243-1676.

Jimmy's (food); open Fri. till 11pm, Sat. till 10pm: 114 W. Housatonic, Pittsfield, 413-499-1288.

Joe's Diner (food); open till midnight; closed Sat. from 6:30pm and all day Sun.: 85 Center St., Rte. 20, Lee, 413-243-9756.

Luau Hale (food); open Fri.–Sat. till 10pm: Pittsfield-Lenox Rd., Rte. 7, Lenox, 413-443-4745.

P.J.'s Convenience Store (food); open Mon.–Sat. till 11:30pm, Sun. till 10pm: S. Main St., Sheffield, 413-229-6610.

Papa Joe's (food); open Fri.–Sat. till 10pm: 107 Newell St., Pittsfield, 413-499-2151.

Price Chopper Supermarkets (food); open till midnight: Stockbridge Rd., Rte. 7, Gt. Barrington, 413-528-8415; Park St., Lee, 413-243-2238; Pittsfield-Lenox Rd., Rte. 7, Lenox, 413-443-5449. Open Mon.–Sat. till midnight, Sun. till 9pm: Rte. 2, N. Adams, 413-663-9415.

Stop & Shop Supermarkets (food); open all night Mon.–Fri., Sat. & Sun. till midnight: Merrill Rd., Pittsfield, 413-499-0745; Dan Fox Dr. (off Pittsfield-Lenox Rd.), Pittsfield, 413-442-7600. Open till midnight every night: Rte. 2, N. Adams, 413-664-8100.

MEDIA: MAGAZINES & NEWSPAPERS; RADIO STATIONS & TELEVISION

MAGAZINES, NEWSPAPERS

Advocate (413-664-6900; 87 Marshall St., N. Adams; Wednesday) Highly readable freebie, well-researched articles, mostly on community-related topics, for northern Berkshire and southern Vermont.

The Berkshire Eagle (413-447-7311; 75 S. Church St., Pittsfield; morning daily) The county's newspaper of record, a Pulitzer Prize–winning publication with extensive world, national, state, and local news, plus features and comics ("Doonesbury"!). The Sunday edition is chockful of interesting features. Each Thursday in season, the *Eagle* also publishes *Berkshires Week*, a supplementary magazine-in-newsprint containing colorful articles, a calendar of events, and lots of ads from local dining and entertainment places.

Berkshire Penny Saver (413-243-2341; 14 Park Pl., Box 300, Lee; Tuesday) Central County's free shopping guide, including classifieds, TV listings, nightlife, comprehensive business service listings.

Berkshire Record (413-528-5380; 271 Main St., Gt. Barrington; weekly) This Southern Berkshire weekly features current affairs and articles of historic note.

Berkshire Trade & Commerce (413-447-7700; 137 North St., Pittsfield; monthly) This freebie is Berkshire's answer to *The Wall Street Journal*. Lively up-to-date news of Berkshire business doings.

Country Journal (413-667-3211; 25 Main St., Huntington, Hampshire County; Thursdays) Covers 16 of the central hilltowns.

The Paper (518-392-2674; P.O.Box 336, Chatham, NY; monthly) A freebie published the first Thursday of the month.

Pittsfield Gazette (413-443-2010; 141 North St., Pittsfield; Thursday) Lively, even acerbic local Pittsfield news.

Shopper's Guide (413-528-0095; 35 Bridge St., Box 89, Gt. Barrington; weekly) Southern Berkshire's free guide, including enticing sections on real estate and automobiles.

South Advocate (413-243-0380; 14 Park St., Lee; Wednesdays). The *Advocate* replated for Lee, Lenox. Distributed free.

Transcript (413-663-3741; American Legion Dr., N. Adams; weekday noons, Saturday morning) Local, some state and national news; covers northern Berkshire County and southern Vermont.

Women's Times (413-528-5303; 323 Main St., Box 390, Gt. Barrington; monthly) A classy, well-written magazine-style paper, with articles by, for, and about Berkshire women. Good reading for men, too. Distributed free.

Yankee Shopper (413-684-1373; 839 Main St., Box 96, Dalton; weekly) Central and northern Berkshire's free shopping guide, including scads of used cars, rototillers, computers, vacuum cleaners, baby bunnies, as well as a business/professional services directory.

RADIO STATIONS

National Public Radio.
There are three stations receivable in the Berkshires:
WAMC-FM, 90.3; 800-323-9262; Albany, NY. Also broadcasts as **WAMQ-FM,** 105.1; 800-323-9262; Gt. Barrington.
WFCR-FM, 88.5; 413-545-0100; Amherst, MA.
WMHT-FM, 89.1; 518-357-1700; Schenectady, NY.

Other Local Radio Stations:

WBEC-AM, 1420; 413-499-3333; Pittsfield. General.
WBEC-FM, 105.5; 413-499-3333; Pittsfield. Rock music.
WBRK-AM, 101; 413-442-1553; Pittsfield. General.
WCFM-FM, 91.9; 413-597-2197; Williams College.
WJJW-FM, 91.1; 413-662-5405; Massachusetts College of Liberal Arts.
WMNB-FM, 100.1; 413-663-6567; N. Adams. General.
WNAW-AM, 1230; 413-663-6567; N. Adams. General.
WNAW-FM, 100.0; 413-663-6567; N. Adams. General.
WSBS-AM, 860; 413-528-0860; Gt. Barrington. General.
WUHN-AM, 1110; 413-499-1100; Pittsfield. General.
WUPE-FM, 96; 413-499-1100; Pittsfield. Rock and other music.

TELEVISION

L ocal public-access televison, run mostly by community volunteers, brings important meetings, events, and opinion to listeners who subscribe to cable television. In addition to live broadcasts of town meetings, city council meetings, and other events of civil and local interest, the locally run stations in each region generate such programs as "Adopt-a-Pet," live viewer call-ins, self-help and religious programs, along with musical and dramatic entertainments by local performers.

Community-based television channels:

Community Television for the Southern Berkshires (CTSB), Adelphia Channel 11 (413-243-8211).

North Berkshire Community Television, Adelphia Channels 15, 16, and 17 (413-663-9006).

Pittsfield Community Television, Warner Cable Channel 3 (413-445-4234).

WilliNet (Williamstown), Adelphia Channels 15, 16, and 17 (413-458-0900)

Consult the *Berkshire Eagle* for schedules.

REAL ESTATE

What's your dream house? An isolated cabin, deep in the woods? A late 20th-century split-level, suburban tract house? A lakeside condo for time-sharing? Or a 40-room Gilded Age mansion that just needs a couple-of-hundred-grand in handyman repairs? Berkshire County has them all.

If you are shopping for Berkshire real estate, you can obtain information as follows.

For lists of realtors, consult the Yellow Pages of the telephone book or, if you're far away, contact any of the three Chambers of Commerce: *Southern Berkshire Chamber of Commerce* (413-528-1510; www.greatbarrington.org; 362 Main St., Gt. Barrington, MA 01230); *Central Berkshire Chamber of Commerce* (413-499-4000; www.berkshirebiz.org; 66 West St., Pittsfield, MA 01201); *Northern Berkshire Chamber of Commerce* (413-663-3735; nberkshirechamber. com; 140 Main St., N. Adams, MA 01247). All three organizations will send lists of their realtor members. The seasonal tourist information brochures from the *Berkshire Visitors Bureau* (413-443-9186; www.berkshires.org; 50 South St., Pittsfield, MA 01201) also list numerous realtors.

Once you're into the process of buying land or a house, it is essential to check with the local town government about zoning laws, building permits, and so forth. Such regulations vary widely from town to town. See "Area Codes" in this chapter for town hall telephone numbers.

You can also follow the real estate market in the newspapers; see "Media," in this chapter. The *Berkshire Home Buyers Guide* is a free monthly publication, distributed in local shops or available from 413-243-2500; 80 Runway, Windsock Industrial Park, Rte. 102; P.O. Box 280, Lee MA 01238.

RELIGIOUS SERVICES & ORGANIZATIONS

Berkshire County has an active and unusually diverse religious community. The best source for information about church and synagogue services is the Saturday edition of the *Berkshire Eagle*. The Berkshire County telephone directory has a comprehensive list of all mainstream religious organizations, under the headings "Churches" and "Synagogues." For nontraditional groups, a helpful publication to consult is New Visions, published seasonally and distributed through various shops. Also, keep an eye on community bulletin boards at the area's colleges and in towns such as Great Barrington, Stockbridge, Lenox, Pittsfield, and Williamstown.

ROAD SERVICE

Emergency road service from AAA, anywhere in the county, can be obtained by calling 413-443-5635, Pittsfield. For non-AAA drivers, the following is a listing of emergency towing services.

South County

Decker's Auto Body, Gt. Barrington	413-528-1432
RW's Inc., Lee	413-243-0946
Stockbridge Motors, Stockbridge	413-298-4780

Central County

All Hours Towing & Repairs, Pittsfield	413-442-8765
Berkshire County Towing, Pittsfield	413-443-0881
County Auto Wrecking, Pittsfield	413-443-6665;
	800-232-5205
Sayers' Auto, Pittsfield	413-443-1635;
	800-323-1635
Scratch-A-Ticket Towing, Pittsfield	413-443-1754
Southgate Motors, Pittsfield	413-445-5971

North County

Al's Service Center, Adams	413-743-9755
Bator's Service & Sales, Cheshire	413-743-3578
Carpinello's Service Center, Williamstown	413-458-2528
Dean's Quality Auto & Truck Repair, N. Adams	413-664-6378
Ernies's Auto Sales, N. Adams	413-663-3503
Mohawk Auto Wrecking, N. Adams	413-664-9191

Ron's Getty, Williamstown	413-458-2238
T&M Auto Sales, N, Adams	413-664-6697
Village Truck Sales, Lanesborough	413-442-0407

SCHOOLS

PUBLIC SCHOOL DISTRICTS

South County

Berkshire Hills Regional School District, Stockbridge, 413-298-3711
Farmington River Regional, Otis, 413-269-4466
Lee Public Schools, 413-243-0276
Southern Berkshire Regional School District, Sheffield, 413-229-8778

Central County

Central Berkshire Regional School District, Dalton, 413-623-5362
Lenox Public Schools, 413-637-5550
Pittsfield Public Schools, 413-499-9512
Richmond Consolidated Schools, 413-698-2207

North County

Adams-Cheshire Regional School District, 413-743-2939
Clarksburg School Department, 413-664-8735
Florida School Department, 413-663-3593
Lanesborough Schools, 413-442-2229
Mount Greylock Regional School District, Williamstown, 413-458-9582
New Ashford School Department, 413-458-5461
N. Adams Public Schools, 413-662-3225
Northern Berkshire Vocational, N. Adams, 413-663-5383
Savoy School Department, 413-743-1992
Williamstown Public Schools, 413-458-5707

PRIVATE & RELIGIOUS SCHOOLS

South County

Berkshire School, Sheffield, 413-229-8511.
De Sisto School, Stockbridge, 413-298-3776.
Kolburne School, New Marlborough, 413-229-8787.
Rudolf Steiner School, Gt. Barrington, 413-528-4015.
St. Mary's School, Lee, 413-243-1079.

Central County

Berkshire Country Day School, Lenox, 413-637-0755
Berkshire County Christian School, Pittsfield, 413-442-4014
Hillcrest Educational Centers, 413-499-7924. Schools in Lenox (2), Gt. Barrington, Pittsfield (2), and Hancock.
Miss Hall's School, Pittsfield, 413-443-6401
Sacred Heart School, Pittsfield, 413-443-6379
St. Agnes School, Dalton, 413-684-3143
St. Joseph's High School, Pittsfield, 413-447-9121

North County

Buxton School, Williamstown, 413-458-3919
Pine Cobble School, Williamstown, 413-458-4680
St. Stanislaus School, Adams, 413-743-1091

COLLEGES

Berkshire Community College, Pittsfield, 413-499-4660. In Gt. Barrington: 413-528-4521.
Massachusetts College of Liberal Arts, N. Adams, 413-662-5000
Simon's Rock College of Bard, Gt. Barrington, 413-528-0771
Williams College, Williamstown, 413-597-3131

TOURIST INFORMATION

Volunteers in several Berkshire towns staff tourist information booths in the summer and early fall. Often information is available at the site even when volunteers are not. Year-round tourist information can be obtained from the *Berkshire Visitors Bureau,* Berkshire Common, bottom level, Crowne Plaza Hotel, 1 West St., Pittsfield (413-443-9186). The bureau is open Mon.–Fri., 8:30–4:30. Lodging information can be obtained through the *Berkshire Bed & Breakfast Reservation Service* (413-268-7244) and from the *Berkshire Lodgings Association* (413-298-4760, 800-298-4760). Chambers of commerce, also listed below, serve the commercial and business needs of the community, and can be the source of information on special town events.

South County

Chamber of Commerce of South Berkshire, Business office, 284 Main St., Gt. Barrington, MA 01230; 413-528-4284. Information booth, 362 Main St., Gt. Barrington; 413-528-1510. Lodging information, 413-528-4006.
Gt. Barrington Information Booth, 362 Main St.; 413-528-1510.

Lee Information Booth, Main St. at the park; 413-243-0852.

Massachusetts Turnpike, Eastbound Mile Marker 8, Lee; 413-243-4929.

Stockbridge Chamber of Commerce, Main office, 7 Elm St., 413-298-5200; www.stockbridgechamber.org. Information booth, Main St., 413-298-5200; self-service, 7 days. Lodging information: 413-298-5327.

W. Stockbridge Information Booth, Rte. 102 at Berkshire Truck Plaza. Self-service, 24 hrs.

Central County

Chamber of Commerce of the Berkshires, 66 West St., Pittsfield, MA 01201; 413-499-4000.

Lenox Chamber of Commerce, 413-637-3646, 800-25-LENOX; www.lenox.org; P.O. Box 646, Lenox, MA 01240. Information office, Lenox Academy, 65 Main St.; summer home: 48 Main St.

Pittsfield Information Booth, Bank Row, Park Sq. Mon.–Thurs., 9–5; Fri.–Sat., 9–8; Sun. 10–2.

North County

Adams Chamber of Commerce, 57 Main St., N. Adams; 413-743-1881.

Northern Berkshire Chamber of Commerce, Main office, 57 Main St., N. Adams; 413-663-3735. Open Mon.–Fri., 9–5. Tour booth, Union St.; 7 days, 10–4.

Williamstown Chamber of Commerce, 413-458-9077. Information booth, jct. Rte. 7 & Main St.; 413-458-4922; attended or self-service, year-round, 24 hrs.

IF TIME IS SHORT

Berkshire offers so much to the visitor that longer sojourns here are most rewarding, but sometimes that isn't possible. Here are some recommendations from the author, the publisher, and the editor from their personal favorites among the multitude of attractions which best exemplify the spirit of the place and might perfectly suit the visitor with only a weekend or a few days available for a first visit.

LODGING

The Red Lion Inn (413-298-5545, Main Street, Stockbridge) Satisfying meals, an excellent range of lodging options, and endless collections of fine furniture and antiques in a rambling, century-old inn in the old style, pleasing visitors and locals since 1793.

The Orchards (413-458-9611; 222 Adams Rd., off Rte. 2, Williamstown) A superb small luxury hotel offering a formal, clublike atmosphere. Huge rooms, many with bay windows and fireplaces; an award-winning restaurant. The service throughout is honed to a fine edge.

RESTAURANTS

Castle Street Café (413 528-5244, 10 Castle St., Gt. Barrington) An American bistro in South County in a charming, brick-walled cafe.

Elm Court Inn (413-528-0325; Rte. 71, N. Egremont) Pleasant inn in South County serving continental cuisine in a cozy traditional setting.

The Mill on the Floss (413-458-9123; Rte. 7, New Ashford) One of the greater gourmet experiences in North County, offering excellent French cuisine in an informal setting.

FOOD PURVEYORS

The Store At Five Corners (413-458-3176; junction of Rtes. 7 & 43, South Williamstown) A wonderful assortment of gourmet foods, wines, oils, jellies for gift baskets, prepared food for picnics, delicious ice creams and yogurt in a renovated Victorian building. Creative cooks will delight in the myriad of offerings and novice cooks will be inspired to experiment. They can even buy the newest cookbooks to assure culinary success. Devoted non-cooks should just stock up on the delicious ready-made salads, casseroles, and baked goods.

CULTURE

MUSEUMS

The Sterling & Francine Clark Art Institute (413-458-9545; 225 South St., Williamstown) Among the museums in the county, the one with the longest-standing national reputation; renowned for its collection of Impressionists, especially Renoir.

Williams College Museum of Art (413-597-2429; Main St., Rte. 2, Williamstown) One of the finest college museums in the country and a leading research center. Emphasis on early art and 20th-century American art, to complement the 19th-century collection at the Clark.

Norman Rockwell Museum (413-298-4100; Rte. 183, Stockbridge) Even connoisseurs of fine art find themselves captivated by Rockwell's evocations of America as we always wanted it to be. A guaranteed hit with every member of the family.

Hancock Shaker Village (413-443-0188; Rte. 20, near Pittsfield / Hancock line) Beautifully restored Shaker village, with numerous exhibits, Shaker buildings, and events for all the family.

SUMMER MUSIC

Tanglewood (413-637-1666 or 413-637-5165; West St., Rte. 183, Lenox) The obvious choice for the visitor with but one evening or day. Shed concerts Friday and Saturday evenings and Sunday afternoons from early July through late August; Wednesday or Thursday evening recitals in Seiji Ozawa Hall; operas in the newly refitted Concert Hall. In addition to world-class concerts by the Boston Symphony Orchestra and visiting soloists, the students of Tanglewood's summer program for aspiring professionals give numerous concerts in all venues seven days a week. Popular or jazz artists often take the stage at the end of August. The grounds, justly famous for their cultivated beauty, are great for a stroll or a picnic.

South Mountain Concerts (413-442-2106; Rtes. 7 & 20, Pittsfield) Chamber music for the serious listener, primarily string quartets but other combinations, too (the annual appearance of the Beaux Arts Trio is a highlight of the season). Concerts are in a historic building built expressly for small ensembles, in a wooded setting above Pittsfield. Five Sunday afternoon concerts during September and early October.

Tannery Pond Concerts (518-794-7887, or for reservations & tickets call 888-846-5848; Rte. 20, New Lebanon, NY) Five chamber concerts, about one a month between late May and early October. Superb rising stars along with internationally renowned performers, in a former Shaker tannery now converted to a rustic and acoustically excellent hall situated in a beautiful meadow on the grounds of Darrow School.

SUMMER THEATER

Berkshire Theatre Festival (413-298-5576, 413-298-5536 off season; E. Main St., Rte. 102, Stockbridge) and **Williamstown Theatre Festival** (413-597-3400; Main St., Williamstown) The two granddaddies of American summer stock theater vie with each other to present superior theater in charming settings. Both offer main stage and studio presentations, traditional and new works from mid-June through Labor Day. Call ahead for schedules and reservations.

Shakespeare & Company at The Mount (413-637-3353 box office, 413-637-1199 off season; Plunkett St., near jct. of Rtes 7 & 7A, Lenox) Shakespeare's classics presented in both conventional and outdoor stagings at Edith Wharton's summer estate, plus a rich array of large- and small-scale works by other writers, including many stage adaptations of Wharton's short works.(Note: Shakespeare & Company will move to new quarters during the next two years.)

RECREATION

Monument Mountain Reservation (413-298-3239; Stockbridge Rd., Rte. 7, Gt. Barrington) 503 acres. A short but rugged climb up Squaw Peak, the reservation's most prominent feature, offers excellent views of three states from a summit 1,642 feet above sea level.

Mount Greylock State Reservation (413-499-4262; Rockwell Rd., off Rte. 7, Lanesborough; also accessible from Notch Road, N. Adams) 12,000 acres, including the state's highest peak, along with 45 miles of trails.

SHOPPING

CLOTHING

Evviva! (413-637-9875; 22 Walker St., Lenox) The clever, ever-changing windows capture the sophistication and variety of clothing and accessories offered. Dresses for special events, romantic hats, unique jewelry, casual country clothes, and hand-painted silks combine to create a feast for the eye. The windows (which change monthly) are fascinating in and of themselves. A recent expansion has added shoes to the mix.

Steven Valenti (413-443-2569; 157 North St., Pittsfield) A men's store with an emphasis on customer satisfaction and stylish yet comfortable clothes for all occasions.

BOOKS

Bookloft (413-528-1521; Barrington Plaza, Stockbridge Rd., Gt. Barrington) a popular source for best sellers and books about the Berkshires with a knowledgeable staff in a pleasant setting.

The Bookstore (413-637-3390; 11 Housatonic St., Lenox) A most knowledgeable owner and a slightly '70s air makes this a great place to browse and chat about books.

GIFTS

The Gingham Rabbit (413-528-0048; 389 Stockbridge Rd., Rte. 7, Gt. Barrington) A large shop with an eclectic mix of giftware, infant ware, indulgent bath and boudoir items just for a treat or to indulge a shut-in. Many of the clothing and gift items can be monogrammed. They also wrap and will delivery locally to hospitals, etc.

Mistral's (413-528-1618; 7 Railroad St., Gt. Barrington) A most elegant, sophisticated collection of tableware, linens, and home furnishings from France. The upstairs houses a collection of items for the bed and bath. A beautiful shop to visit for an infusion of French chic.

Pamela Loring Gifts and Interiors (413-243-2689; 40 Main St., Lee) Very attractive shop on Main St. with excellent service, they will wrap packages and provide gift cards. Mostly giftware with an emphasis on floral, pretty gifts for women, and seasonal merchandise.

B. Mango & Bird (413-637-2611; 74 Main St., Lenox) Deep red walls set off an eclectic collection of accessories for home and table. Witty tapes, clever cards, and toys for adults round out the offerings in this shop.

FOR FUN ...

Homegoods (413-236-6996; 676 Merrill Rd., Pittsfield) and **Sappa** (413-528-9592; 308 Main St., Gt. Barrington) are at different ends of the spectrum in relationship to style, but each is fun in its own way for shopping.

Index

LODGING BY PRICE CODE

RESTAURANTS BY PRICE CODE

RESTAURANTS BY CUISINE

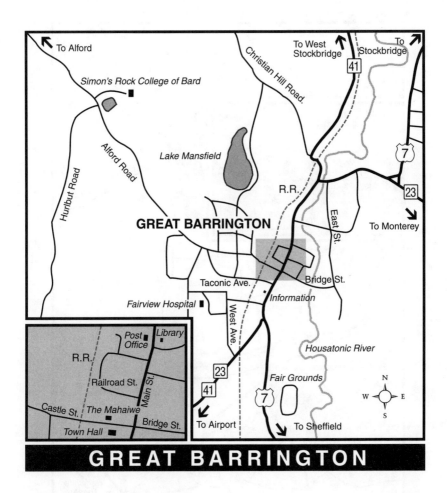

GREAT BARRINGTON

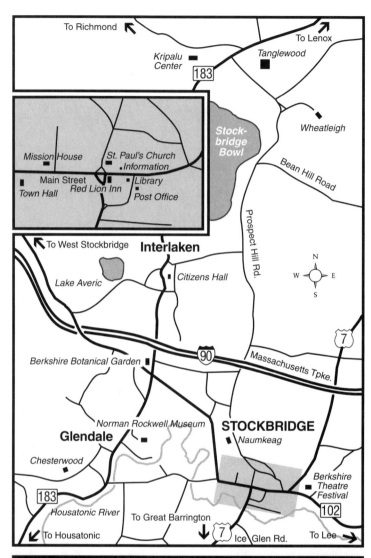

STOCKBRIDGE

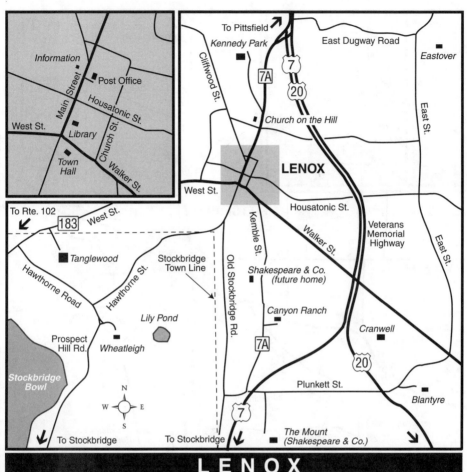

LENOX

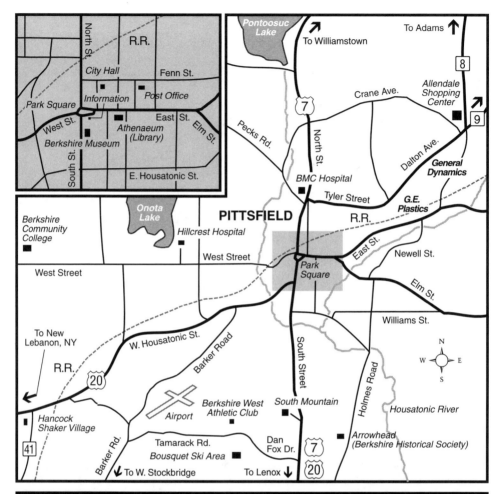

PITTSFIELD

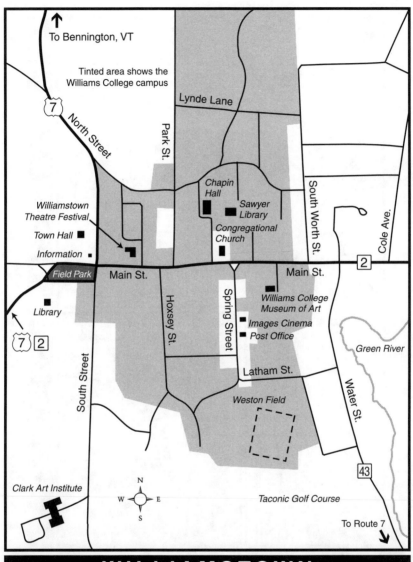

To Bennington, VT

Tinted area shows the
Williams College campus

7

North Street

Lynde Lane

Park St.

Chapin
Hall

Sawyer
Library

Congregational
Church

South Worth St.

Cole Ave.

Williamstown
Theatre Festival

Town Hall

Information

Field Park

Main St.

Main St.

2

Library

7 2

South Street

Hoxsey St.

Spring Street

Williams College
Museum of Art

Images Cinema

Post Office

Green River

Latham St.

Weston Field

Water St.

Clark Art Institute

N
W E
S

Taconic Golf Course

43

To Route 7

WILLIAMSTOWN

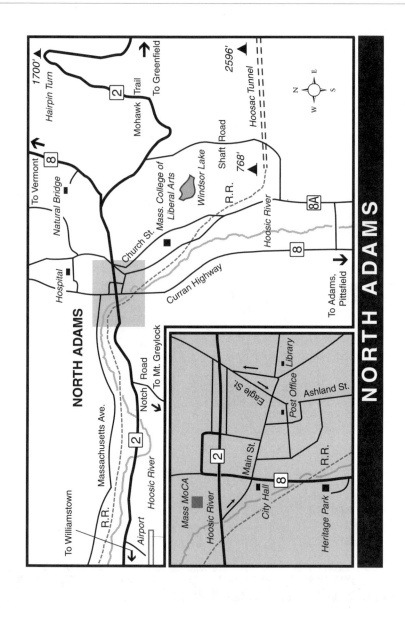

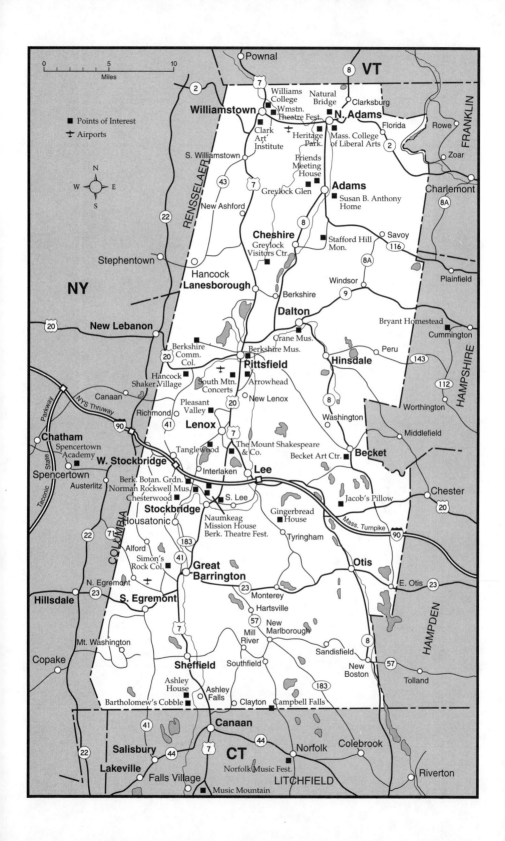

About Lauren R. Stevens

Judith Monachina

Lauren R. Stevens is the author, with Richard W. Babcock, of *Old Barns in the New World* and, with Deborah E. Burns, of *Most Excellent Majesty: A History of Mount Greylock*. A resident of Williamstown and an avid hiker, he is also author of *Hikes & Walks in the Berkshire Hills* and of *Skiing in the Berkshire Hills*. Founder in 1981 of *The Advocate*, a county-wide weekly newspaper, he is now a freelancer who has written on the environment for most Berkshire periodicals, as well as several longer studies as an environmental consultant. His novel, *The Double Axe*, was published by Scribner's.